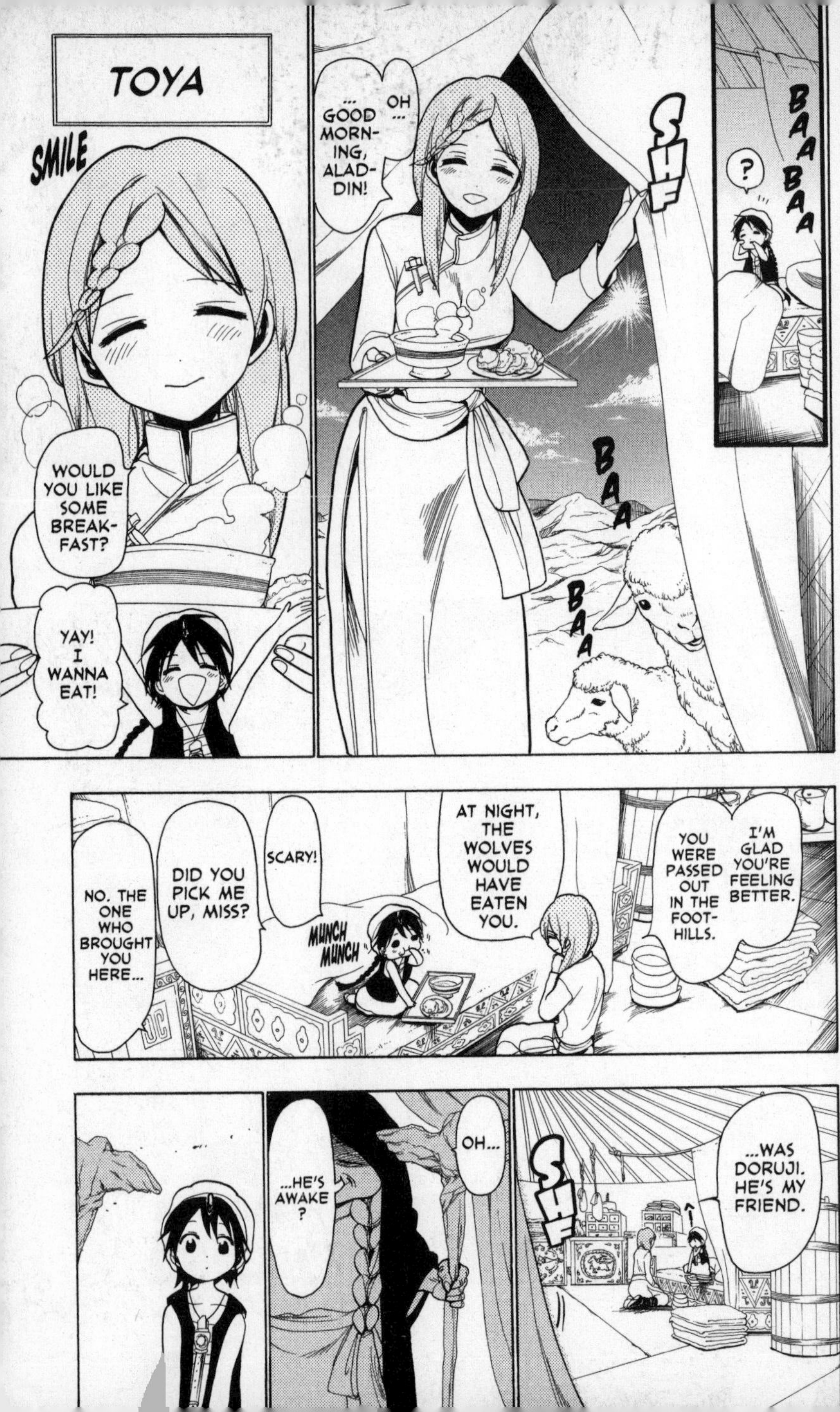
BAA BAA BAA
?
OH ... ... GOOD MORNING, ALADDIN!
SHF
BAA
BAA
TOYA
SMILE
WOULD YOU LIKE SOME BREAKFAST?
YAY! I WANNA EAT!
I'M GLAD YOU'RE FEELING BETTER.
YOU WERE PASSED OUT IN THE FOOTHILLS.
AT NIGHT, THE WOLVES WOULD HAVE EATEN YOU.
SCARY!
MUNCH MUNCH
DID YOU PICK ME UP, MISS?
NO. THE ONE WHO BROUGHT YOU HERE...
...WAS DORUJI. HE'S MY FRIEND.
SHF
OH...
...HE'S AWAKE?

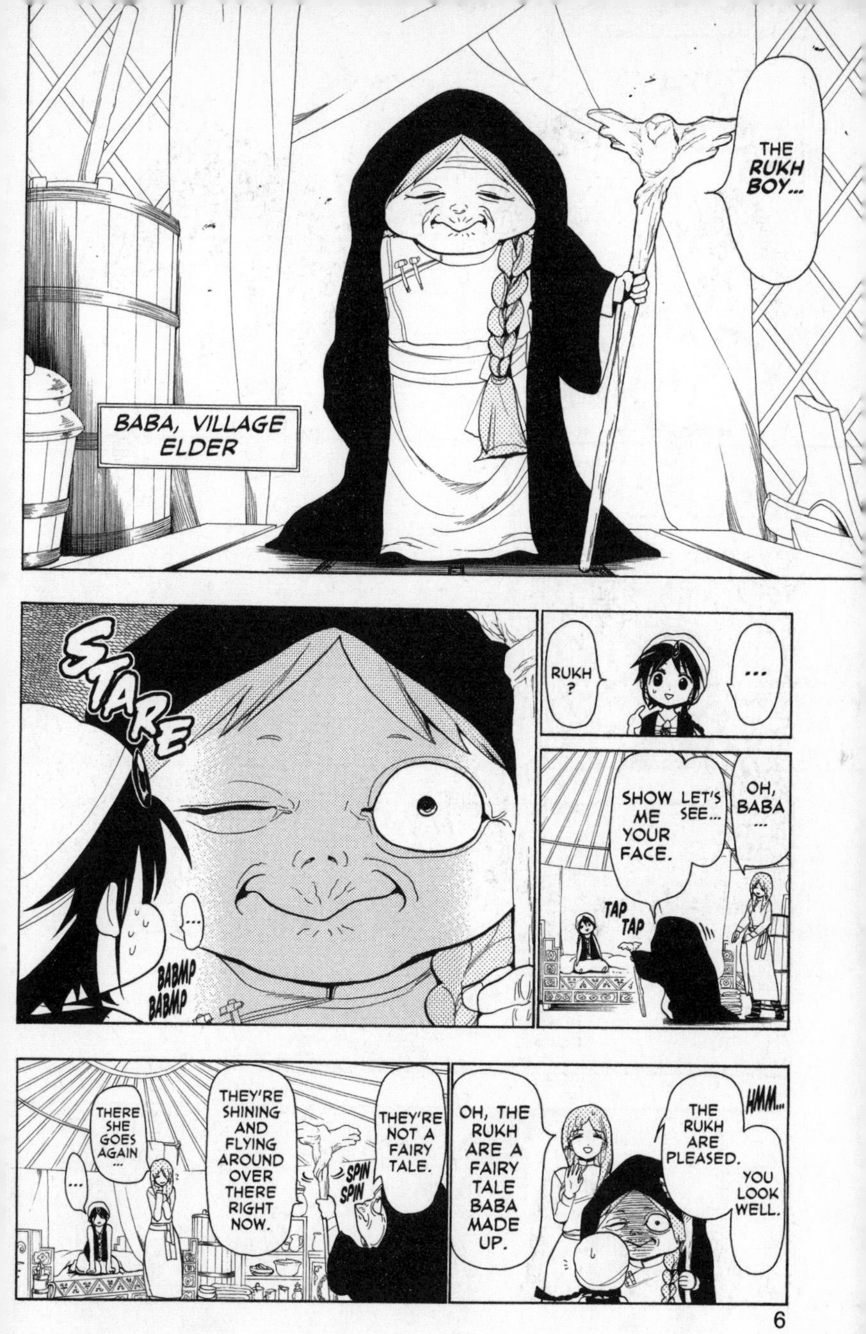
THE RUKH BOY...
BABA, VILLAGE ELDER
...
RUKH ?
OH, BABA ...
LET'S SEE...
SHOW ME YOUR FACE.
TAP TAP
STARE
...
BABMP BABMP
HMM...
THE RUKH ARE PLEASED.
YOU LOOK WELL.
OH, THE RUKH ARE A FAIRY TALE BABA MADE UP.
THEY'RE NOT A FAIRY TALE.
SPIN SPIN
THEY'RE SHINING AND FLYING AROUND OVER THERE RIGHT NOW.
THERE SHE GOES AGAIN ...
...

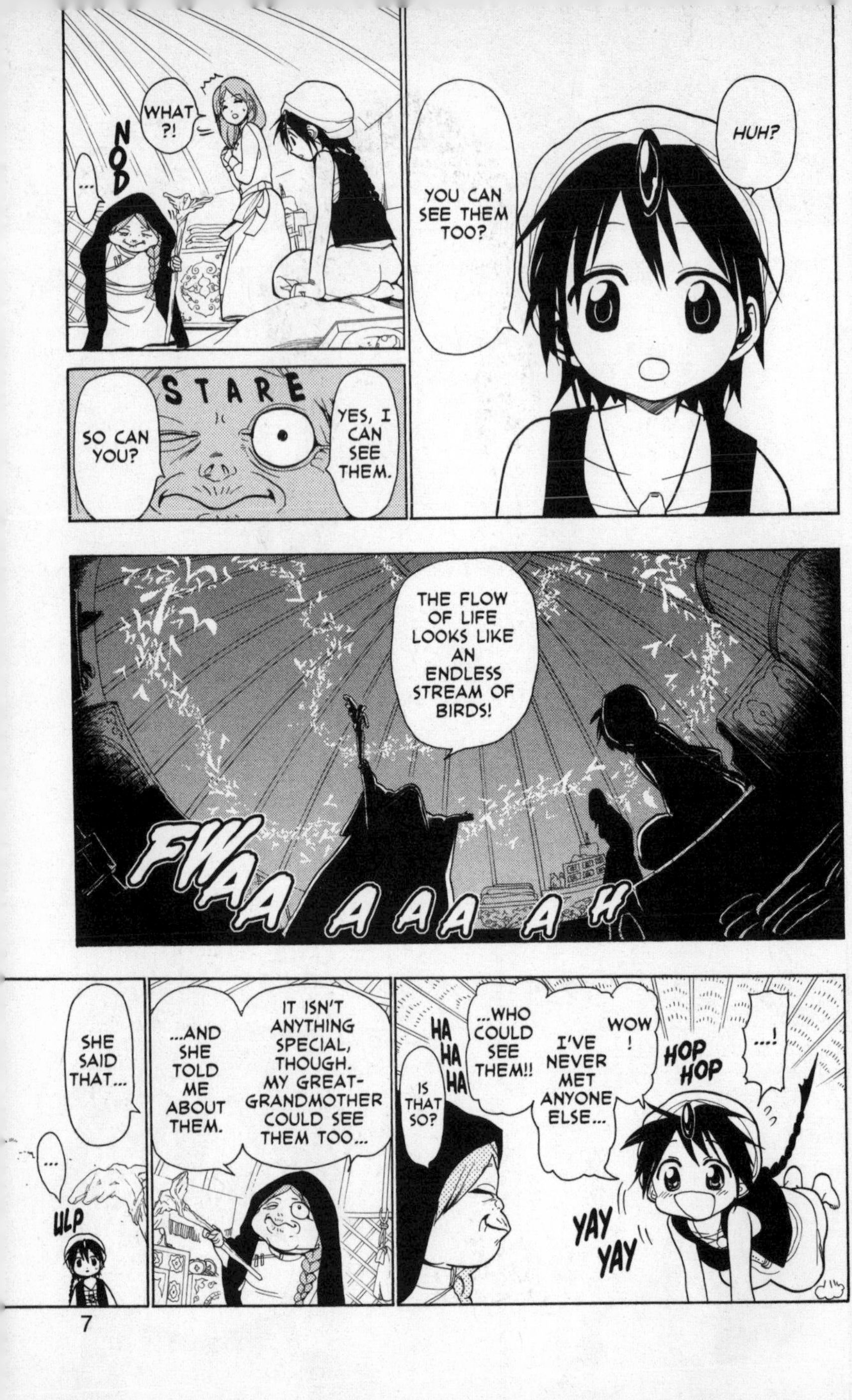
HUH?
YOU CAN SEE THEM TOO?
WHAT?!
NOD
...
STARE
YES, I CAN SEE THEM.
SO CAN YOU?
THE FLOW OF LIFE LOOKS LIKE AN ENDLESS STREAM OF BIRDS!
FWAAAAAAAH
...!
HOP HOP
WOW!
I'VE NEVER MET ANYONE ELSE...
...WHO COULD SEE THEM!!
YAY YAY
HA HA HA
IS THAT SO?
IT ISN'T ANYTHING SPECIAL, THOUGH. MY GREAT-GRANDMOTHER COULD SEE THEM TOO...
...AND SHE TOLD ME ABOUT THEM.
SHE SAID THAT...
...
ULP

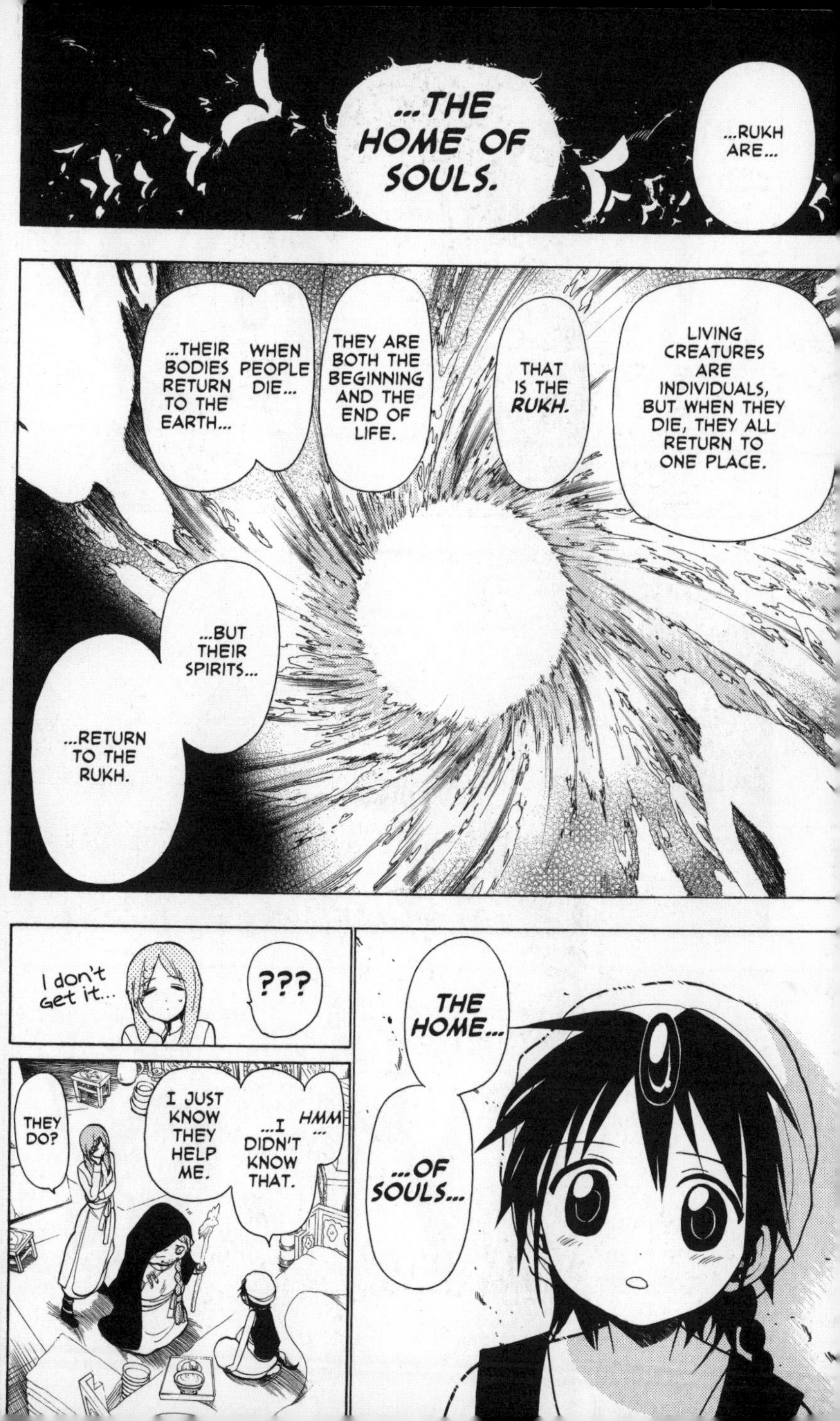
...RUKH ARE...
...THE HOME OF SOULS.
LIVING CREATURES ARE INDIVIDUALS, BUT WHEN THEY DIE, THEY ALL RETURN TO ONE PLACE.
THAT IS THE *RUKH.*
THEY ARE BOTH THE BEGINNING AND THE END OF LIFE.
WHEN PEOPLE DIE...
...THEIR BODIES RETURN TO THE EARTH...
...BUT THEIR SPIRITS...
...RETURN TO THE RUKH.
THE HOME...
...OF SOULS...
???
I don't get it...
HMM...
...I DIDN'T KNOW THAT.
I JUST KNOW THEY HELP ME.
THEY DO?

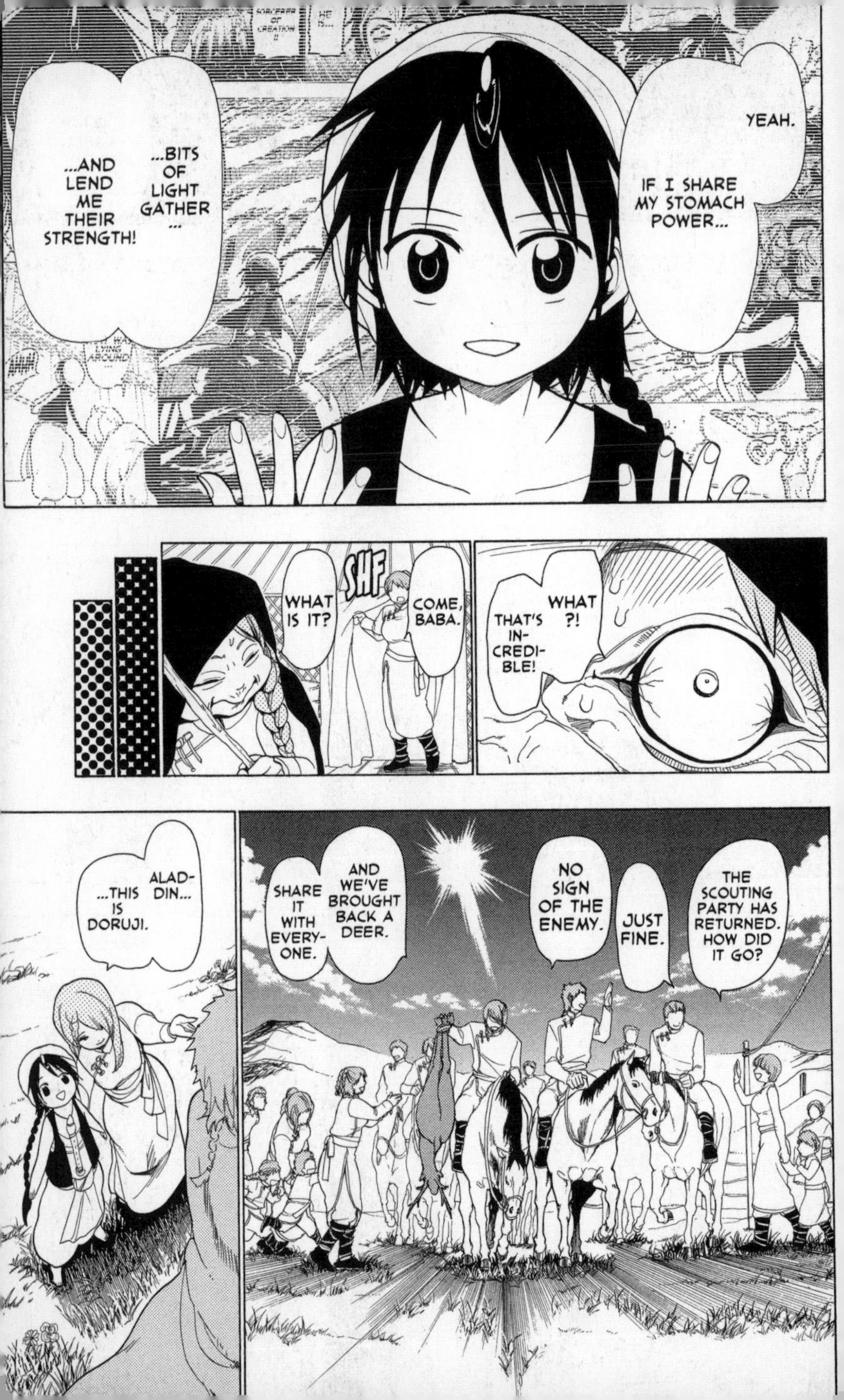
YEAH.
IF I SHARE MY STOMACH POWER...
...BITS OF LIGHT GATHER...
...AND LEND ME THEIR STRENGTH!
WHAT ?!
THAT'S IN-CREDI-BLE!
COME, BABA.
SHF
WHAT IS IT?
THE SCOUTING PARTY HAS RETURNED. HOW DID IT GO?
JUST FINE.
NO SIGN OF THE ENEMY.
AND WE'VE BROUGHT BACK A DEER.
SHARE IT WITH EVERY-ONE.
ALAD-DIN...
...THIS IS DORUJI.

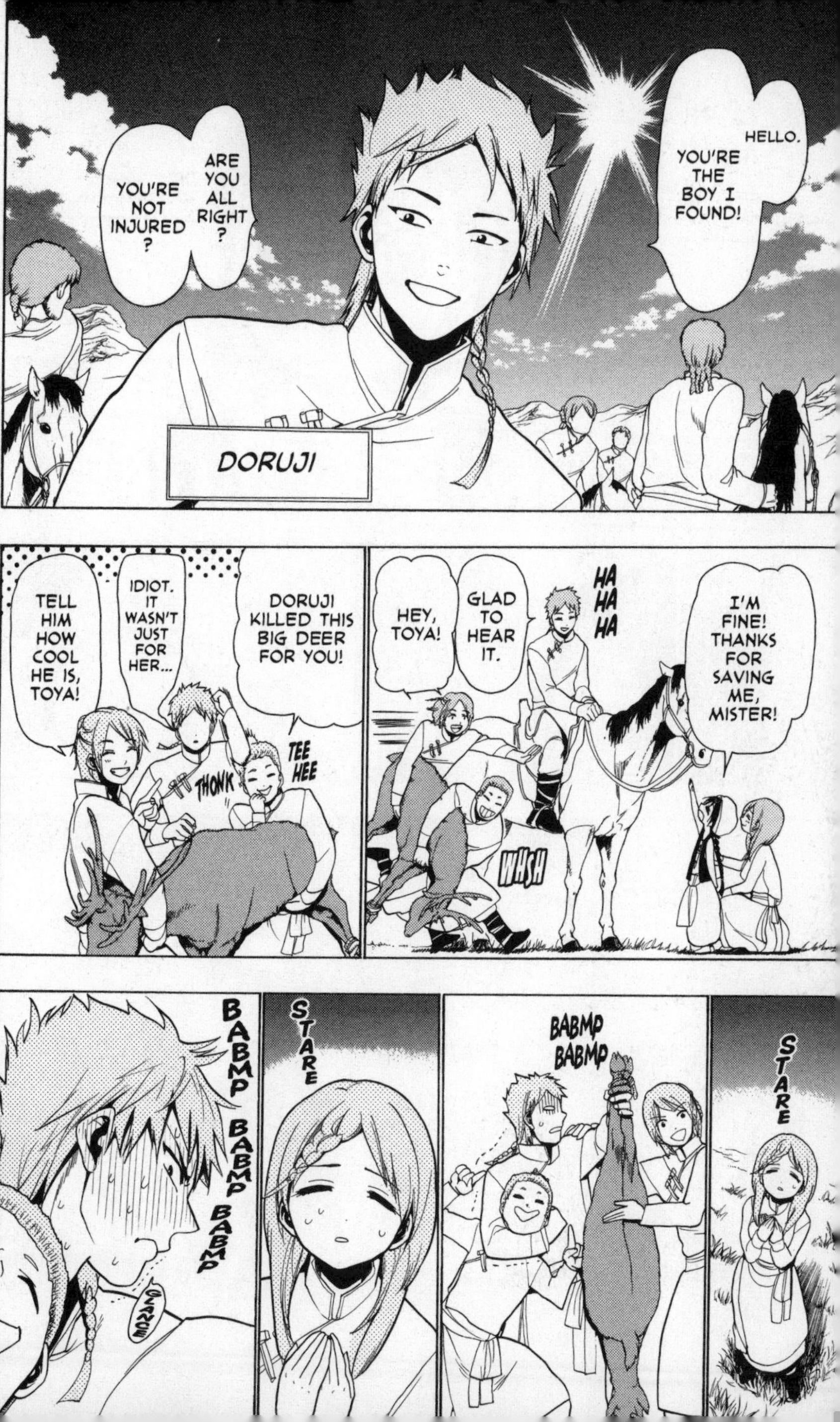
HELLO.
YOU'RE THE BOY I FOUND!
ARE YOU ALL RIGHT?
YOU'RE NOT INJURED?
DORUJI
I'M FINE! THANKS FOR SAVING ME, MISTER!
HA HA HA
GLAD TO HEAR IT.
HEY, TOYA!
WHSH
DORUJI KILLED THIS BIG DEER FOR YOU!
TEE HEE
IDIOT. IT WASN'T JUST FOR HER...
THONK
TELL HIM HOW COOL HE IS, TOYA!
STARE
BABMP BABMP
STARE
BABMP BABMP BABMP BABMP
GLANCE

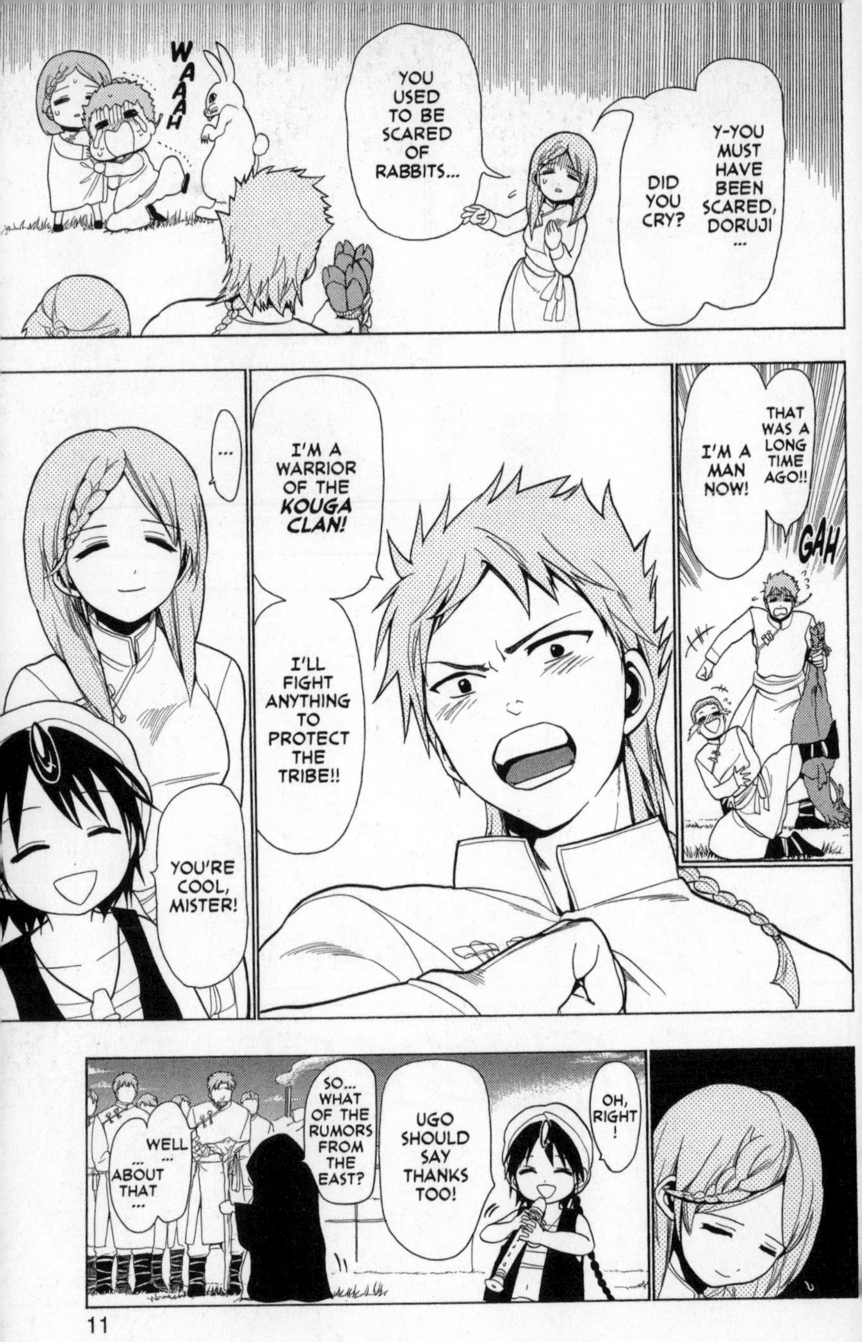
Y-YOU MUST HAVE BEEN SCARED, DORUJI ...
DID YOU CRY?
YOU USED TO BE SCARED OF RABBITS...
WAAAH
THAT WAS A LONG TIME AGO!!
I'M A MAN NOW!
GAH
I'M A WARRIOR OF THE *KOUGA CLAN!*
I'LL FIGHT ANYTHING TO PROTECT THE TRIBE!!
...
YOU'RE COOL, MISTER!
OH, RIGHT!
UGO SHOULD SAY THANKS TOO!
SO... WHAT OF THE RUMORS FROM THE EAST?
WELL ... ABOUT THAT ...

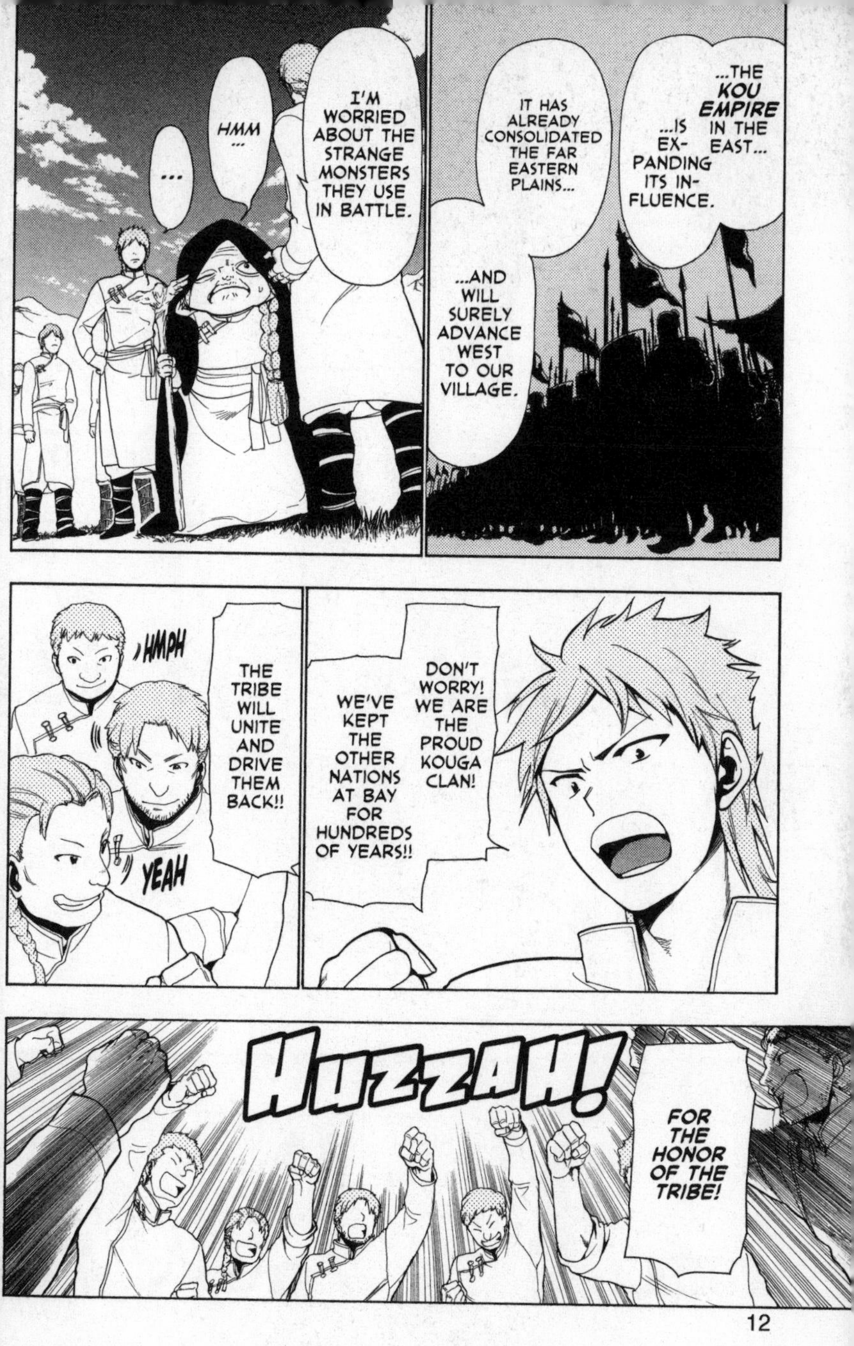
...THE KOU EMPIRE IN THE EAST...
...IS EXPANDING ITS INFLUENCE.
IT HAS ALREADY CONSOLIDATED THE FAR EASTERN PLAINS...
...AND WILL SURELY ADVANCE WEST TO OUR VILLAGE.
I'M WORRIED ABOUT THE STRANGE MONSTERS THEY USE IN BATTLE.
HMM...
...
DON'T WORRY! WE ARE THE PROUD KOUGA CLAN!
WE'VE KEPT THE OTHER NATIONS AT BAY FOR HUNDREDS OF YEARS!!
HMPH
THE TRIBE WILL UNITE AND DRIVE THEM BACK!!
YEAH
FOR THE HONOR OF THE TRIBE!
HUZZAH!

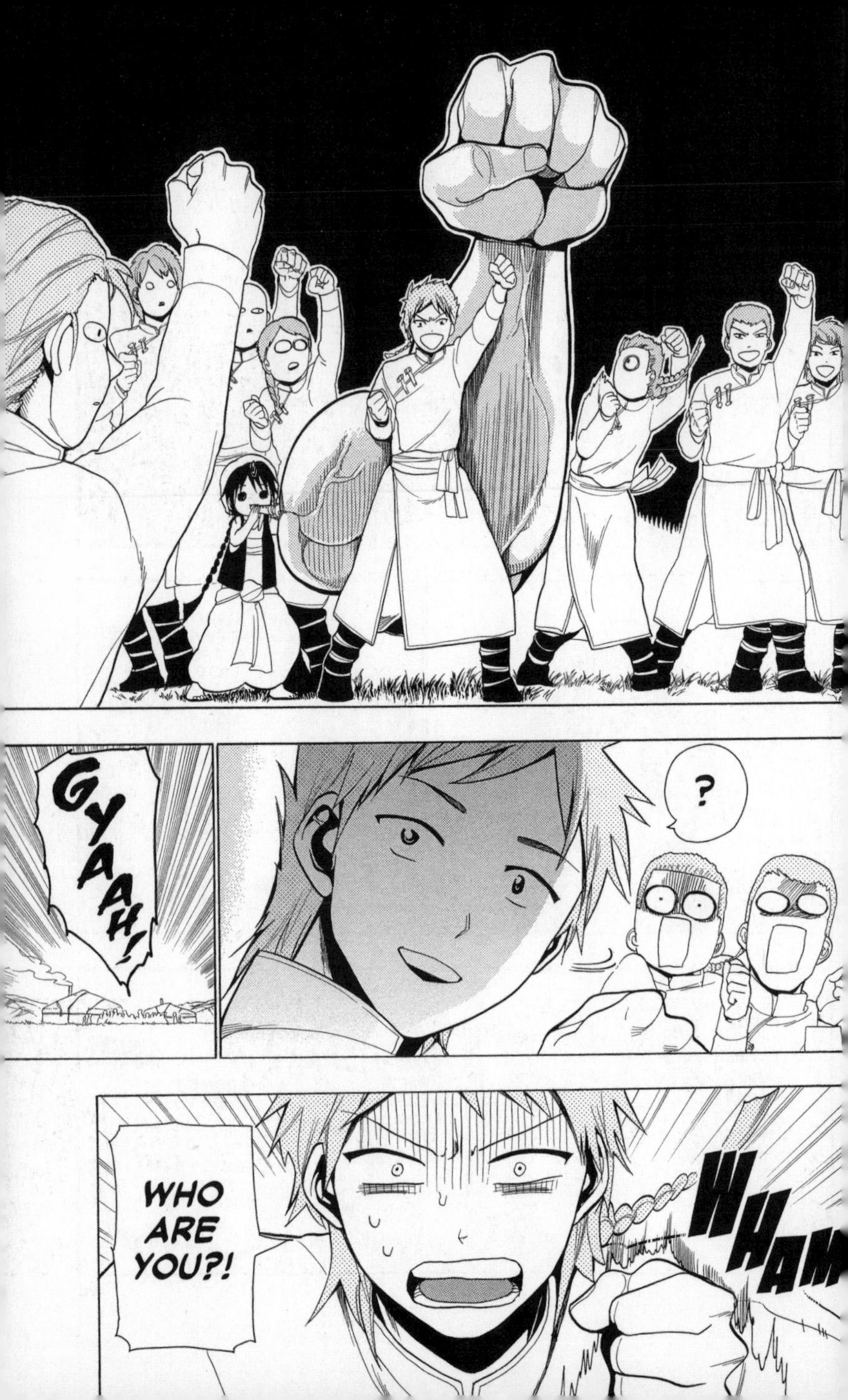
?
GYAAH!
WHAM
WHO ARE YOU?!

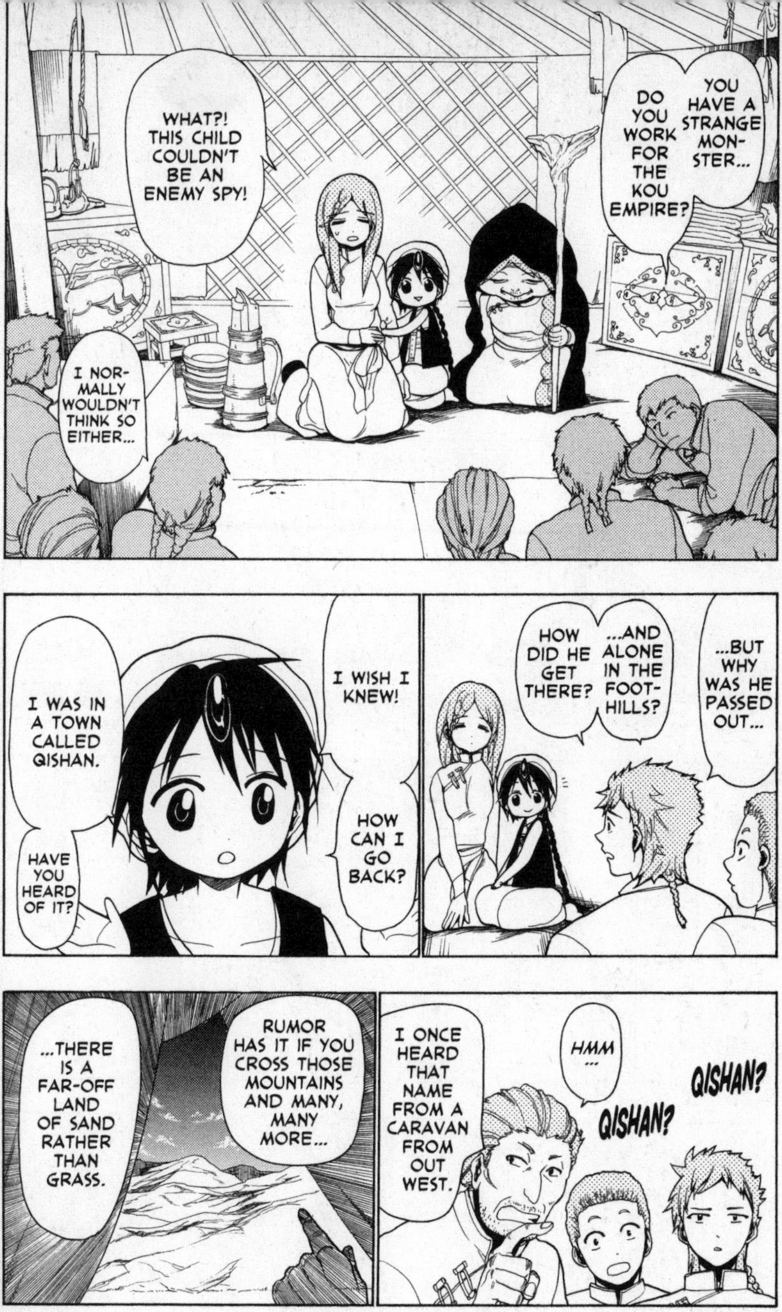
YOU HAVE A STRANGE MONSTER...
DO YOU WORK FOR THE KOU EMPIRE?
WHAT?! THIS CHILD COULDN'T BE AN ENEMY SPY!
I NORMALLY WOULDN'T THINK SO EITHER...
...BUT WHY WAS HE PASSED OUT...
...AND ALONE IN THE FOOTHILLS?
HOW DID HE GET THERE?
I WISH I KNEW!
HOW CAN I GO BACK?
I WAS IN A TOWN CALLED QISHAN.
HAVE YOU HEARD OF IT?
QISHAN?
QISHAN?
HMM...
I ONCE HEARD THAT NAME FROM A CARAVAN FROM OUT WEST.
RUMOR HAS IT IF YOU CROSS THOSE MOUNTAINS AND MANY, MANY MORE...
...THERE IS A FAR-OFF LAND OF SAND RATHER THAN GRASS.

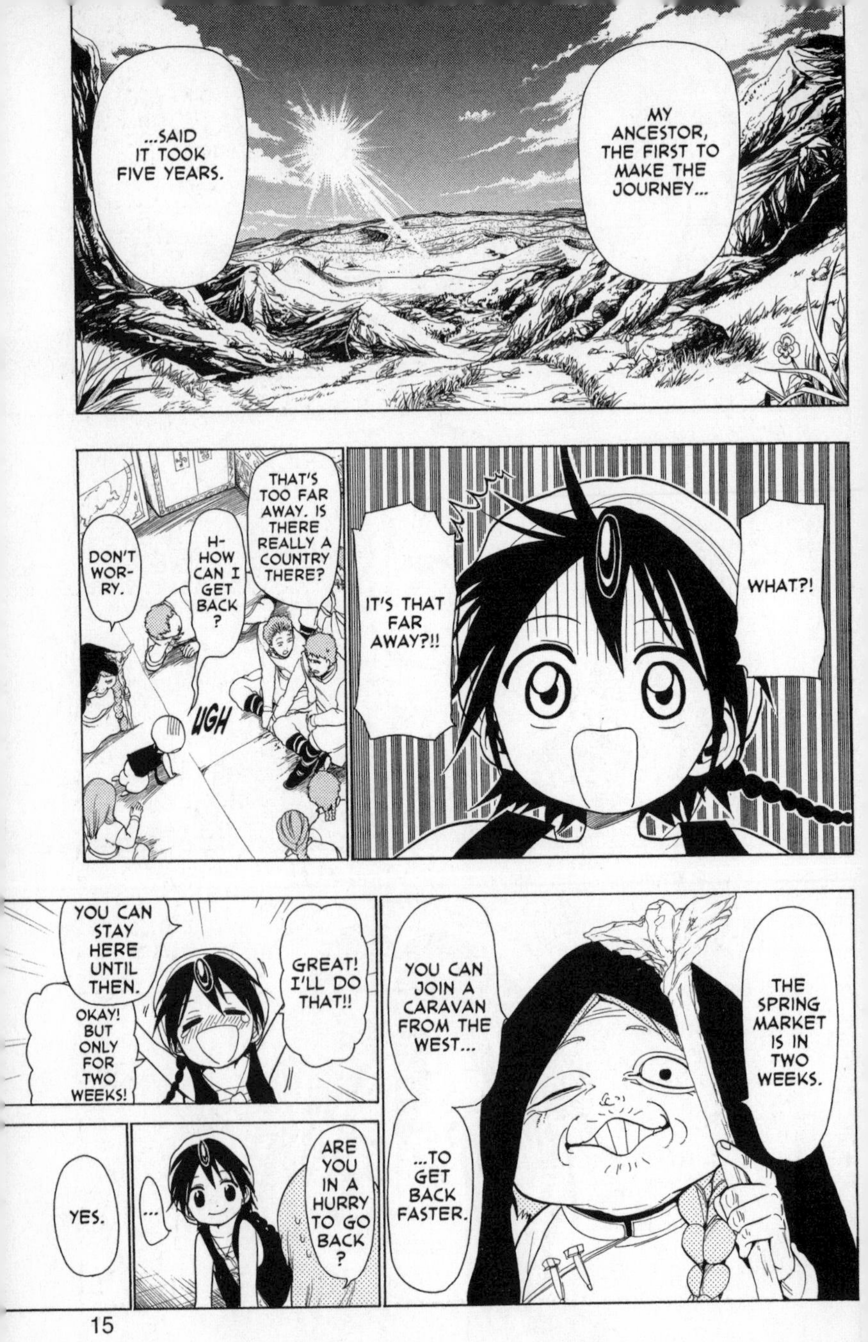
MY ANCESTOR, THE FIRST TO MAKE THE JOURNEY...
...SAID IT TOOK FIVE YEARS.
WHAT?!
IT'S THAT FAR AWAY?!!
THAT'S TOO FAR AWAY. IS THERE REALLY A COUNTRY THERE?
H-HOW CAN I GET BACK?
DON'T WOR-RY.
UGH
THE SPRING MARKET IS IN TWO WEEKS.
YOU CAN JOIN A CARAVAN FROM THE WEST...
...TO GET BACK FASTER.
GREAT! I'LL DO THAT!!
YOU CAN STAY HERE UNTIL THEN.
OKAY! BUT ONLY FOR TWO WEEKS!
ARE YOU IN A HURRY TO GO BACK?
...
YES.

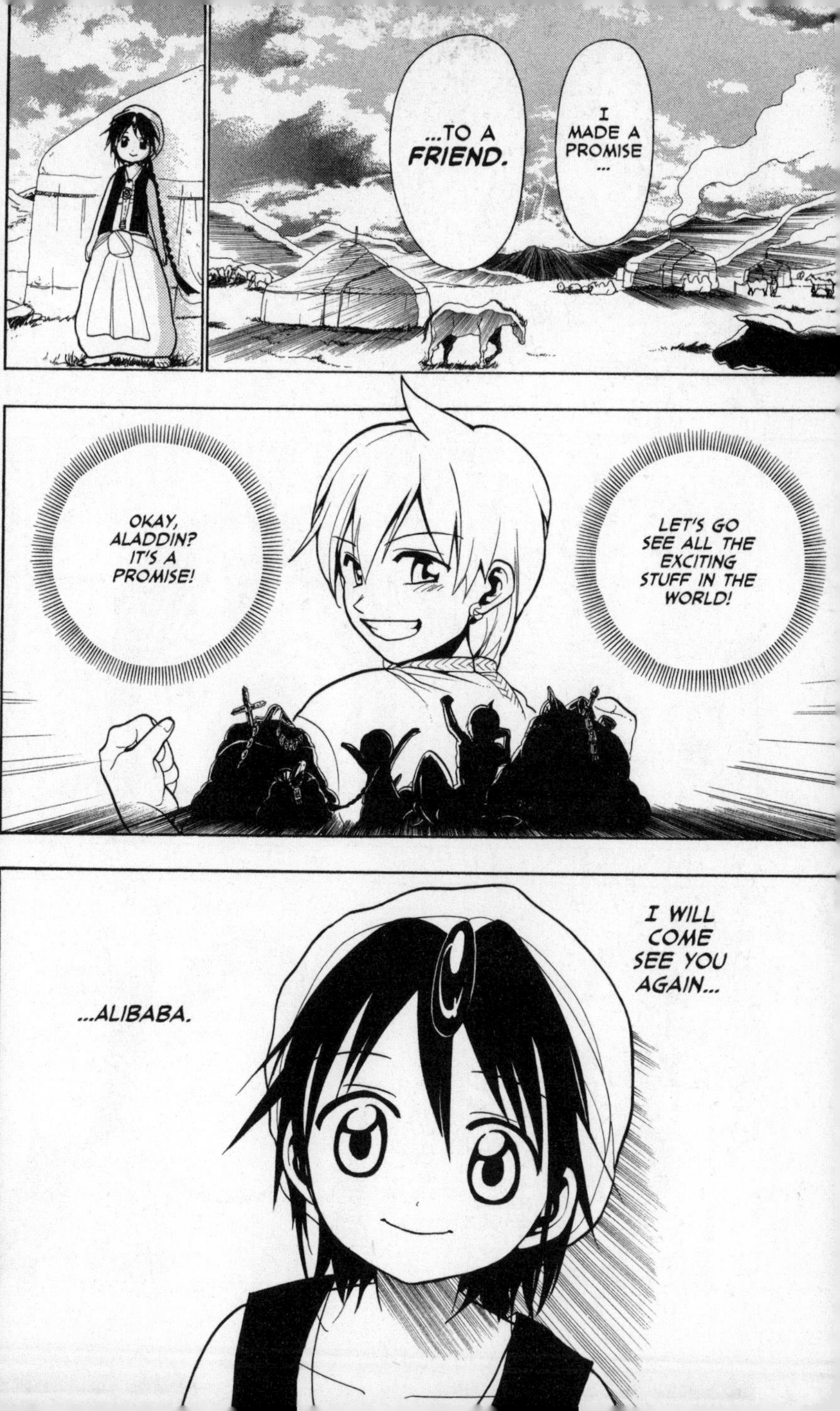
I MADE A PROMISE...
...TO A FRIEND.
LET'S GO SEE ALL THE EXCITING STUFF IN THE WORLD!
OKAY, ALADDIN? IT'S A PROMISE!
I WILL COME SEE YOU AGAIN...
...ALIBABA.

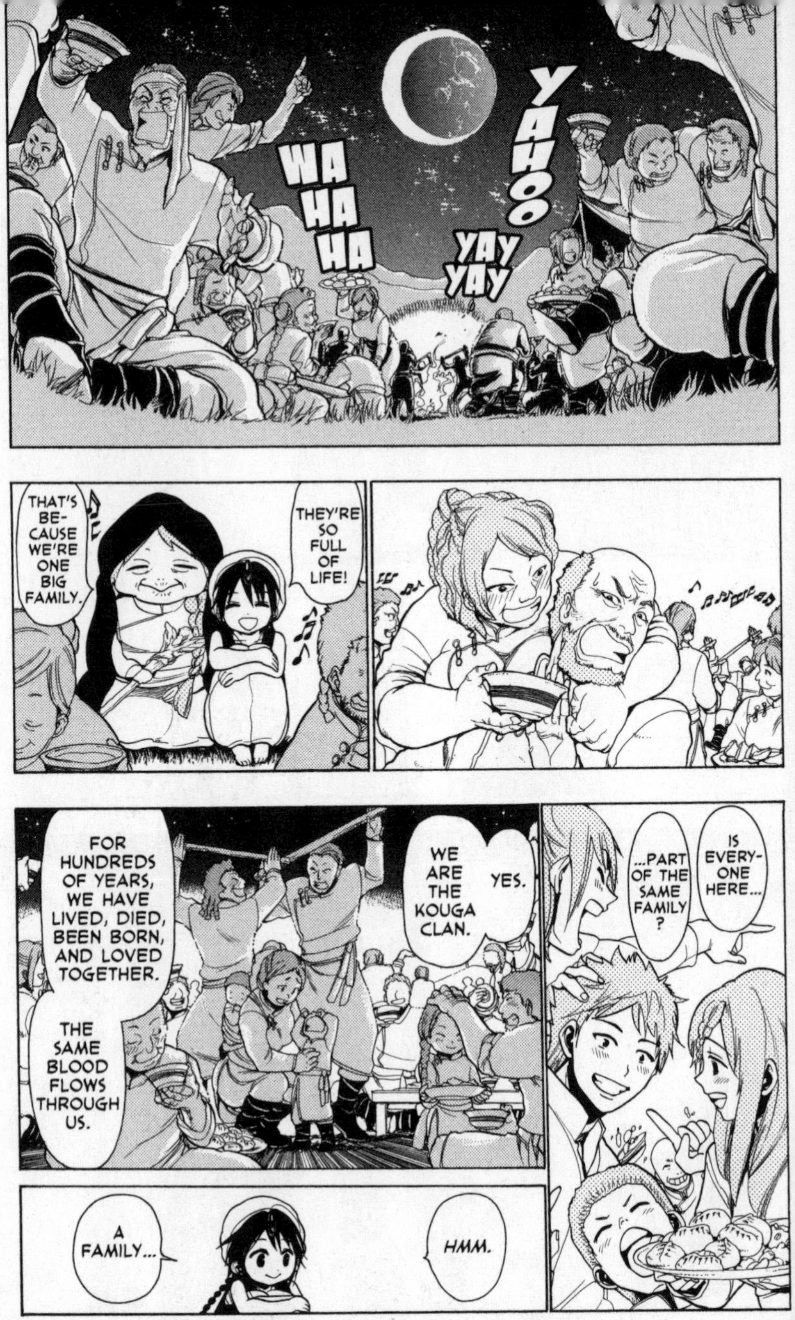
YAHOO
WA HA HA
YAY YAY
THEY'RE SO FULL OF LIFE!
THAT'S BE-CAUSE WE'RE ONE BIG FAMILY.
IS EVERY-ONE HERE...
...PART OF THE SAME FAMILY?
YES.
WE ARE THE KOUGA CLAN.
FOR HUNDREDS OF YEARS, WE HAVE LIVED, DIED, BEEN BORN, AND LOVED TOGETHER.
THE SAME BLOOD FLOWS THROUGH US.
HMM.
A FAMILY...

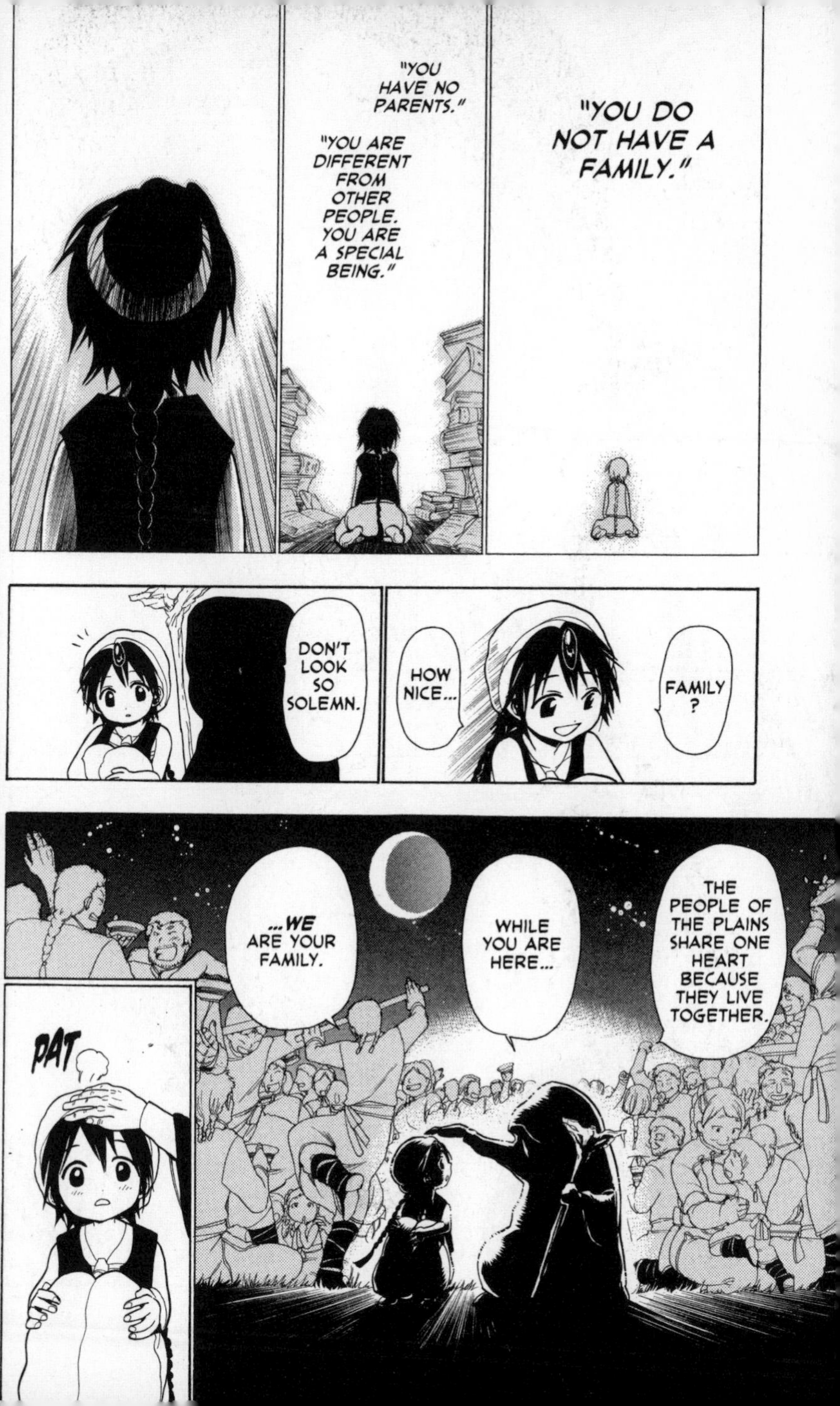
"YOU DO NOT HAVE A FAMILY."
"YOU HAVE NO PARENTS."
"YOU ARE DIFFERENT FROM OTHER PEOPLE. YOU ARE A SPECIAL BEING."
FAMILY?
HOW NICE...
DON'T LOOK SO SOLEMN.
THE PEOPLE OF THE PLAINS SHARE ONE HEART BECAUSE THEY LIVE TOGETHER.
WHILE YOU ARE HERE...
...WE ARE YOUR FAMILY.
PAT

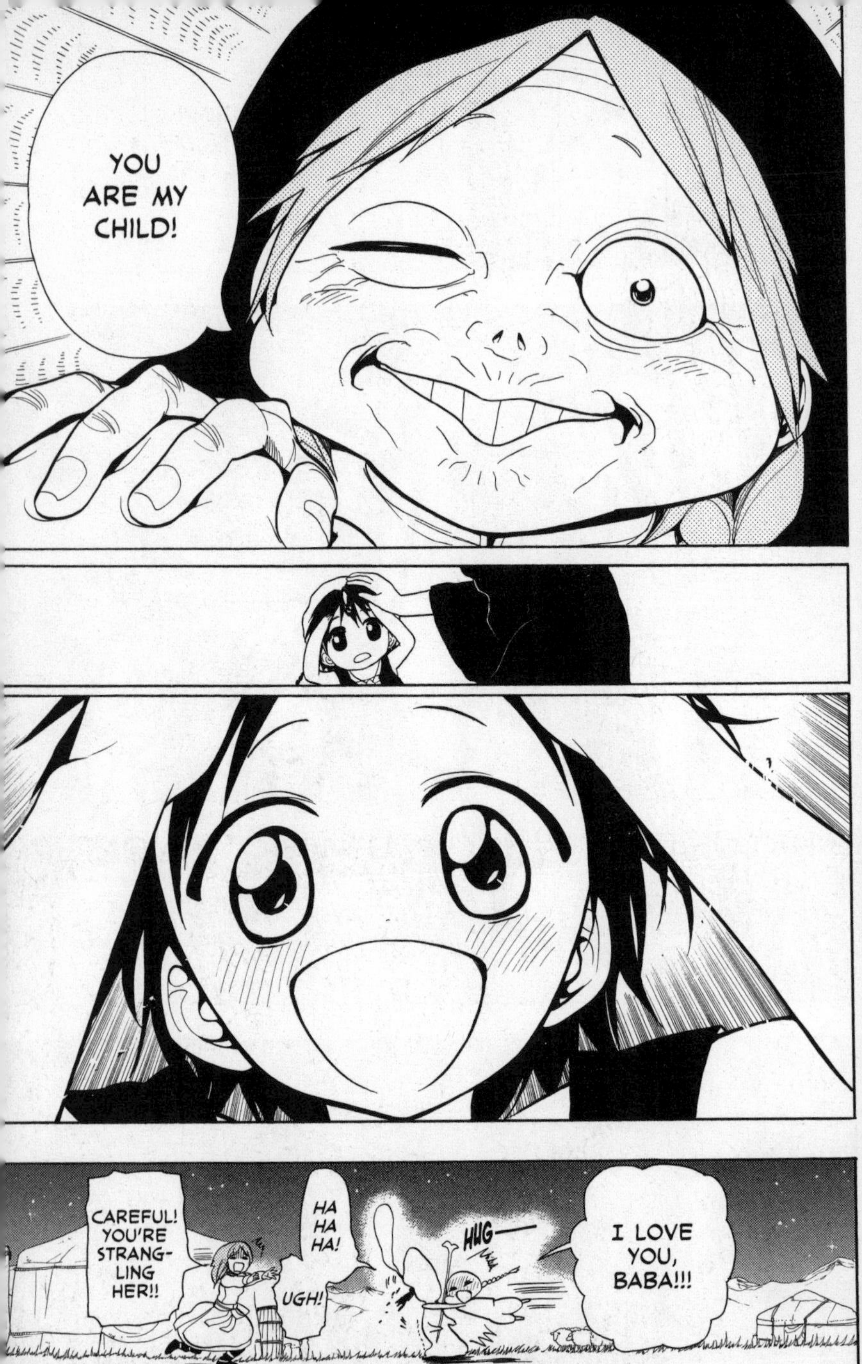
YOU ARE MY CHILD!
I LOVE YOU, BABA!!!
HUG—
HA HA HA!
UGH!
CAREFUL! YOU'RE STRANG-LING HER!!

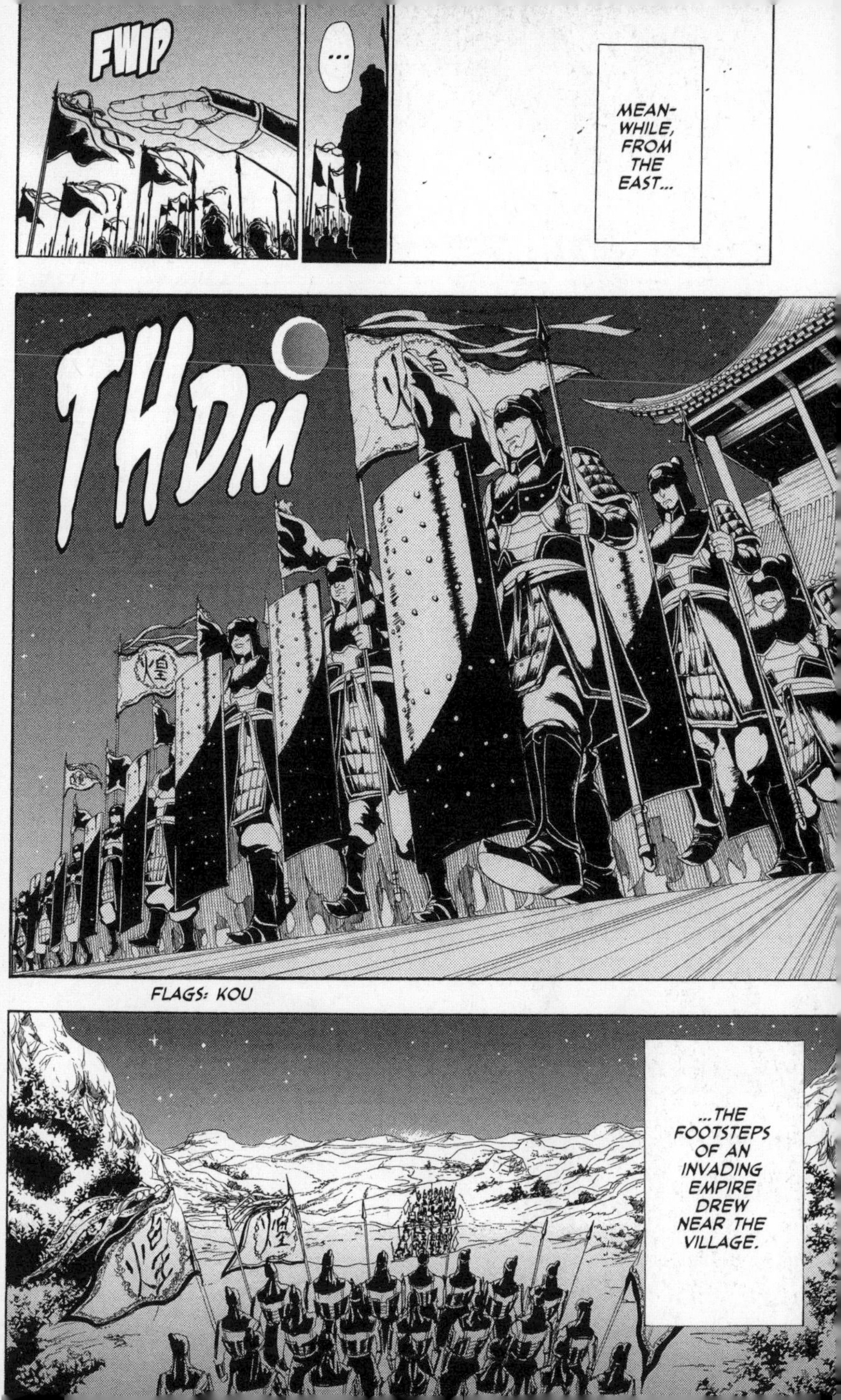
MEAN-WHILE, FROM THE EAST...
...
FWIP
THDM
FLAGS: KOU
...THE FOOTSTEPS OF AN INVADING EMPIRE DREW NEAR THE VILLAGE.

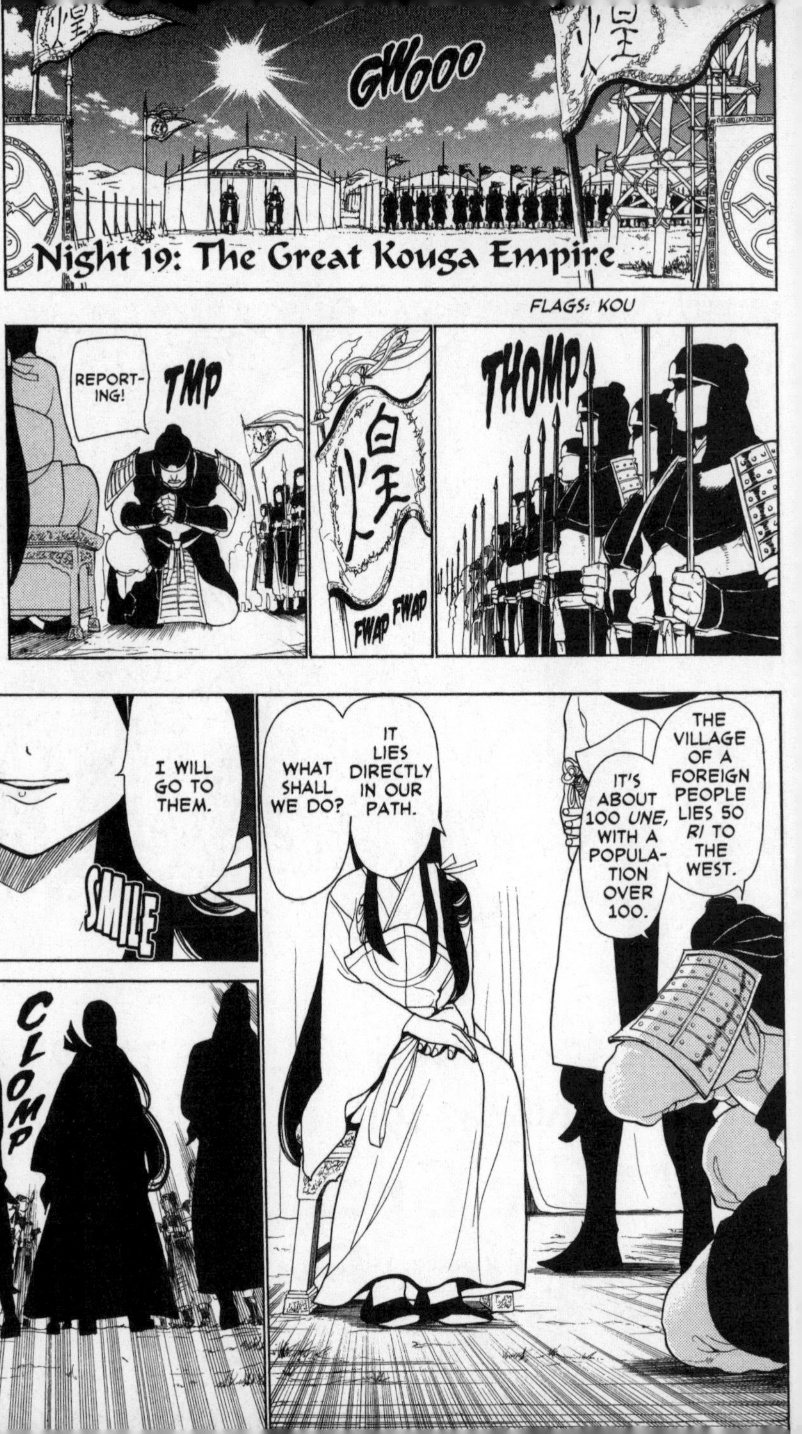
GWOOO
Night 19: The Great Kouga Empire
FLAGS: KOU
THOMP
FWAP FWAP
REPORTING!
TMP
THE VILLAGE OF A FOREIGN PEOPLE LIES 50 *RI* TO THE WEST.
IT'S ABOUT 100 *UNE*, WITH A POPULATION OVER 100.
IT LIES DIRECTLY IN OUR PATH.
WHAT SHALL WE DO?
I WILL GO TO THEM.
SMILE
CLOMP

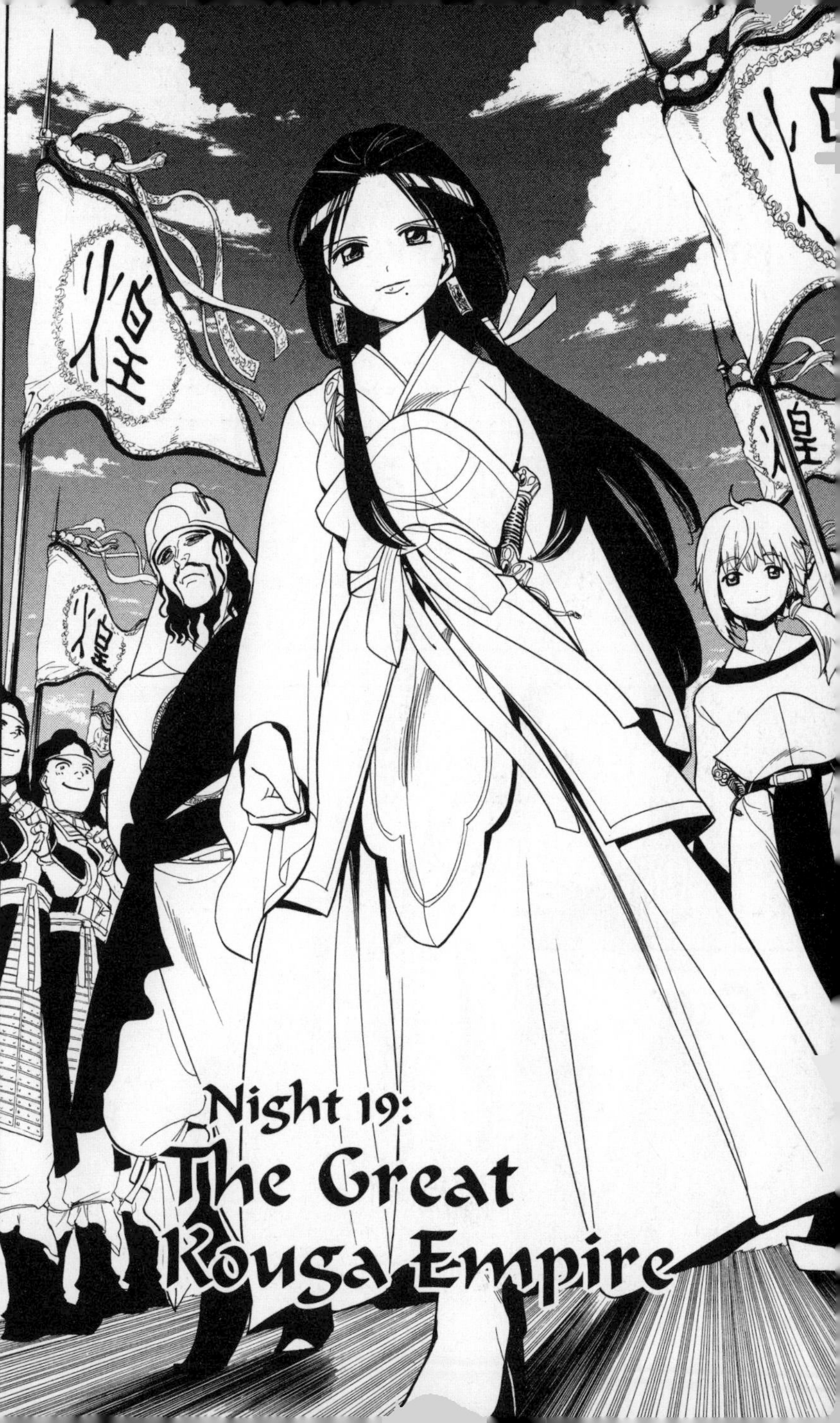
Night 19:
The Great Kouga Empire

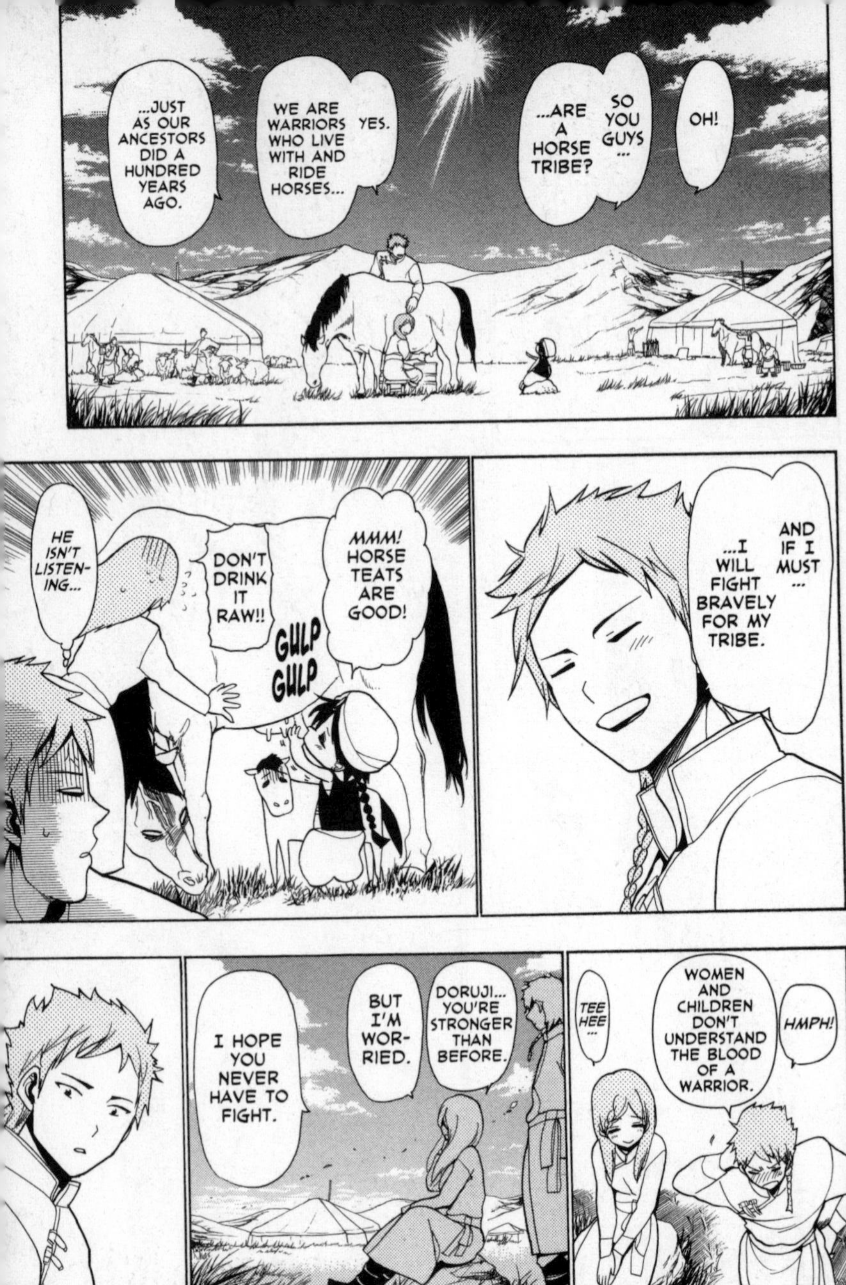
OH!
SO YOU GUYS...
...ARE A HORSE TRIBE?
YES.
WE ARE WARRIORS WHO LIVE WITH AND RIDE HORSES...
...JUST AS OUR ANCESTORS DID A HUNDRED YEARS AGO.
AND IF I MUST...
...I WILL FIGHT BRAVELY FOR MY TRIBE.
MMM! HORSE TEATS ARE GOOD!
GULP GULP
DON'T DRINK IT RAW!!
HE ISN'T LISTENING...
HMPH!
WOMEN AND CHILDREN DON'T UNDERSTAND THE BLOOD OF A WARRIOR.
TEE HEE...
DORUJI... YOU'RE STRONGER THAN BEFORE.
BUT I'M WORRIED.
I HOPE YOU NEVER HAVE TO FIGHT.

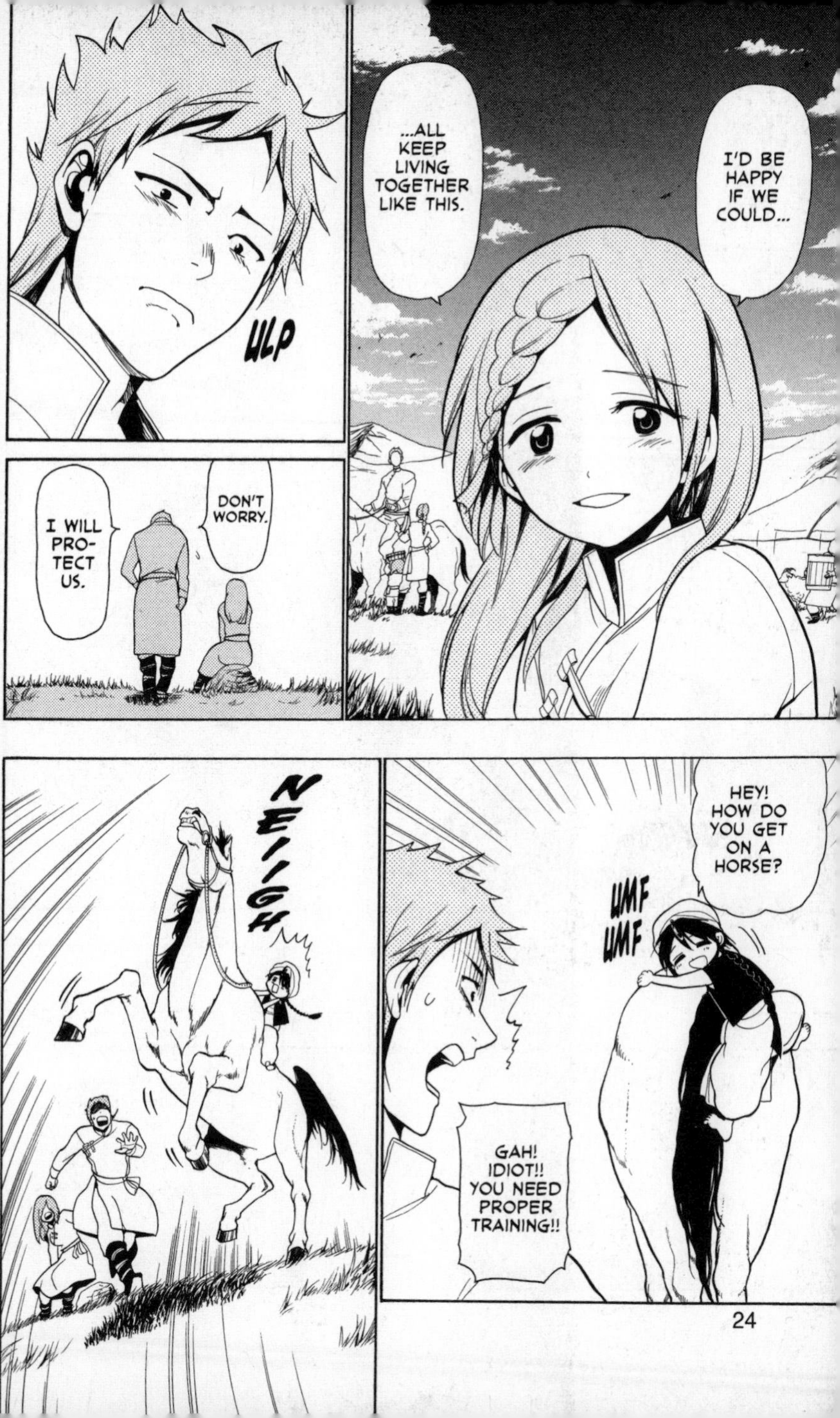
I'D BE HAPPY IF WE COULD...
...ALL KEEP LIVING TOGETHER LIKE THIS.
ULP
DON'T WORRY.
I WILL PRO-TECT US.
HEY! HOW DO YOU GET ON A HORSE?
UMF UMF
GAH! IDIOT!! YOU NEED PROPER TRAINING!!
NEIIGH

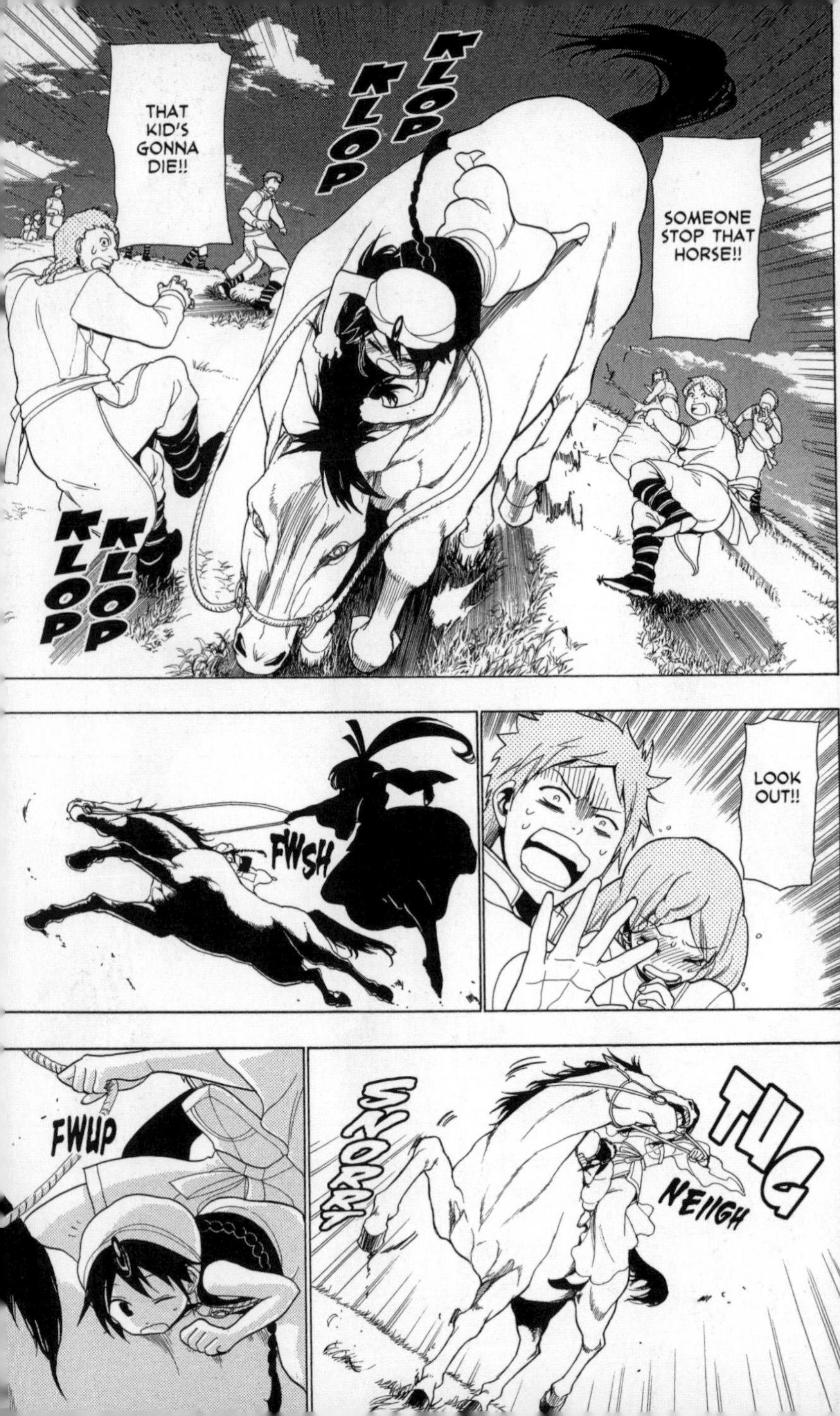
SOMEONE STOP THAT HORSE!!
KLOP KLOP
THAT KID'S GONNA DIE!!
KLOP KLOP
LOOK OUT!!
FWSH
TUG
NEIIGH
SNORR
FWUP

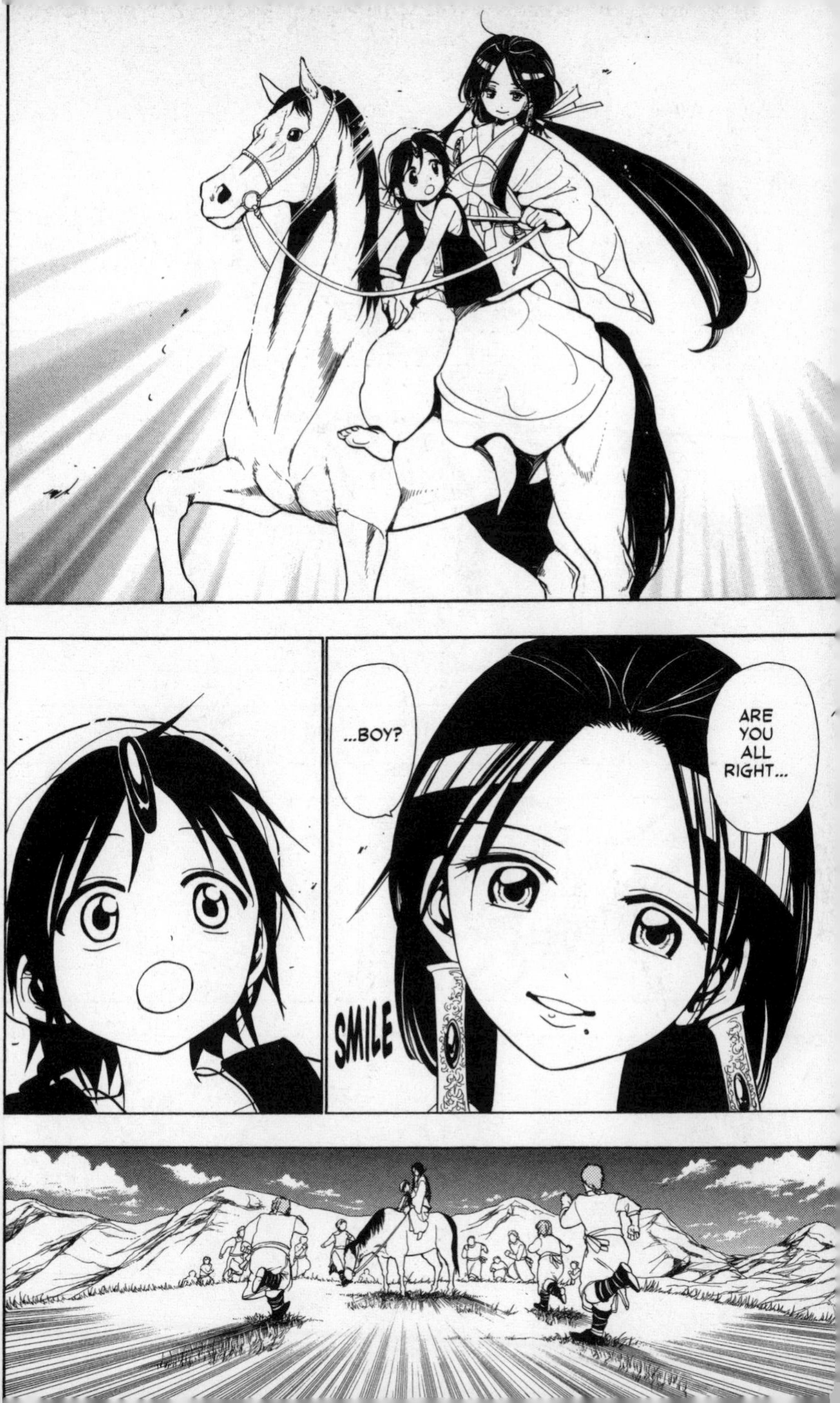
ARE YOU ALL RIGHT...
...BOY?
SMILE

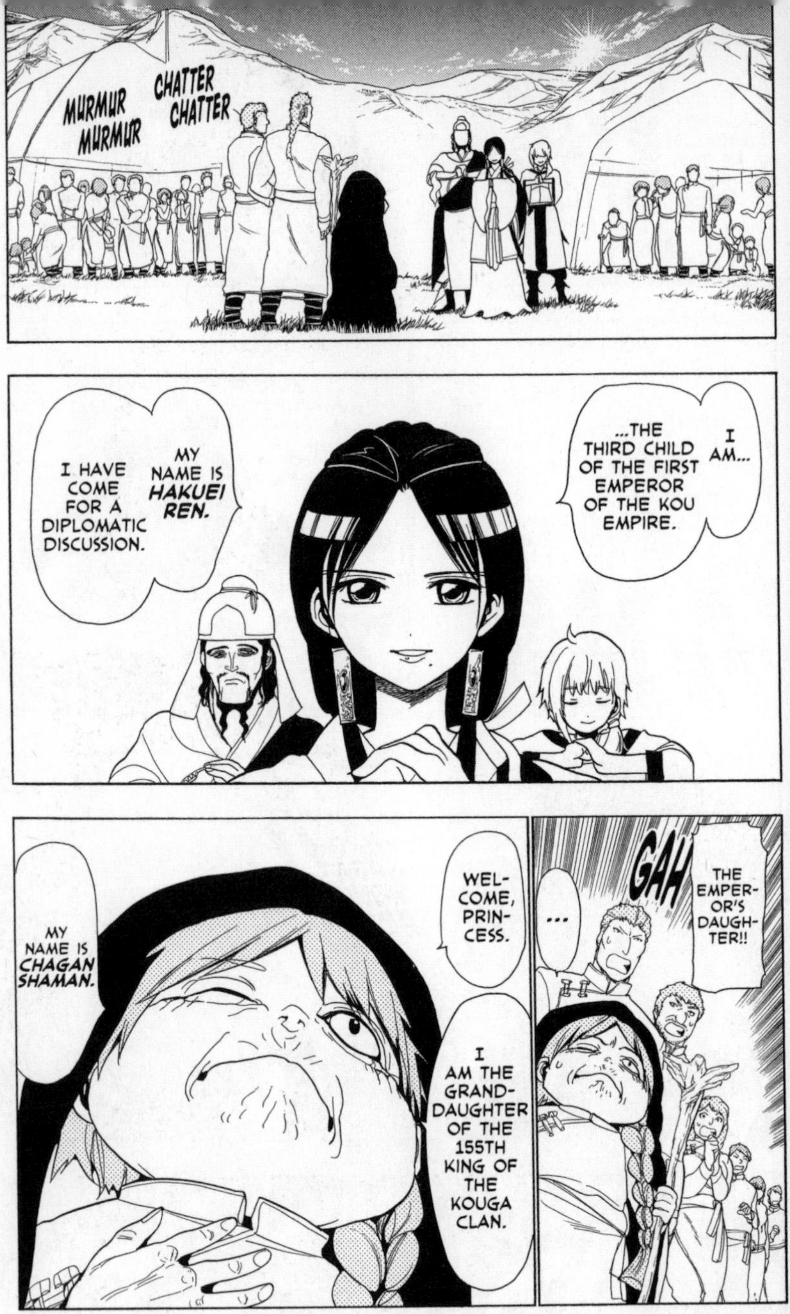
CHATTER CHATTER
MURMUR MURMUR
I AM...
...THE THIRD CHILD OF THE FIRST EMPEROR OF THE KOU EMPIRE.
MY NAME IS HAKUEI REN.
I HAVE COME FOR A DIPLOMATIC DISCUSSION.
GAH
THE EMPEROR'S DAUGHTER!!
...
WELCOME, PRINCESS.
I AM THE GRANDDAUGHTER OF THE 155TH KING OF THE KOUGA CLAN.
MY NAME IS CHAGAN SHAMAN.

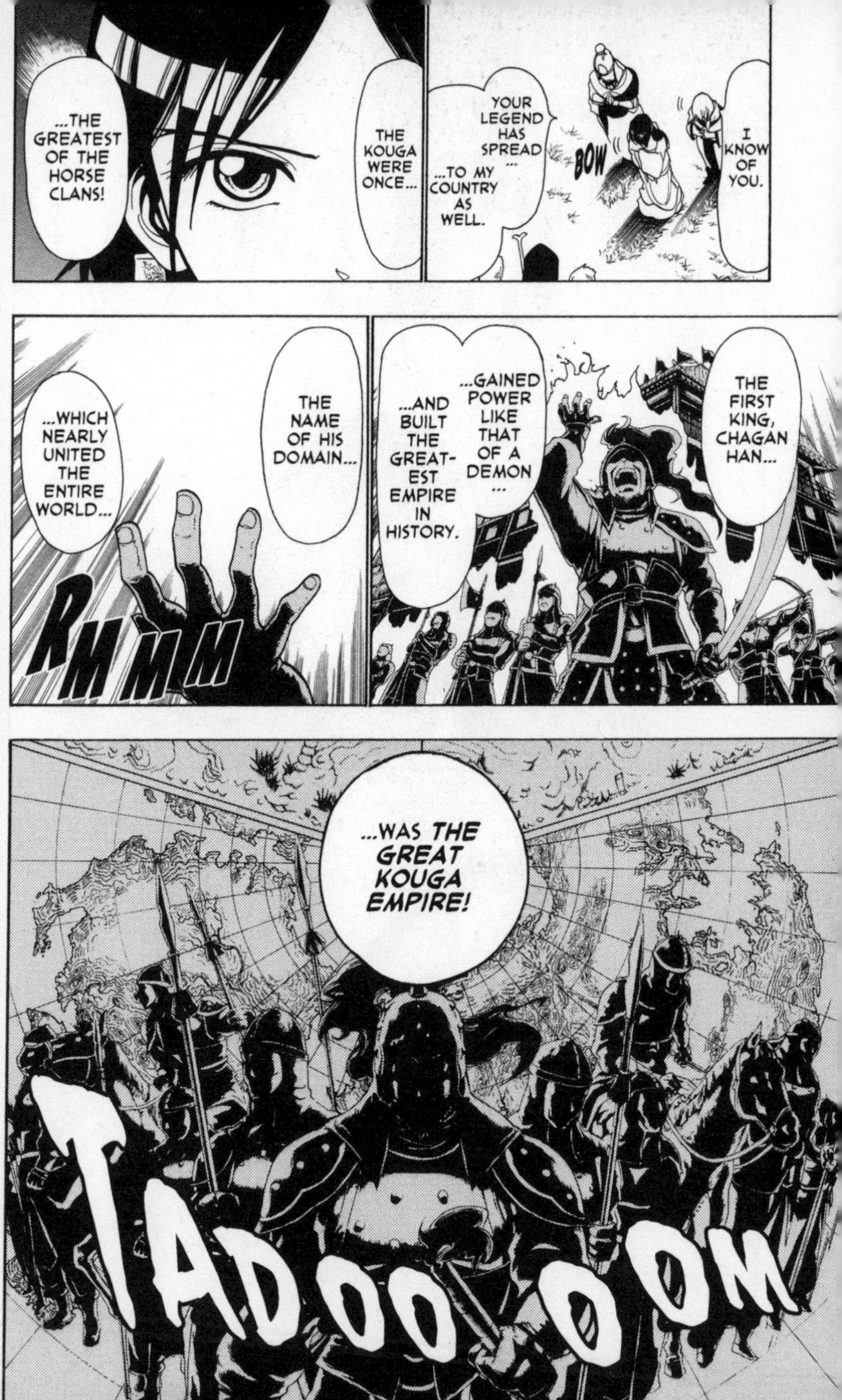
I KNOW OF YOU.
BOW
YOUR LEGEND HAS SPREAD...
...TO MY COUNTRY AS WELL.
THE KOUGA WERE ONCE...
...THE GREATEST OF THE HORSE CLANS!
THE FIRST KING, CHAGAN HAN...
...GAINED POWER LIKE THAT OF A DEMON...
...AND BUILT THE GREAT-EST EMPIRE IN HISTORY.
THE NAME OF HIS DOMAIN...
...WHICH NEARLY UNITED THE ENTIRE WORLD...
RMMMM
...WAS THE GREAT KOUGA EMPIRE!
TADOOOOOM

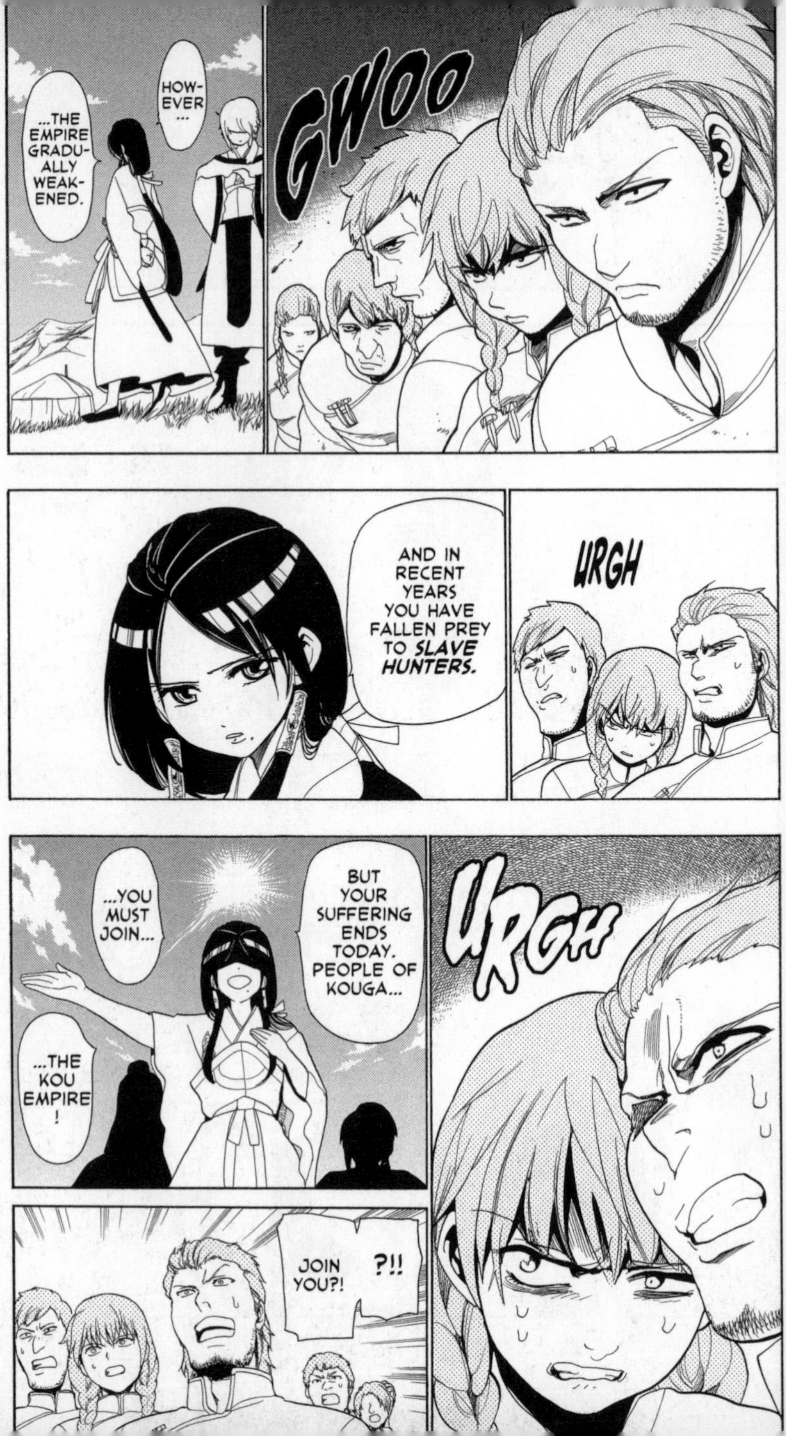
GWOO
HOW-EVER...
...THE EMPIRE GRADU-ALLY WEAK-ENED.
URGH
AND IN RECENT YEARS YOU HAVE FALLEN PREY TO *SLAVE HUNTERS.*
URGH
BUT YOUR SUFFERING ENDS TODAY. PEOPLE OF KOUGA...
...YOU MUST JOIN...
...THE KOU EMPIRE!
?!!
JOIN YOU?!

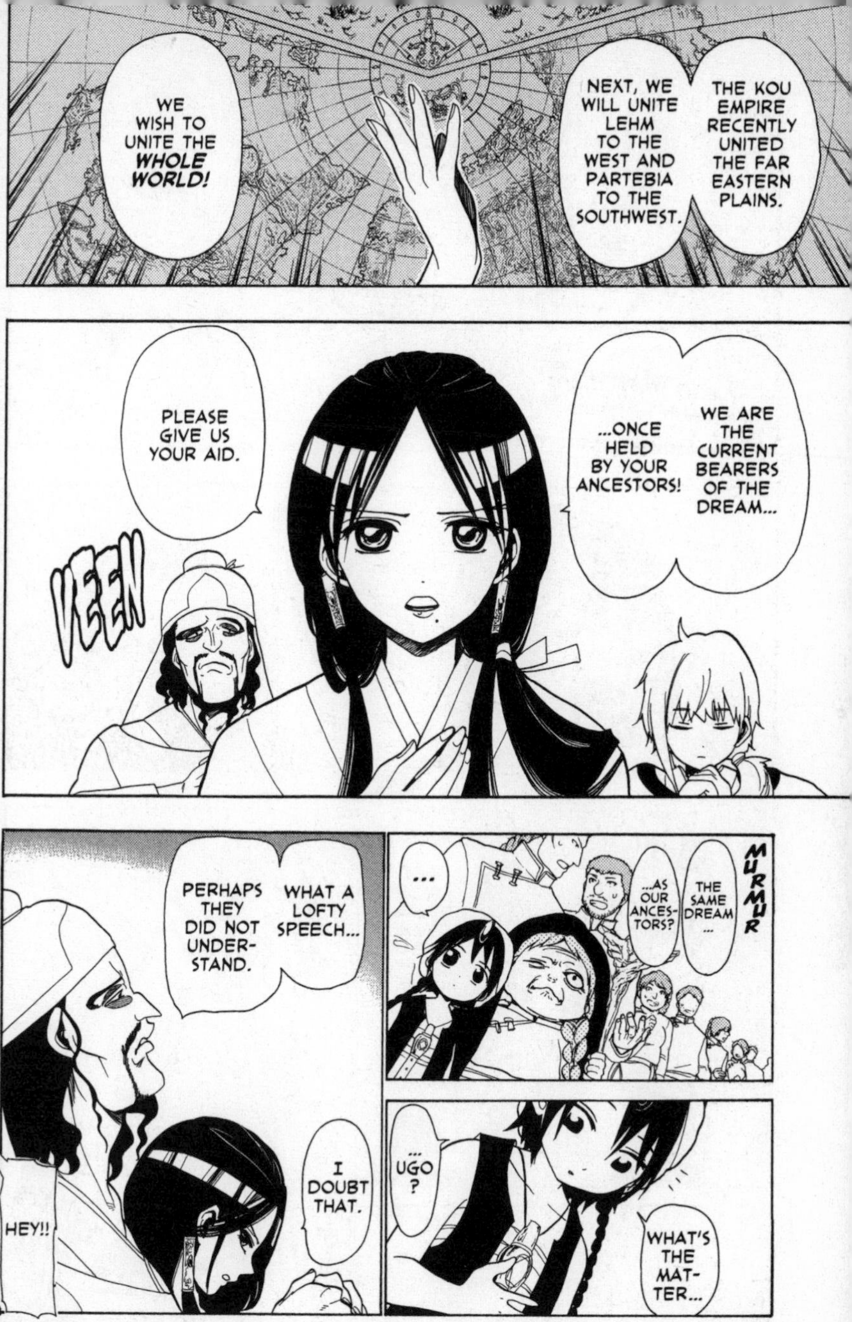
THE KOU EMPIRE RECENTLY UNITED THE FAR EASTERN PLAINS.
NEXT, WE WILL UNITE LEHM TO THE WEST AND PARTEBIA TO THE SOUTHWEST.
WE WISH TO UNITE THE ***WHOLE WORLD!***
WE ARE THE CURRENT BEARERS OF THE DREAM...
...ONCE HELD BY YOUR ANCESTORS!
PLEASE GIVE US YOUR AID.
VEEN
MURMUR
THE SAME DREAM...
...AS OUR ANCESTORS?
...
WHAT'S THE MATTER...
...UGO?
WHAT A LOFTY SPEECH...
PERHAPS THEY DID NOT UNDERSTAND.
I DOUBT THAT.
HEY!!

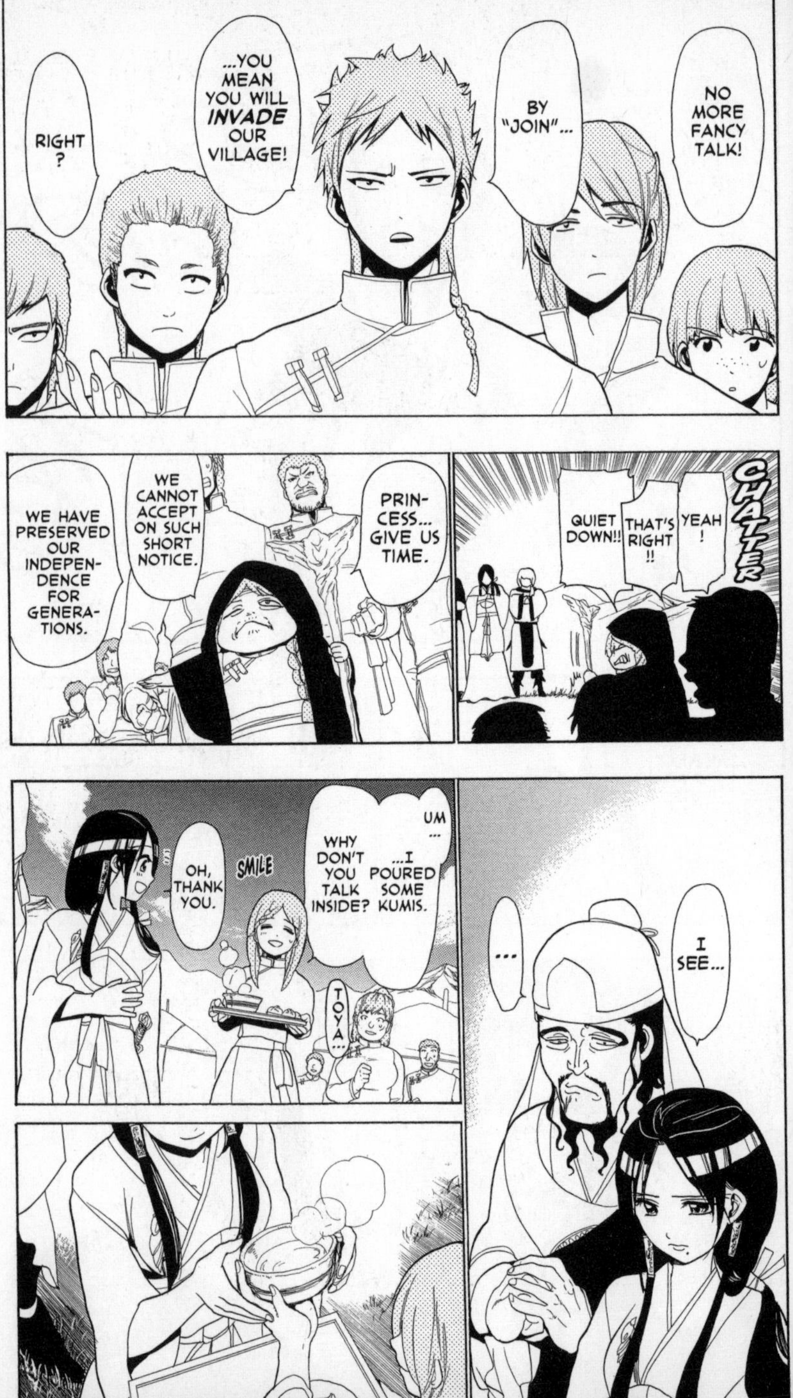
NO MORE FANCY TALK!
BY "JOIN"...
...YOU MEAN YOU WILL *INVADE* OUR VILLAGE!
RIGHT?
CHATTER
YEAH!
THAT'S RIGHT!!
QUIET DOWN!!
PRINCESS... GIVE US TIME.
WE CANNOT ACCEPT ON SUCH SHORT NOTICE.
WE HAVE PRESERVED OUR INDEPENDENCE FOR GENERATIONS.
I SEE...
...
UM...
...I POURED SOME KUMIS.
WHY DON'T YOU TALK INSIDE?
SMILE
OH, THANK YOU.
TOYA...

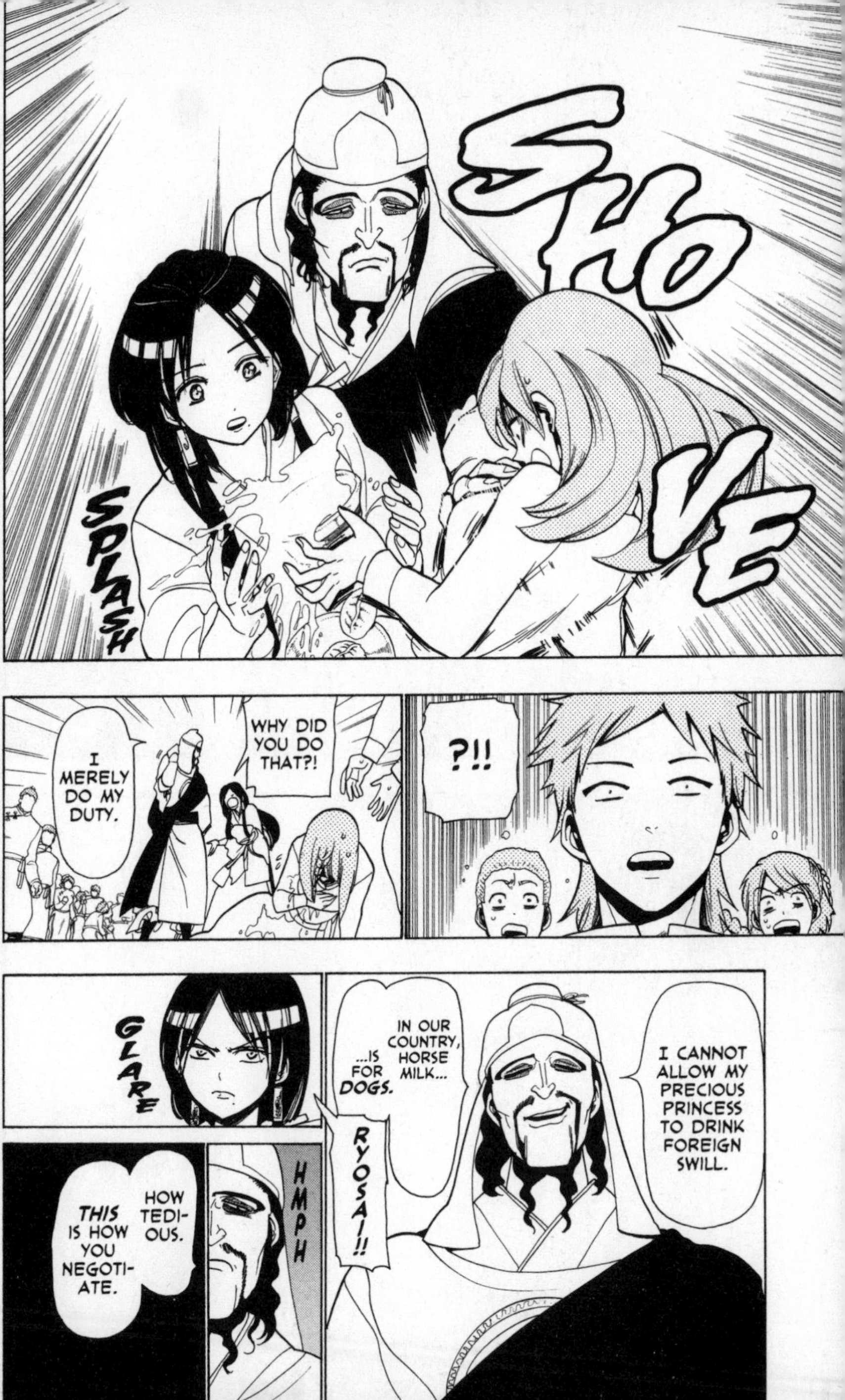

SHOVE
SPLASH
?!!
WHY DID YOU DO THAT?!
I MERELY DO MY DUTY.
I CANNOT ALLOW MY PRECIOUS PRINCESS TO DRINK FOREIGN SWILL.
IN OUR COUNTRY, HORSE MILK...
...IS FOR *DOGS.*
RYOSAI!!
GLARE
HMPH
HOW TEDIOUS.
THIS IS HOW YOU NEGOTIATE.

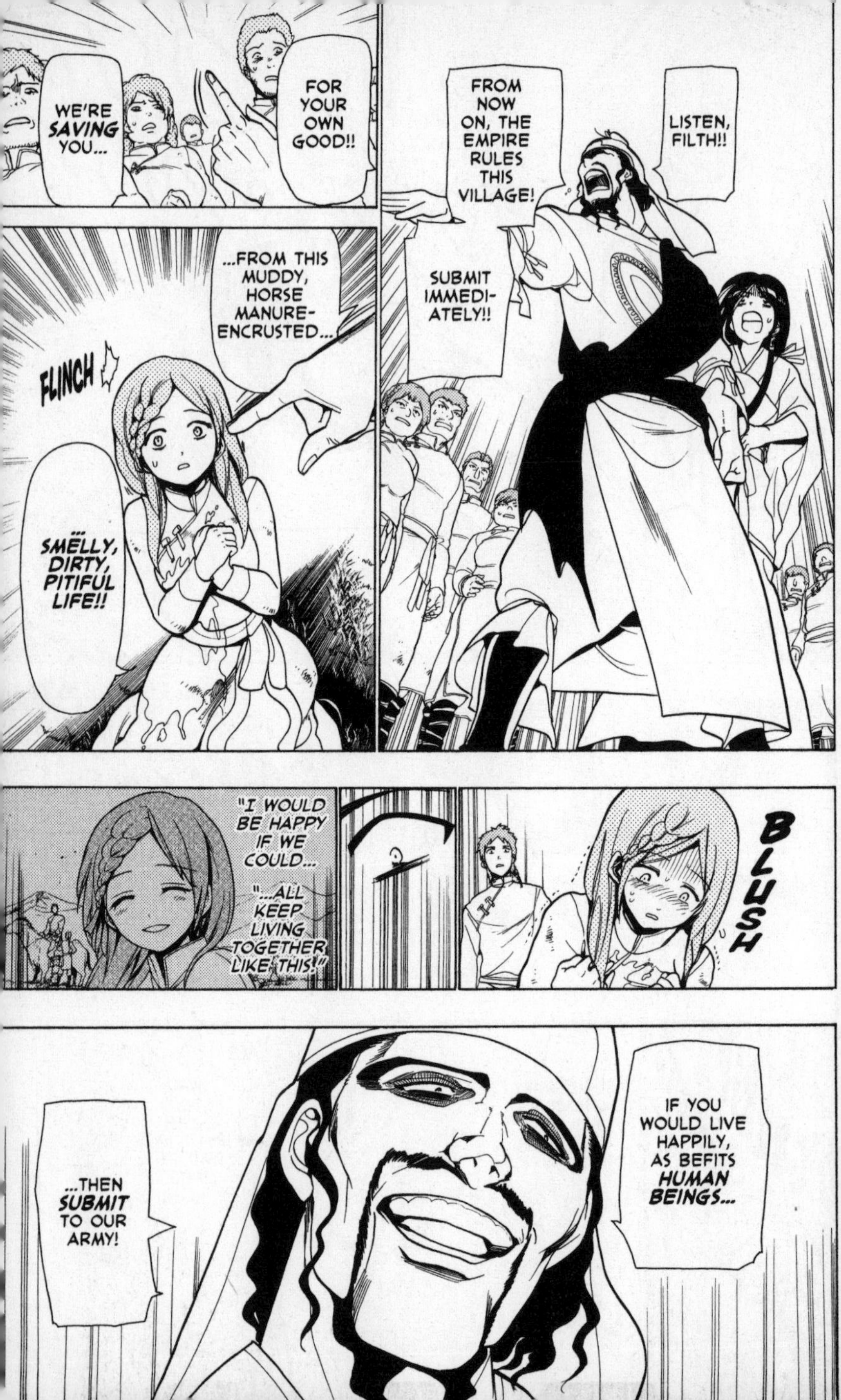
LISTEN, FILTH!!
FROM NOW ON, THE EMPIRE RULES THIS VILLAGE!
SUBMIT IMMEDIATELY!!
FOR YOUR OWN GOOD!!
WE'RE SAVING YOU...
...FROM THIS MUDDY, HORSE MANURE-ENCRUSTED...
FLINCH
...SMELLY, DIRTY, PITIFUL LIFE!!
BLUSH
"I WOULD BE HAPPY IF WE COULD...
"...ALL KEEP LIVING TOGETHER LIKE THIS!"
IF YOU WOULD LIVE HAPPILY, AS BEFITS HUMAN BEINGS...
...THEN SUBMIT TO OUR ARMY!

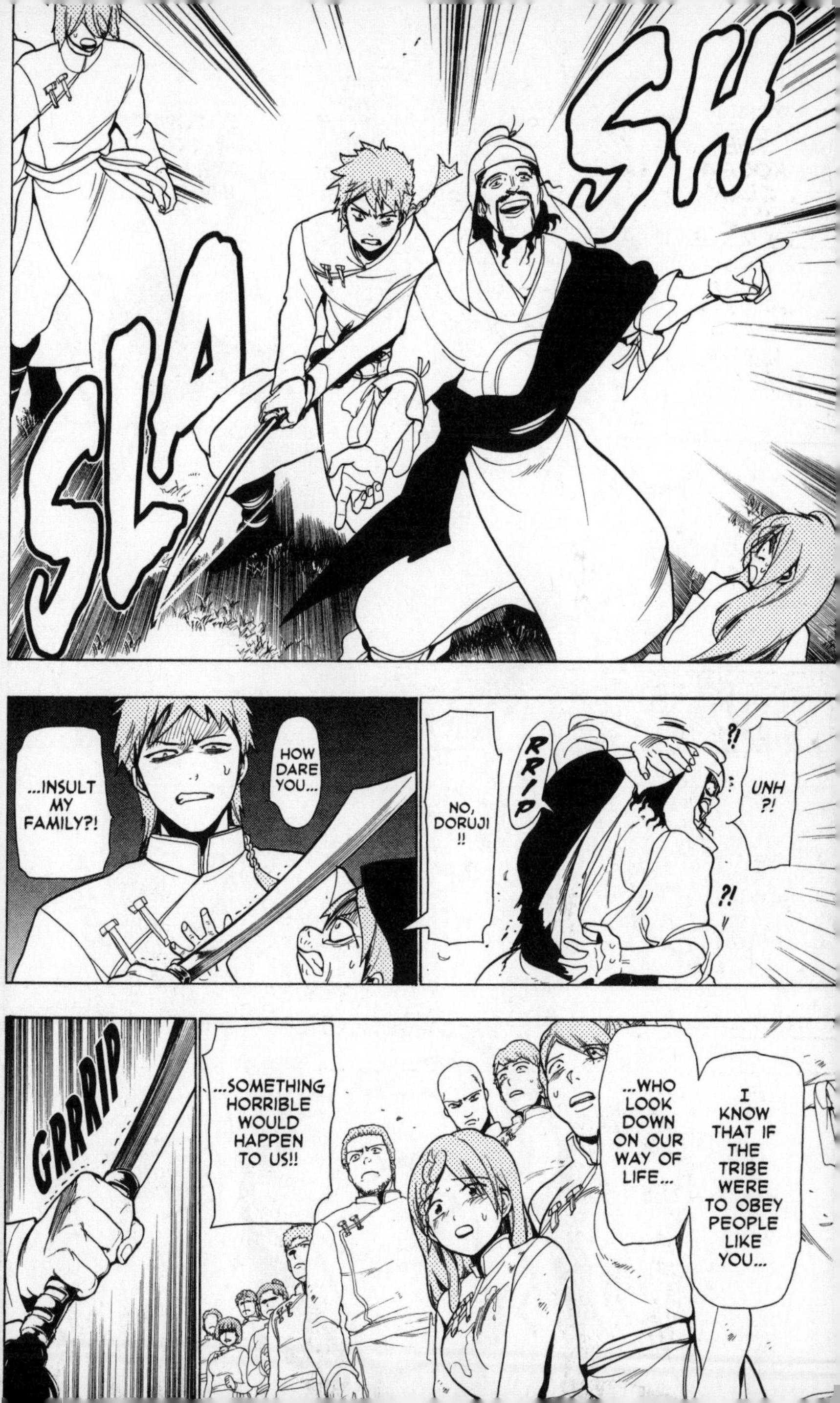

SH
SLA
UNH ?!
?!
?!
RRIP
NO, DORUJI !!
HOW DARE YOU...
...INSULT MY FAMILY?!
I KNOW THAT IF THE TRIBE WERE TO OBEY PEOPLE LIKE YOU...
...WHO LOOK DOWN ON OUR WAY OF LIFE...
...SOMETHING HORRIBLE WOULD HAPPEN TO US!!
GRRRIP

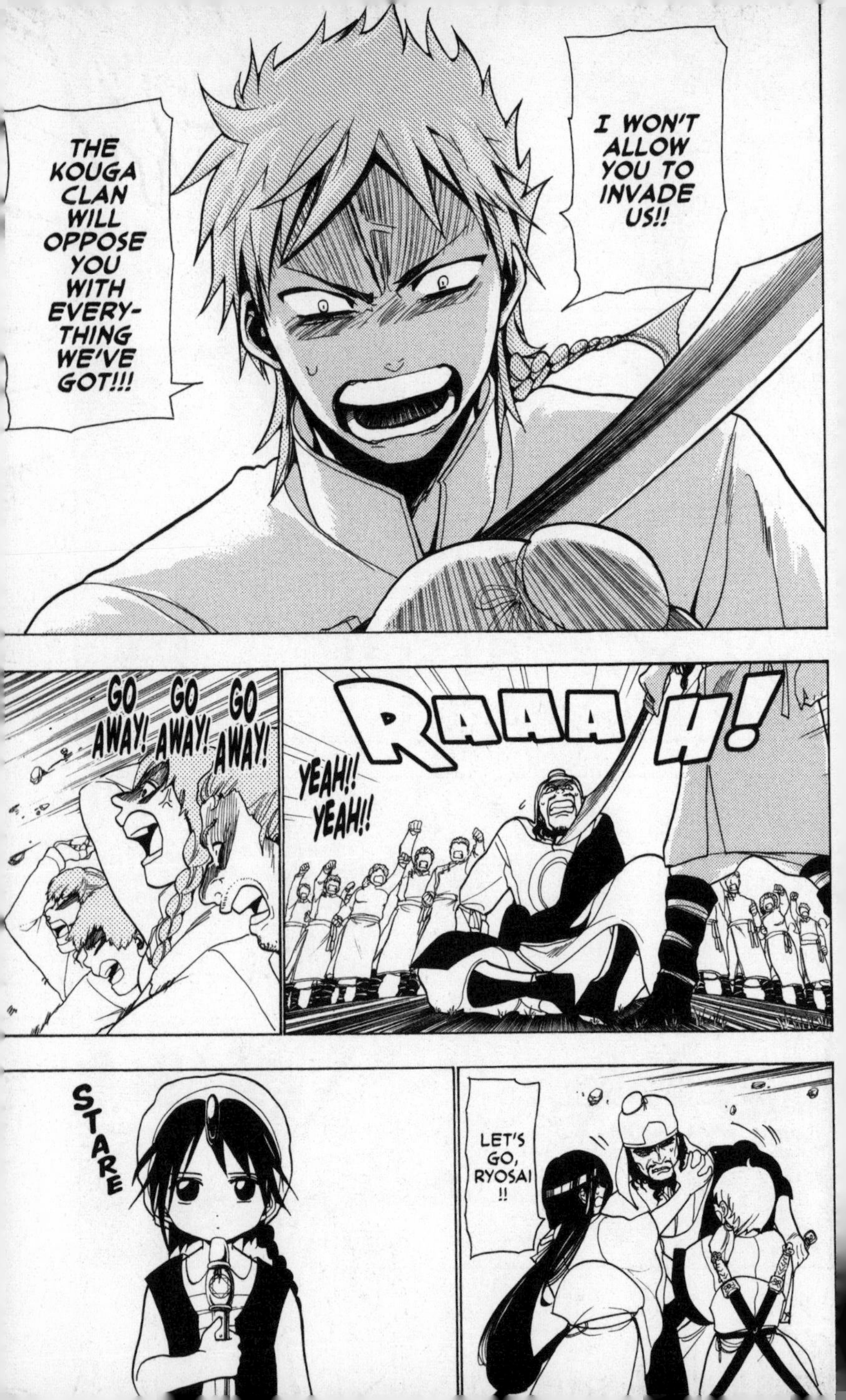
I WON'T ALLOW YOU TO INVADE US!!
THE KOUGA CLAN WILL OPPOSE YOU WITH EVERY-THING WE'VE GOT!!!
RAAAAH!
YEAH!! YEAH!!
GO AWAY! GO AWAY! GO AWAY!
LET'S GO, RYOSAI!!
STARE

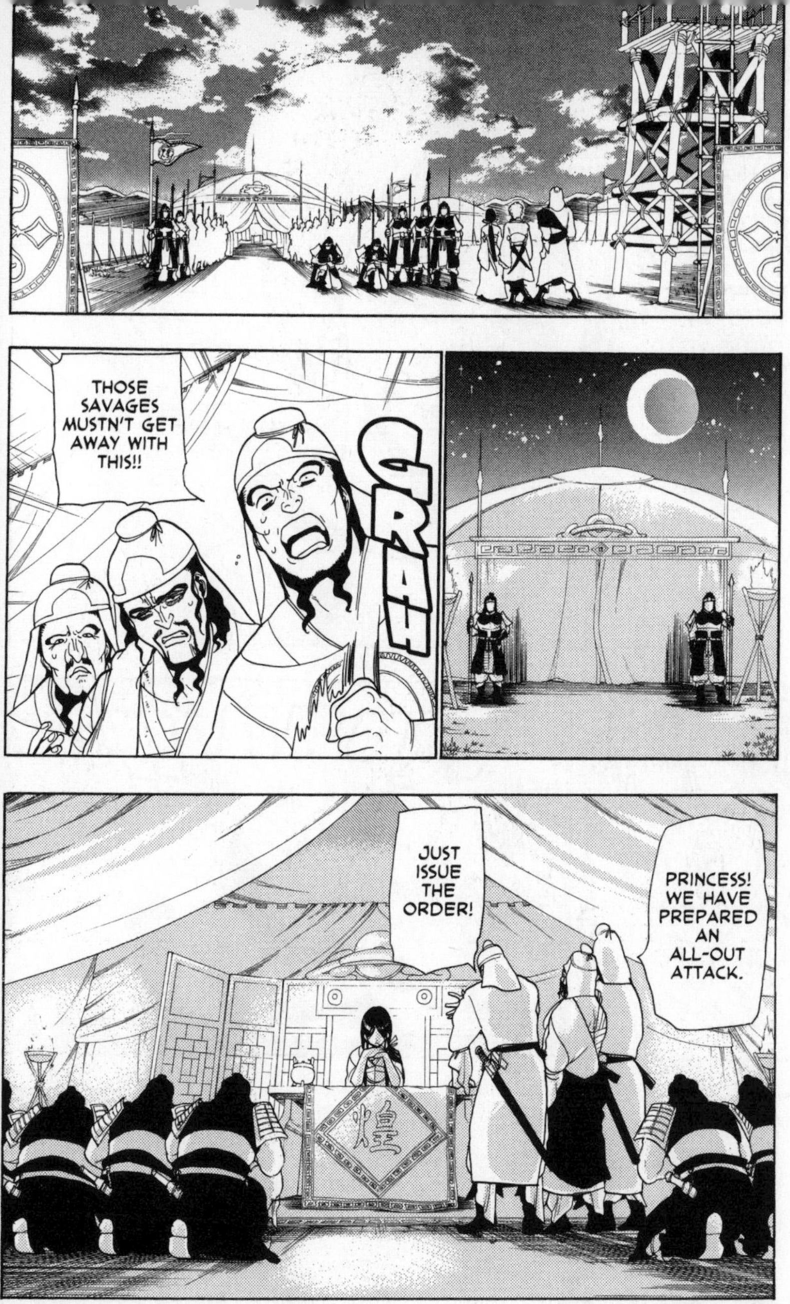
THOSE SAVAGES MUSTN'T GET AWAY WITH THIS!!
GRAH
PRINCESS! WE HAVE PREPARED AN ALL-OUT ATTACK.
JUST ISSUE THE ORDER!
煌

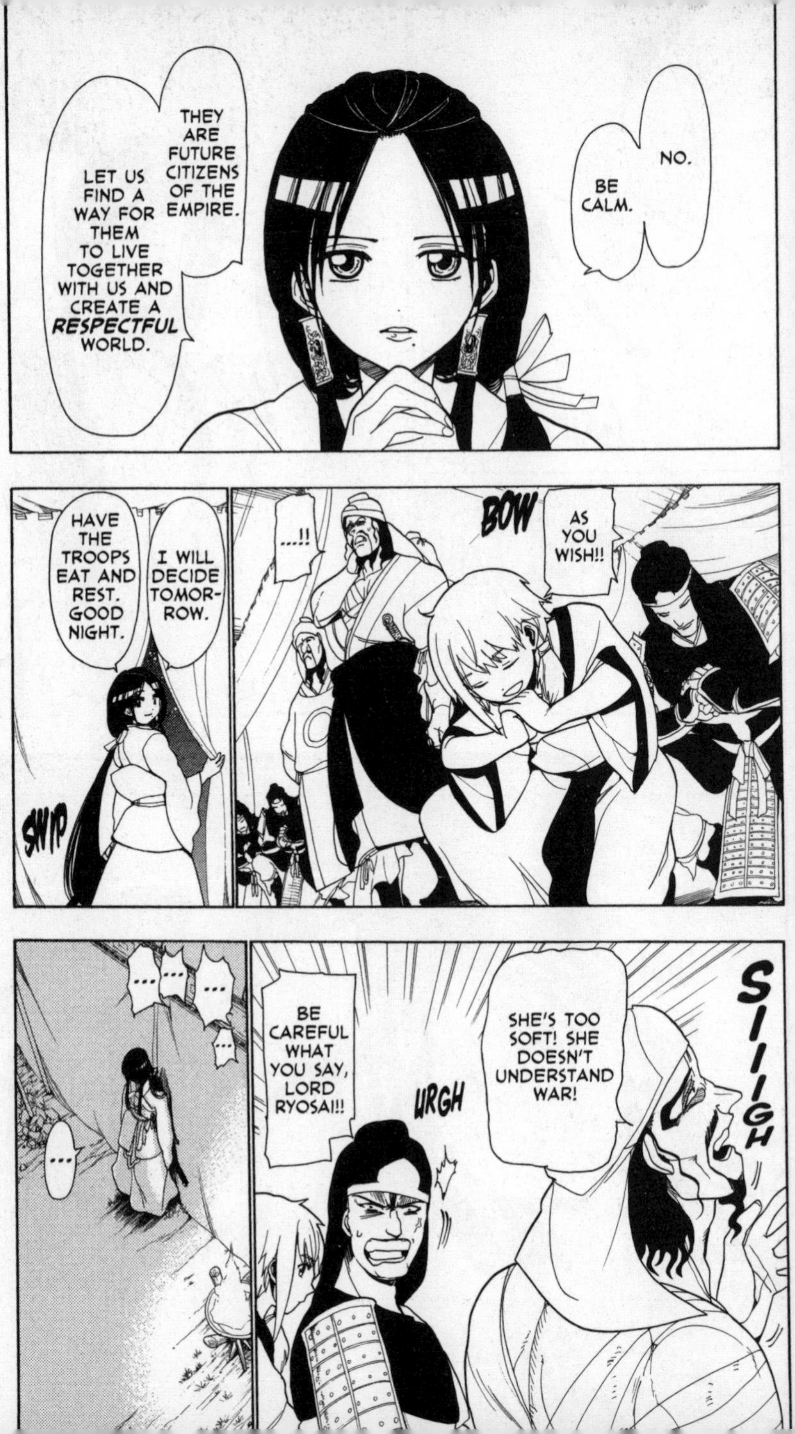
NO.
BE CALM.
THEY ARE FUTURE CITIZENS OF THE EMPIRE.
LET US FIND A WAY FOR THEM TO LIVE TOGETHER WITH US AND CREATE A *RESPECTFUL* WORLD.
AS YOU WISH!!
BOW
...!!
I WILL DECIDE TOMORROW.
HAVE THE TROOPS EAT AND REST. GOOD NIGHT.
SNIP
SIIIGH
SHE'S TOO SOFT! SHE DOESN'T UNDERSTAND WAR!
URGH
BE CAREFUL WHAT YOU SAY, LORD RYOSAI!!
...
...
...
...
...

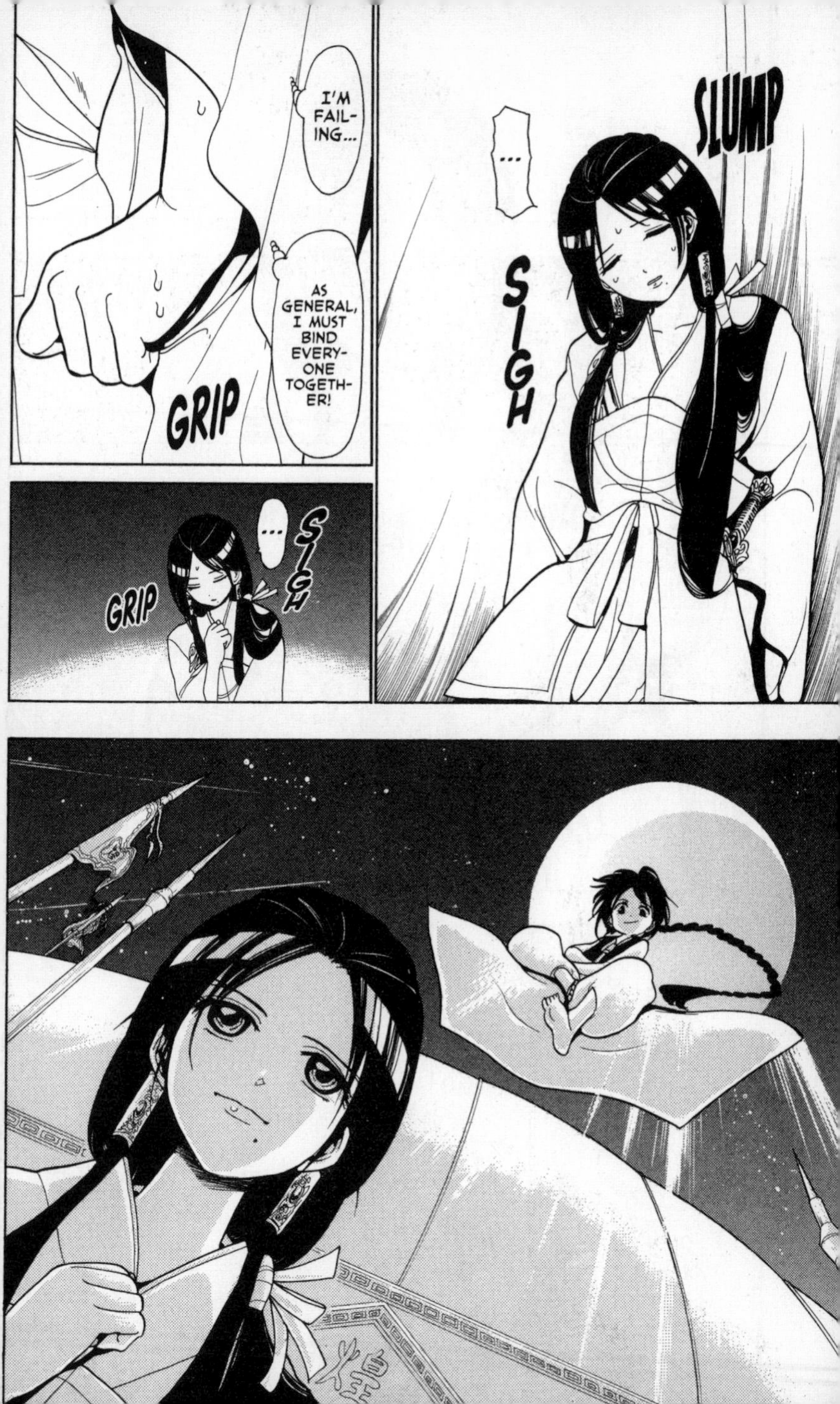
SLUMP
...
SIGH
I'M FAILING...
AS GENERAL, I MUST BIND EVERYONE TOGETHER!
GRIP
...
SIGH
GRIP

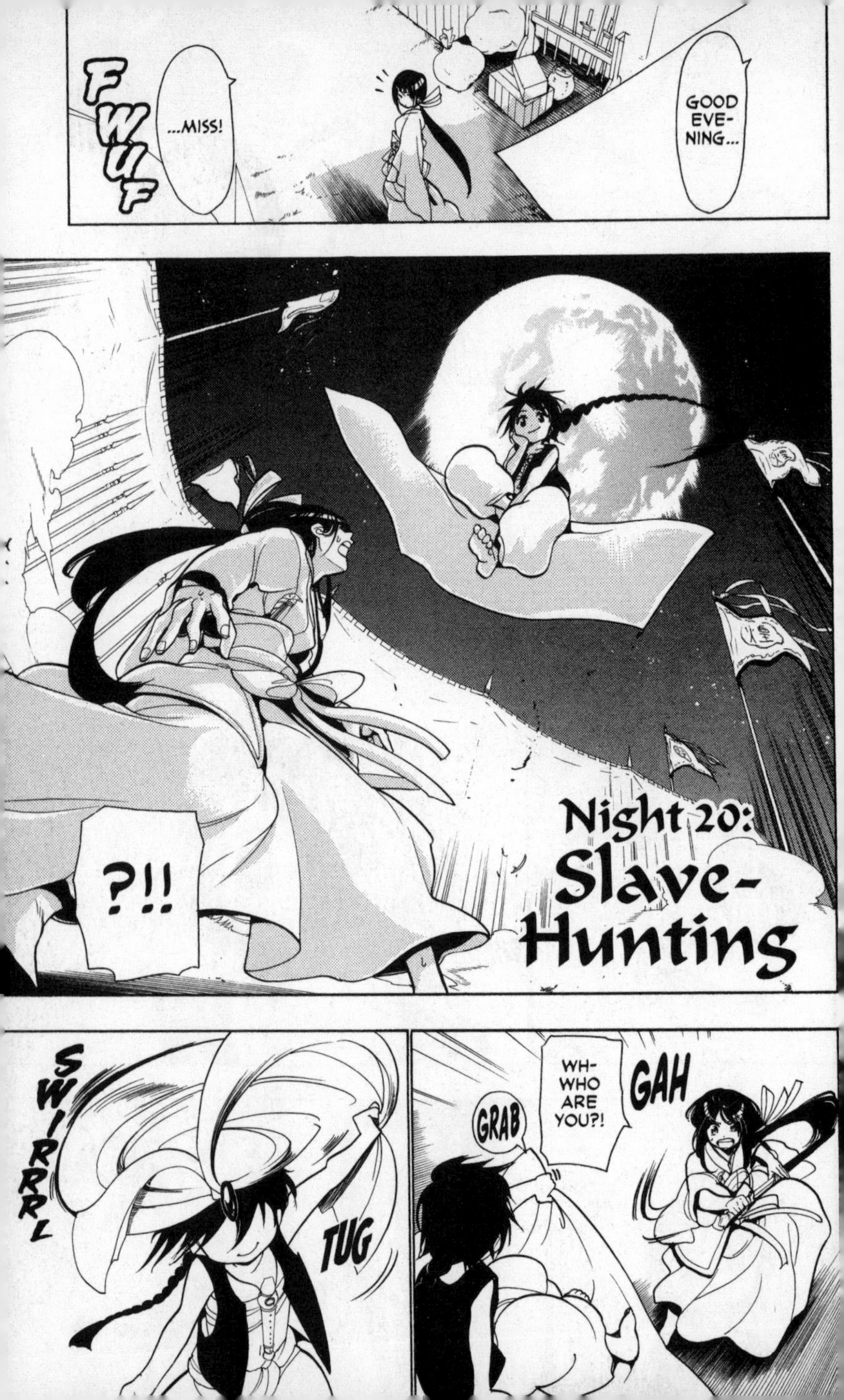
GOOD EVE-NING...
...MISS!
FWUF
Night 20: Slave-Hunting
?!!
GAH
WH-WHO ARE YOU?!
GRAB
SWIRRRL
TUG

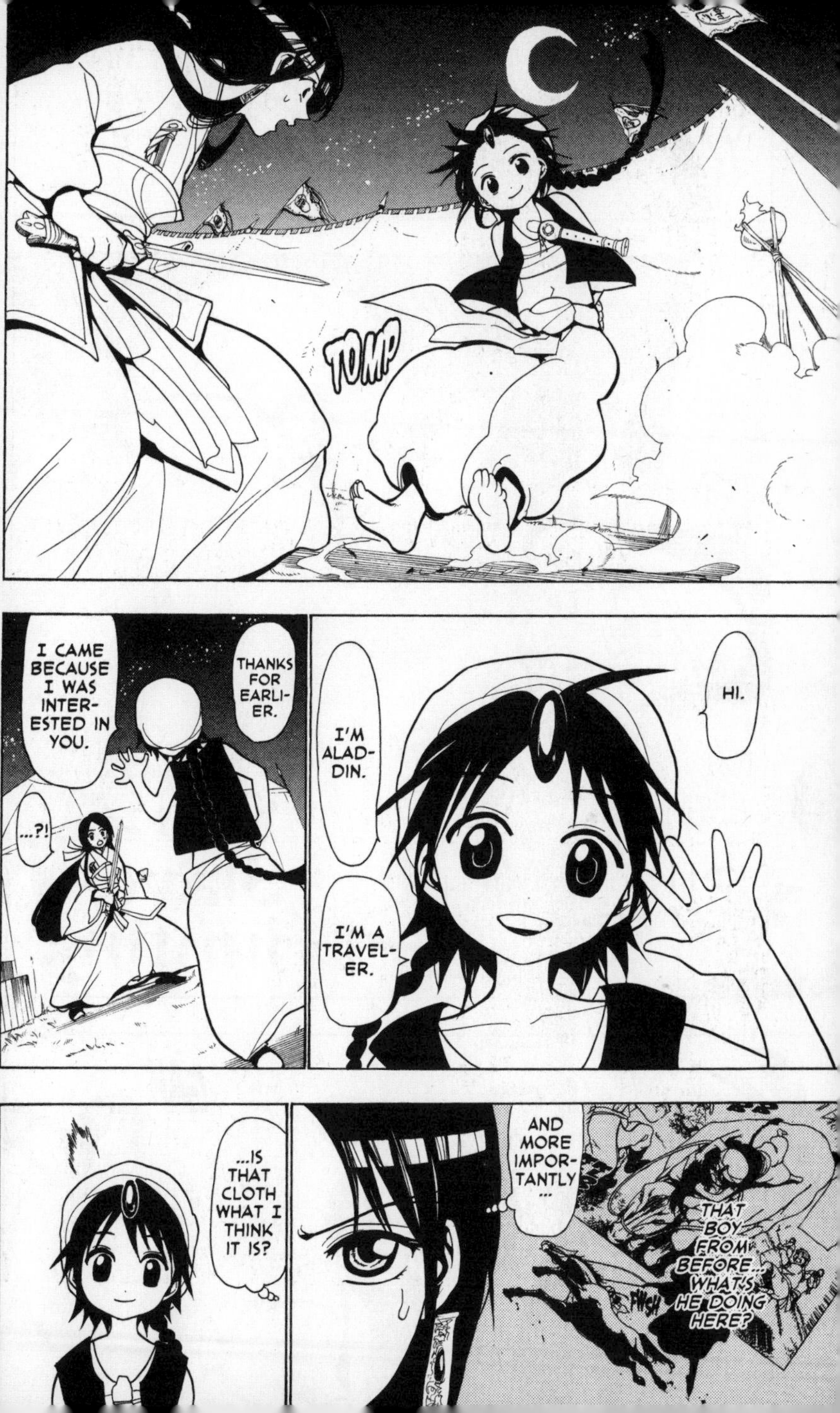
TOMP
HI.
I'M ALAD-DIN.
I'M A TRAVEL-ER.
THANKS FOR EARLI-ER.
I CAME BECAUSE I WAS INTER-ESTED IN YOU.
...?!
THAT BOY FROM BEFORE... WHAT'S HE DOING HERE?
FWSH
AND MORE IMPOR-TANTLY ...
...IS THAT CLOTH WHAT I THINK IT IS?

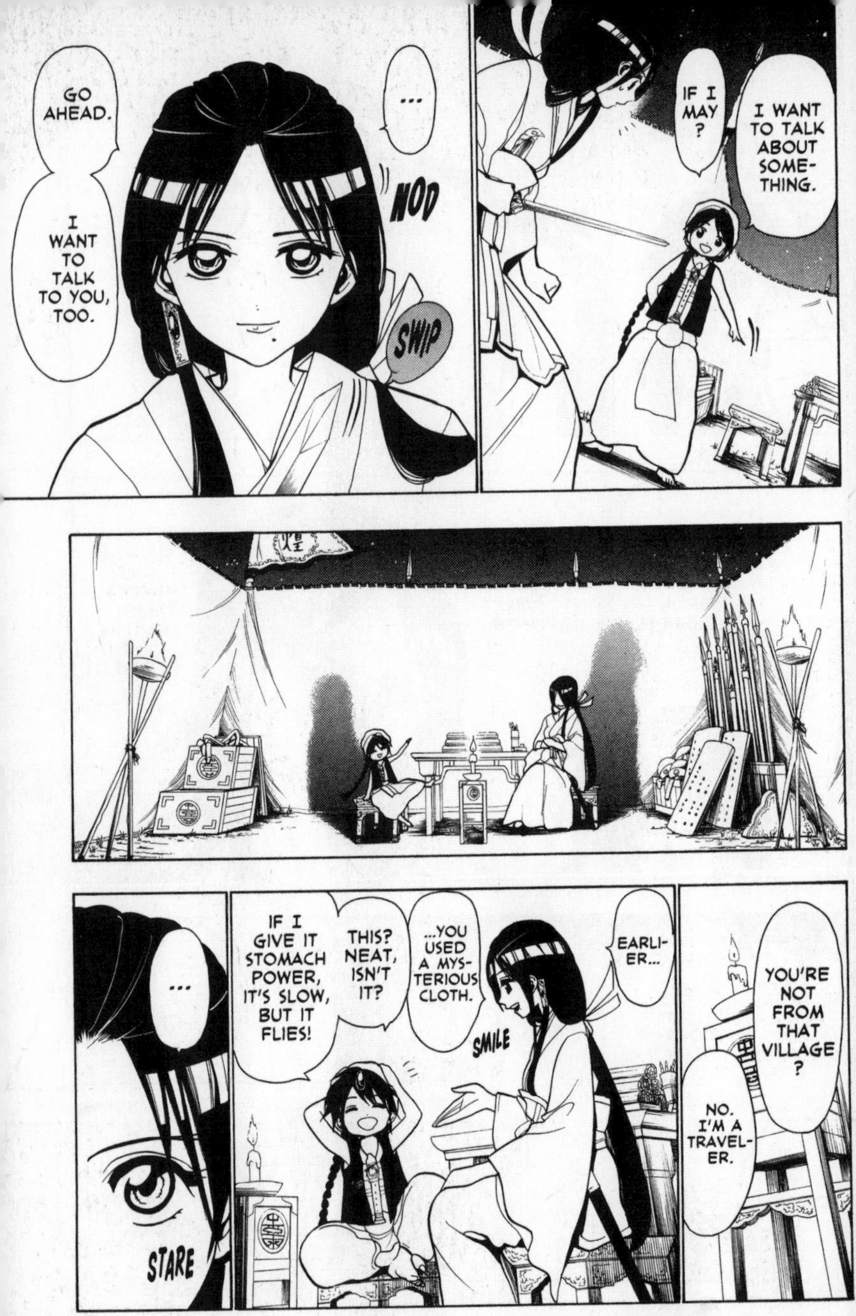
I WANT TO TALK ABOUT SOME-THING.
IF I MAY?
...
NOD
SWIP
GO AHEAD.
I WANT TO TALK TO YOU, TOO.
YOU'RE NOT FROM THAT VILLAGE?
NO. I'M A TRAVEL-ER.
EARLI-ER...
...YOU USED A MYS-TERIOUS CLOTH.
SMILE
THIS? NEAT, ISN'T IT?
IF I GIVE IT STOMACH POWER, IT'S SLOW, BUT IT FLIES!
...
STARE

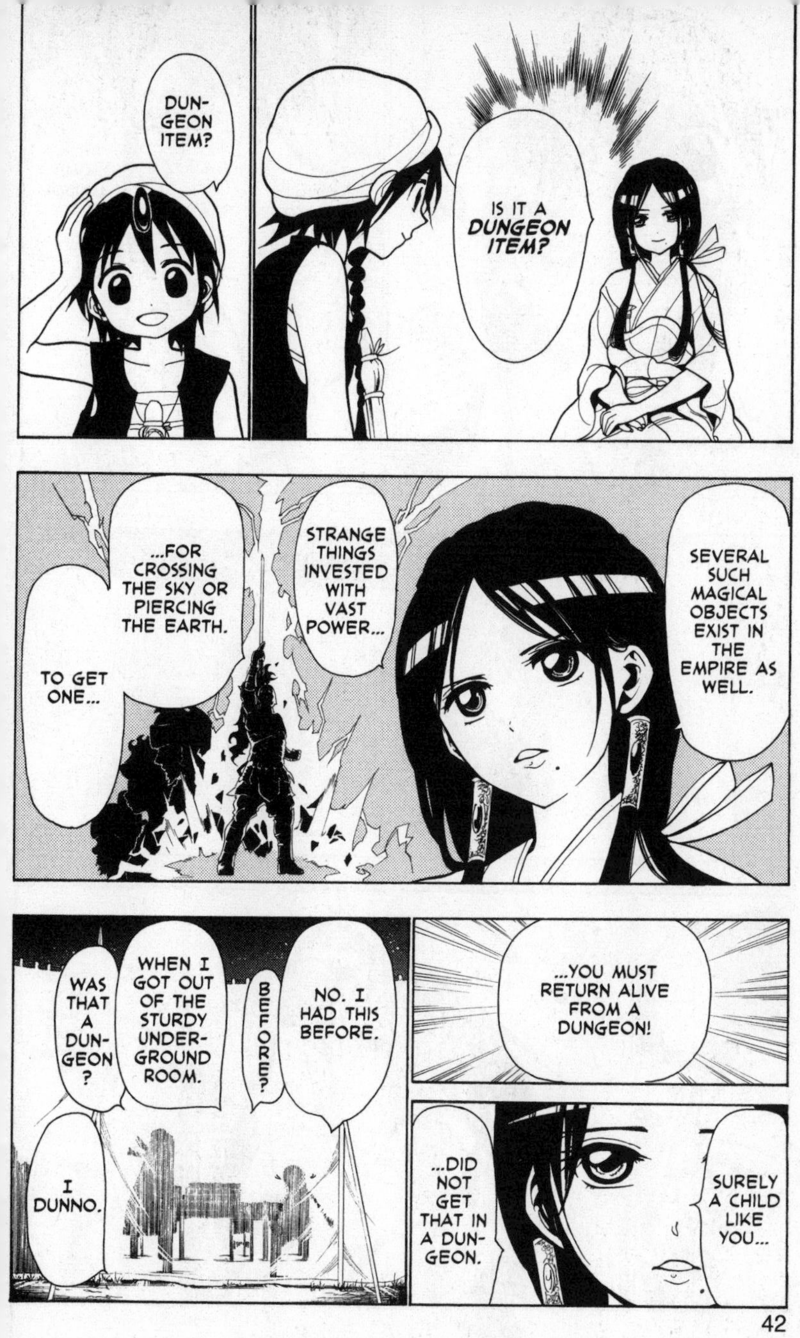
IS IT A DUNGEON ITEM?
DUN-GEON ITEM?
SEVERAL SUCH MAGICAL OBJECTS EXIST IN THE EMPIRE AS WELL.
STRANGE THINGS INVESTED WITH VAST POWER...
...FOR CROSSING THE SKY OR PIERCING THE EARTH.
TO GET ONE...
...YOU MUST RETURN ALIVE FROM A DUNGEON!
SURELY A CHILD LIKE YOU...
...DID NOT GET THAT IN A DUN-GEON.
NO. I HAD THIS BEFORE.
BEFORE?
WHEN I GOT OUT OF THE STURDY UNDER-GROUND ROOM.
WAS THAT A DUN-GEON?
I DUNNO.

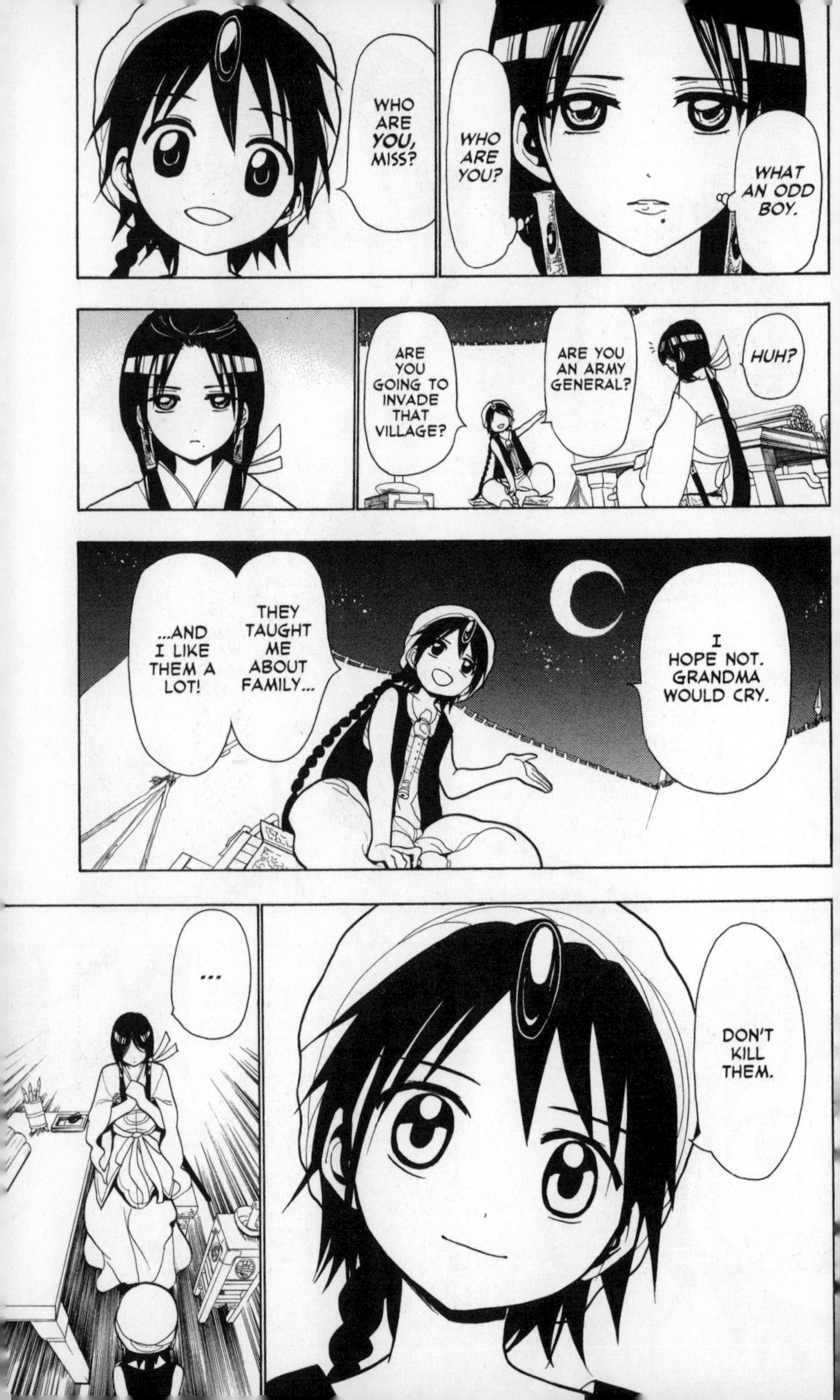
WHAT AN ODD BOY.
WHO ARE YOU?
WHO ARE YOU, MISS?
HUH?
ARE YOU AN ARMY GENERAL?
ARE YOU GOING TO INVADE THAT VILLAGE?
I HOPE NOT. GRANDMA WOULD CRY.
THEY TAUGHT ME ABOUT FAMILY...
...AND I LIKE THEM A LOT!
DON'T KILL THEM.
...

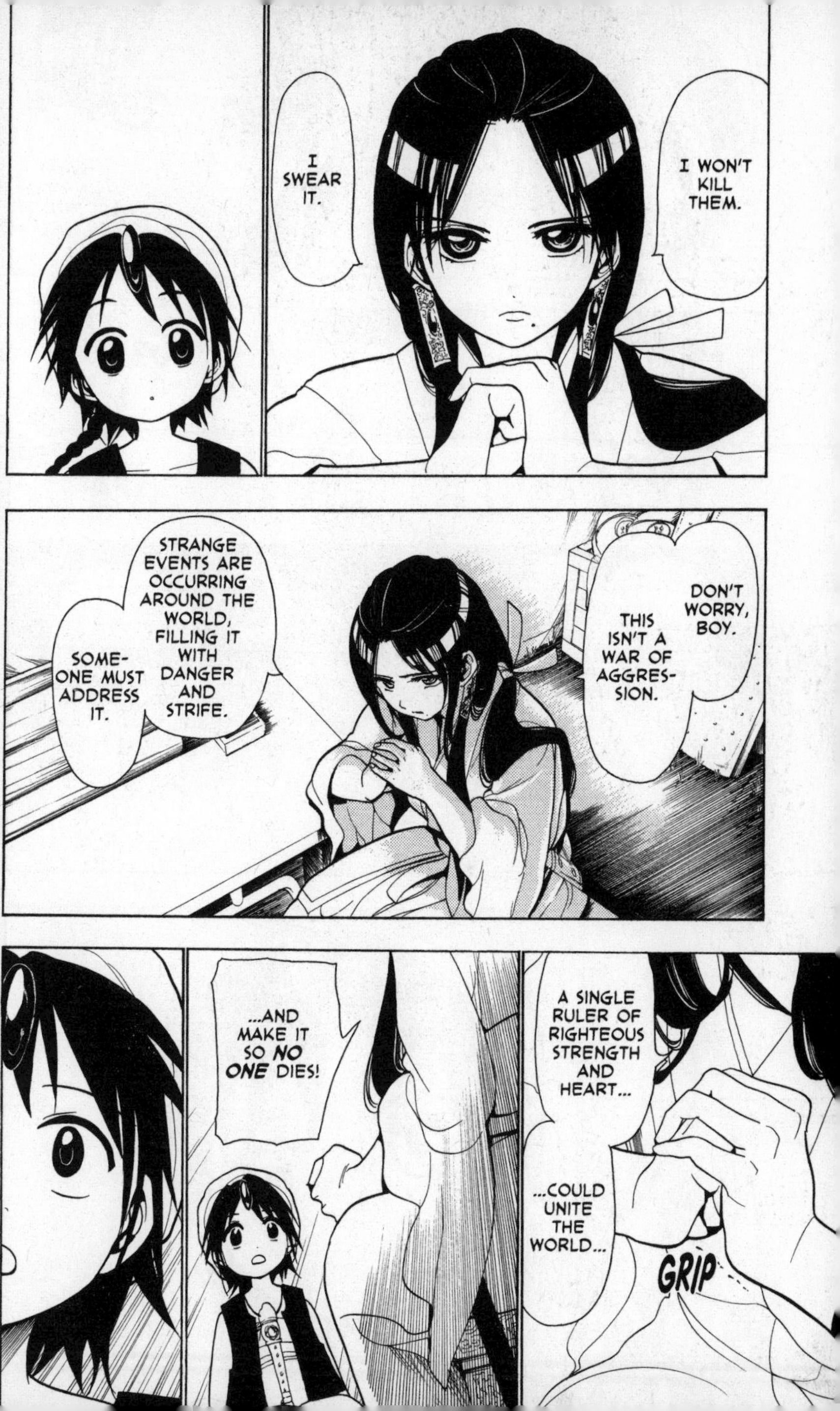
I WON'T KILL THEM.
I SWEAR IT.
DON'T WORRY, BOY.
THIS ISN'T A WAR OF AGGRESSION.
STRANGE EVENTS ARE OCCURRING AROUND THE WORLD, FILLING IT WITH DANGER AND STRIFE.
SOMEONE MUST ADDRESS IT.
A SINGLE RULER OF RIGHTEOUS STRENGTH AND HEART...
...COULD UNITE THE WORLD...
GRIP
...AND MAKE IT SO **NO ONE** DIES!

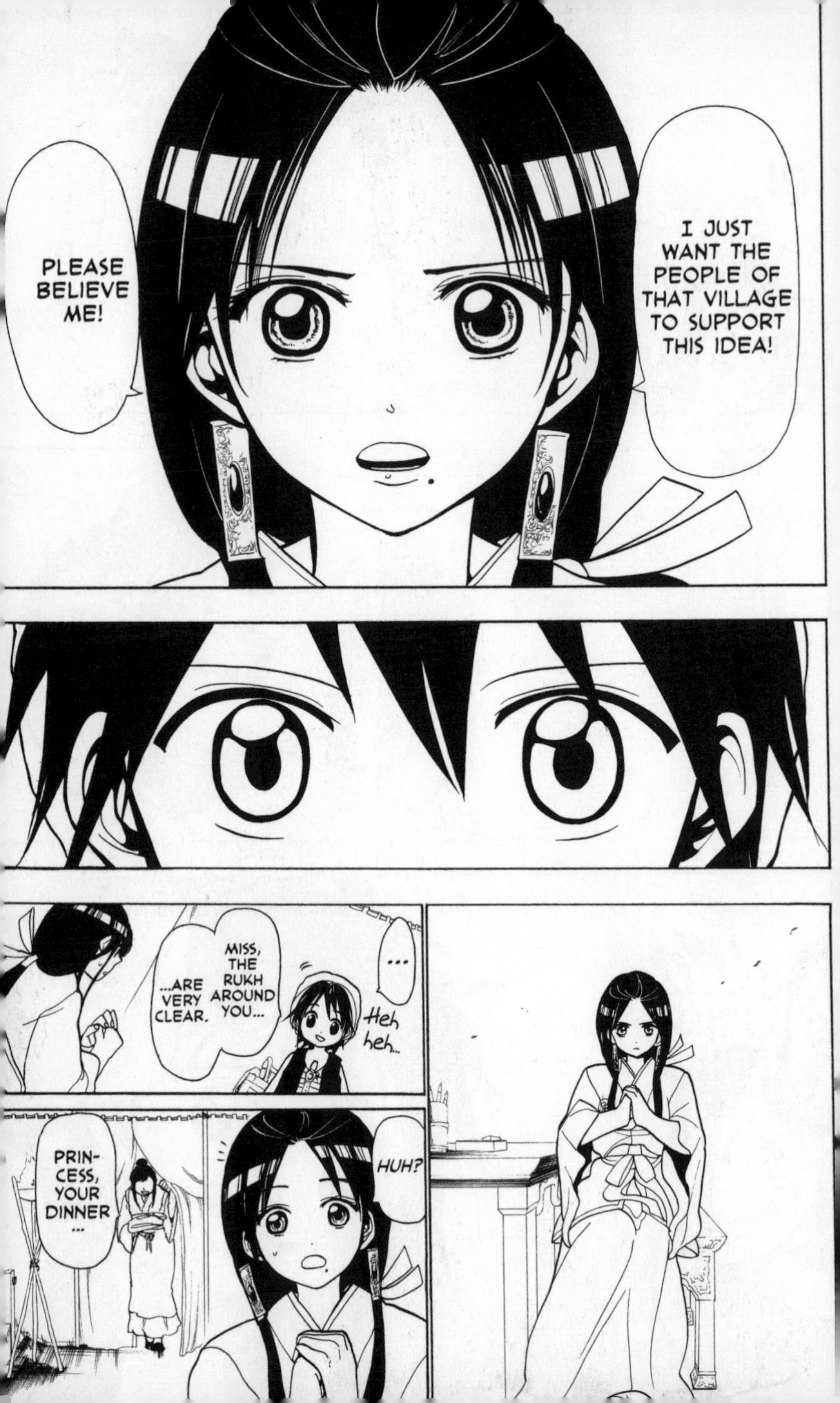

I JUST WANT THE PEOPLE OF THAT VILLAGE TO SUPPORT THIS IDEA!
PLEASE BELIEVE ME!
...
MISS, THE RUKH AROUND YOU...
...ARE VERY CLEAR.
Heh heh...
HUH?
PRIN-CESS, YOUR DINNER ...

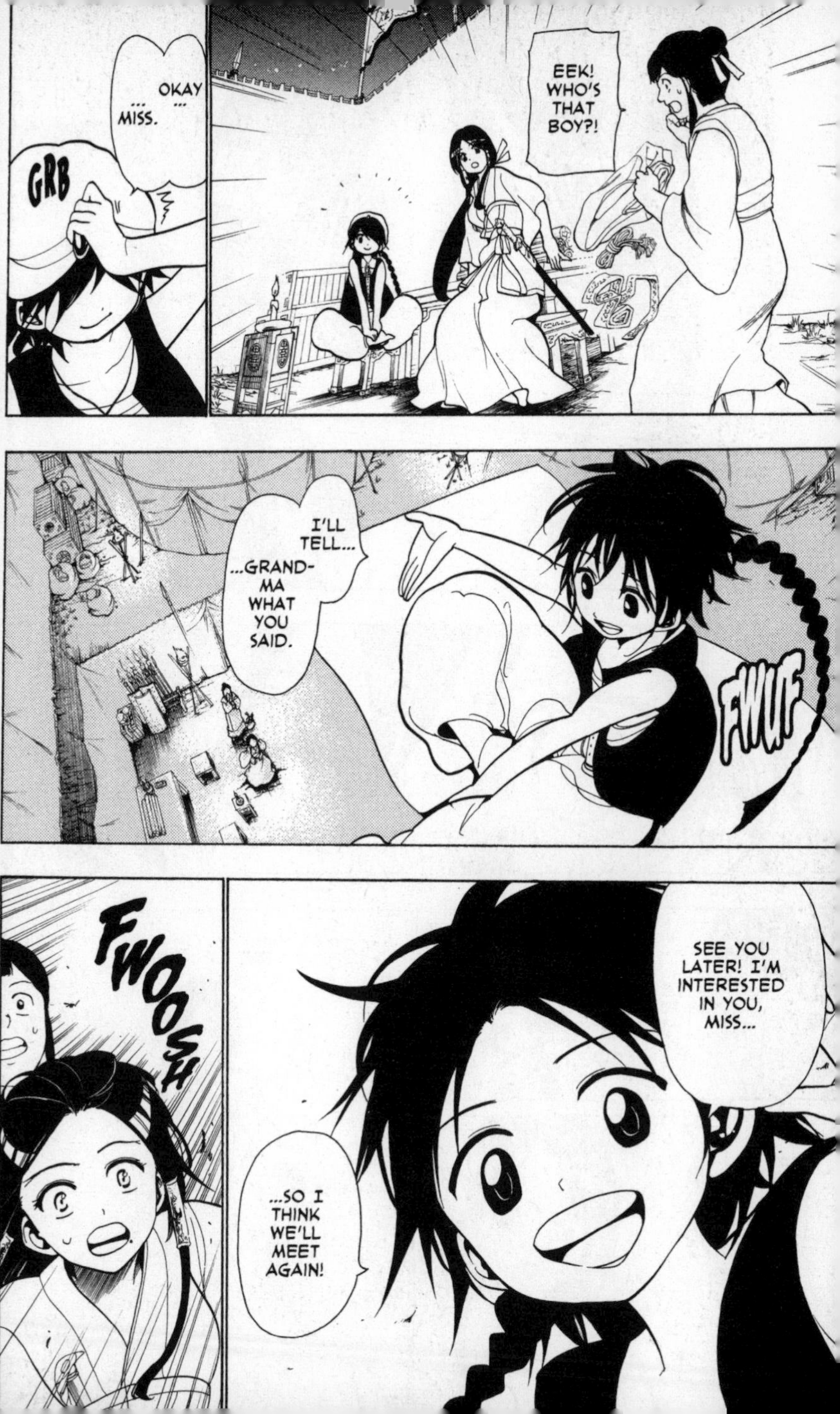
EEK! WHO'S THAT BOY?!
GRB
OKAY ... ... MISS.
FWUF
I'LL TELL... ...GRAND-MA WHAT YOU SAID.
SEE YOU LATER! I'M INTERESTED IN YOU, MISS...
...SO I THINK WE'LL MEET AGAIN!
FWOOSH

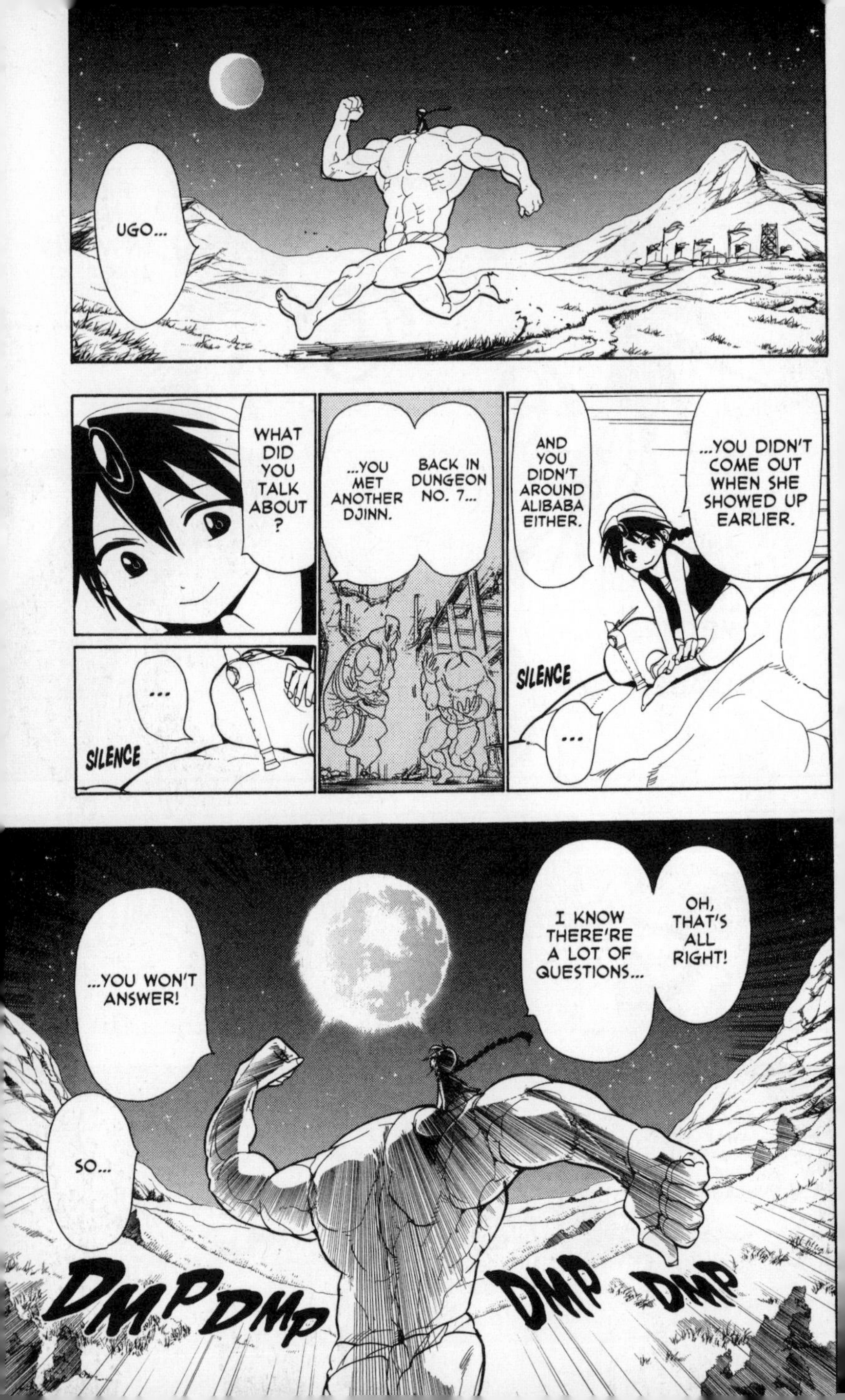
UGO...
...YOU DIDN'T COME OUT WHEN SHE SHOWED UP EARLIER.
AND YOU DIDN'T AROUND ALIBABA EITHER.
SILENCE
...
BACK IN DUNGEON NO. 7...
...YOU MET ANOTHER DJINN.
WHAT DID YOU TALK ABOUT?
...
SILENCE
OH, THAT'S ALL RIGHT!
I KNOW THERE'RE A LOT OF QUESTIONS...
...YOU WON'T ANSWER!
SO...
DMP DMP
DMP
DMP
DMP

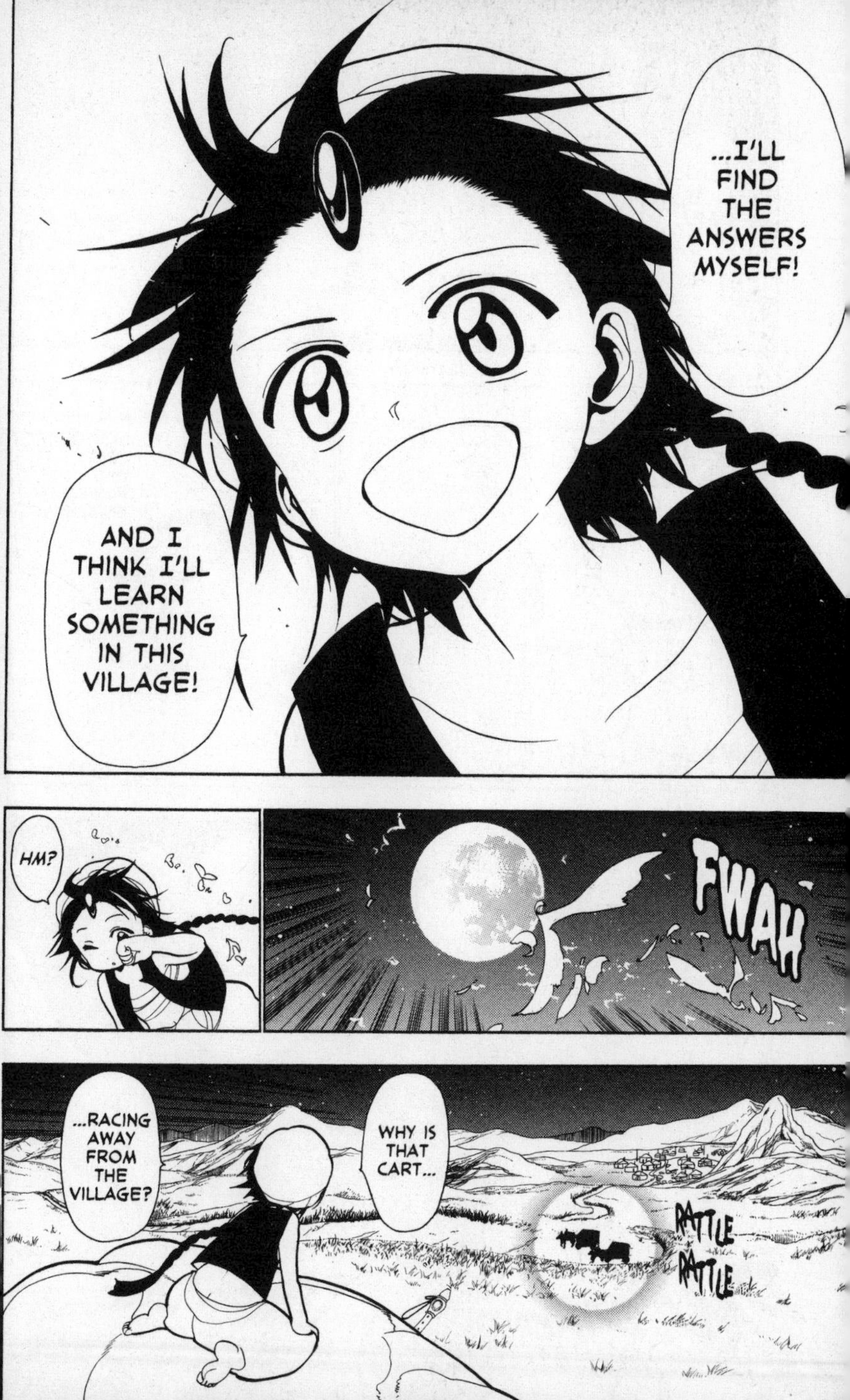
...I'LL FIND THE ANSWERS MYSELF!
AND I THINK I'LL LEARN SOMETHING IN THIS VILLAGE!
FWAH
HM?
WHY IS THAT CART...
...RACING AWAY FROM THE VILLAGE?
RATTLE RATTLE

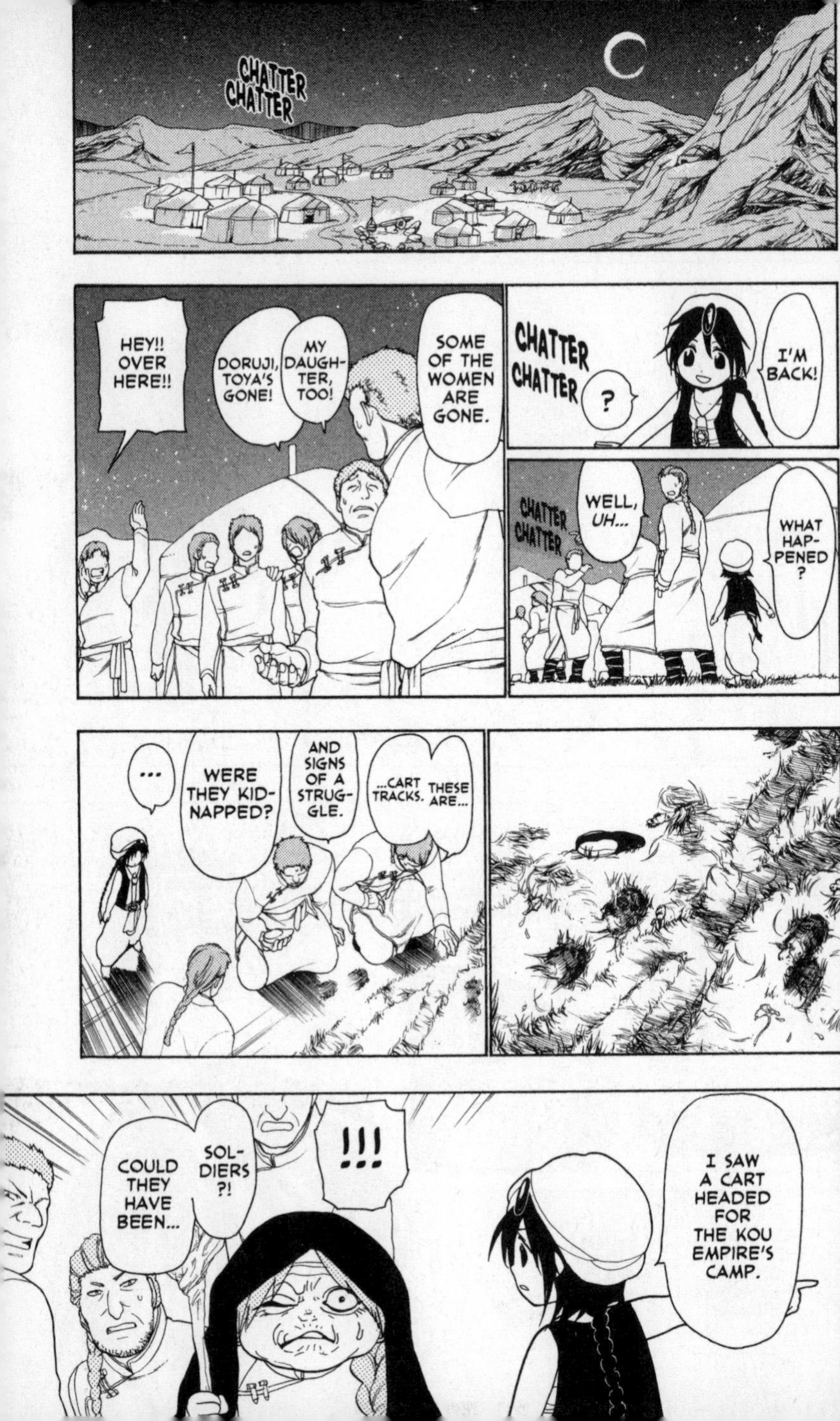
CHATTER CHATTER
I'M BACK!
?
CHATTER CHATTER
WHAT HAPPENED?
WELL, UH...
CHATTER CHATTER
SOME OF THE WOMEN ARE GONE.
MY DAUGHTER, TOO!
DORUJI, TOYA'S GONE!
HEY!! OVER HERE!!
THESE ARE...
...CART TRACKS.
AND SIGNS OF A STRUGGLE.
WERE THEY KIDNAPPED?
...
I SAW A CART HEADED FOR THE KOU EMPIRE'S CAMP.
!!!
SOLDIERS?!
COULD THEY HAVE BEEN...

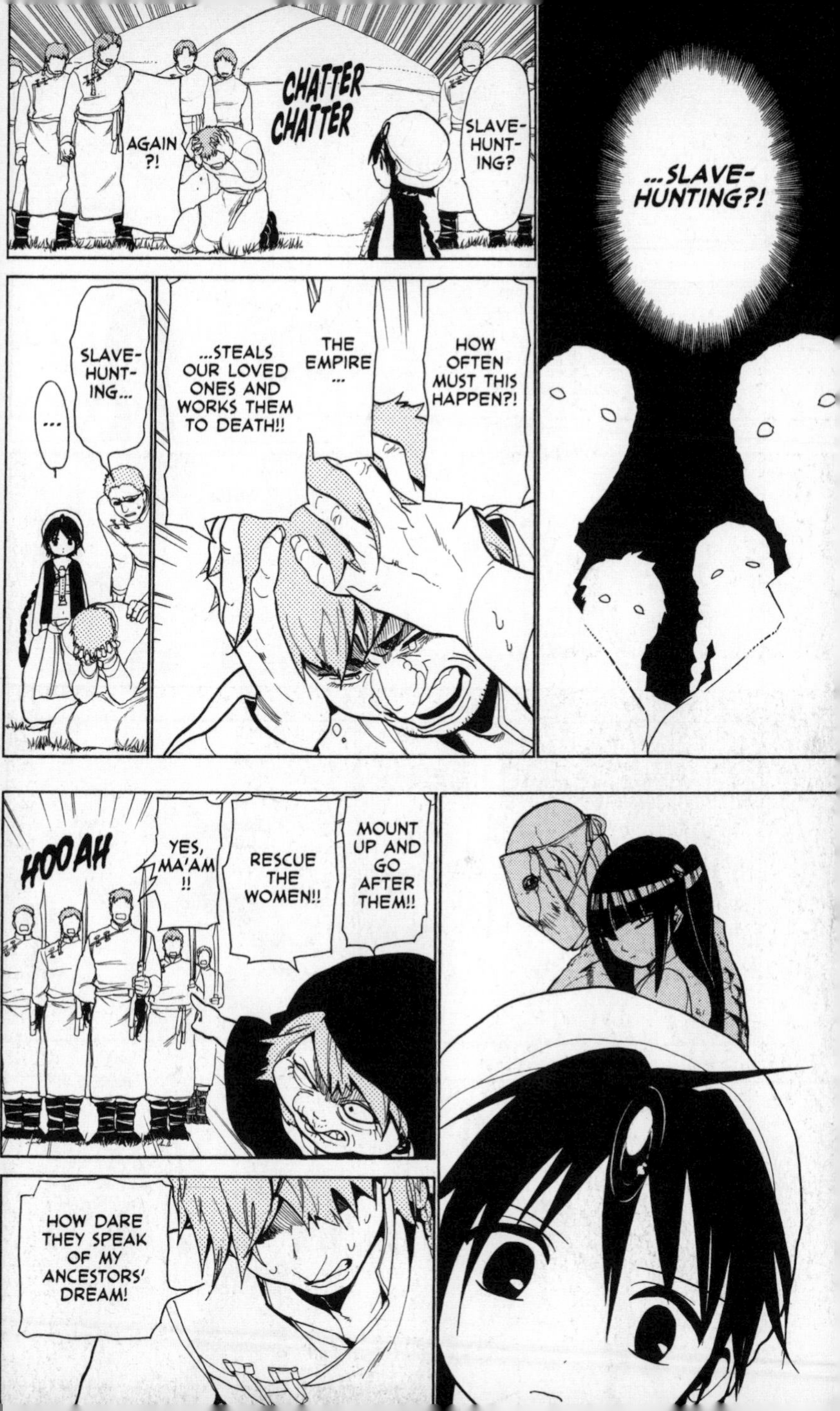
...SLAVE-HUNTING?!
CHATTER CHATTER
SLAVE-HUNTING?
AGAIN?!
HOW OFTEN MUST THIS HAPPEN?!
THE EMPIRE...
...STEALS OUR LOVED ONES AND WORKS THEM TO DEATH!!
SLAVE-HUNTING...
...
MOUNT UP AND GO AFTER THEM!!
RESCUE THE WOMEN!!
YES, MA'AM!!
HOOAH
HOW DARE THEY SPEAK OF MY ANCESTORS' DREAM!

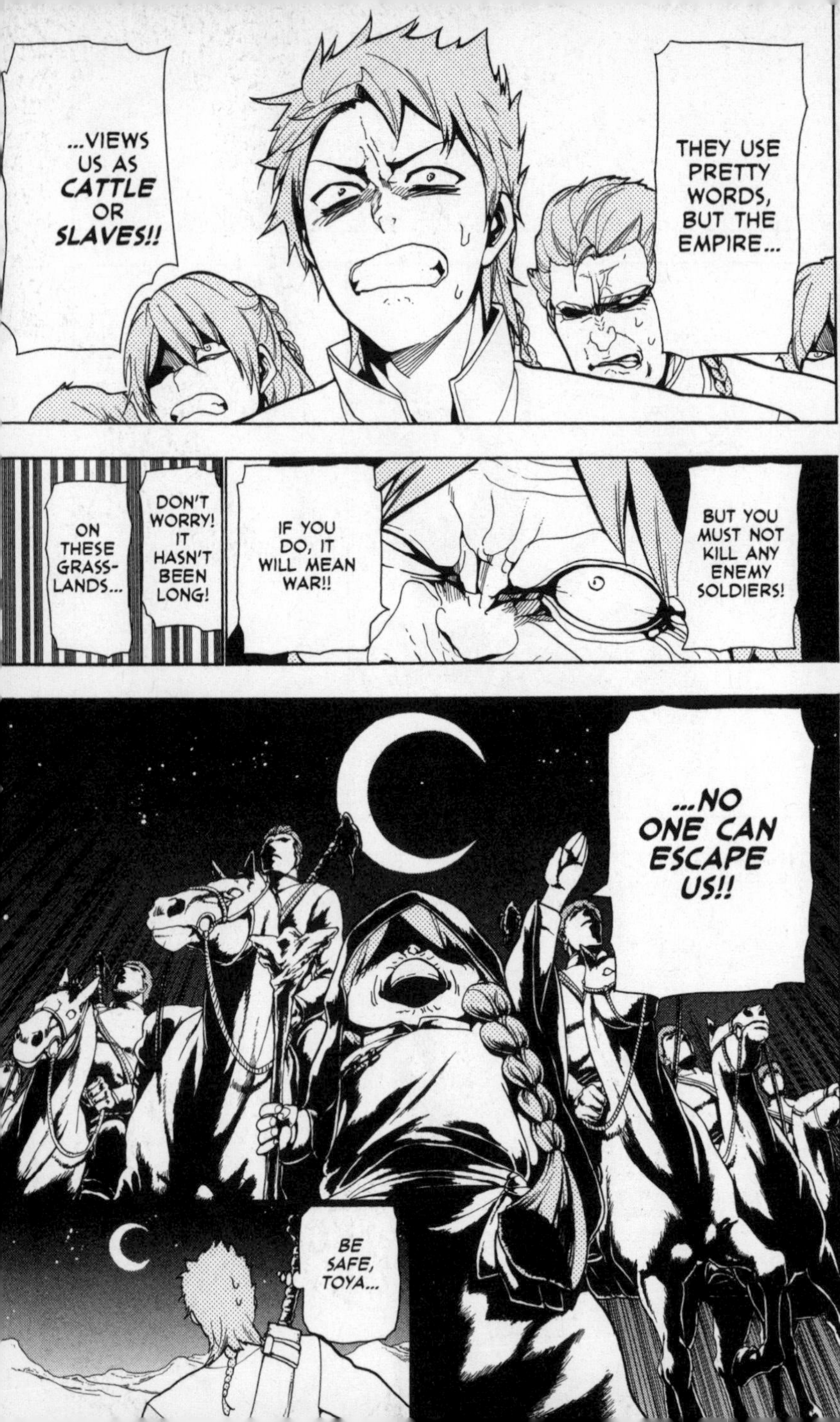
THEY USE PRETTY WORDS, BUT THE EMPIRE...
...VIEWS US AS CATTLE OR SLAVES!!
BUT YOU MUST NOT KILL ANY ENEMY SOLDIERS!
IF YOU DO, IT WILL MEAN WAR!!
DON'T WORRY! IT HASN'T BEEN LONG!
ON THESE GRASS-LANDS...
...NO ONE CAN ESCAPE US!!
BE SAFE, TOYA...

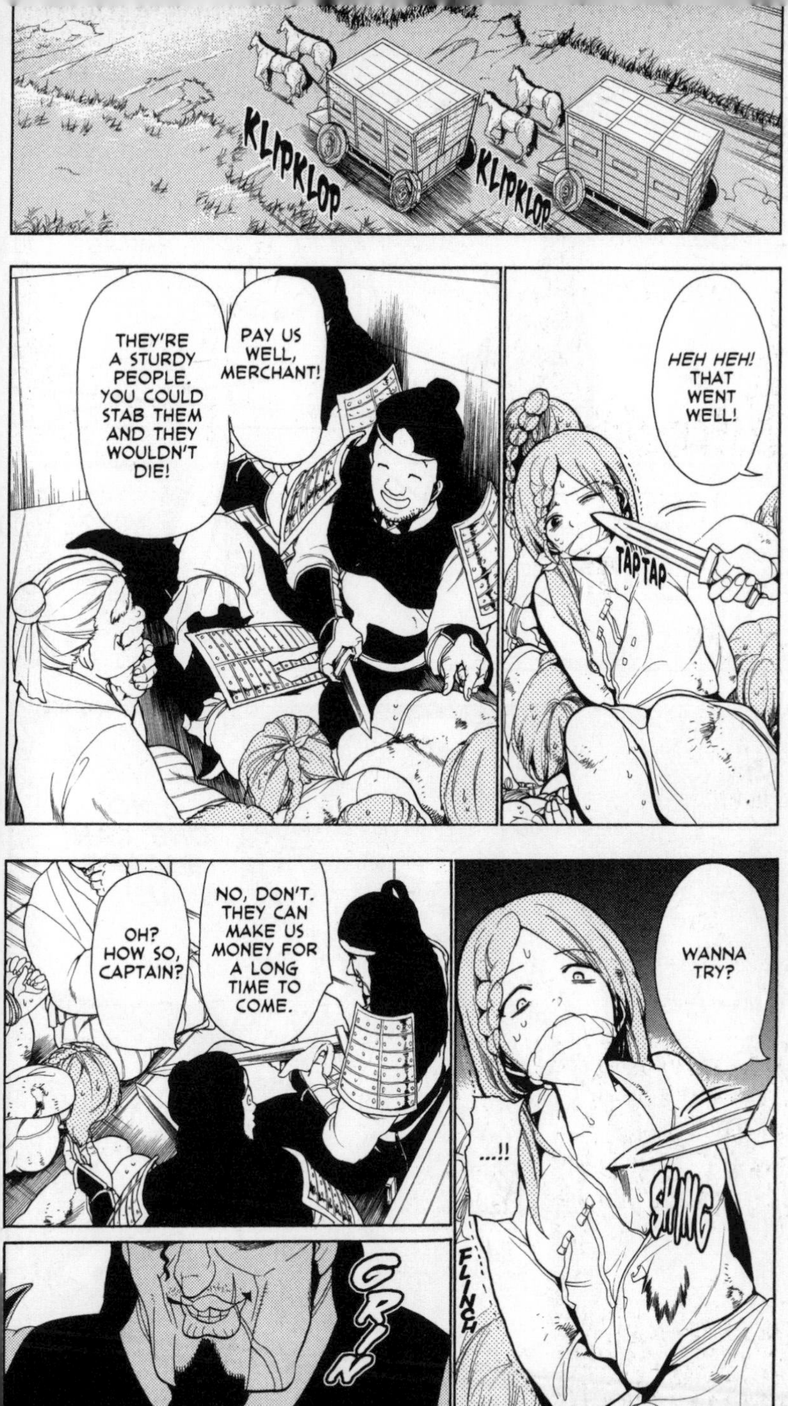
KLIPKLOP
KLIPKLOP
HEH HEH! THAT WENT WELL!
TAPTAP
PAY US WELL, MERCHANT!
THEY'RE A STURDY PEOPLE. YOU COULD STAB THEM AND THEY WOULDN'T DIE!
WANNA TRY?
...!!
SHING
FLINCH
NO, DON'T. THEY CAN MAKE US MONEY FOR A LONG TIME TO COME.
OH? HOW SO, CAPTAIN?
GRIN

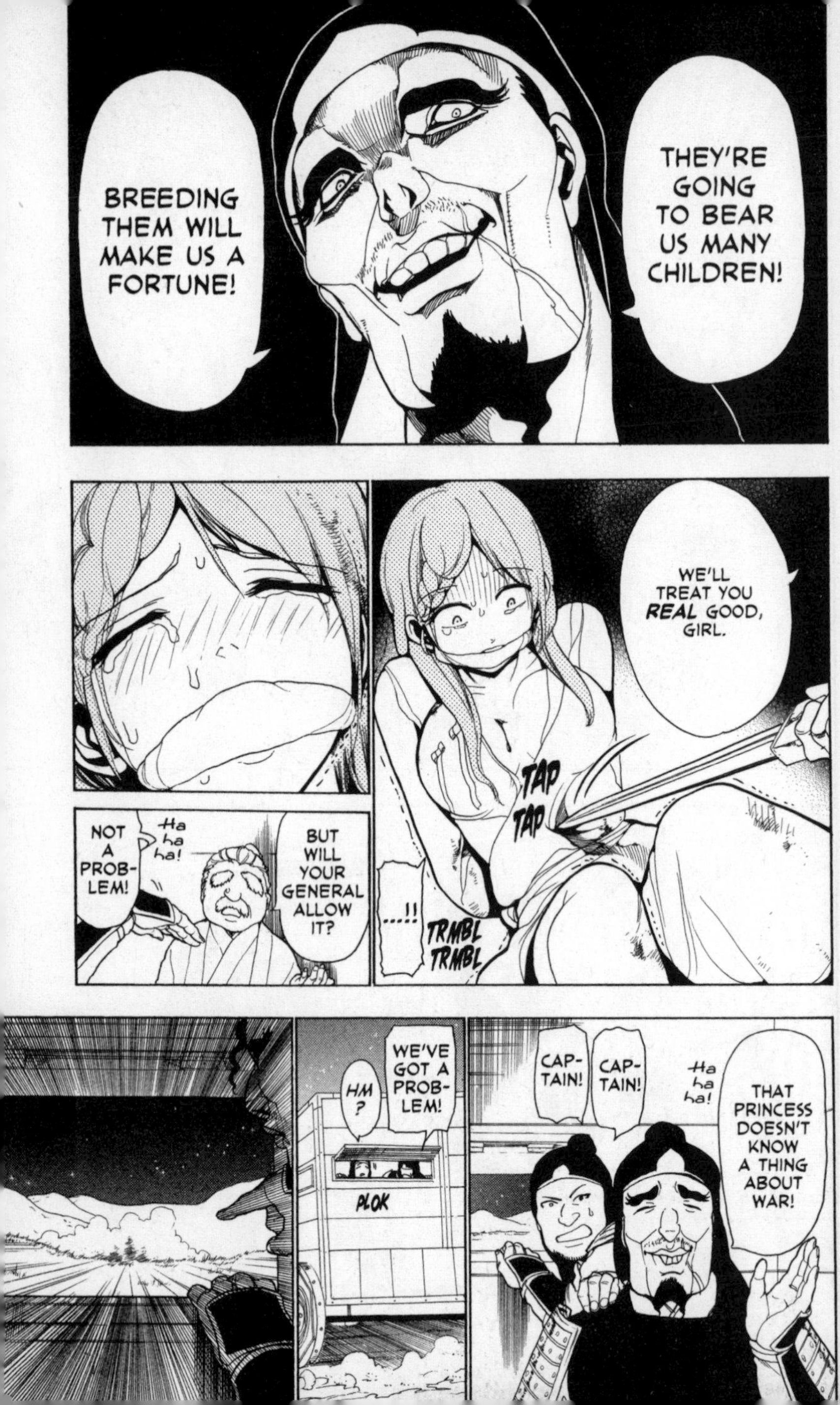
THEY'RE GOING TO BEAR US MANY CHILDREN!
BREEDING THEM WILL MAKE US A FORTUNE!
WE'LL TREAT YOU REAL GOOD, GIRL.
TAP TAP
....!!
TRMBL TRMBL
BUT WILL YOUR GENERAL ALLOW IT?
Ha ha ha!
NOT A PROBLEM!
THAT PRINCESS DOESN'T KNOW A THING ABOUT WAR!
Ha ha ha!
CAPTAIN!
CAPTAIN!
WE'VE GOT A PROBLEM!
HM?
PLOK

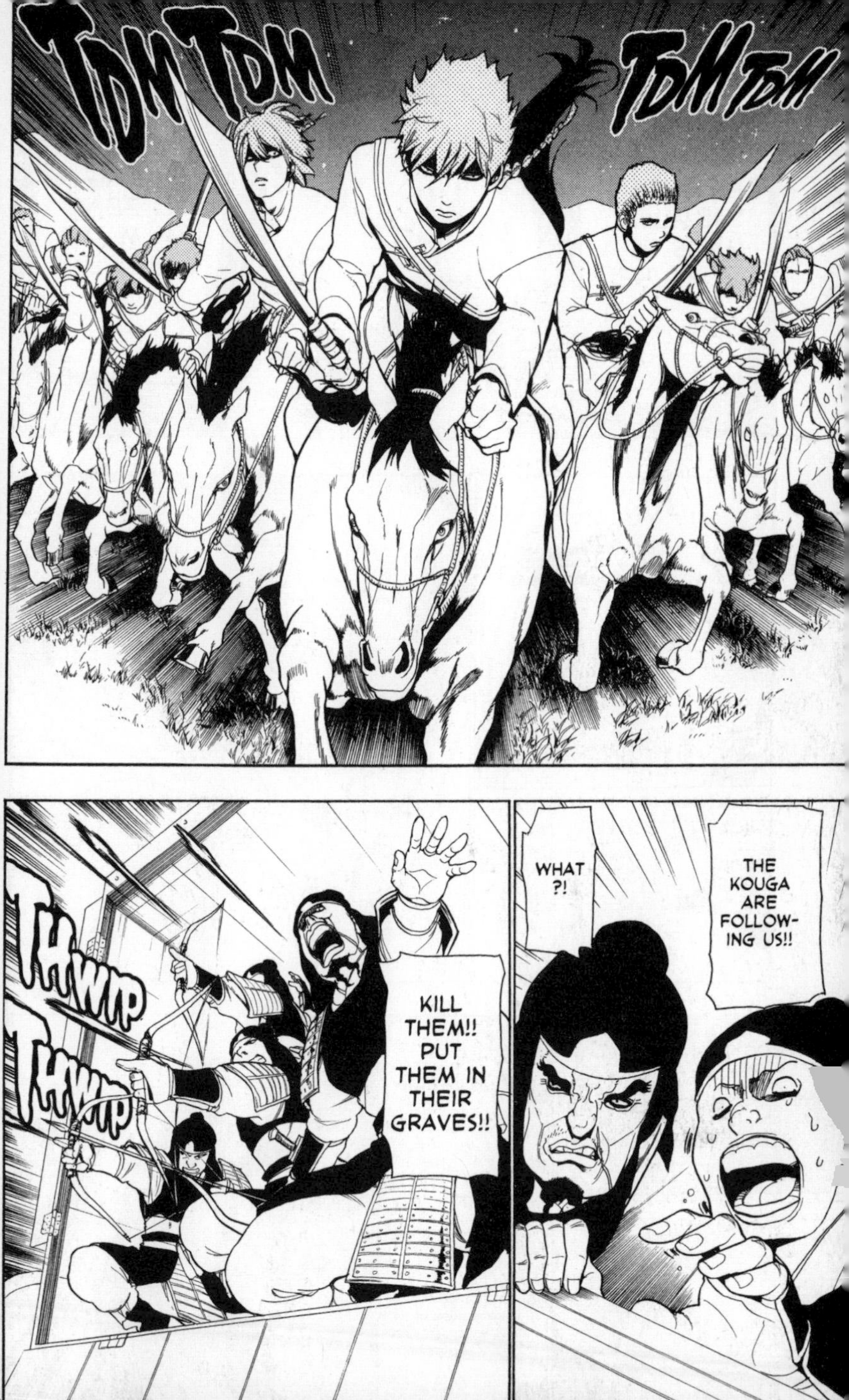
TOM TOM
TOM TOM
THE KOUGA ARE FOLLOW-ING US!!
WHAT ?!
KILL THEM!! PUT THEM IN THEIR GRAVES!!
THWIP
THWIP

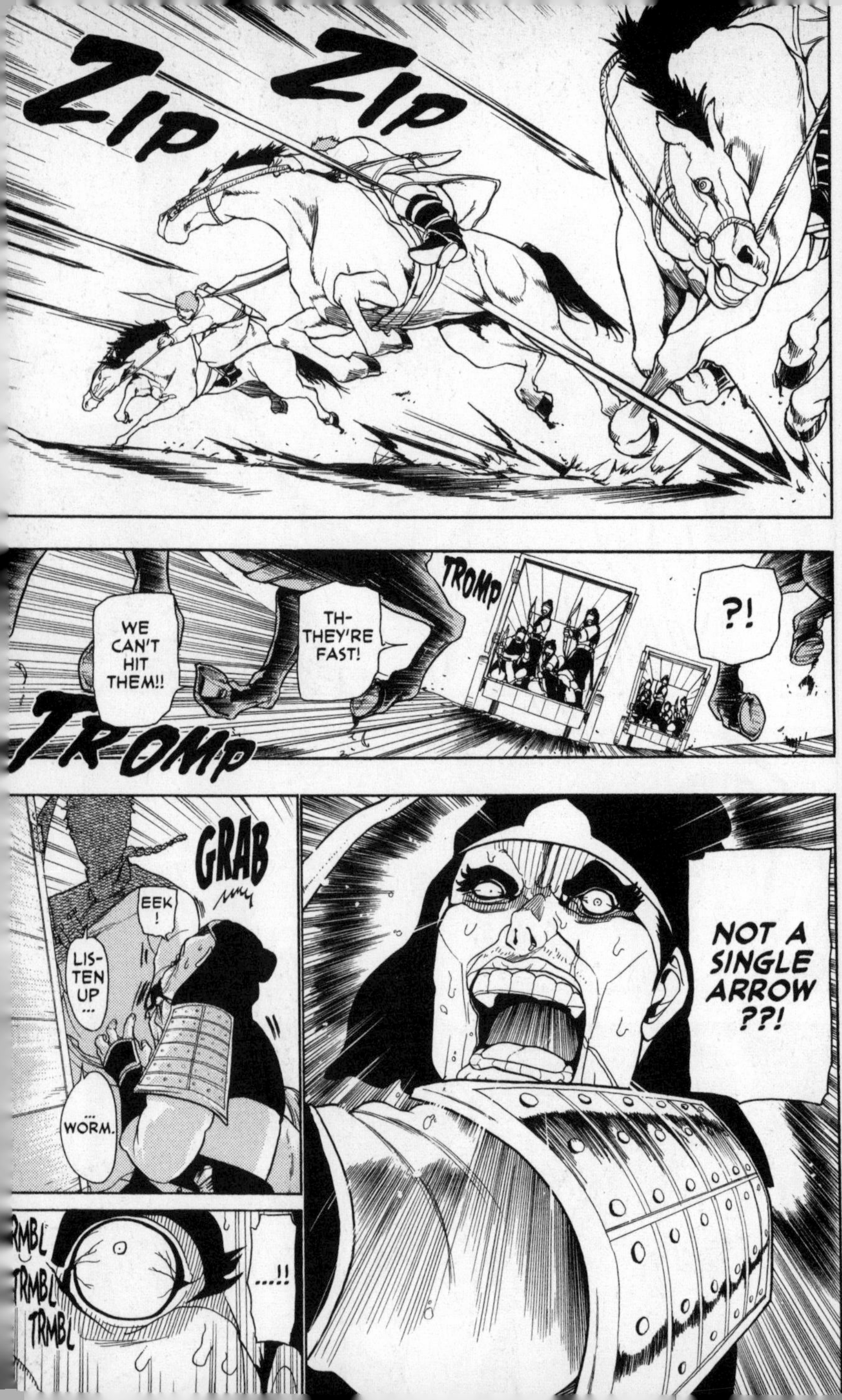
ZIP
ZIP
?!
TROMP
TH-THEY'RE FAST!
WE CAN'T HIT THEM!!
TROMP
NOT A SINGLE ARROW ??!
GRAB
EEK!
LIS-TEN UP...
...WORM.
...!!
TRMBL TRMBL TRMBL

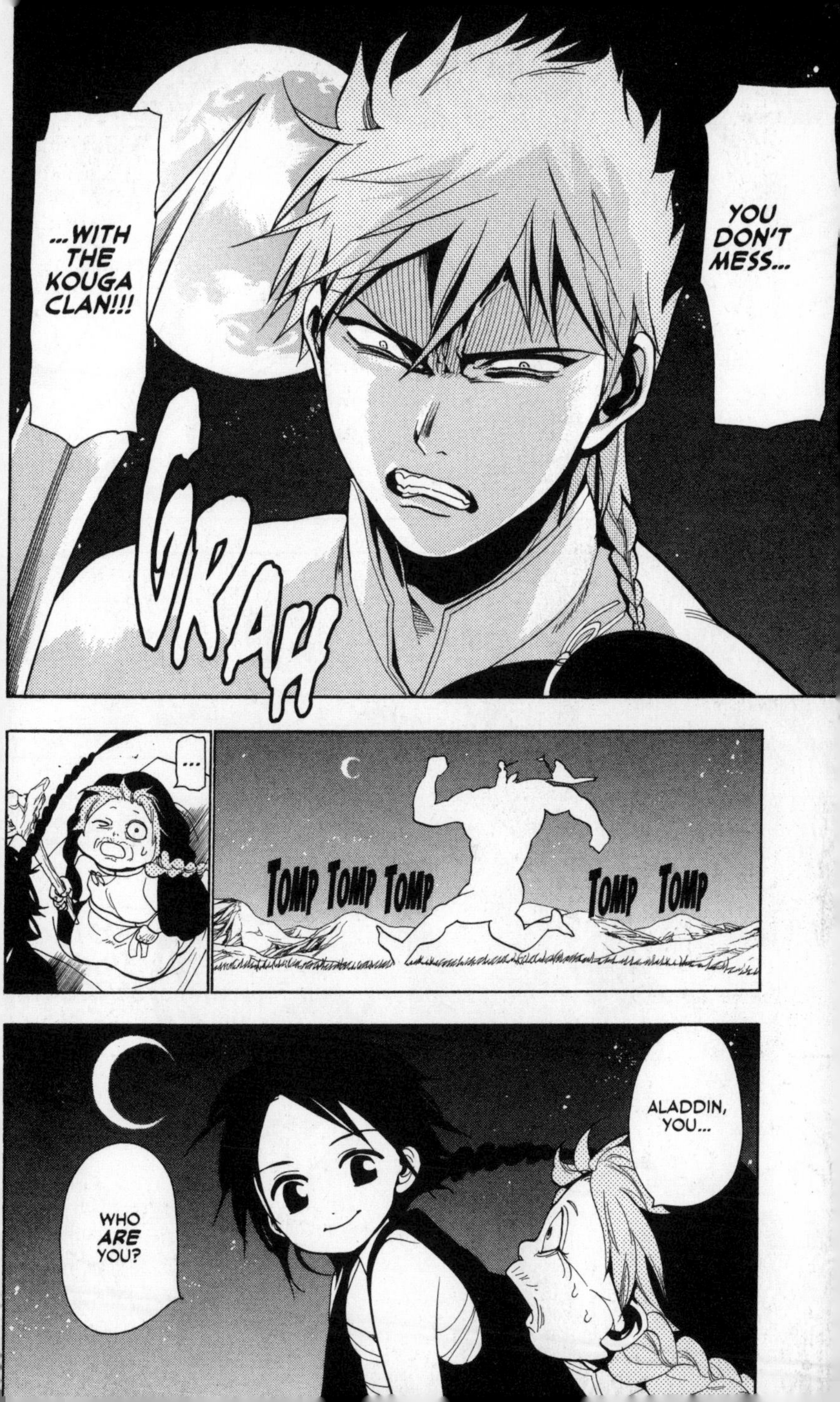
YOU DON'T MESS...
...WITH THE KOUGA CLAN!!!
GRAH
TOMP TOMP TOMP TOMP TOMP
...
ALADDIN, YOU...
WHO ARE YOU?

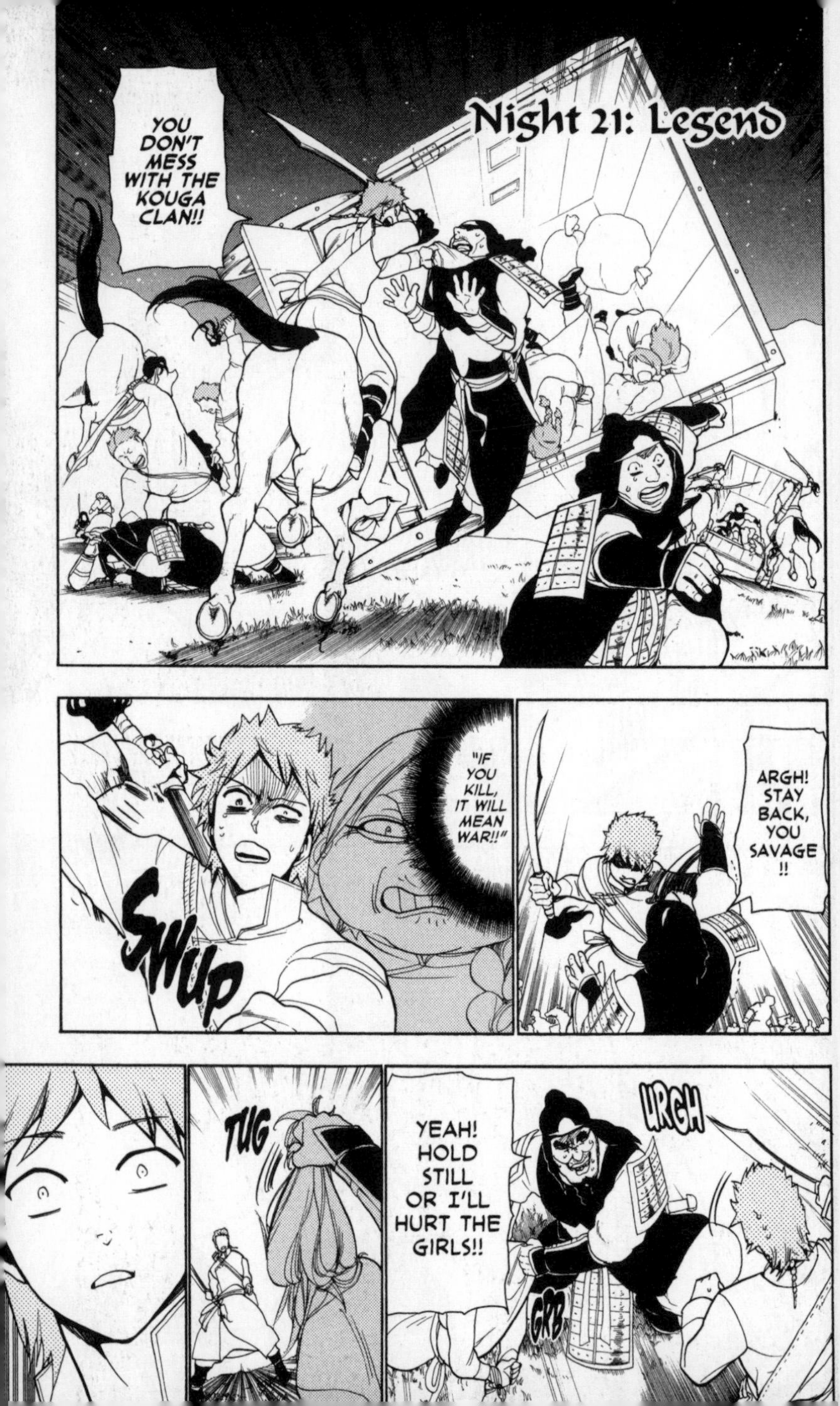
Night 21: Legend
YOU DON'T MESS WITH THE KOUGA CLAN!!
ARGH! STAY BACK, YOU SAVAGE!!
"IF YOU KILL, IT WILL MEAN WAR!!"
SWUP
URGH
YEAH! HOLD STILL OR I'LL HURT THE GIRLS!!
GRB
TUG

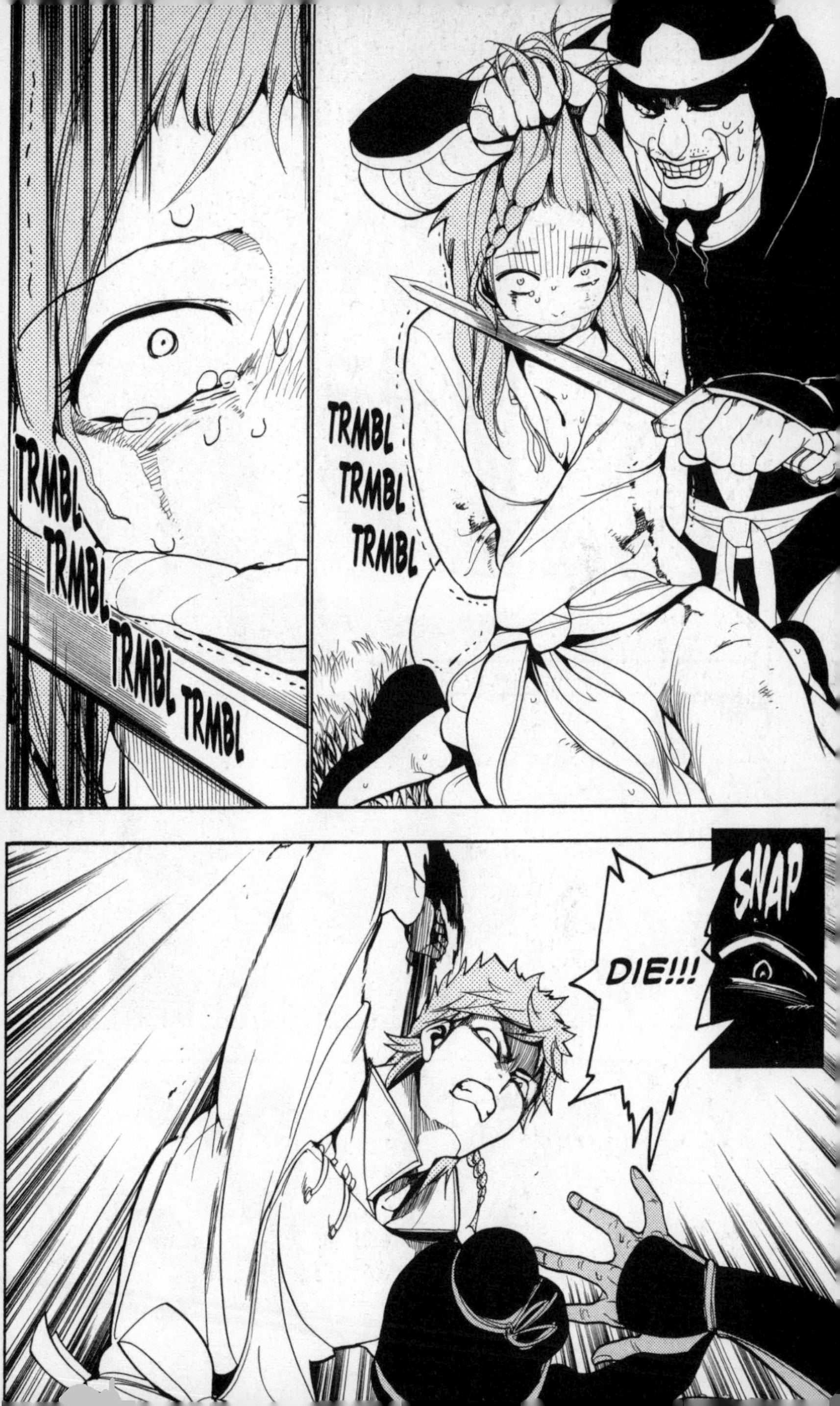
TRMBL
TRMBL
TRMBL
TRMBL
TRMBL
TRMBL
TRMBL
TRMBL
SNAP
DIE!!!

Night 21: Legend

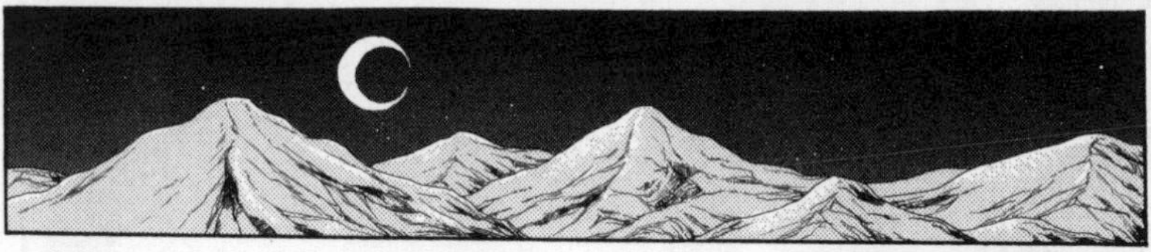

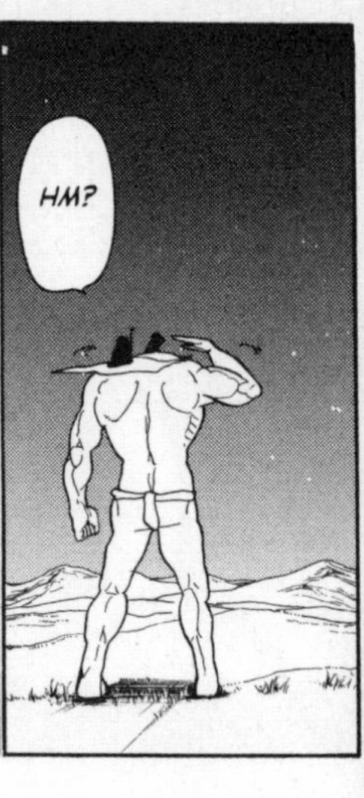
HM?

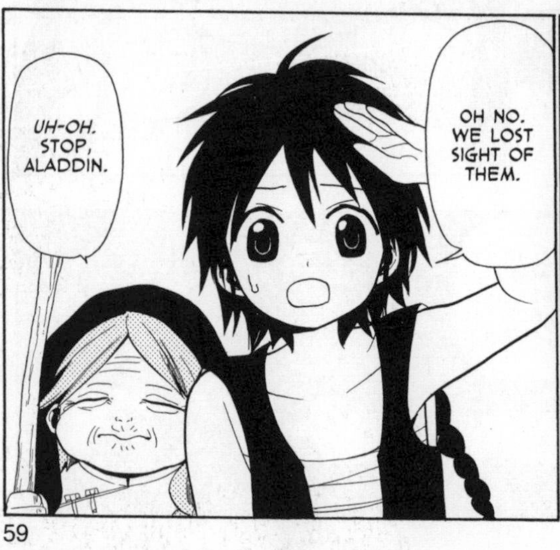
OH NO. WE LOST SIGHT OF THEM.
UH-OH. STOP, ALADDIN.

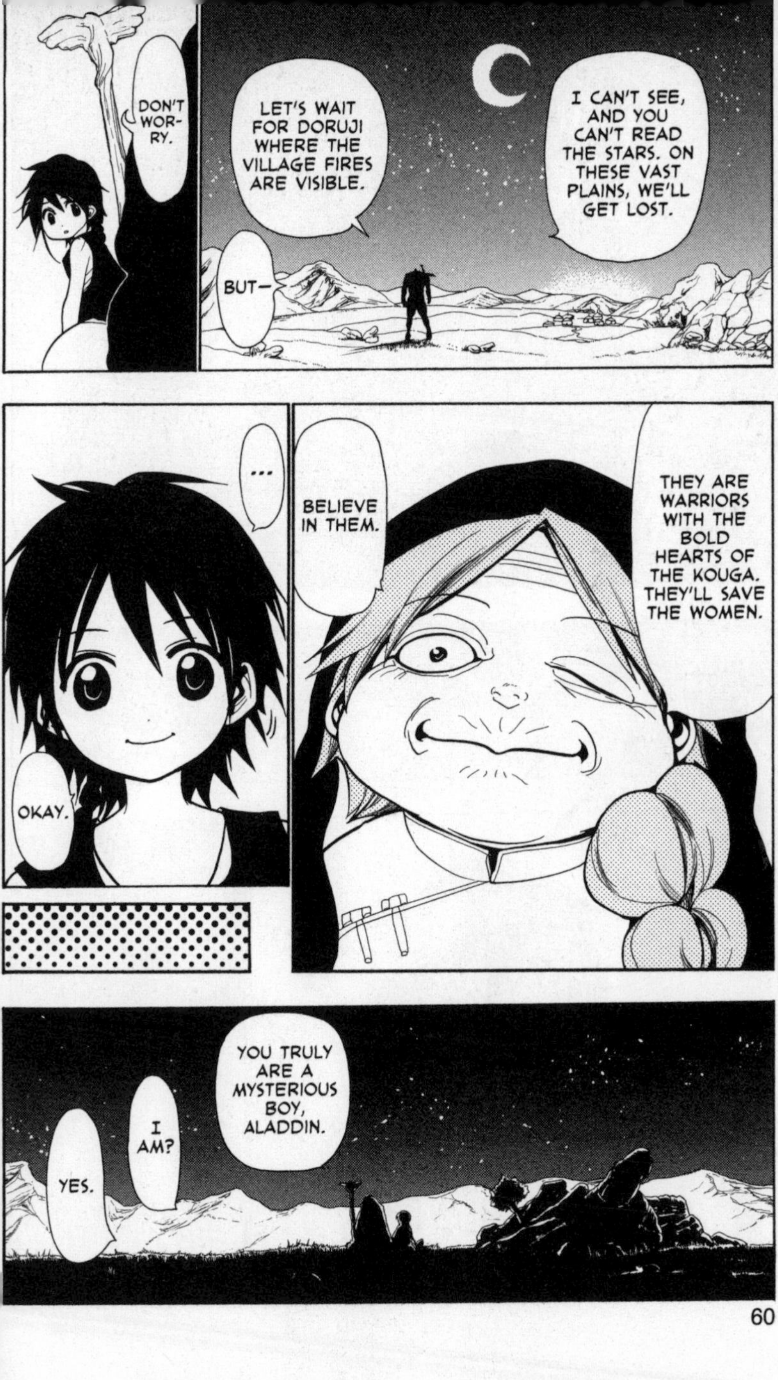
I CAN'T SEE, AND YOU CAN'T READ THE STARS. ON THESE VAST PLAINS, WE'LL GET LOST.
LET'S WAIT FOR DORUJI WHERE THE VILLAGE FIRES ARE VISIBLE.
BUT—
DON'T WOR-RY.
THEY ARE WARRIORS WITH THE BOLD HEARTS OF THE KOUGA. THEY'LL SAVE THE WOMEN.
BELIEVE IN THEM.
...
OKAY.
YOU TRULY ARE A MYSTERIOUS BOY, ALADDIN.
I AM?
YES.

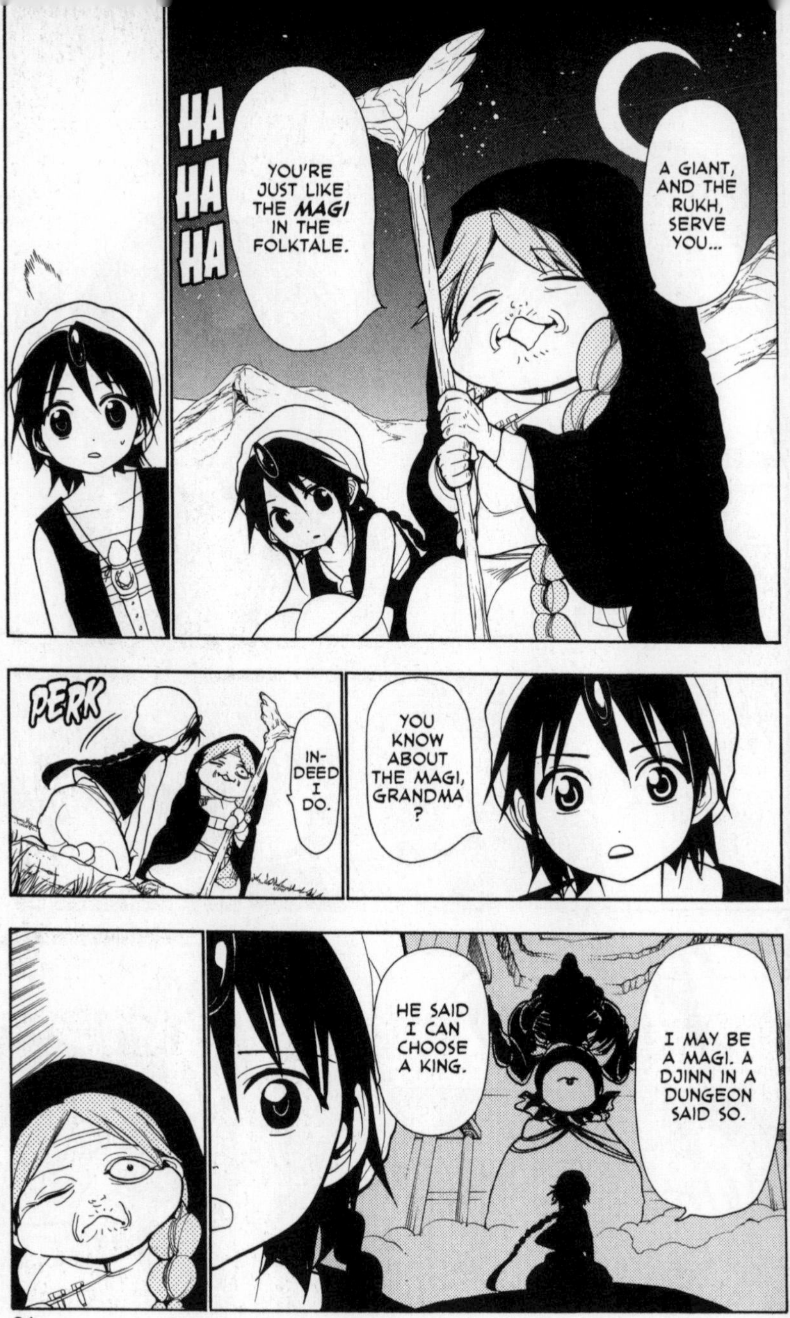
A GIANT, AND THE RUKH, SERVE YOU...
YOU'RE JUST LIKE THE *MAGI* IN THE FOLKTALE.
HA HA HA
YOU KNOW ABOUT THE MAGI, GRANDMA?
IN-DEED I DO.
PERK
I MAY BE A MAGI. A DJINN IN A DUNGEON SAID SO.
HE SAID I CAN CHOOSE A KING.

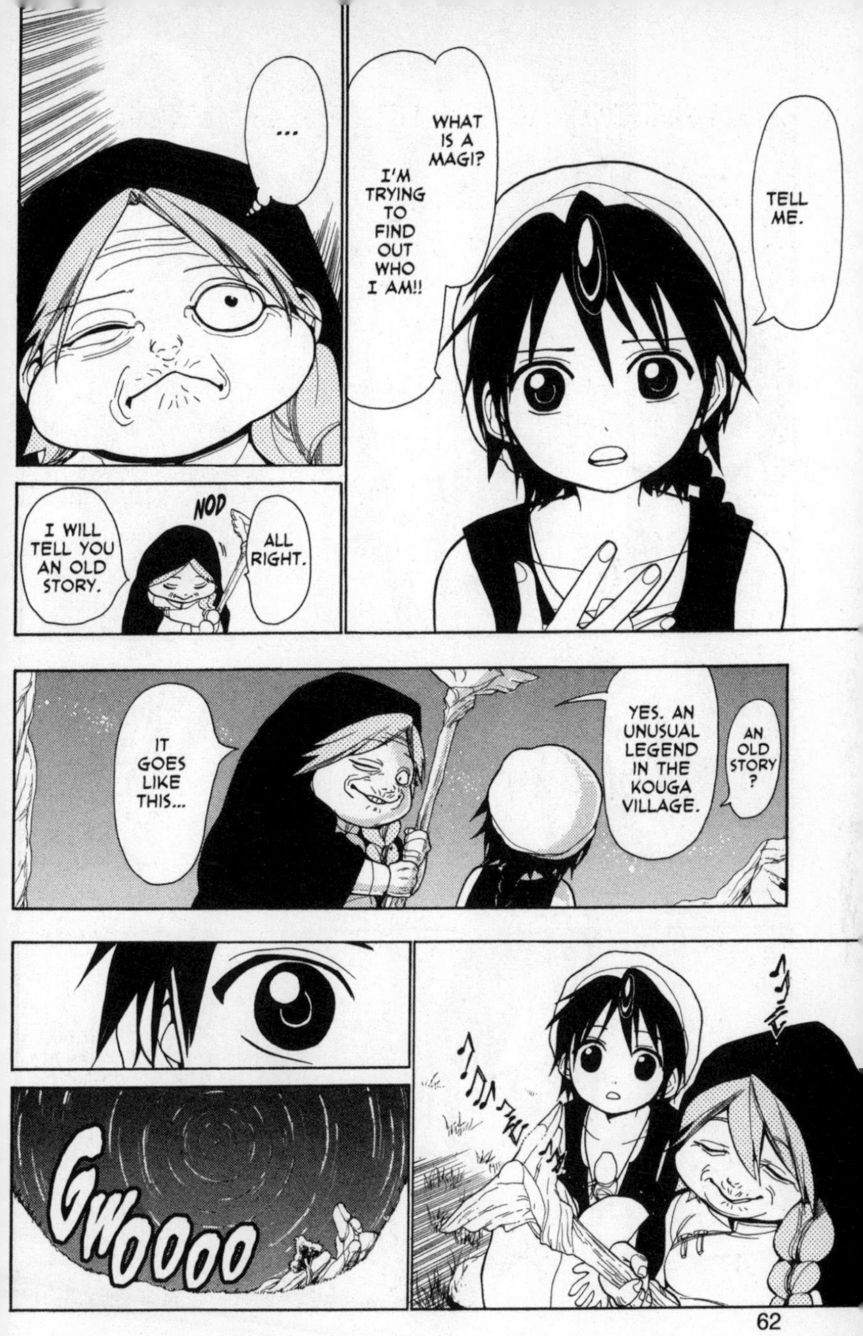
TELL ME.
WHAT IS A MAGI?
I'M TRYING TO FIND OUT WHO I AM!!
...
ALL RIGHT.
NOD
I WILL TELL YOU AN OLD STORY.
AN OLD STORY?
YES. AN UNUSUAL LEGEND IN THE KOUGA VILLAGE.
IT GOES LIKE THIS...
GWOOOO

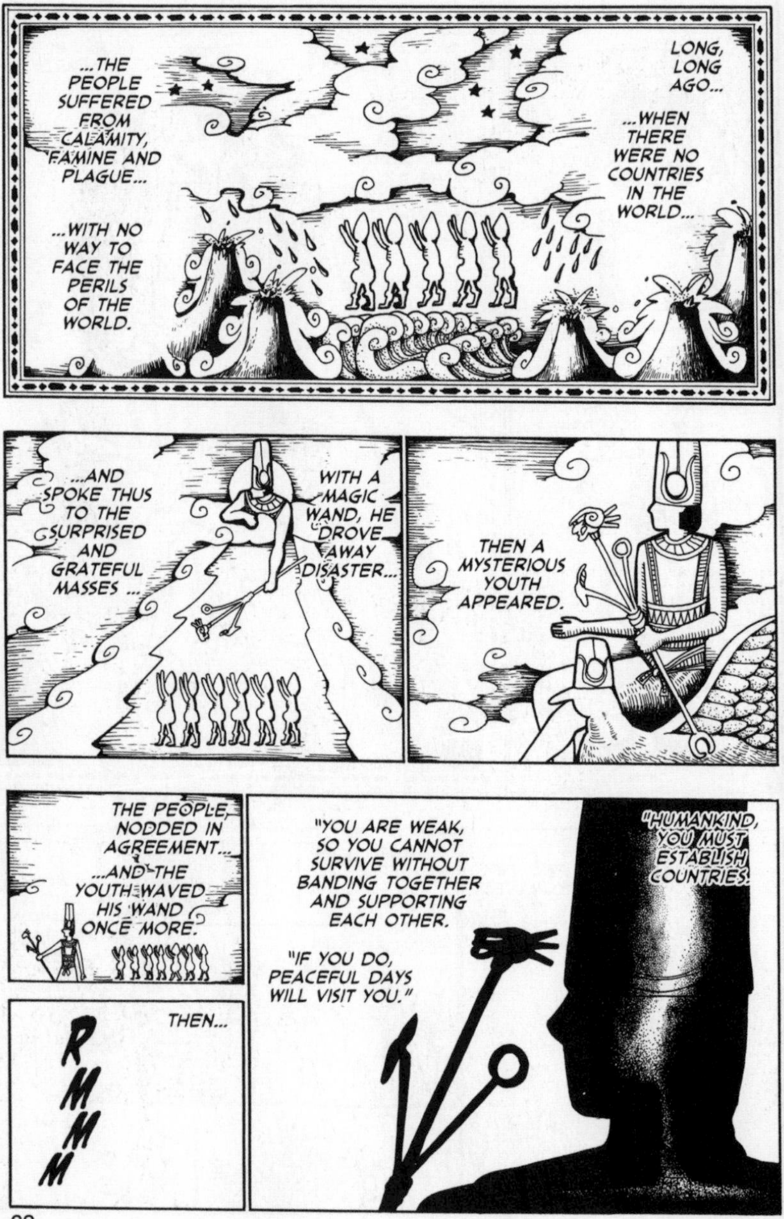
LONG, LONG AGO...
...WHEN THERE WERE NO COUNTRIES IN THE WORLD...
...THE PEOPLE SUFFERED FROM CALAMITY, FAMINE AND PLAGUE...
...WITH NO WAY TO FACE THE PERILS OF THE WORLD.
THEN A MYSTERIOUS YOUTH APPEARED.
WITH A MAGIC WAND, HE DROVE AWAY DISASTER...
...AND SPOKE THUS TO THE SURPRISED AND GRATEFUL MASSES ...
"HUMANKIND, YOU MUST ESTABLISH COUNTRIES.
"YOU ARE WEAK, SO YOU CANNOT SURVIVE WITHOUT BANDING TOGETHER AND SUPPORTING EACH OTHER.
"IF YOU DO, PEACEFUL DAYS WILL VISIT YOU."
THE PEOPLE NODDED IN AGREEMENT...
...AND THE YOUTH WAVED HIS WAND ONCE MORE.
THEN...
RMMM

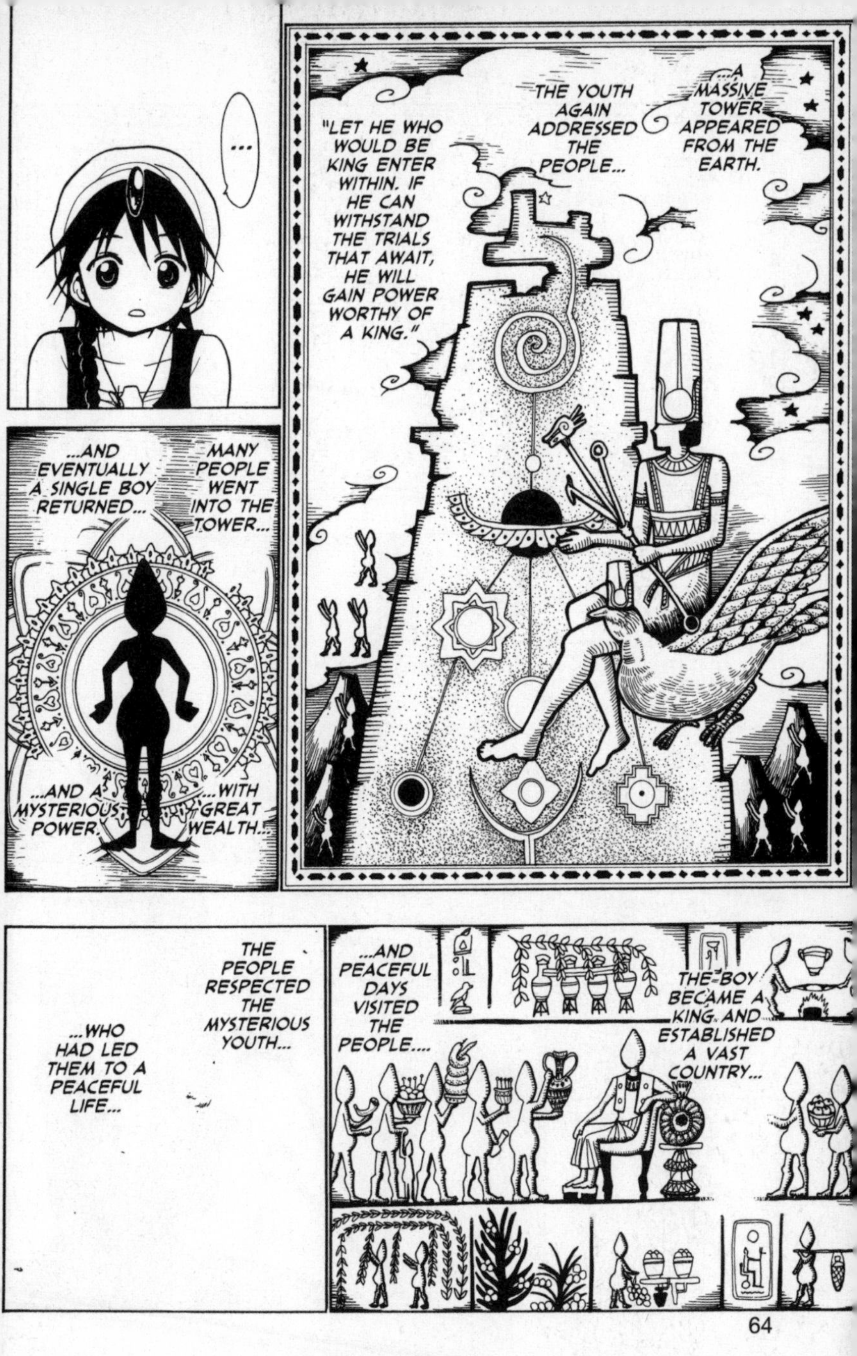
...A MASSIVE TOWER APPEARED FROM THE EARTH.
THE YOUTH AGAIN ADDRESSED THE PEOPLE...
"LET HE WHO WOULD BE KING ENTER WITHIN. IF HE CAN WITHSTAND THE TRIALS THAT AWAIT, HE WILL GAIN POWER WORTHY OF A KING."
...
MANY PEOPLE WENT INTO THE TOWER...
...AND EVENTUALLY A SINGLE BOY RETURNED...
...WITH GREAT WEALTH...
...AND A MYSTERIOUS POWER.
THE BOY BECAME A KING AND ESTABLISHED A VAST COUNTRY...
...AND PEACEFUL DAYS VISITED THE PEOPLE....
THE PEOPLE RESPECTED THE MYSTERIOUS YOUTH...
...WHO HAD LED THEM TO A PEACEFUL LIFE...

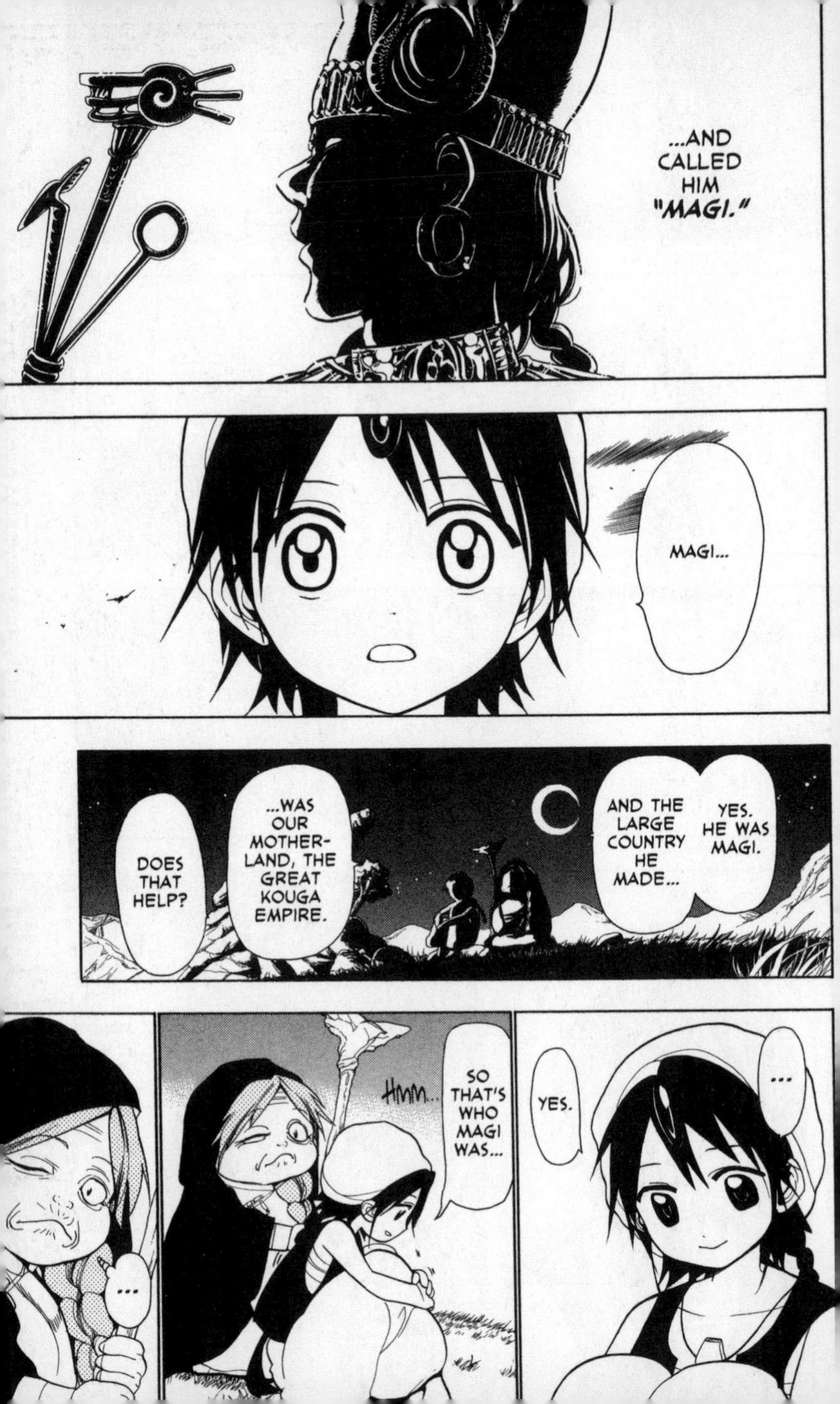
...AND CALLED HIM "MAGI."
MAGI...
YES. HE WAS MAGI.
AND THE LARGE COUNTRY HE MADE...
...WAS OUR MOTHER-LAND, THE GREAT KOUGA EMPIRE.
DOES THAT HELP?
...
YES.
SO THAT'S WHO MAGI WAS...
Hmm...
...

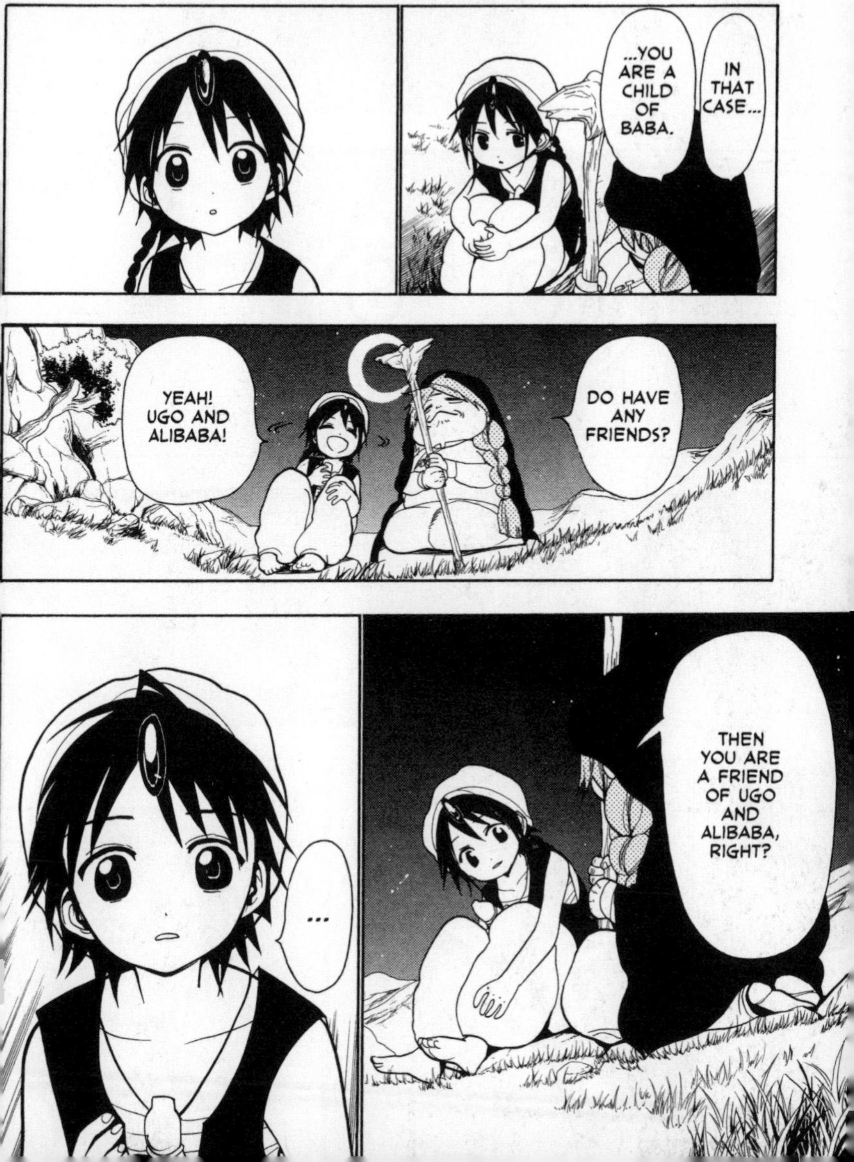
IN THAT CASE...
...YOU ARE A CHILD OF BABA.
DO HAVE ANY FRIENDS?
YEAH! UGO AND ALIBABA!
THEN YOU ARE A FRIEND OF UGO AND ALIBABA, RIGHT?
...

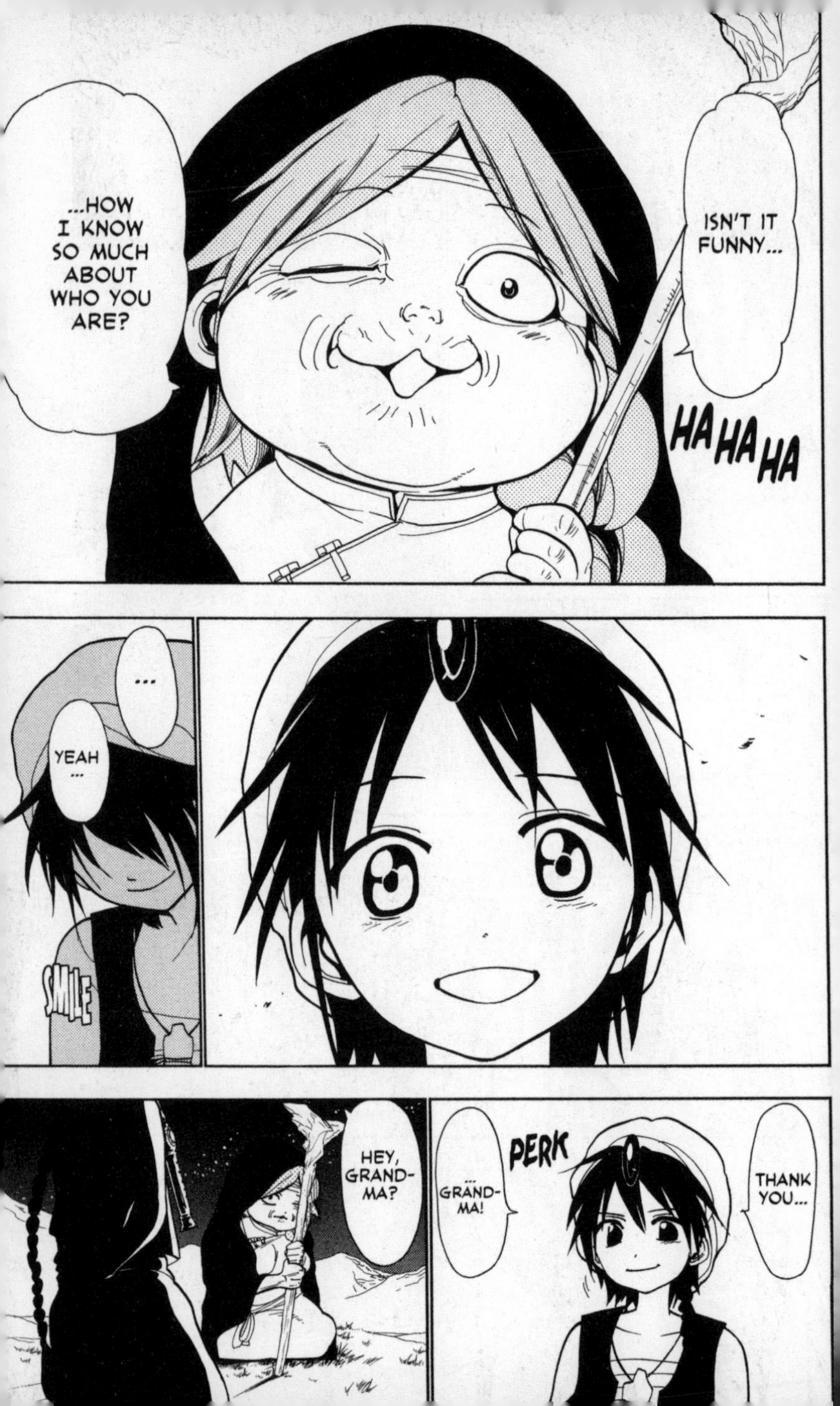
ISN'T IT FUNNY...
...HOW I KNOW SO MUCH ABOUT WHO YOU ARE?
HA HA HA
...
YEAH ...
SMILE
THANK YOU...
PERK
...GRAND-MA!
HEY, GRAND-MA?

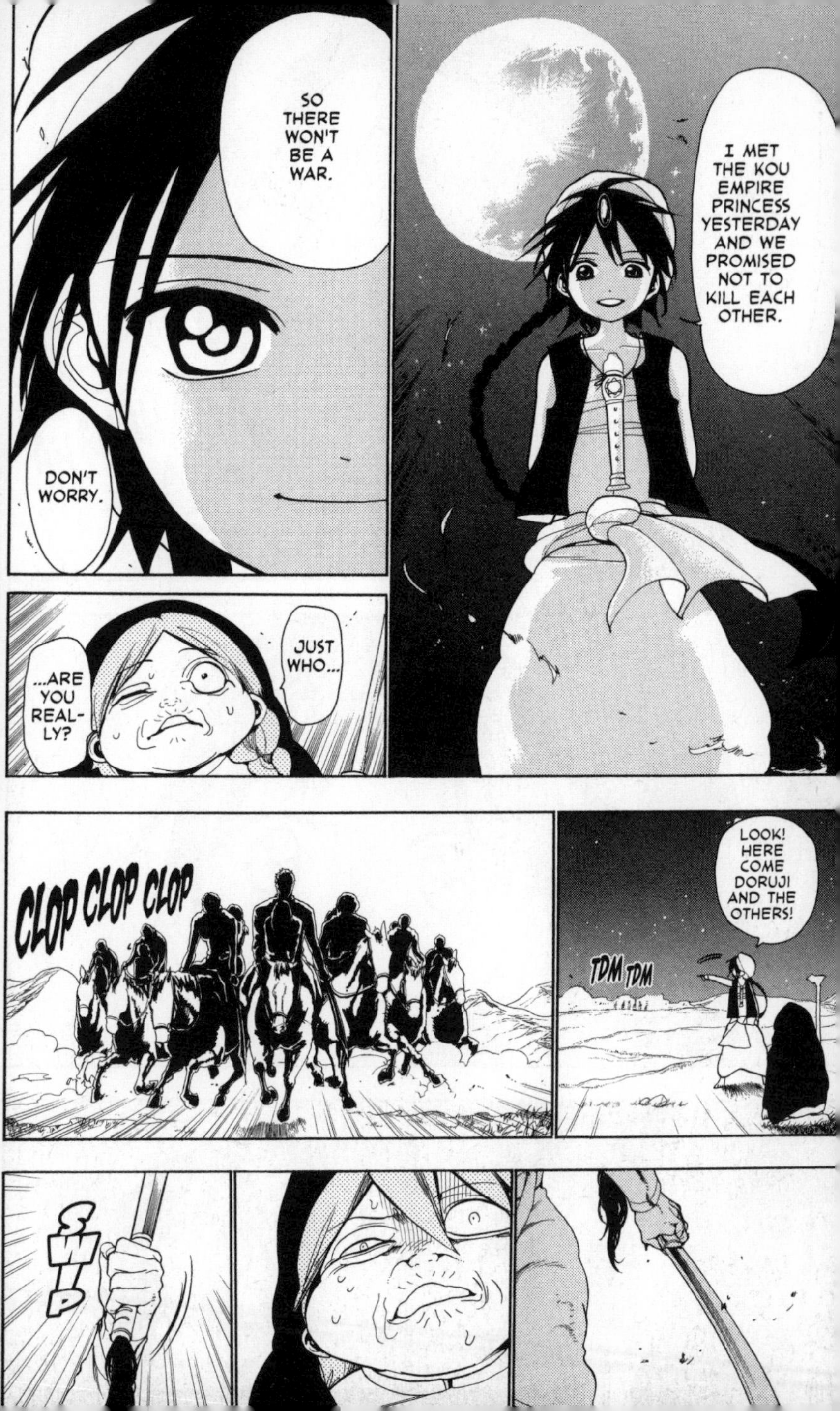
I MET THE KOU EMPIRE PRINCESS YESTERDAY AND WE PROMISED NOT TO KILL EACH OTHER.
SO THERE WON'T BE A WAR.
DON'T WORRY.
JUST WHO...
...ARE YOU REAL-LY?
LOOK! HERE COME DORUJI AND THE OTHERS!
TDM TDM
CLOP CLOP CLOP
SWIP

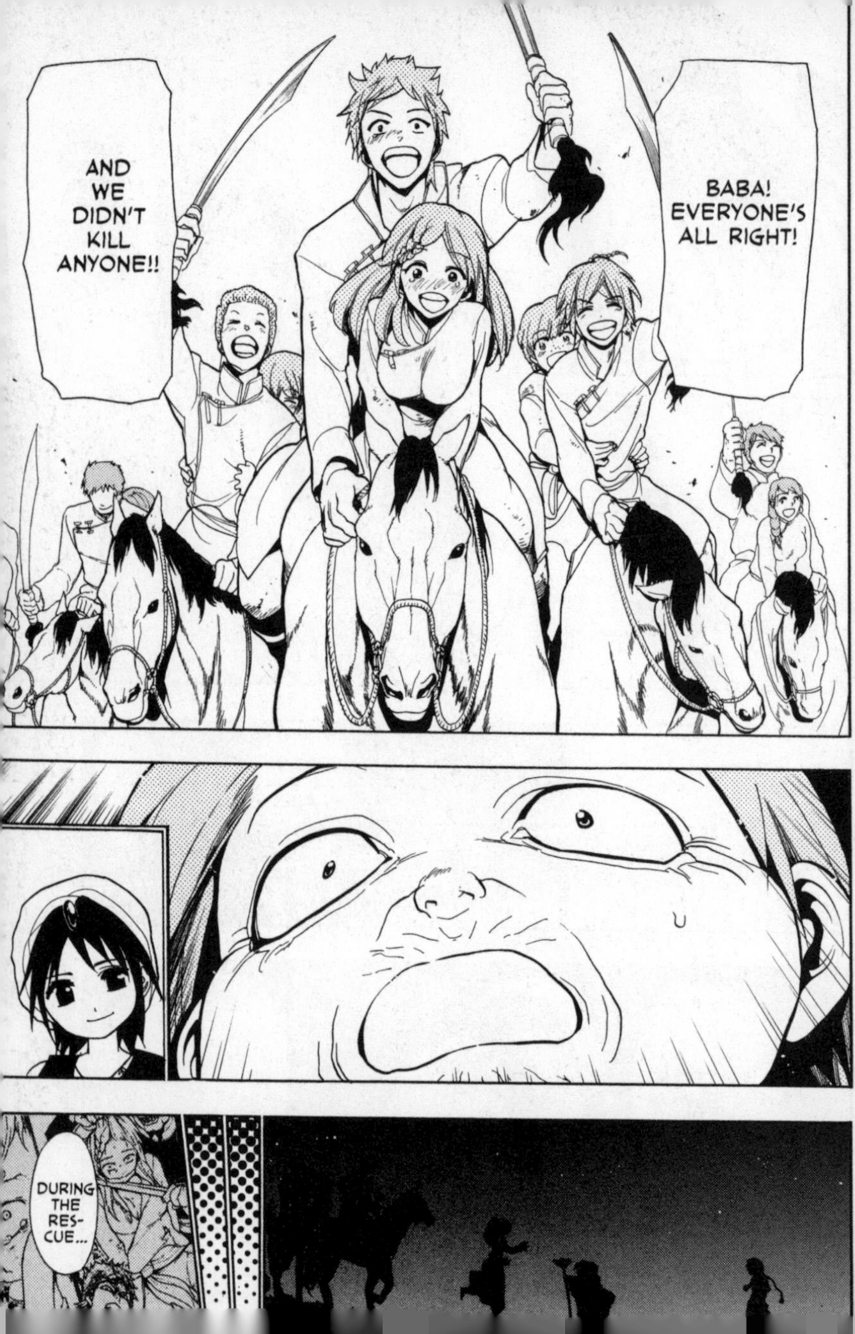
BABA! EVERYONE'S ALL RIGHT!
AND WE DIDN'T KILL ANYONE!!
DURING THE RES- CUE...

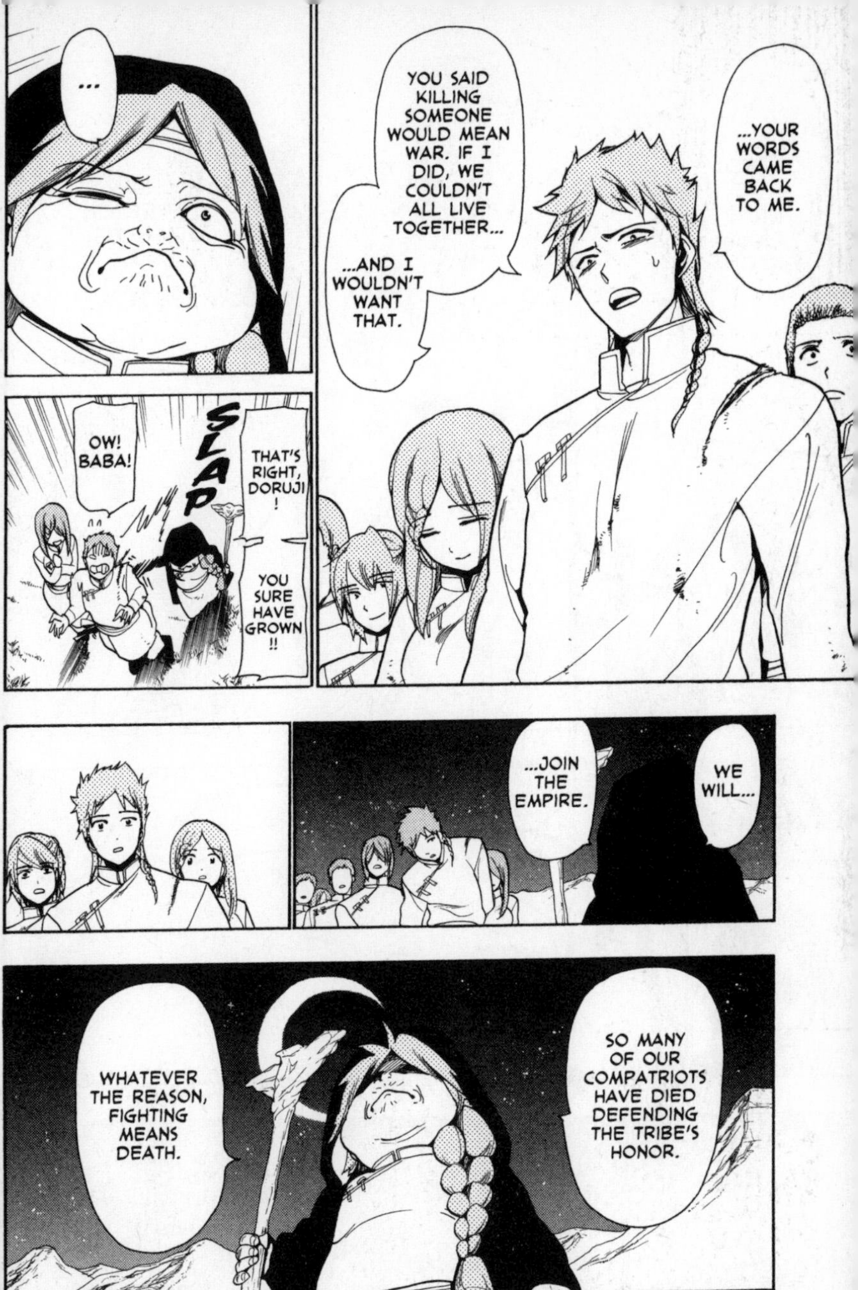
...YOUR WORDS CAME BACK TO ME.
YOU SAID KILLING SOMEONE WOULD MEAN WAR. IF I DID, WE COULDN'T ALL LIVE TOGETHER...
...AND I WOULDN'T WANT THAT.
...
THAT'S RIGHT, DORUJI! YOU SURE HAVE GROWN!!
SLAP
OW! BABA!
WE WILL...
...JOIN THE EMPIRE.
SO MANY OF OUR COMPATRIOTS HAVE DIED DEFENDING THE TRIBE'S HONOR.
WHATEVER THE REASON, FIGHTING MEANS DEATH.

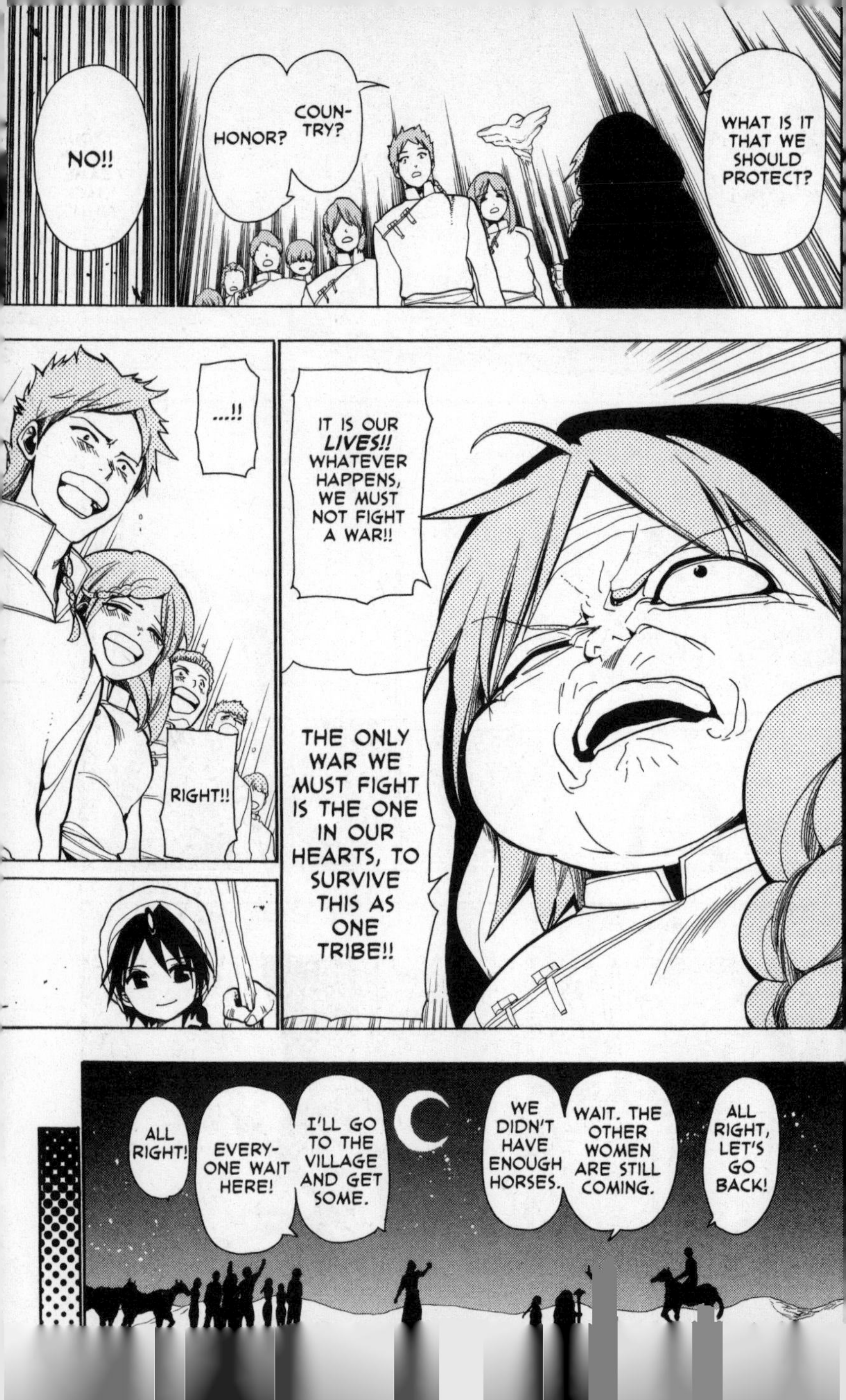
WHAT IS IT THAT WE SHOULD PROTECT?
COUNTRY?
HONOR?
NO!!
IT IS OUR *LIVES!!* WHATEVER HAPPENS, WE MUST NOT FIGHT A WAR!!
THE ONLY WAR WE MUST FIGHT IS THE ONE IN OUR HEARTS, TO SURVIVE THIS AS ONE TRIBE!!
...!!
RIGHT!!
ALL RIGHT, LET'S GO BACK!
WAIT. THE OTHER WOMEN ARE STILL COMING.
WE DIDN'T HAVE ENOUGH HORSES.
I'LL GO TO THE VILLAGE AND GET SOME.
EVERYONE WAIT HERE!
ALL RIGHT!

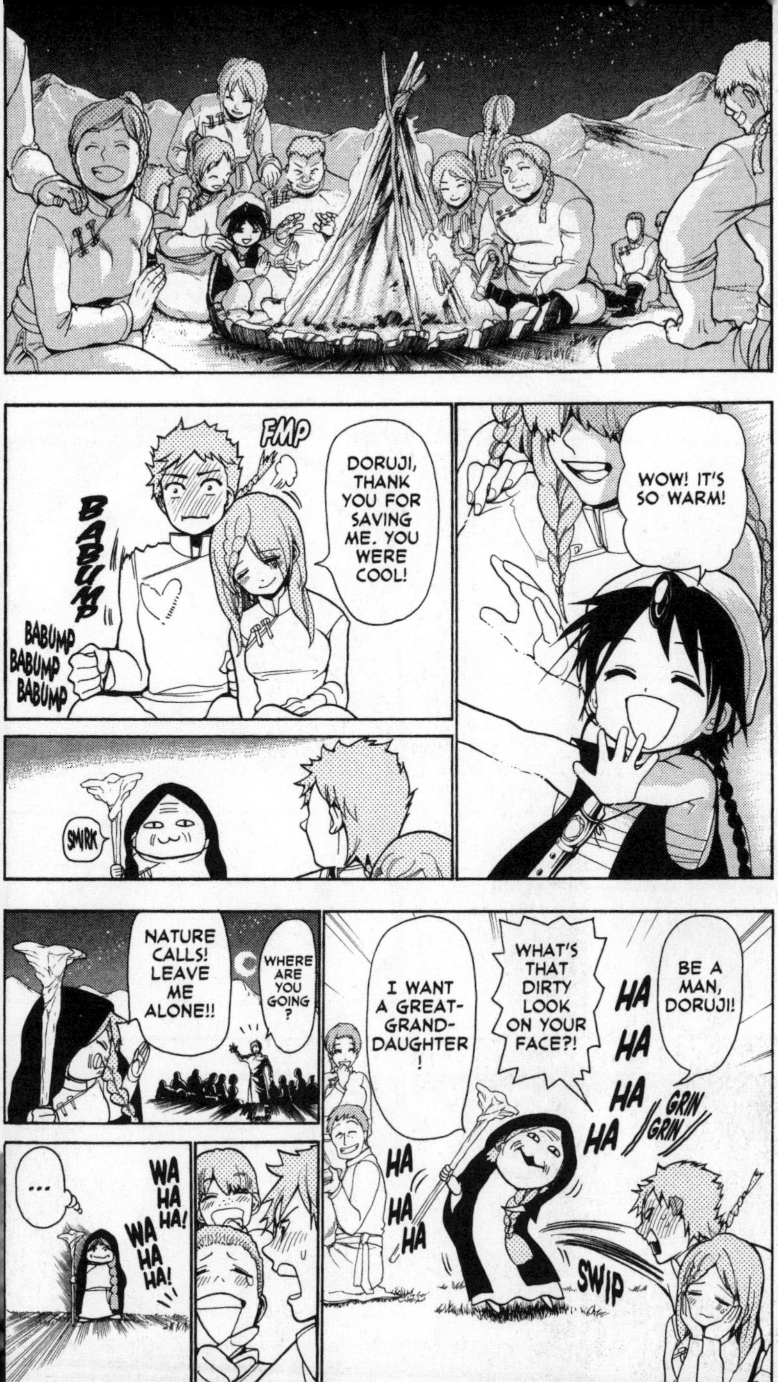
WOW! IT'S SO WARM!
FMP
DORUJI, THANK YOU FOR SAVING ME. YOU WERE COOL!
BABUMP
BABUMP BABUMP BABUMP
SMIRK
BE A MAN, DORUJI!
GRIN GRIN
HA HA HA HA
WHAT'S THAT DIRTY LOOK ON YOUR FACE?!
I WANT A GREAT-GRANDDAUGHTER!
HA HA HA
SWIP
WHERE ARE YOU GOING?
NATURE CALLS! LEAVE ME ALONE!!
WA HA HA!
WA HA HA!
...

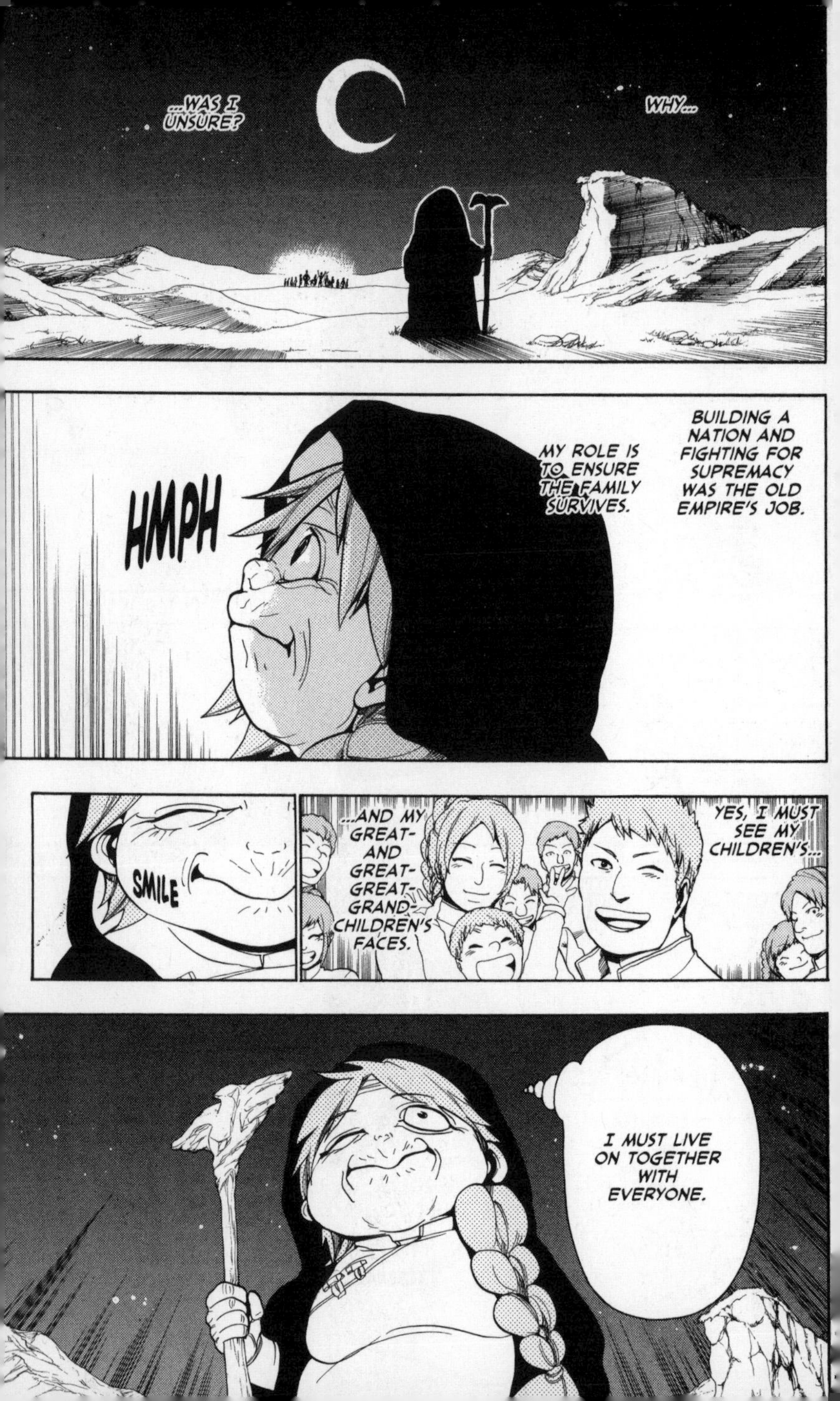
WHY...
...WAS I UNSURE?
BUILDING A NATION AND FIGHTING FOR SUPREMACY WAS THE OLD EMPIRE'S JOB.
MY ROLE IS TO ENSURE THE FAMILY SURVIVES.
HMPH
YES, I MUST SEE MY CHILDREN'S...
...AND MY GREAT- AND GREAT-GREAT-GRAND-CHILDREN'S FACES.
SMILE
I MUST LIVE ON TOGETHER WITH EVERYONE.

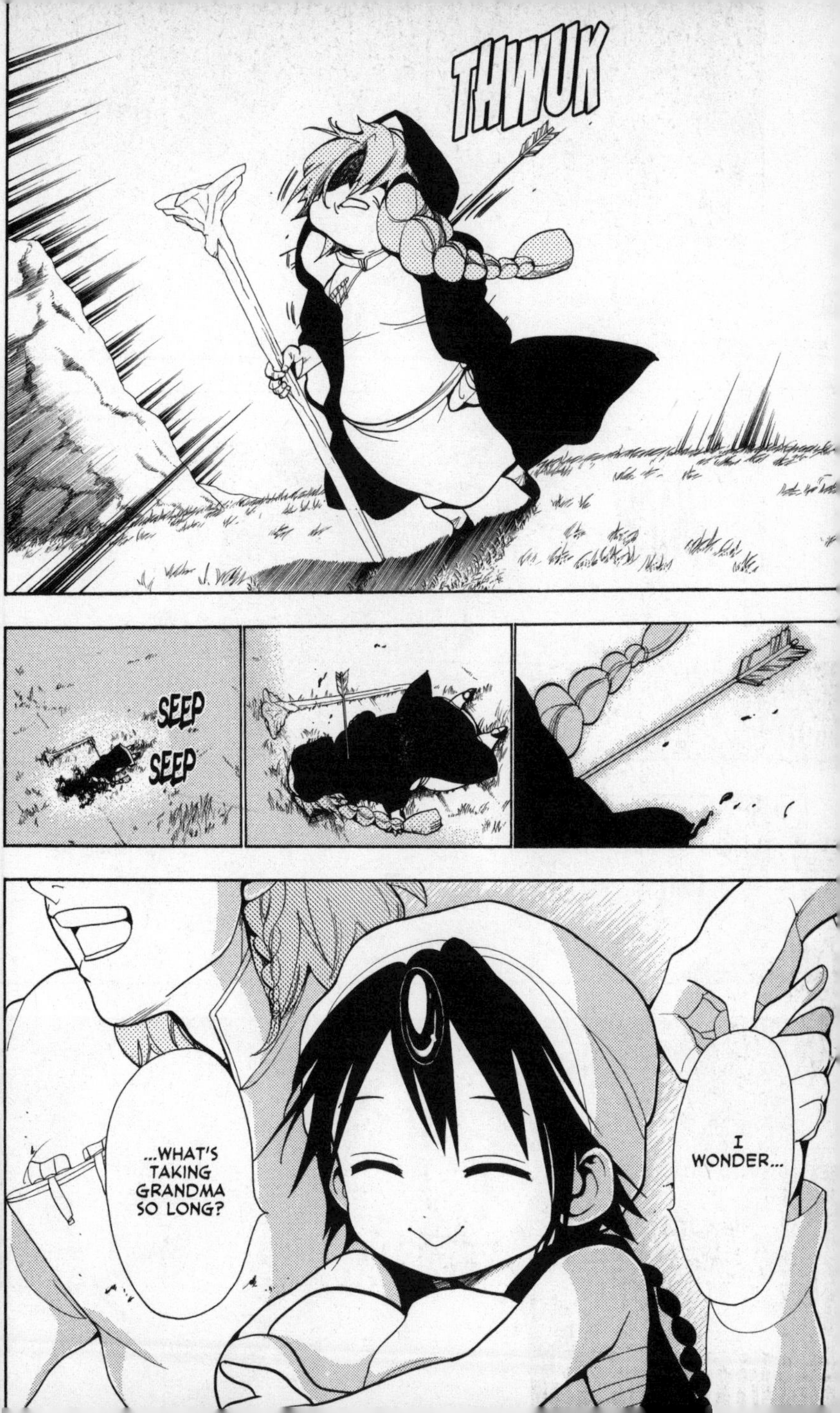
THWUK
SEEP
SEEP
I WONDER...
...WHAT'S TAKING GRANDMA SO LONG?

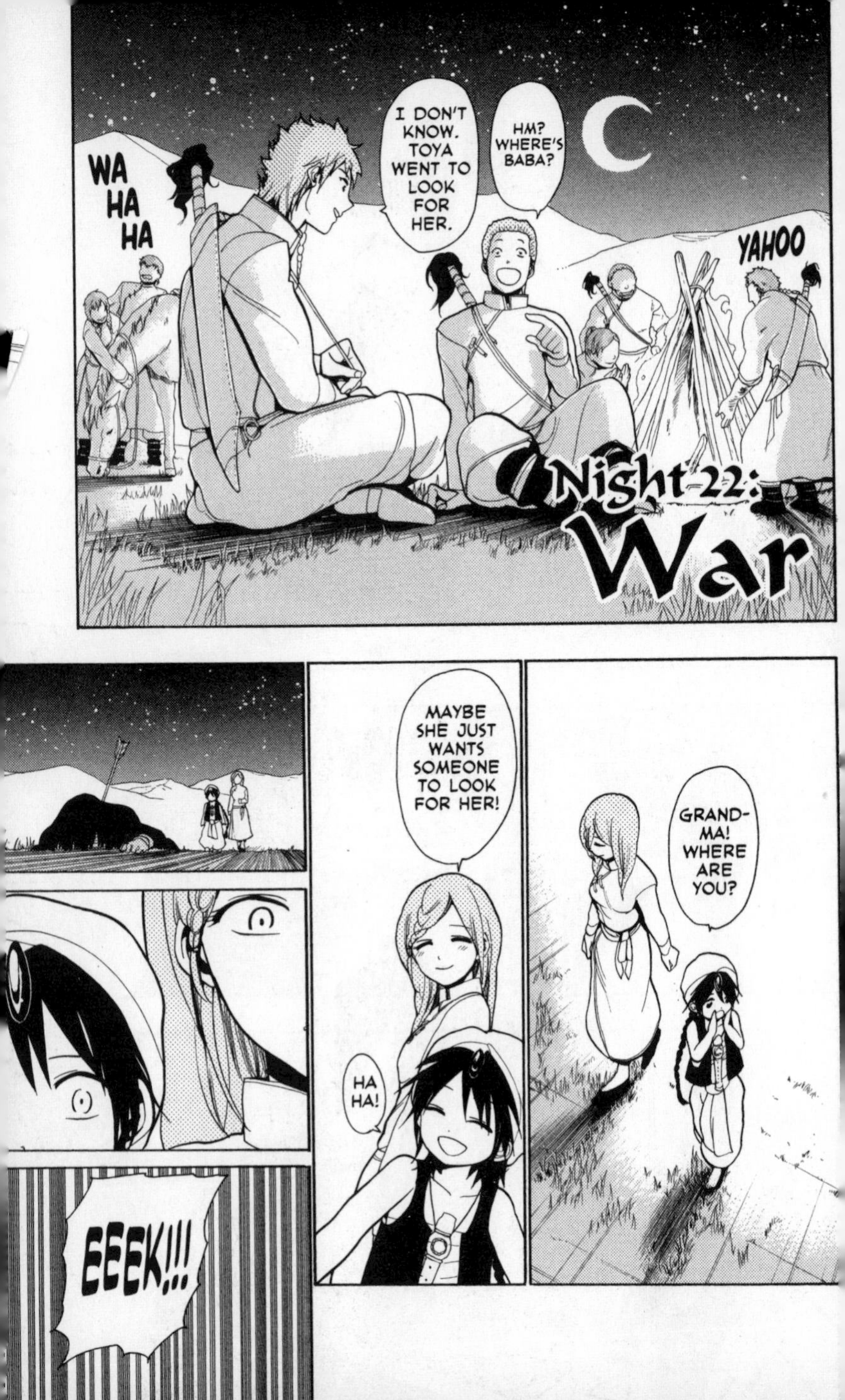
HM? WHERE'S BABA?
I DON'T KNOW. TOYA WENT TO LOOK FOR HER.
YAHOO
WA HA HA
Night 22: War
GRAND-MA! WHERE ARE YOU?
MAYBE SHE JUST WANTS SOMEONE TO LOOK FOR HER!
HA HA!
EEEK!!!

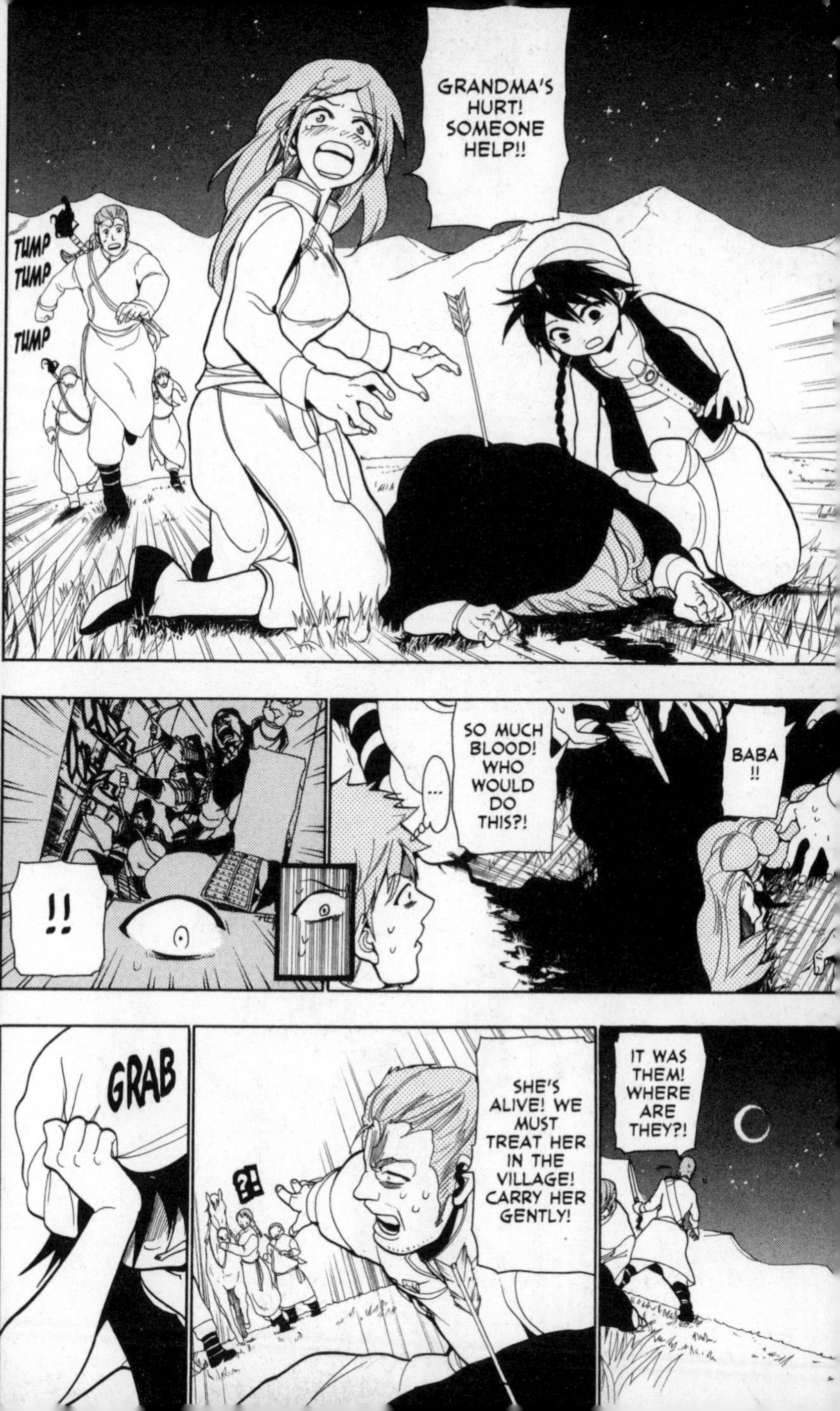
GRANDMA'S HURT! SOMEONE HELP!!
TUMP TUMP TUMP
BABA !!
SO MUCH BLOOD! WHO WOULD DO THIS?!
...
!!
IT WAS THEM! WHERE ARE THEY?!
SHE'S ALIVE! WE MUST TREAT HER IN THE VILLAGE! CARRY HER GENTLY!
?!
GRAB

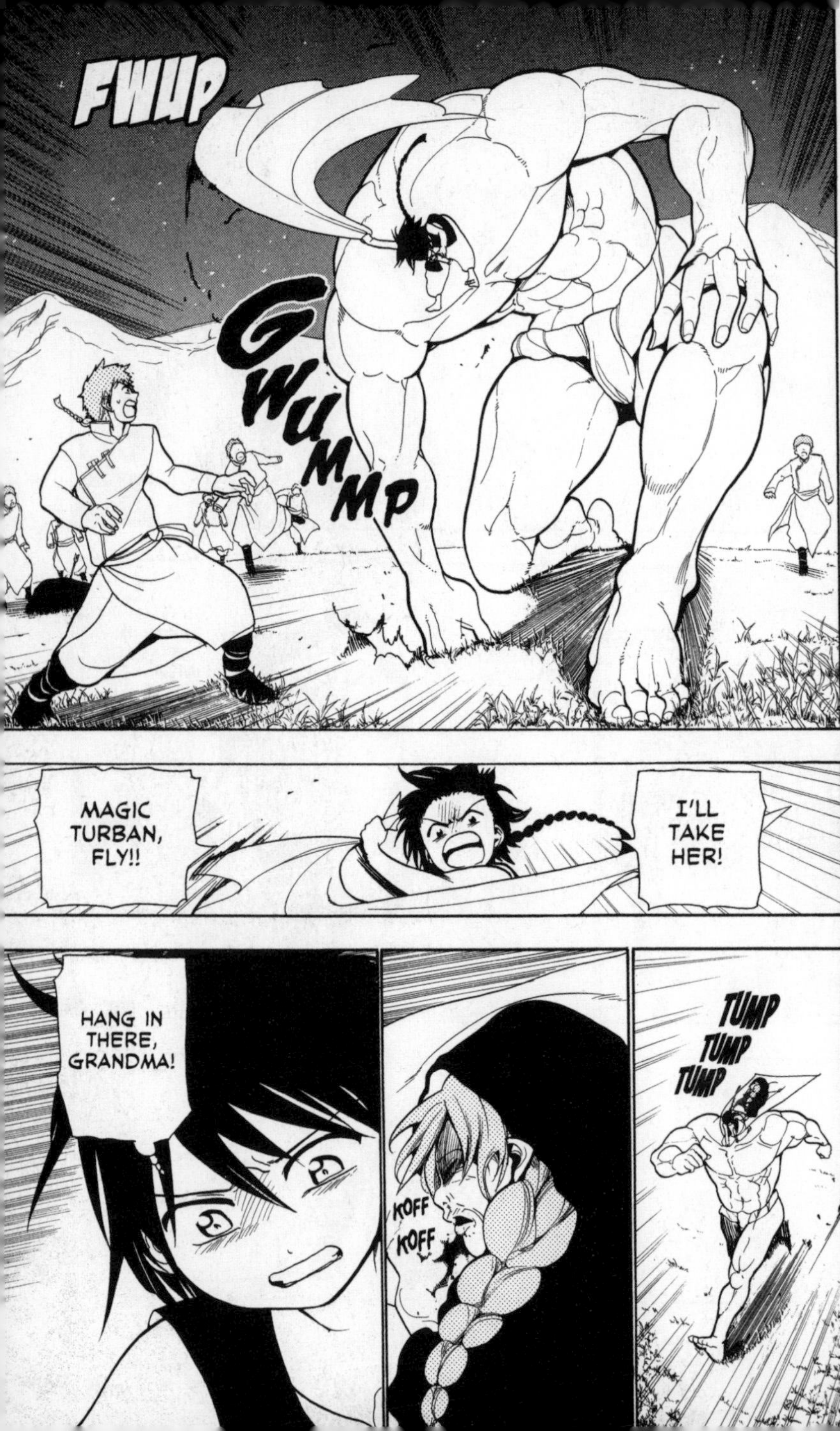
FWUP
GWUMMP
I'LL TAKE HER!
MAGIC TURBAN, FLY!!
TUMP TUMP TUMP
KOFF KOFF
HANG IN THERE, GRANDMA!

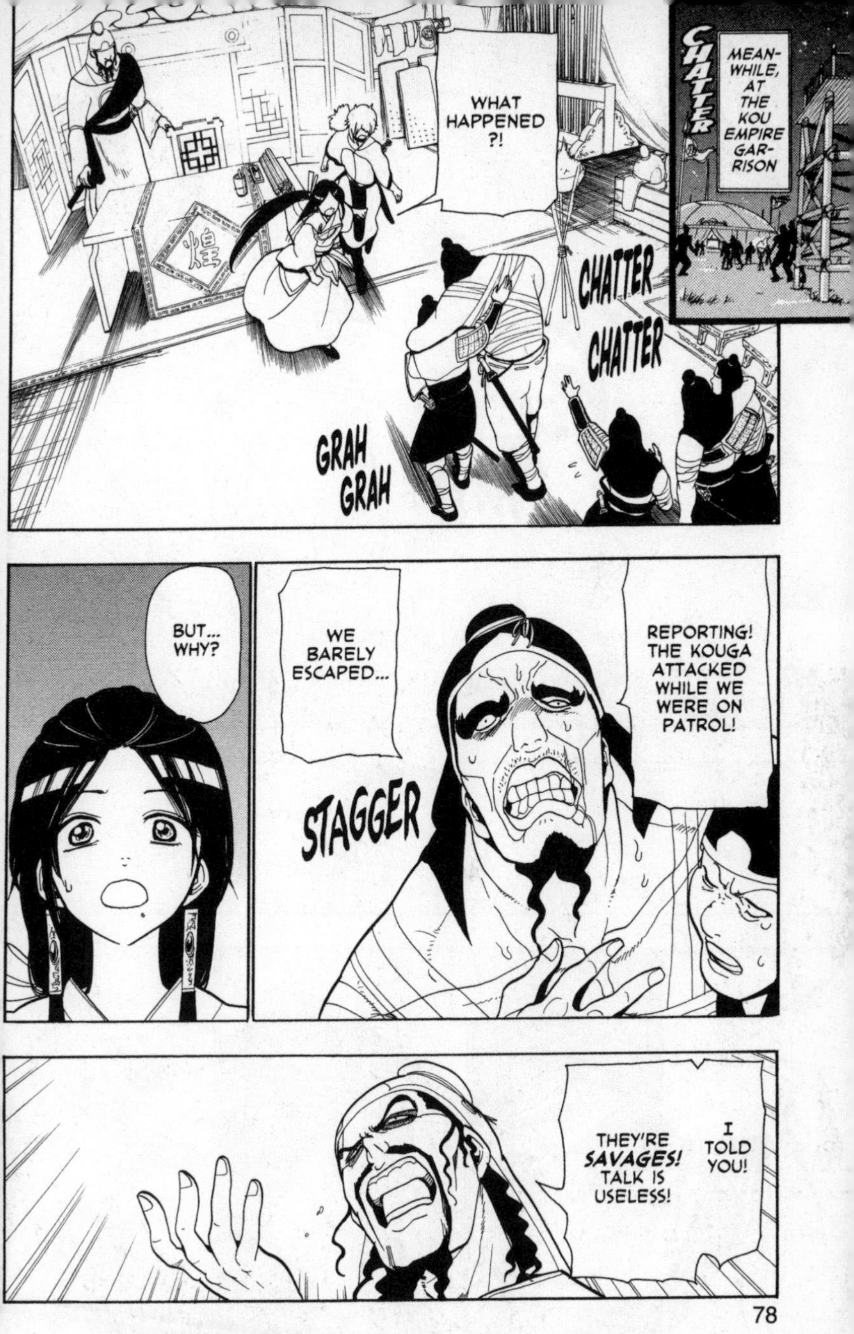
CHATTER
MEAN-WHILE, AT THE KOU EMPIRE GAR-RISON
WHAT HAPPENED?!
CHATTER
CHATTER
GRAH GRAH
REPORTING! THE KOUGA ATTACKED WHILE WE WERE ON PATROL!
WE BARELY ESCAPED...
STAGGER
BUT... WHY?
I TOLD YOU!
THEY'RE SAVAGES! TALK IS USELESS!

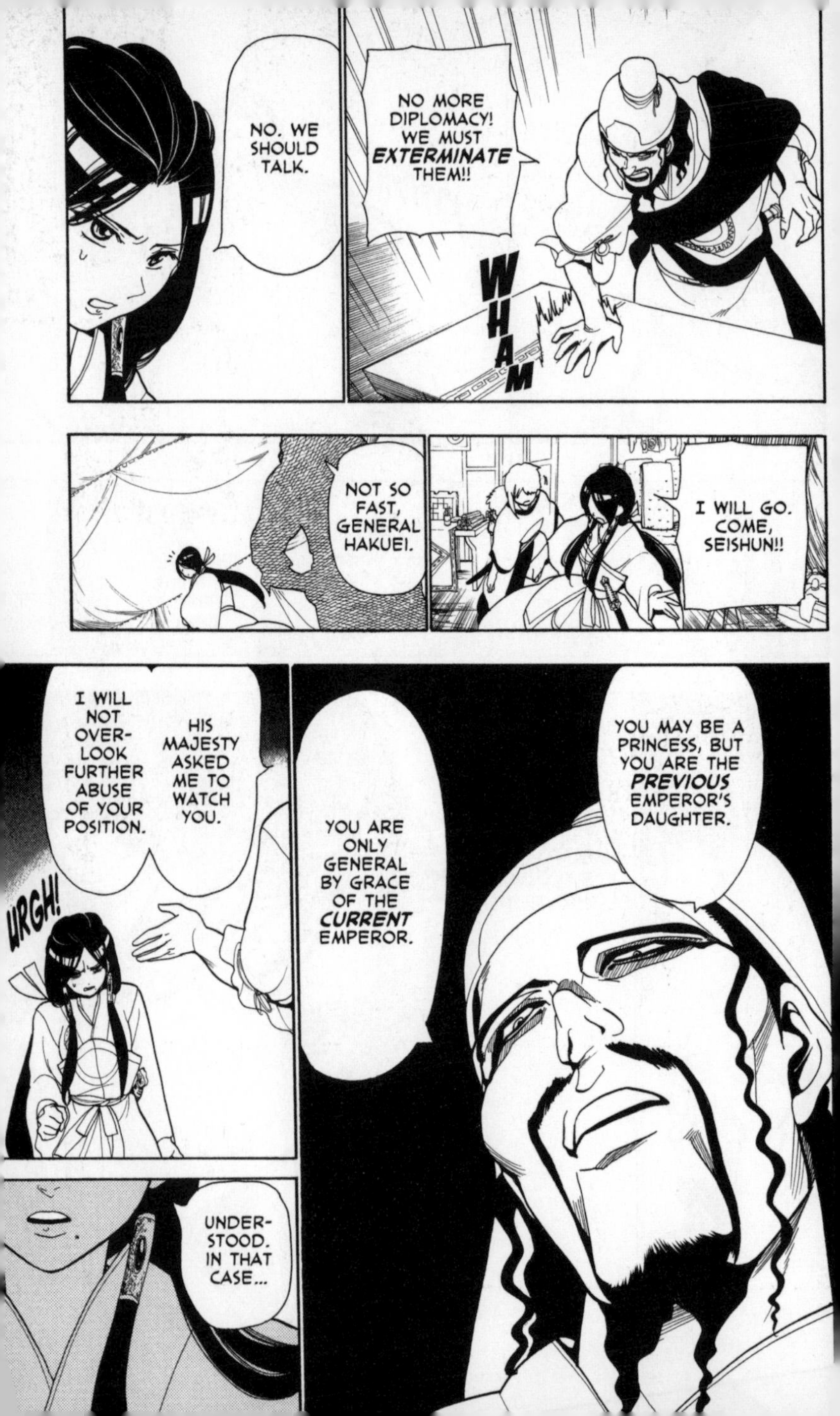
NO MORE DIPLOMACY! WE MUST EXTERMINATE THEM!!
WHAM
NO. WE SHOULD TALK.
I WILL GO. COME, SEISHUN!!
NOT SO FAST, GENERAL HAKUEI.
YOU MAY BE A PRINCESS, BUT YOU ARE THE PREVIOUS EMPEROR'S DAUGHTER.
YOU ARE ONLY GENERAL BY GRACE OF THE CURRENT EMPEROR.
HIS MAJESTY ASKED ME TO WATCH YOU.
I WILL NOT OVER-LOOK FURTHER ABUSE OF YOUR POSITION.
URGH!
UNDER-STOOD. IN THAT CASE...

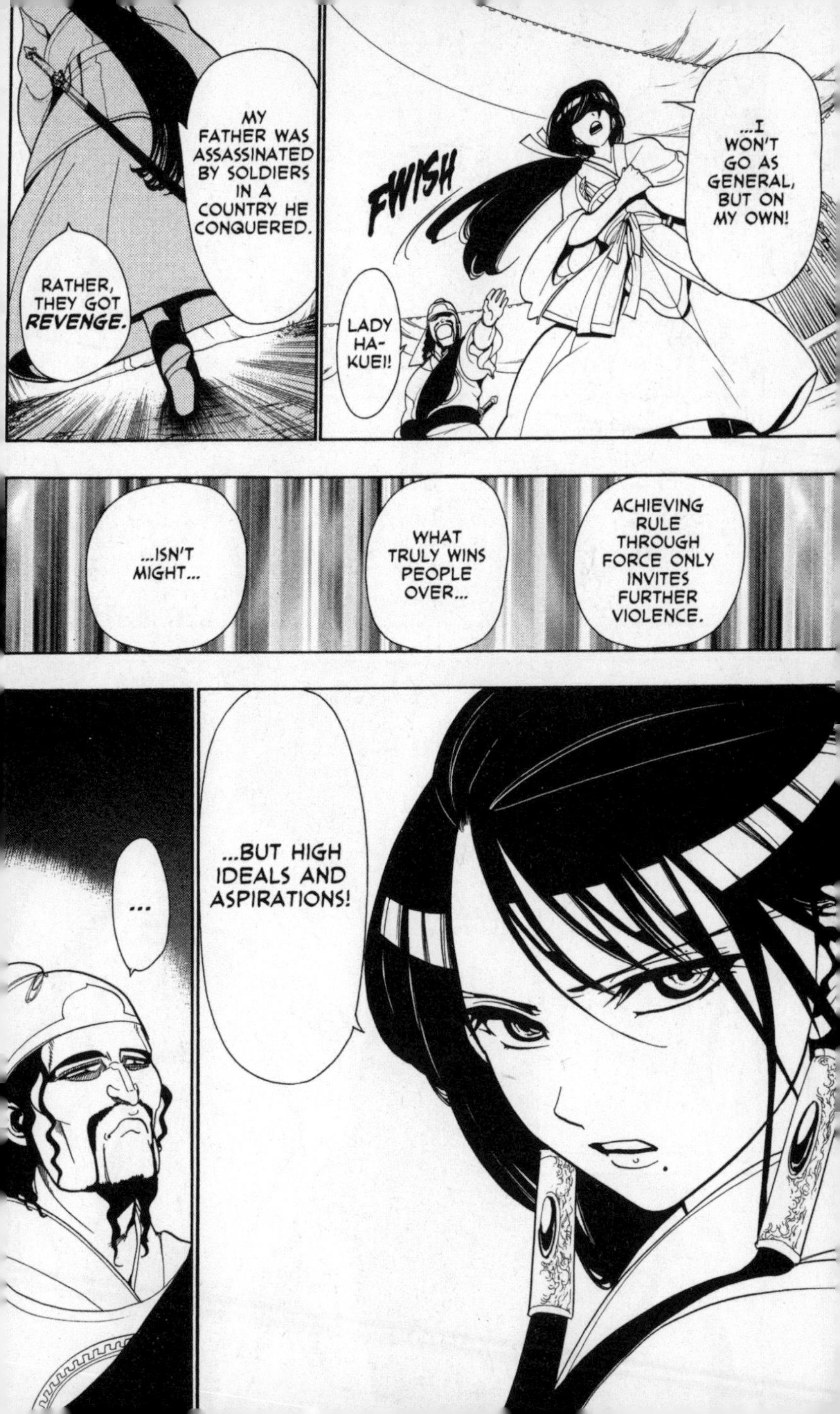
...I WON'T GO AS GENERAL, BUT ON MY OWN!
FWISH
LADY HA-KUEI!
MY FATHER WAS ASSASSINATED BY SOLDIERS IN A COUNTRY HE CONQUERED.
RATHER, THEY GOT *REVENGE.*
ACHIEVING RULE THROUGH FORCE ONLY INVITES FURTHER VIOLENCE.
WHAT TRULY WINS PEOPLE OVER...
...ISN'T MIGHT...
...BUT HIGH IDEALS AND ASPIRATIONS!
...

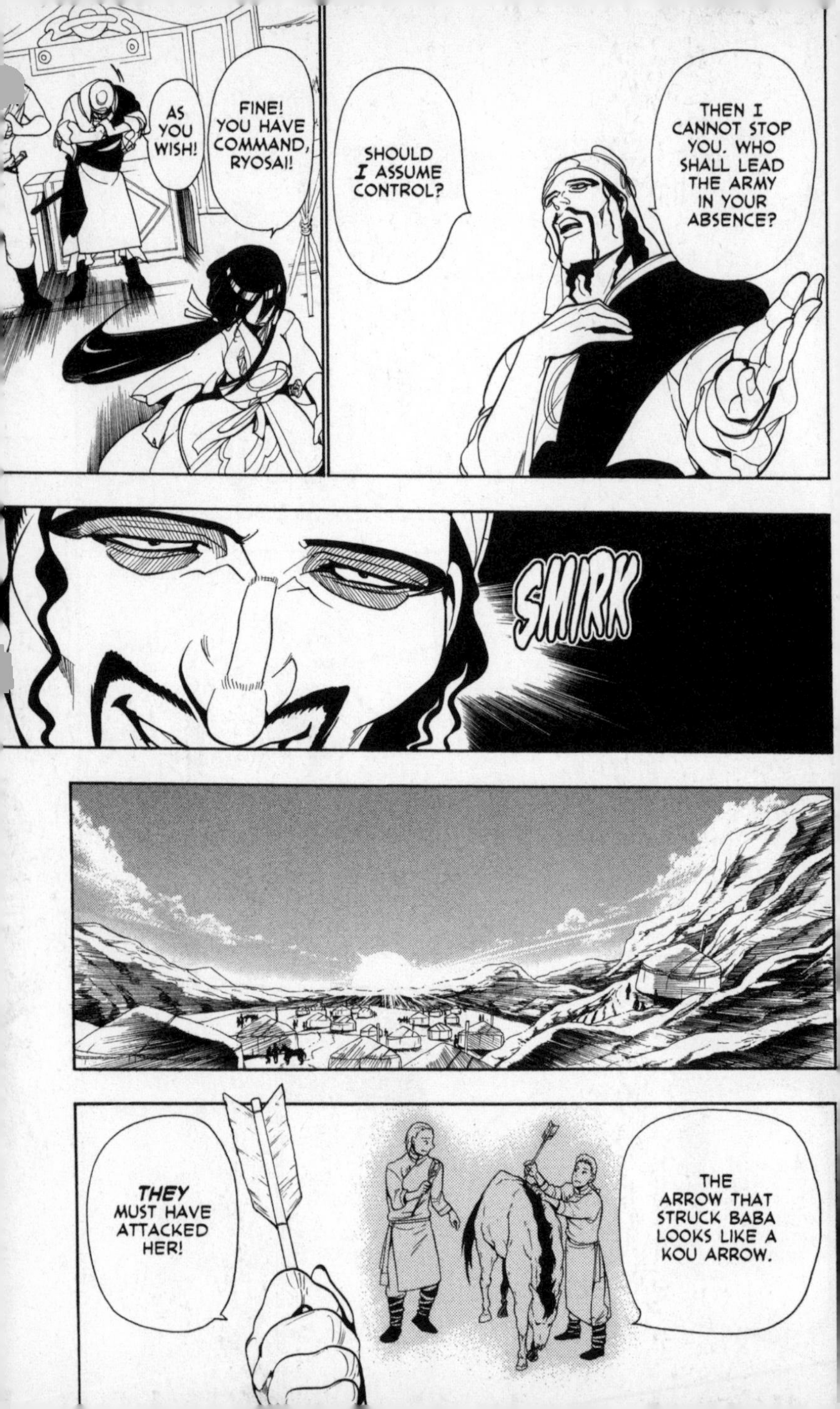
THEN I CANNOT STOP YOU. WHO SHALL LEAD THE ARMY IN YOUR ABSENCE?
SHOULD *I* ASSUME CONTROL?
FINE! YOU HAVE COMMAND, RYOSAI!
AS YOU WISH!
SMIRK
THE ARROW THAT STRUCK BABA LOOKS LIKE A KOU ARROW.
THEY MUST HAVE ATTACKED HER!

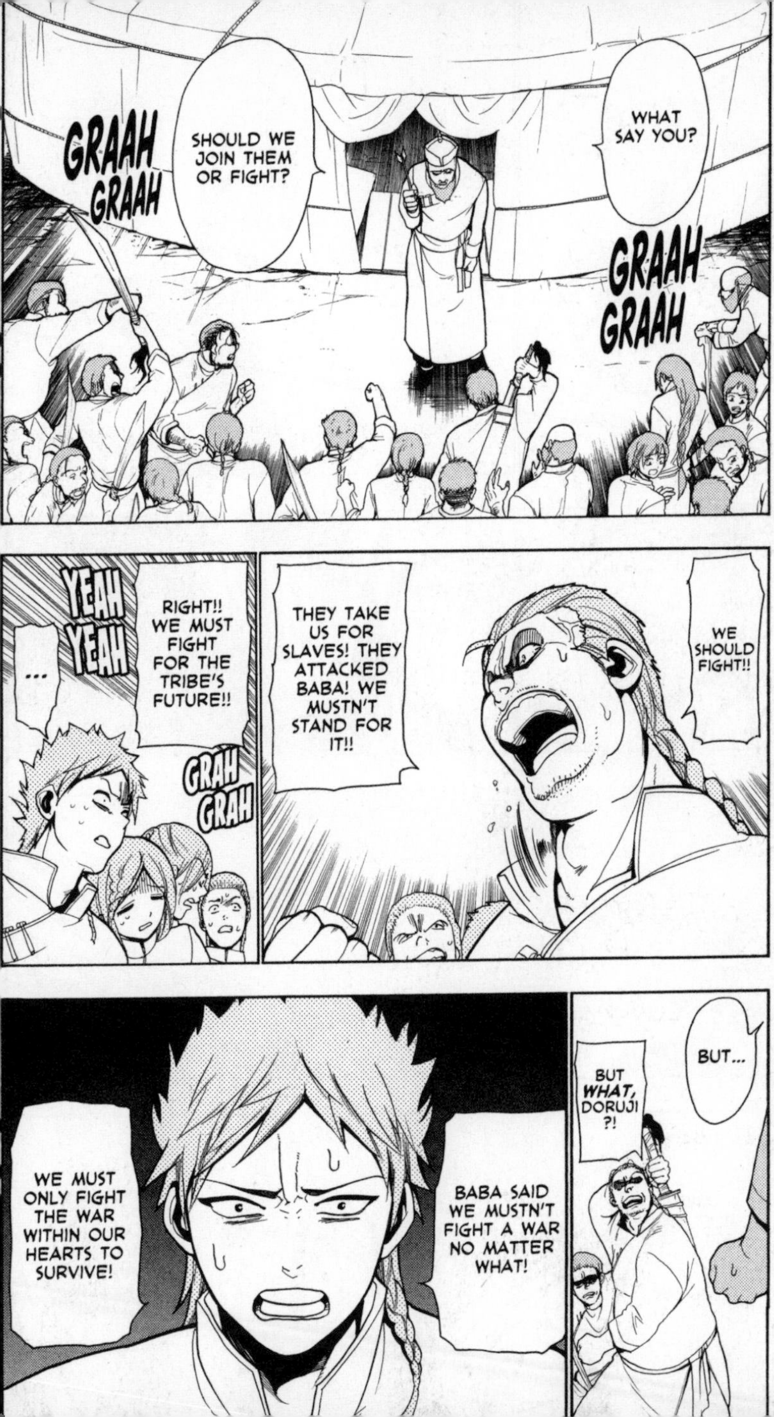
WHAT SAY YOU?
GRAAH GRAAH
SHOULD WE JOIN THEM OR FIGHT?
GRAAH GRAAH
WE SHOULD FIGHT!!
THEY TAKE US FOR SLAVES! THEY ATTACKED BABA! WE MUSTN'T STAND FOR IT!!
RIGHT!! WE MUST FIGHT FOR THE TRIBE'S FUTURE!!
YEAH YEAH
...
GRAH GRAH
BUT...
BUT WHAT, DORUJI?!
BABA SAID WE MUSTN'T FIGHT A WAR NO MATTER WHAT!
WE MUST ONLY FIGHT THE WAR WITHIN OUR HEARTS TO SURVIVE!

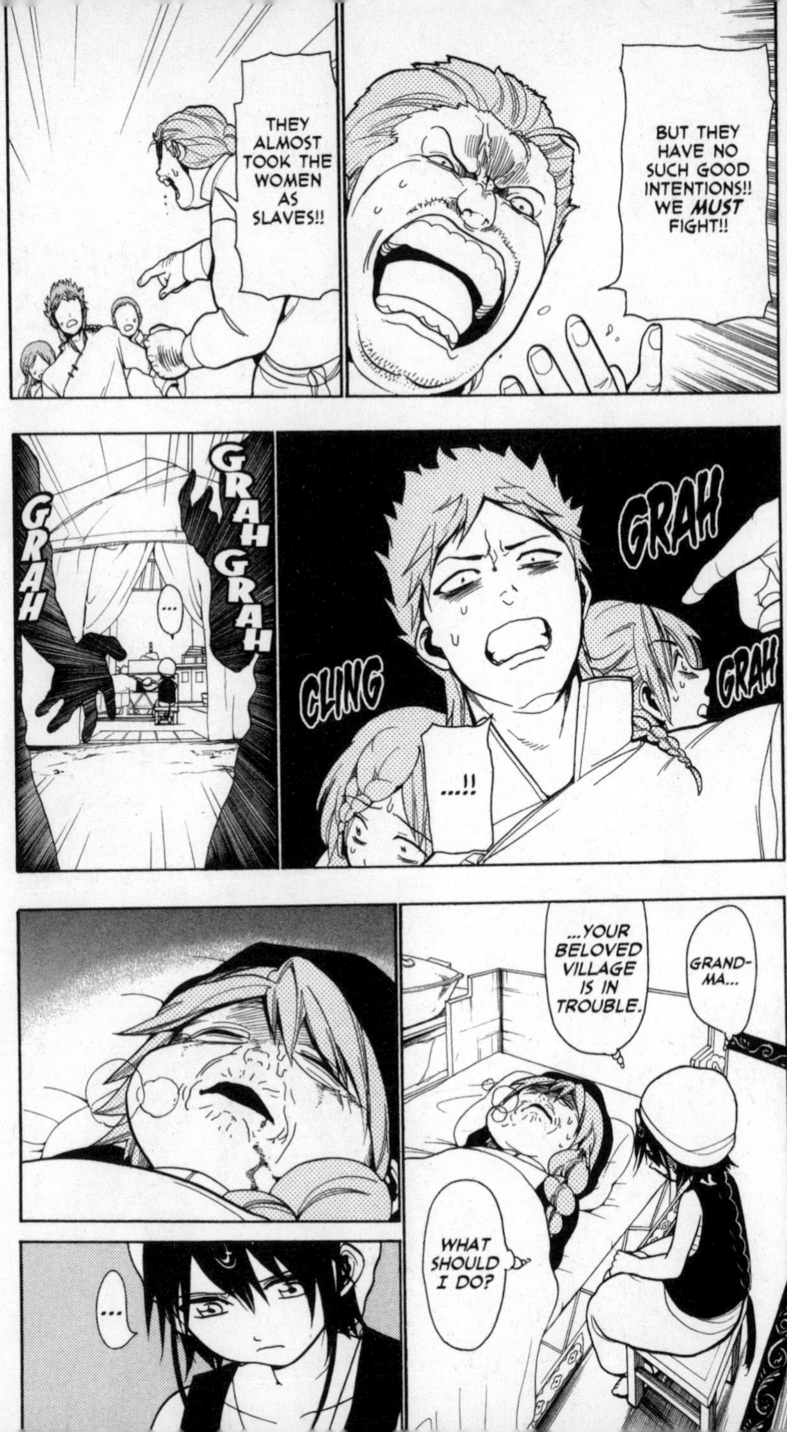
BUT THEY HAVE NO SUCH GOOD INTENTIONS!! WE *MUST* FIGHT!!
THEY ALMOST TOOK THE WOMEN AS SLAVES!!
GRAH
GRAH
CLING
...!!
GRAH GRAH
GRAH
GRAH
...
GRAND-MA...
...YOUR BELOVED VILLAGE IS IN TROUBLE.
WHAT SHOULD I DO?
...

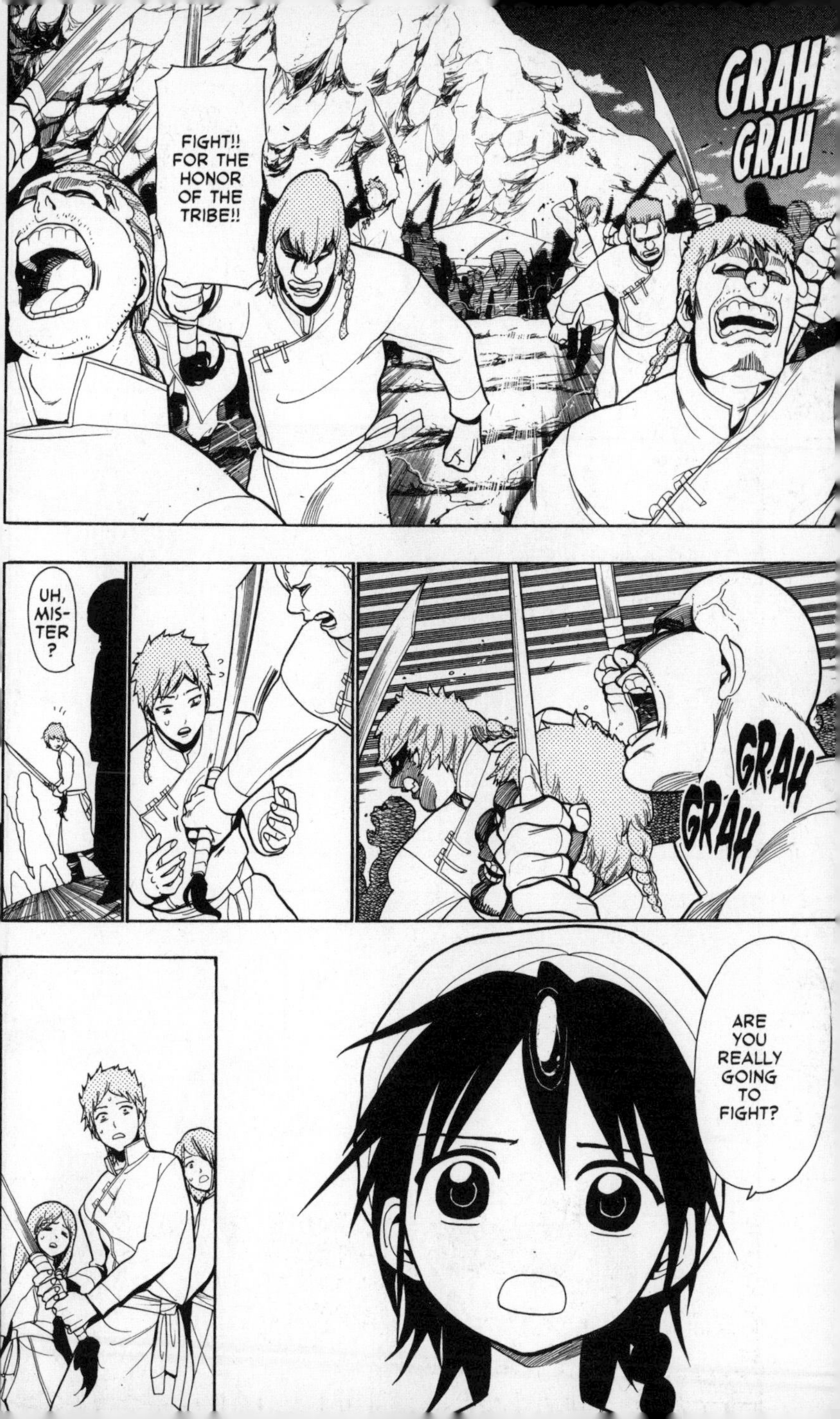
GRAH GRAH
FIGHT!! FOR THE HONOR OF THE TRIBE!!
GRAH GRAH
UH, MIS-TER?
ARE YOU REALLY GOING TO FIGHT?

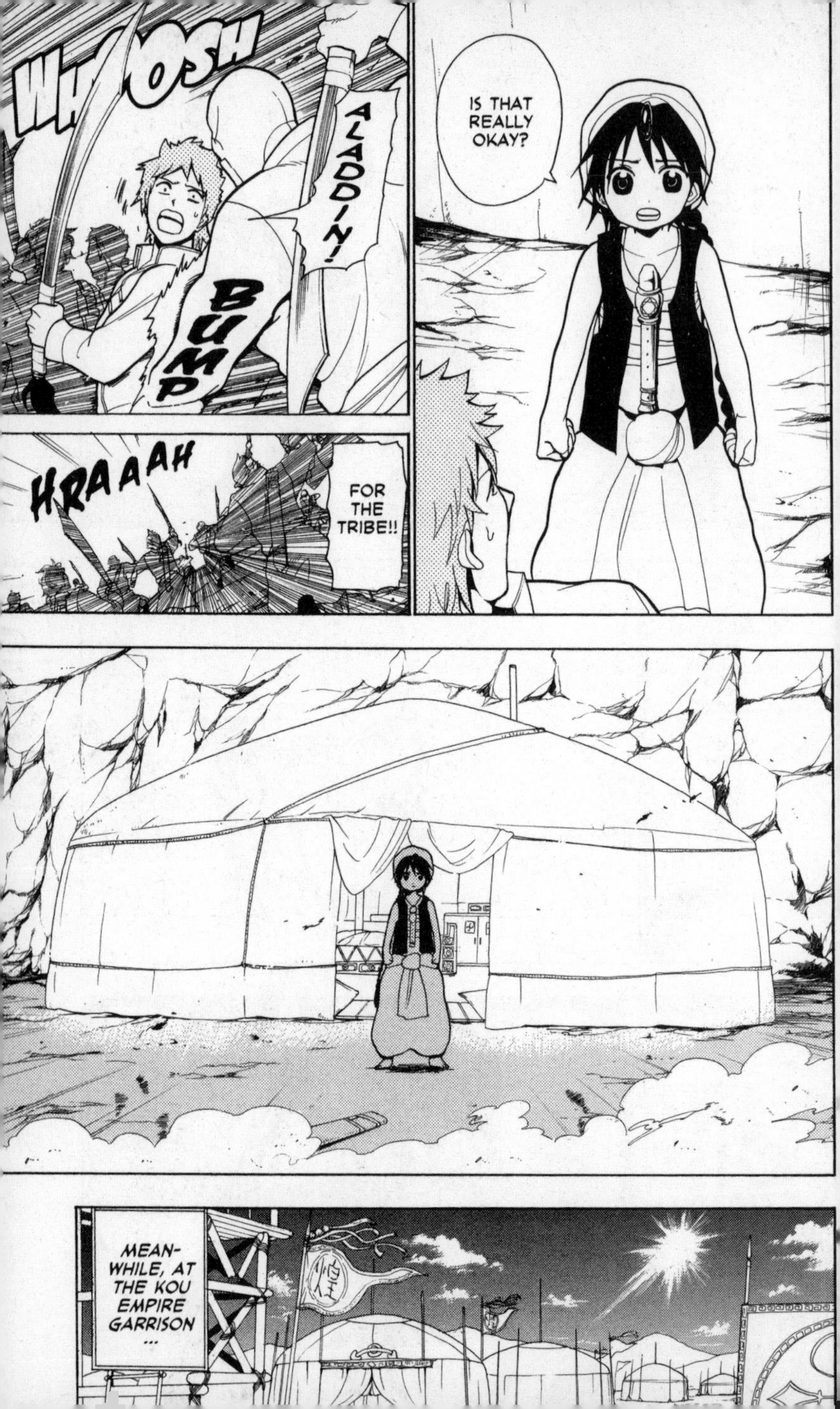

IS THAT REALLY OKAY?
WHOOSH
ALADDIN!
BUMP
FOR THE TRIBE!!
HRAAAH
MEAN-WHILE, AT THE KOU EMPIRE GARRISON ...

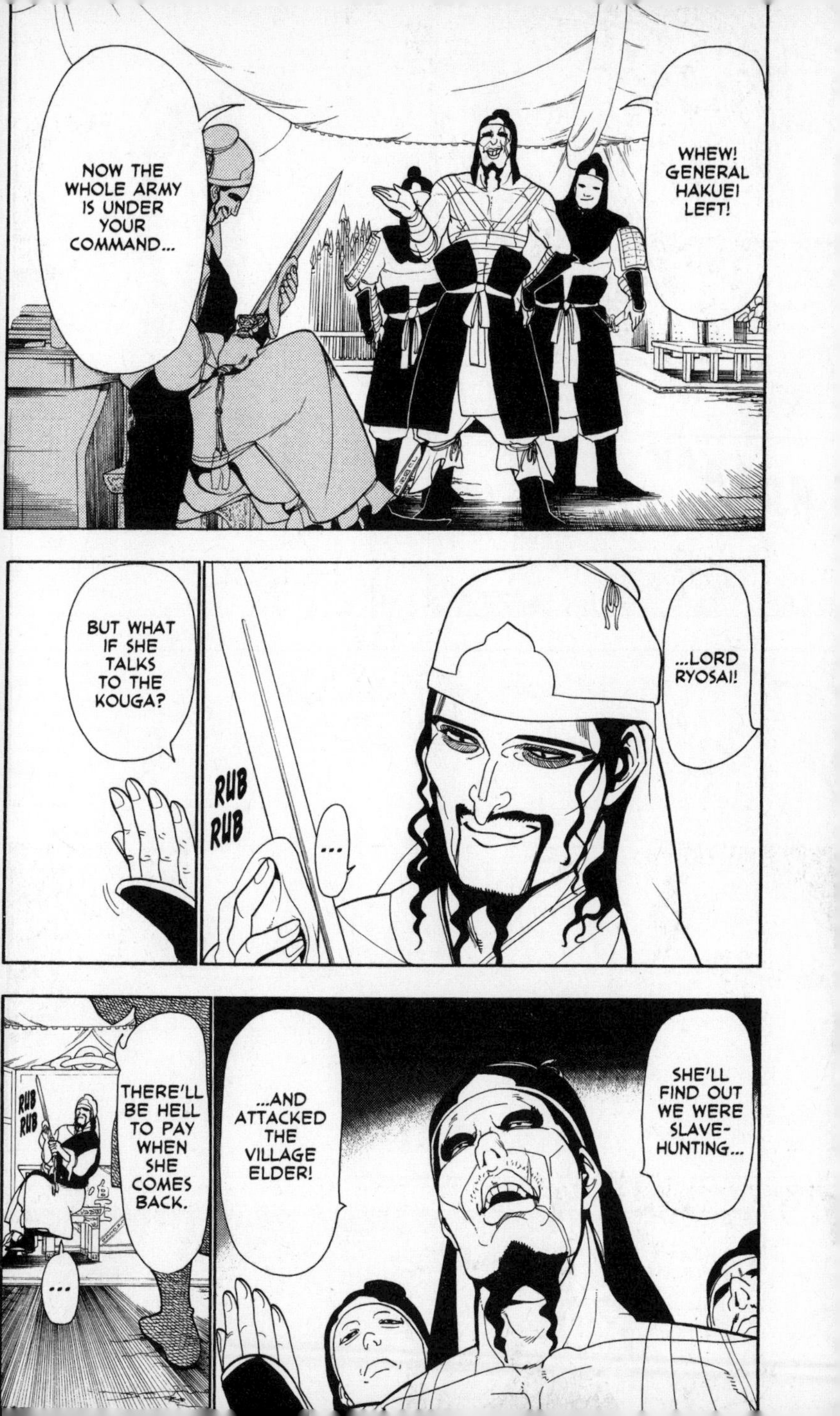
WHEW! GENERAL HAKUEI LEFT!
NOW THE WHOLE ARMY IS UNDER YOUR COMMAND...
...LORD RYOSAI!
RUB RUB
...
BUT WHAT IF SHE TALKS TO THE KOUGA?
SHE'LL FIND OUT WE WERE SLAVE-HUNTING...
...AND ATTACKED THE VILLAGE ELDER!
THERE'LL BE HELL TO PAY WHEN SHE COMES BACK.
RUB RUB
...

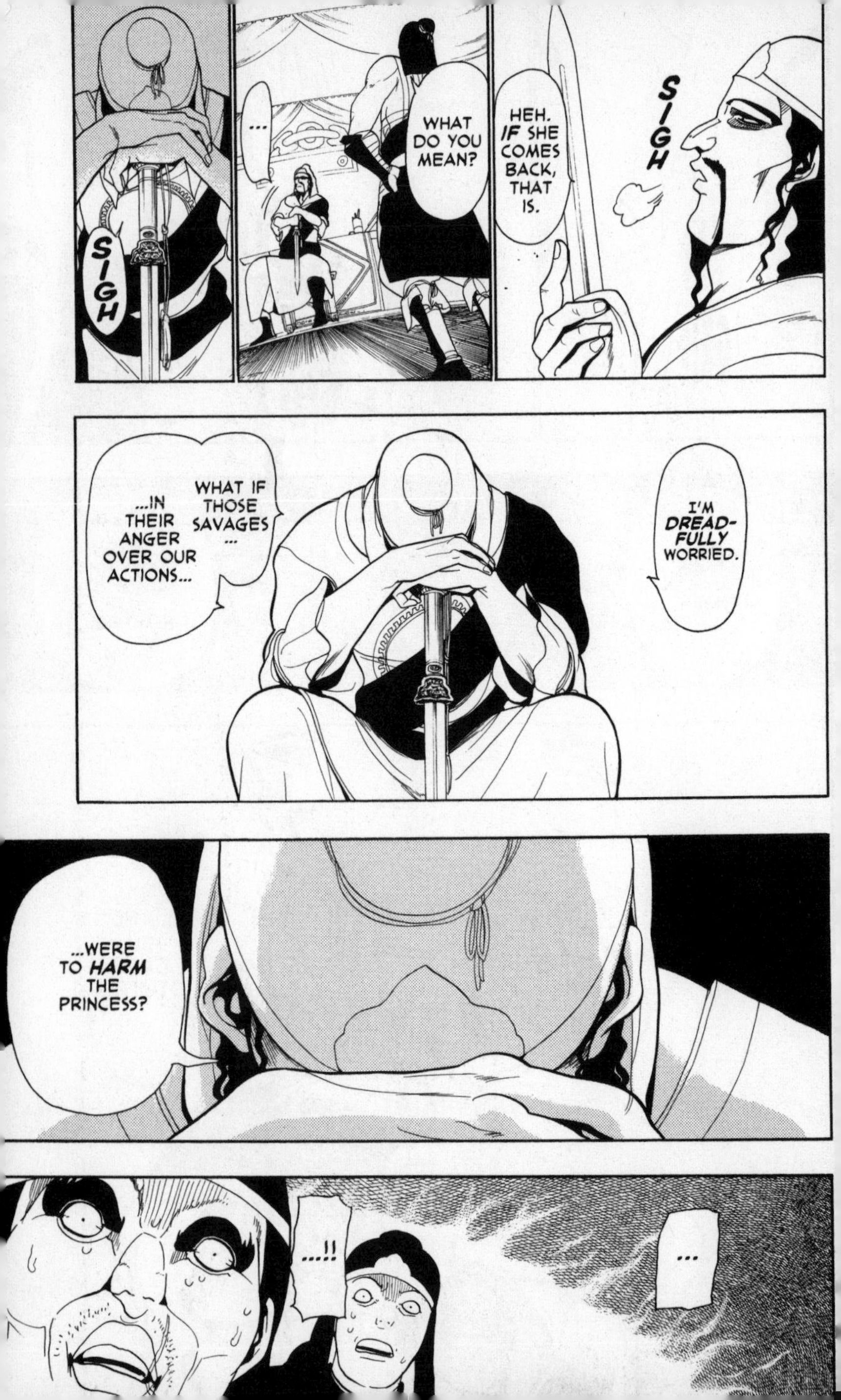
SIGH
HEH. IF SHE COMES BACK, THAT IS.
WHAT DO YOU MEAN?
...
SIGH
I'M DREADFULLY WORRIED.
WHAT IF THOSE SAVAGES...
...IN THEIR ANGER OVER OUR ACTIONS...
...WERE TO HARM THE PRINCESS?
...
...!!

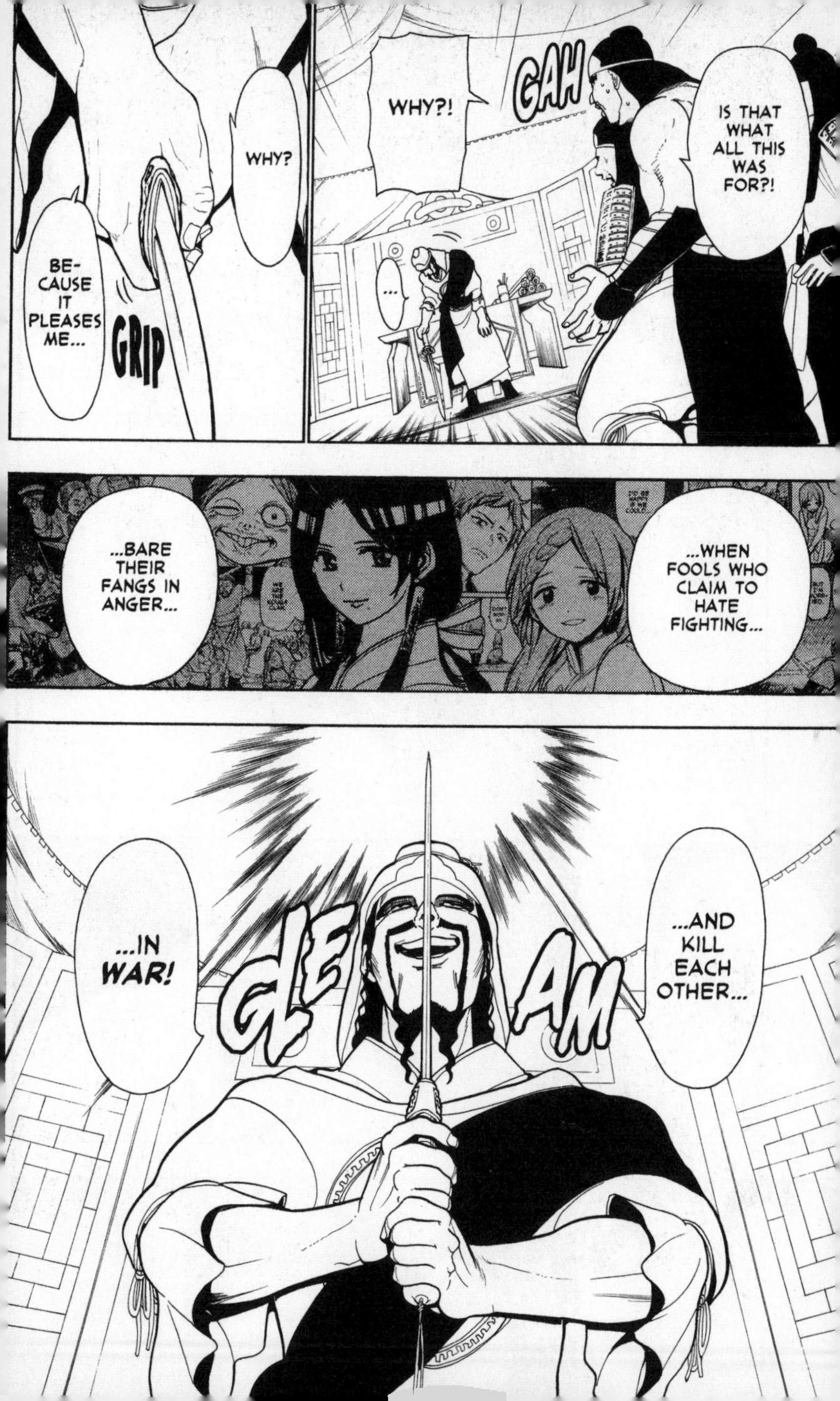
IS THAT WHAT ALL THIS WAS FOR?!
GAH
WHY?!
...
WHY?
BE-CAUSE IT PLEASES ME...
GRIP
...WHEN FOOLS WHO CLAIM TO HATE FIGHTING...
...BARE THEIR FANGS IN ANGER...
...AND KILL EACH OTHER...
GLEAM
...IN WAR!

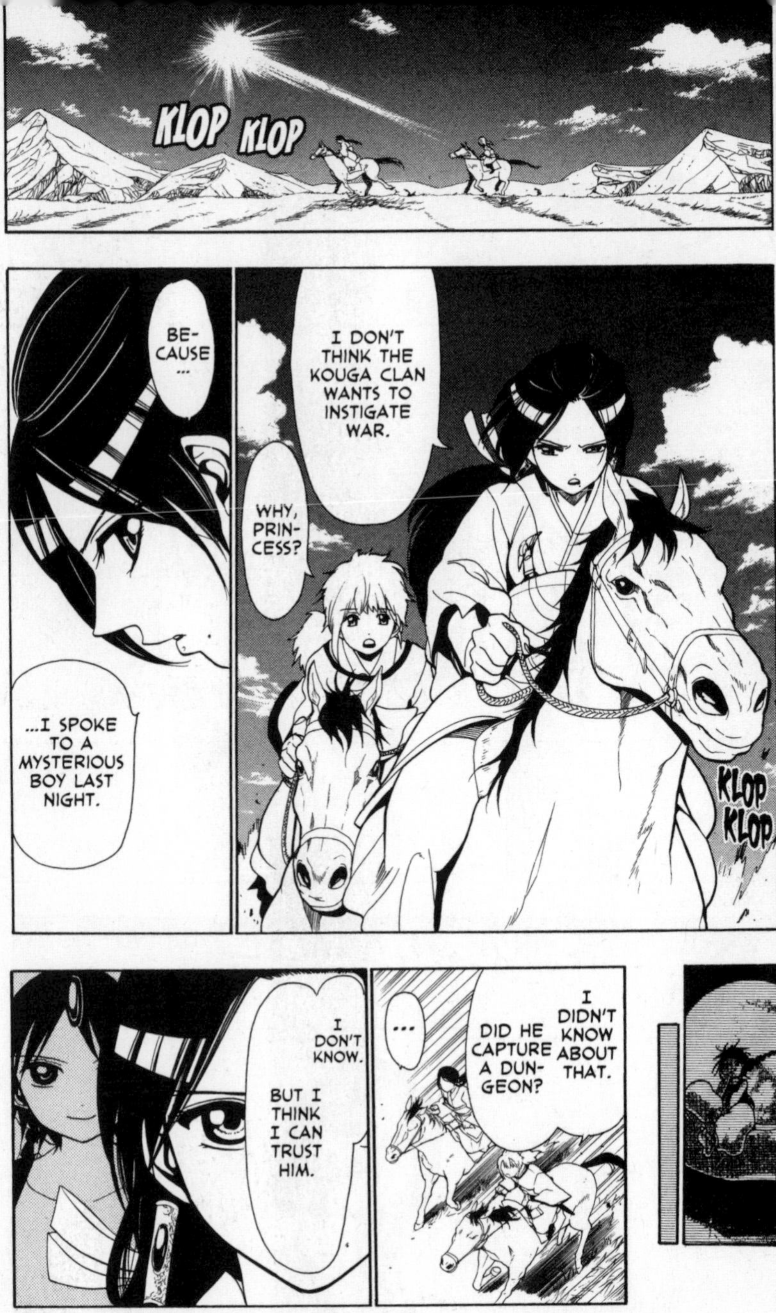
KLOP KLOP
I DON'T THINK THE KOUGA CLAN WANTS TO INSTIGATE WAR.
WHY, PRINCESS?
KLOP KLOP
BE-CAUSE...
...I SPOKE TO A MYSTERIOUS BOY LAST NIGHT.
I DIDN'T KNOW ABOUT THAT.
DID HE CAPTURE A DUN-GEON?
...
I DON'T KNOW.
BUT I THINK I CAN TRUST HIM.

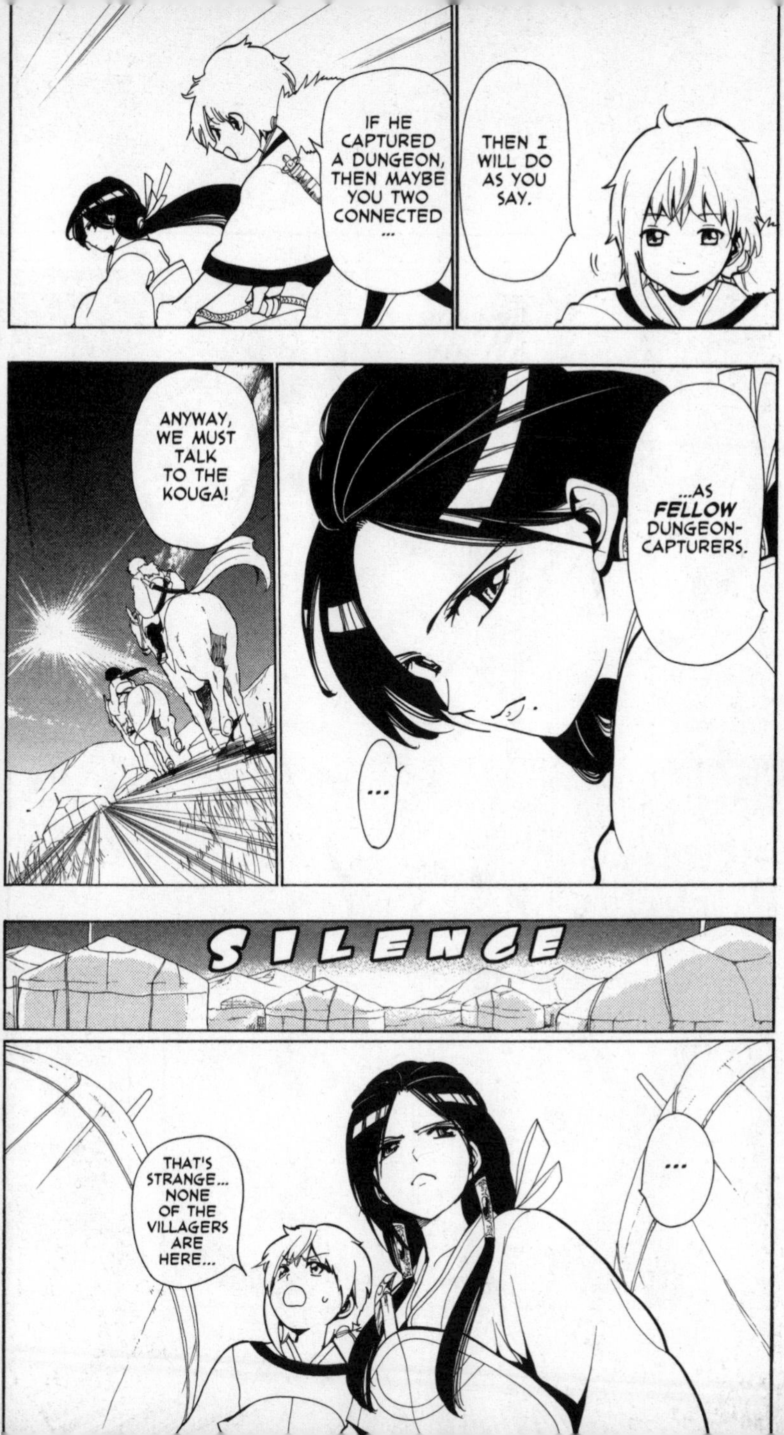
THEN I WILL DO AS YOU SAY.
IF HE CAPTURED A DUNGEON, THEN MAYBE YOU TWO CONNECTED ...
...AS FELLOW DUNGEON-CAPTURERS.
...
ANYWAY, WE MUST TALK TO THE KOUGA!
SILENCE
...
THAT'S STRANGE... NONE OF THE VILLAGERS ARE HERE...

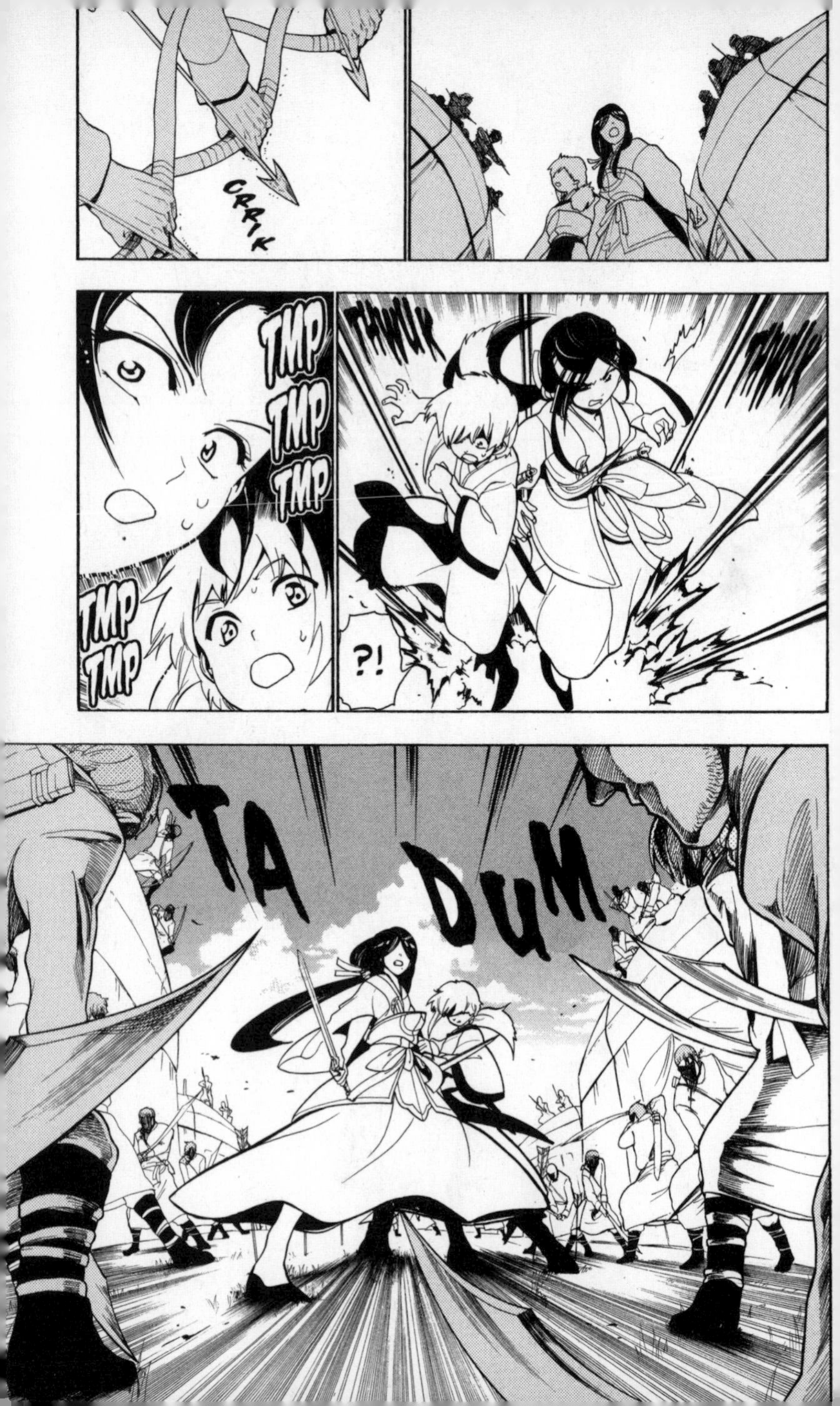
CRRIK
THWUK
THWUK
?!
TMP TMP TMP
TMP TMP
TA DUM

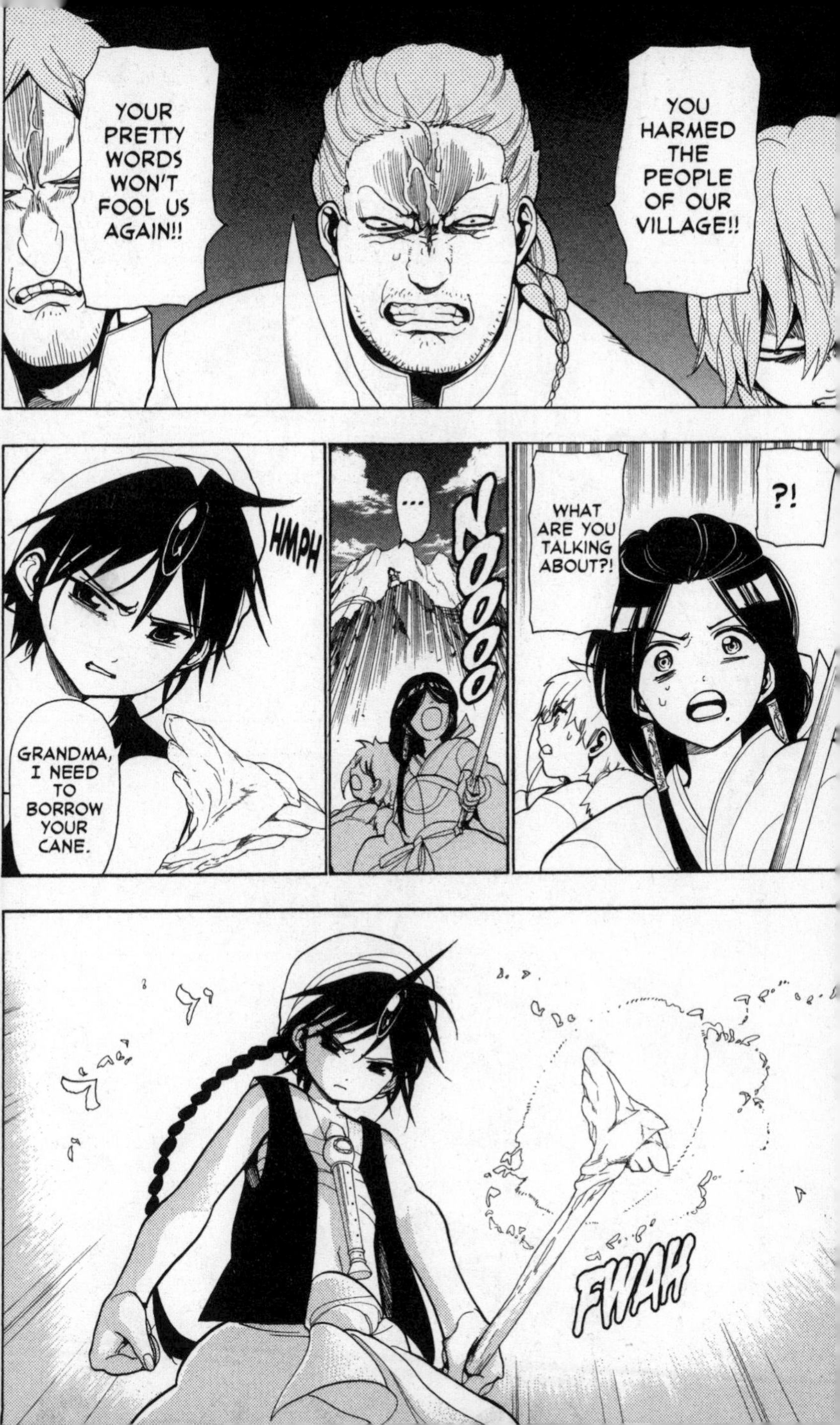
YOU HARMED THE PEOPLE OF OUR VILLAGE!!
YOUR PRETTY WORDS WON'T FOOL US AGAIN!!
?!
WHAT ARE YOU TALKING ABOUT?!
...
NOOOOO
HMPH
GRANDMA, I NEED TO BORROW YOUR CANE.
FWAH

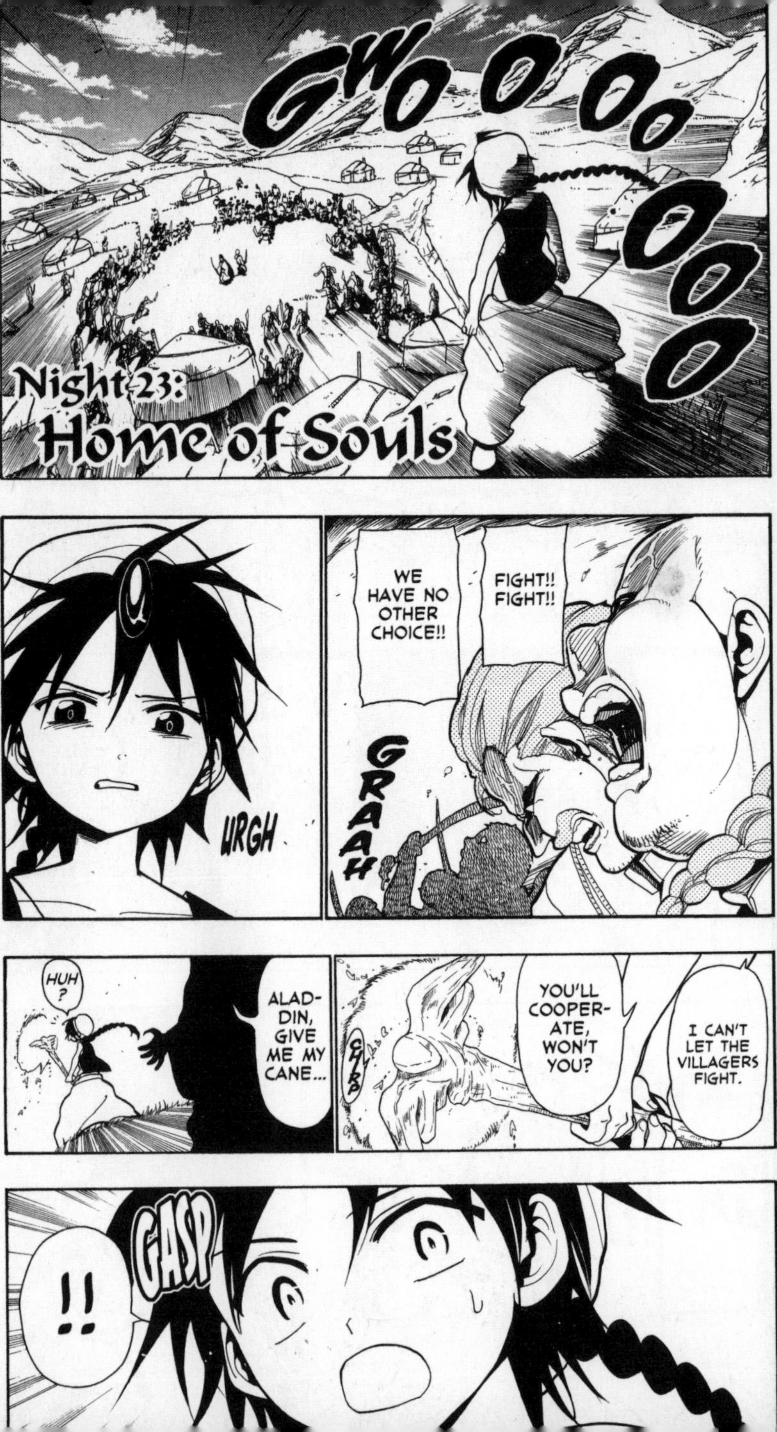
GWOOOOOOOO
Night 23:
Home of Souls
FIGHT!! FIGHT!!
WE HAVE NO OTHER CHOICE!!
GRAAAH
URGH
I CAN'T LET THE VILLAGERS FIGHT.
YOU'LL COOPER-ATE, WON'T YOU?
CHIRP
ALAD-DIN, GIVE ME MY CANE...
HUH?
GASP
!!

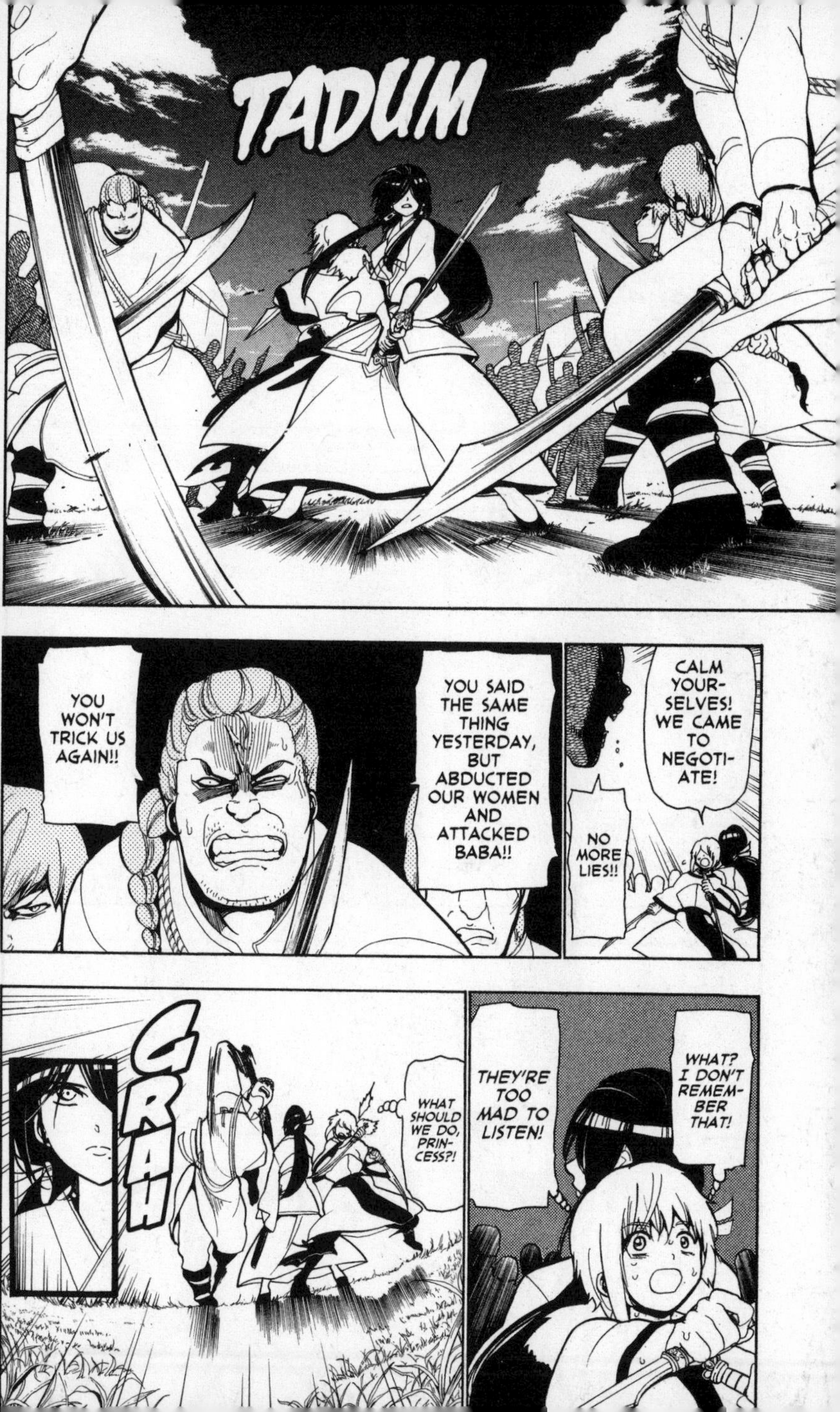
TADUM
CALM YOUR-SELVES! WE CAME TO NEGOTI-ATE!
NO MORE LIES!!
YOU SAID THE SAME THING YESTERDAY, BUT ABDUCTED OUR WOMEN AND ATTACKED BABA!!
YOU WON'T TRICK US AGAIN!!
WHAT? I DON'T REMEM-BER THAT!
THEY'RE TOO MAD TO LISTEN!
WHAT SHOULD WE DO, PRIN-CESS?!
GRAH

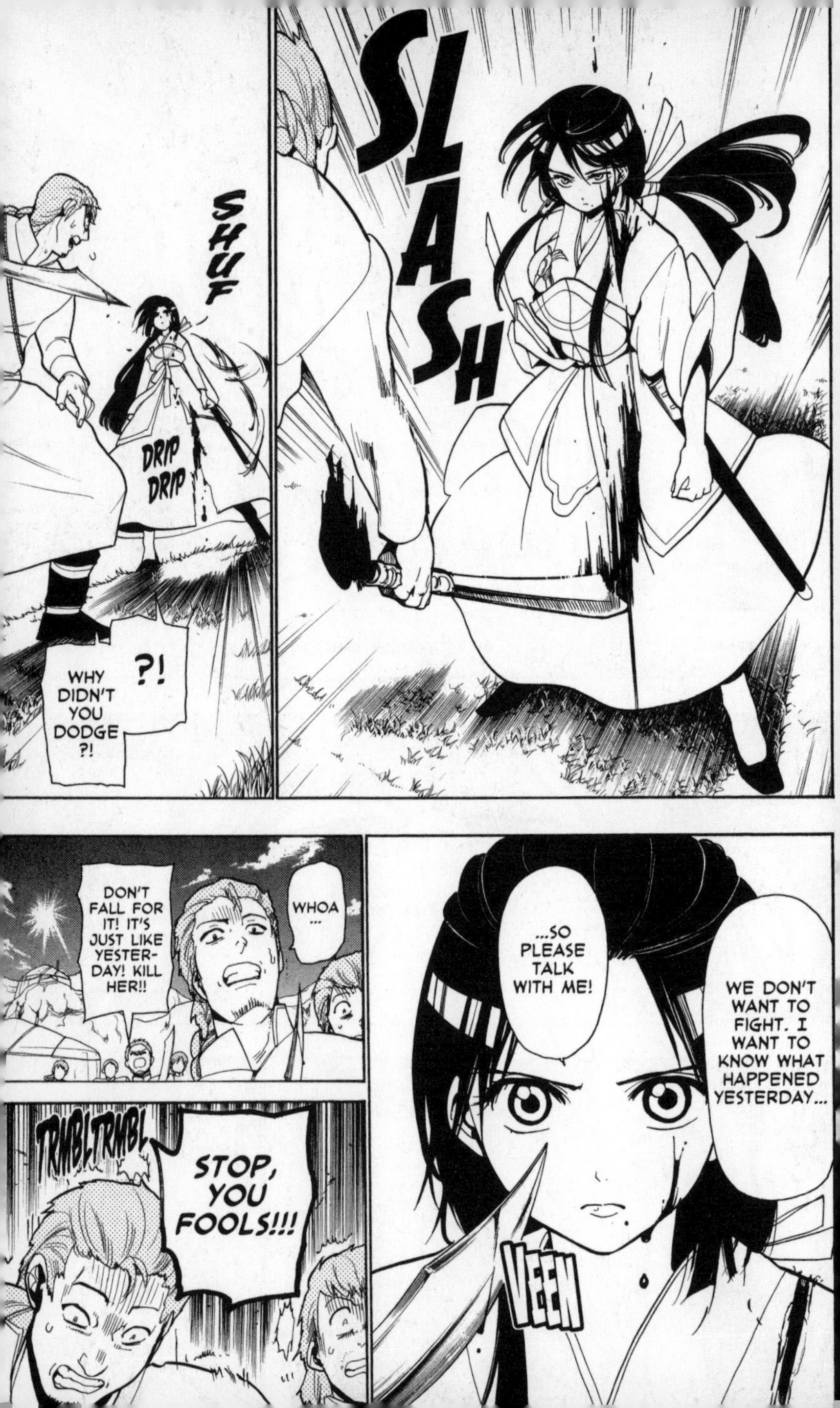
SLASH
SHUF
DRIP DRIP
?!
WHY DIDN'T YOU DODGE?!
WE DON'T WANT TO FIGHT. I WANT TO KNOW WHAT HAPPENED YESTERDAY...
...SO PLEASE TALK WITH ME!
VEEN
WHOA...
DON'T FALL FOR IT! IT'S JUST LIKE YESTER-DAY! KILL HER!!
TRMBL TRMBL
STOP, YOU FOOLS!!!

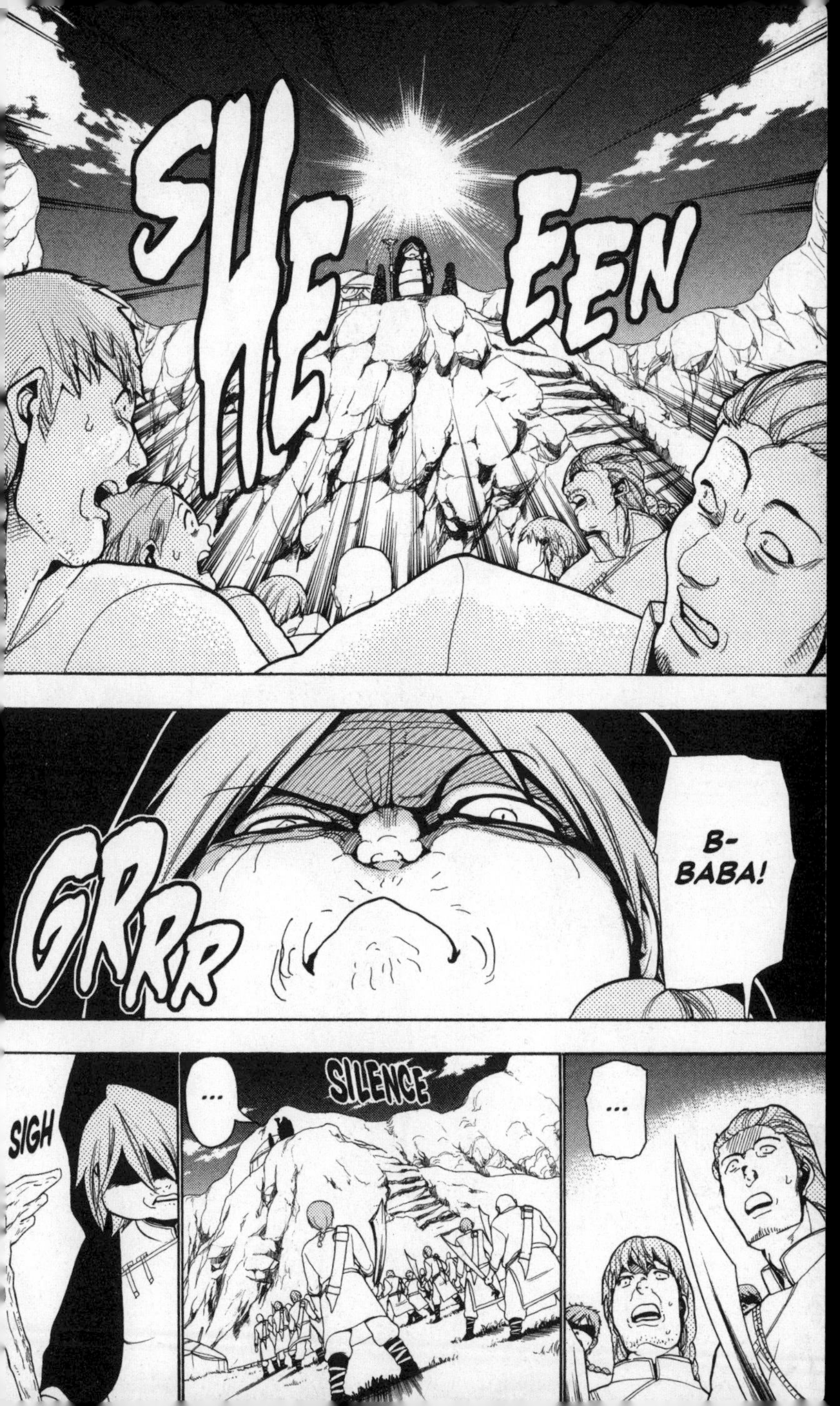
SHEEEN
B-BABA!
GRRR
...
...
SILENCE
SIGH

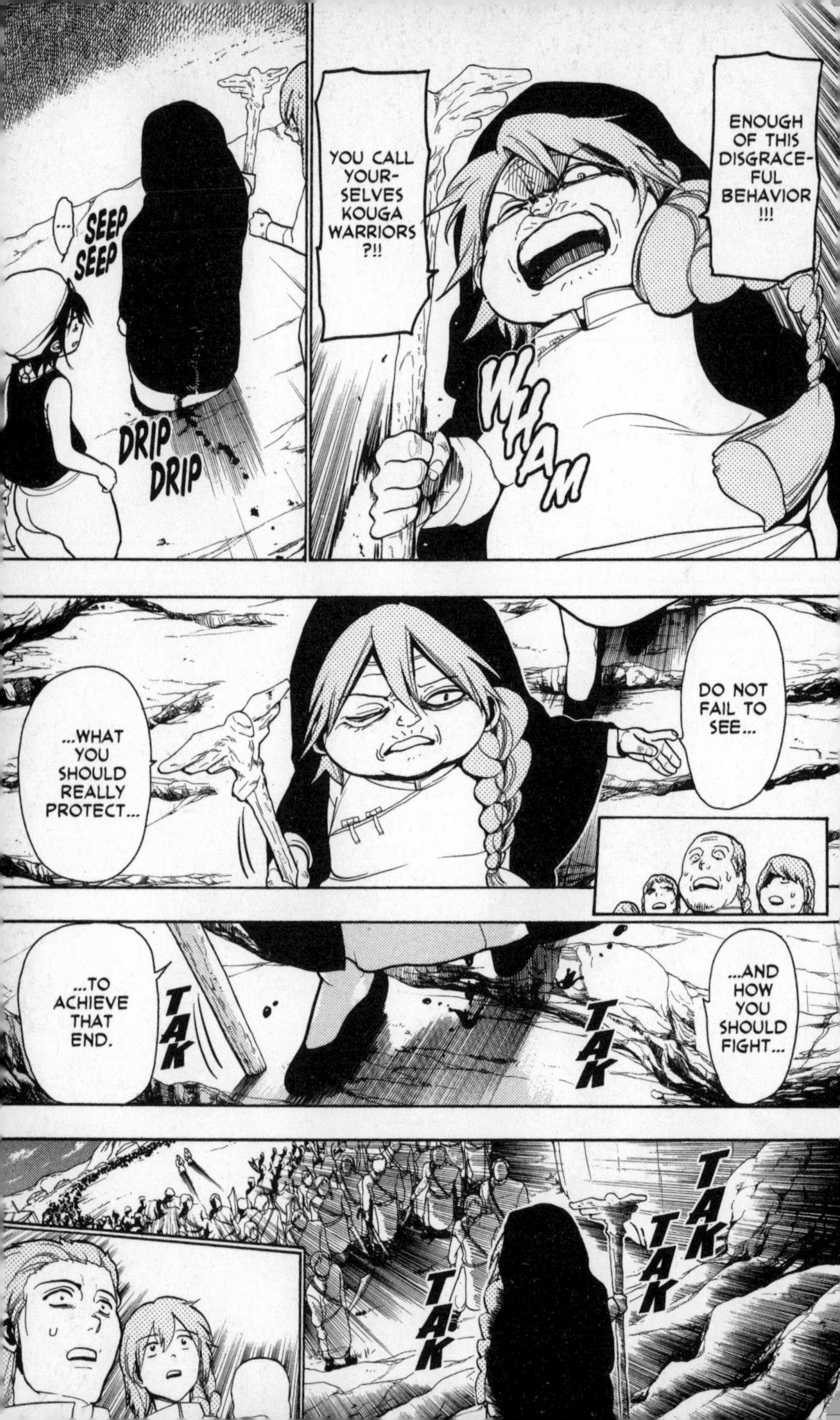
ENOUGH OF THIS DISGRACEFUL BEHAVIOR!!!
YOU CALL YOURSELVES KOUGA WARRIORS?!!
WHAM
...
SEEP SEEP
DRIP DRIP
DO NOT FAIL TO SEE...
...WHAT YOU SHOULD REALLY PROTECT...
...AND HOW YOU SHOULD FIGHT...
TAK TAK
...TO ACHIEVE THAT END.
TAK
TAK TAK
TAK TAK

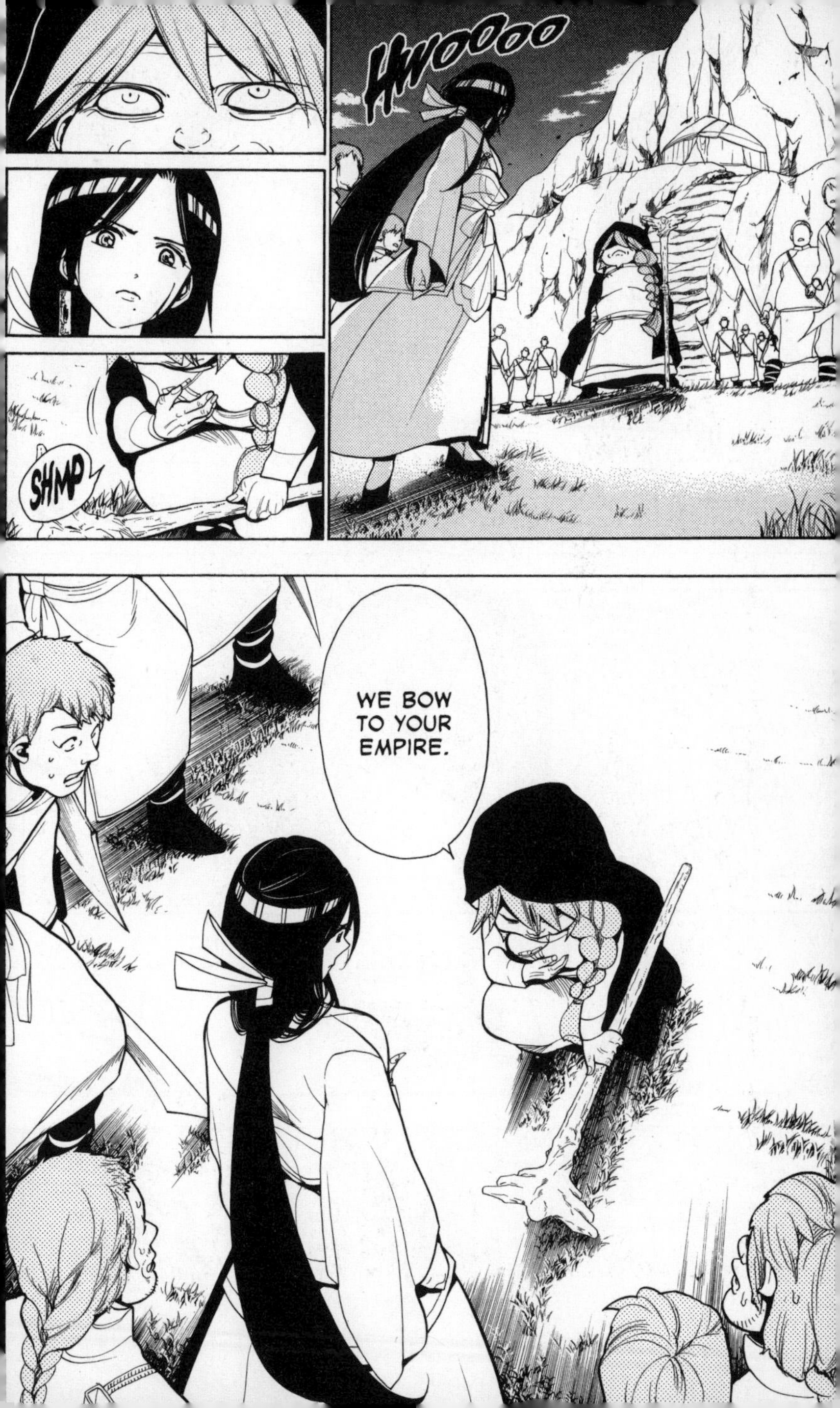
HWOOOO
SHMP
WE BOW TO YOUR EMPIRE.

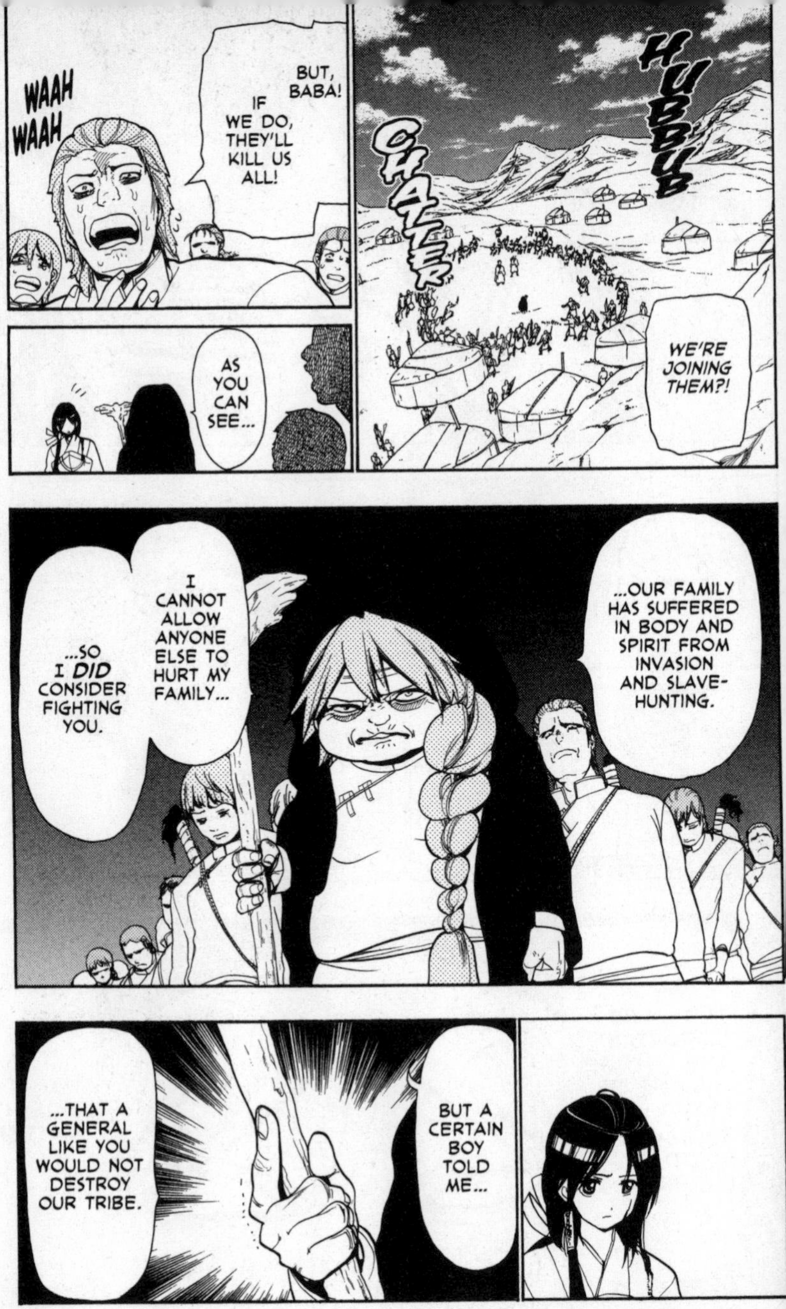
HUBBUB
CHATTER
WE'RE JOINING THEM?!
BUT, BABA!
IF WE DO, THEY'LL KILL US ALL!
WAAH WAAH
AS YOU CAN SEE...
...OUR FAMILY HAS SUFFERED IN BODY AND SPIRIT FROM INVASION AND SLAVE-HUNTING.
I CANNOT ALLOW ANYONE ELSE TO HURT MY FAMILY...
...SO I *DID* CONSIDER FIGHTING YOU.
BUT A CERTAIN BOY TOLD ME...
...THAT A GENERAL LIKE YOU WOULD NOT DESTROY OUR TRIBE.

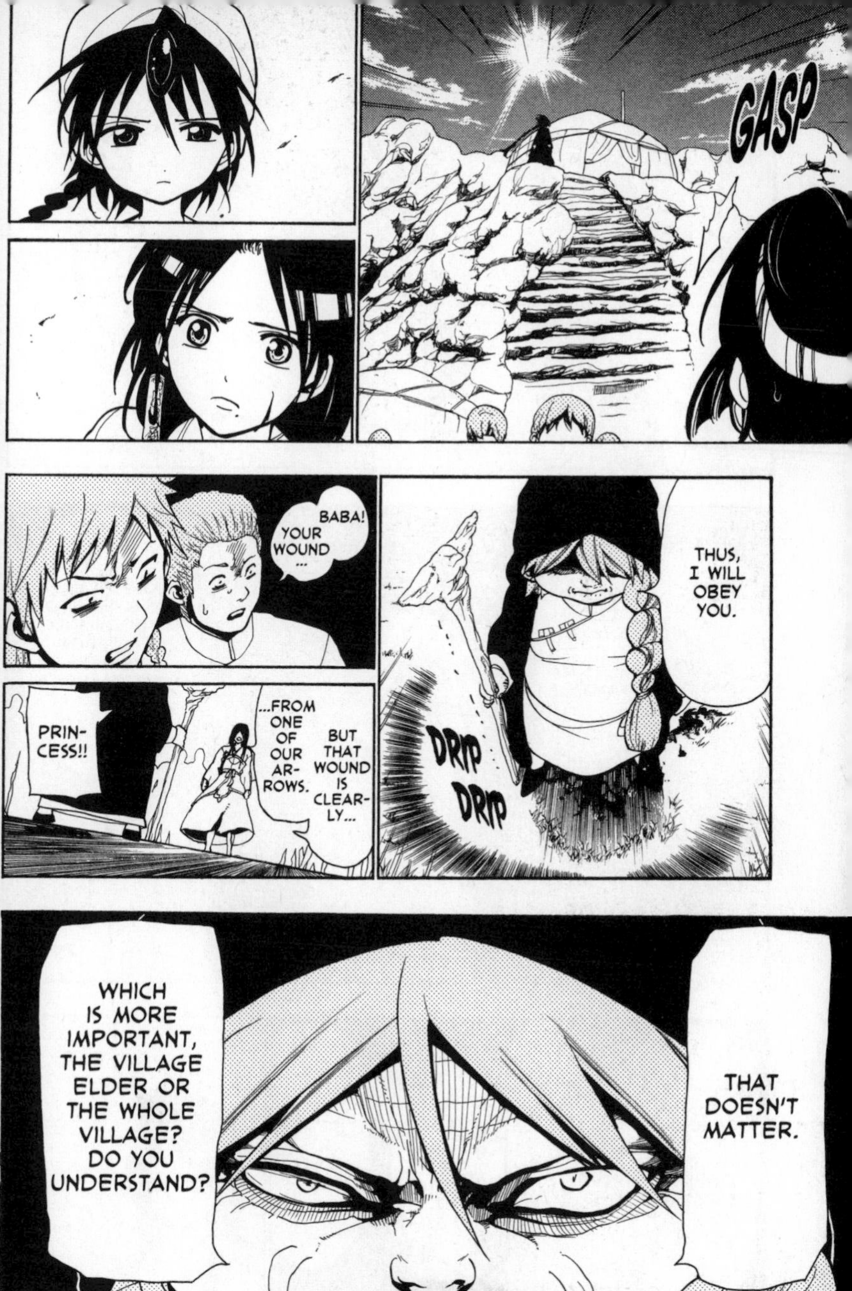
GASP
THUS, I WILL OBEY YOU.
DRIP
DRIP
BABA! YOUR WOUND ...
BUT THAT WOUND IS CLEARLY...
...FROM ONE OF OUR ARROWS.
PRINCESS!!
THAT DOESN'T MATTER.
WHICH IS MORE IMPORTANT, THE VILLAGE ELDER OR THE WHOLE VILLAGE? DO YOU UNDERSTAND?

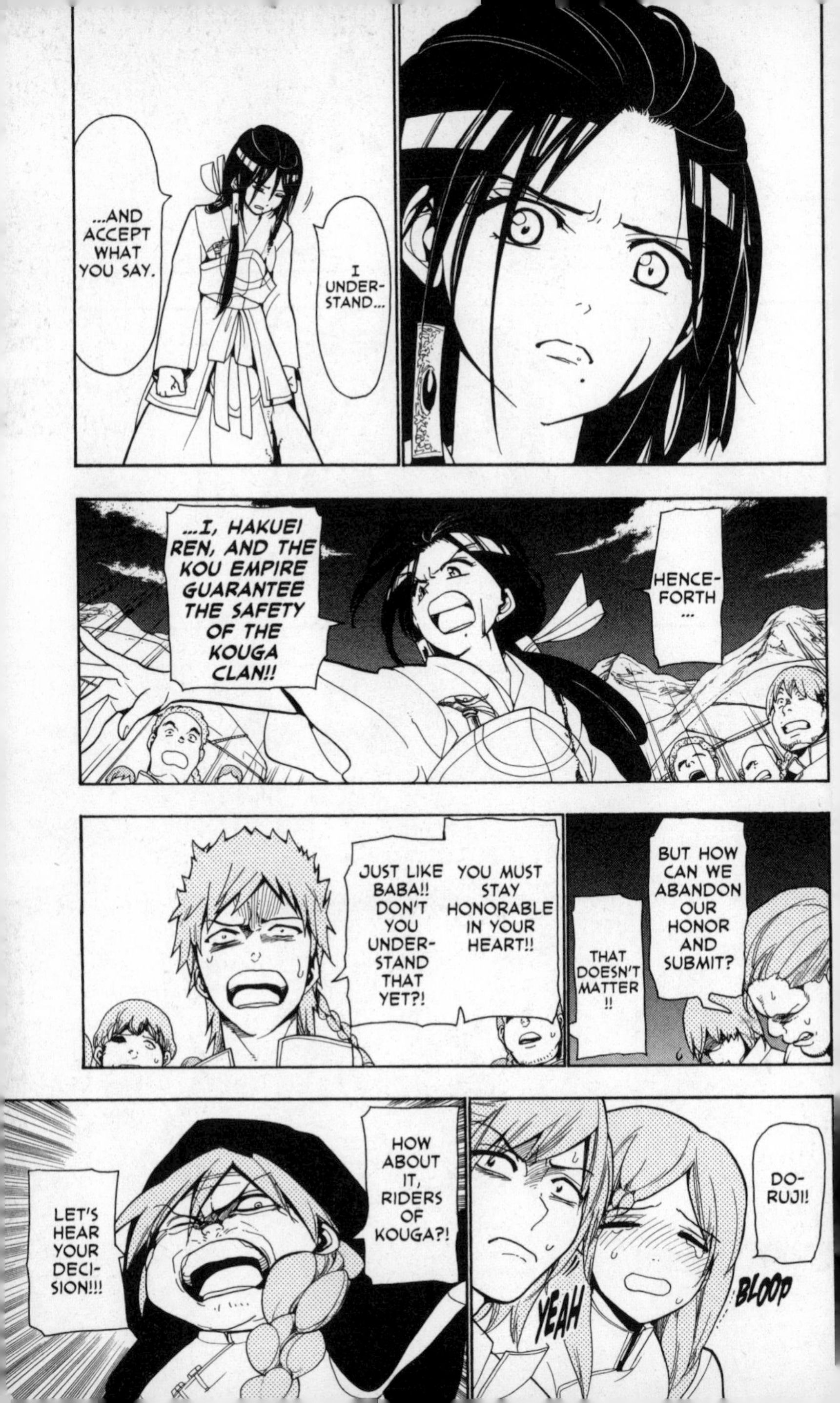
I UNDERSTAND...
...AND ACCEPT WHAT YOU SAY.
HENCEFORTH ...
...I, HAKUEI REN, AND THE KOU EMPIRE GUARANTEE THE SAFETY OF THE KOUGA CLAN!!
BUT HOW CAN WE ABANDON OUR HONOR AND SUBMIT?
THAT DOESN'T MATTER !!
YOU MUST STAY HONORABLE IN YOUR HEART!!
JUST LIKE BABA!! DON'T YOU UNDERSTAND THAT YET?!
DORUJI!
BLOOP
YEAH
HOW ABOUT IT, RIDERS OF KOUGA?!
LET'S HEAR YOUR DECISION!!!

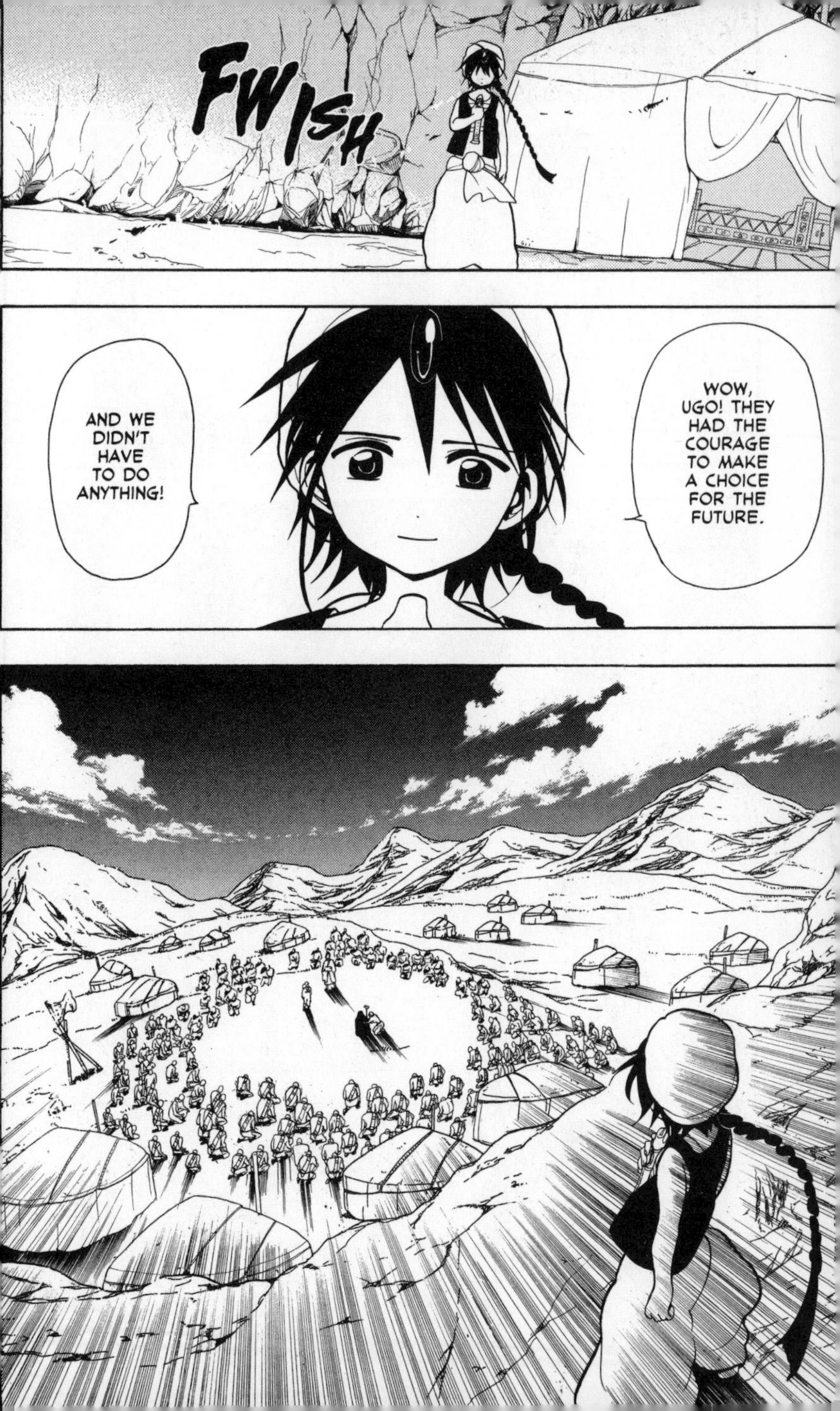
FWISH
WOW, UGO! THEY HAD THE COURAGE TO MAKE A CHOICE FOR THE FUTURE.
AND WE DIDN'T HAVE TO DO ANYTHING!

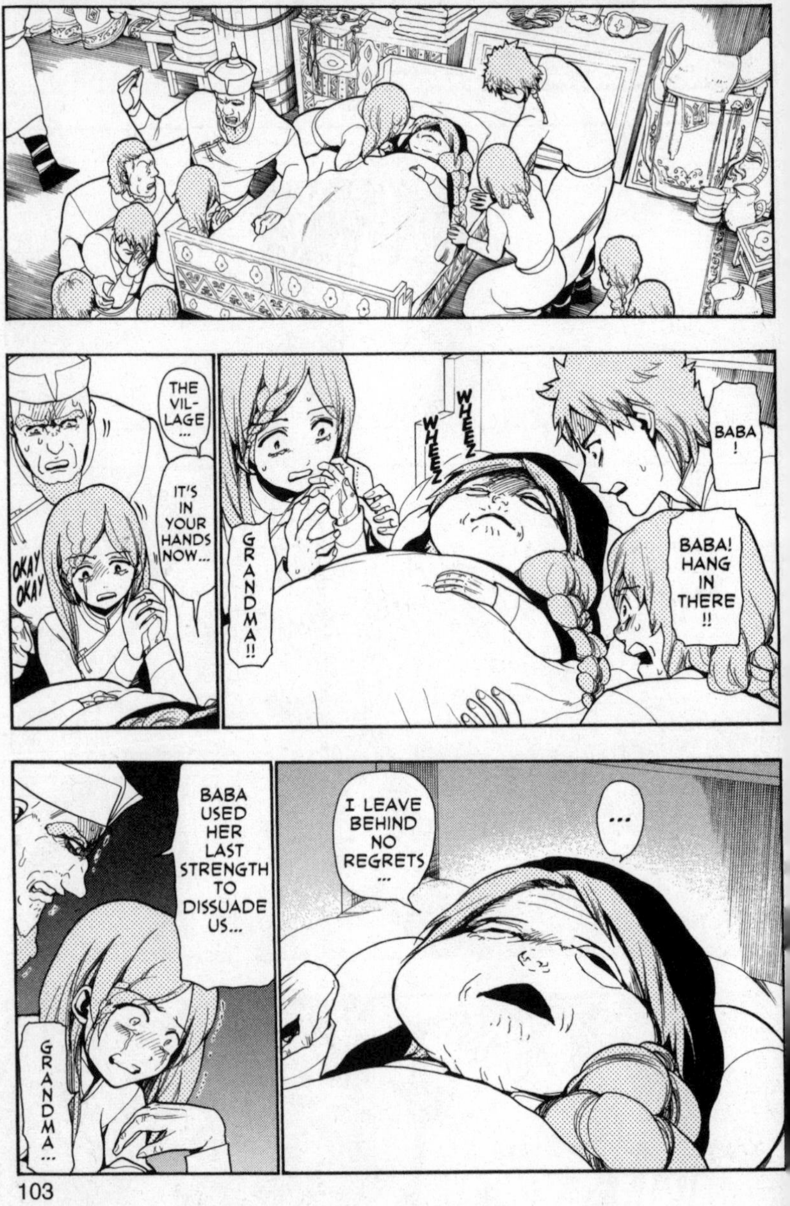
BABA!
BABA! HANG IN THERE!!
WHEEZ WHEEZ
GRANDMA!!
THE VIL-LAGE...
IT'S IN YOUR HANDS NOW...
OKAY OKAY
...
I LEAVE BEHIND NO REGRETS...
BABA USED HER LAST STRENGTH TO DISSUADE US...
GRANDMA...

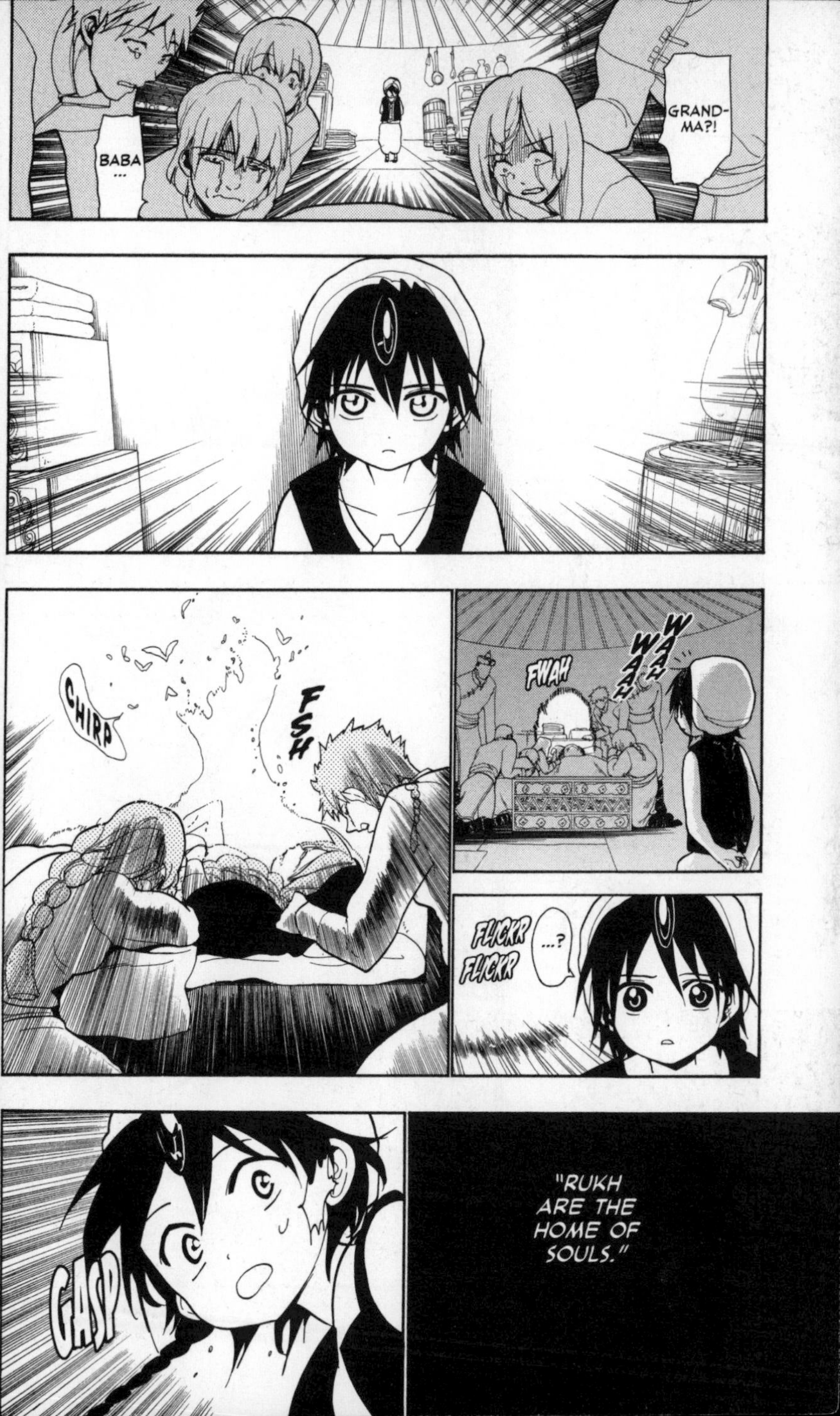
GRAND-MA?!
BABA...
WAAH WAAH
FWAH
...?
FLICKR FLICKR
FSH
CHIRP
"RUKH ARE THE HOME OF SOULS."
GASP

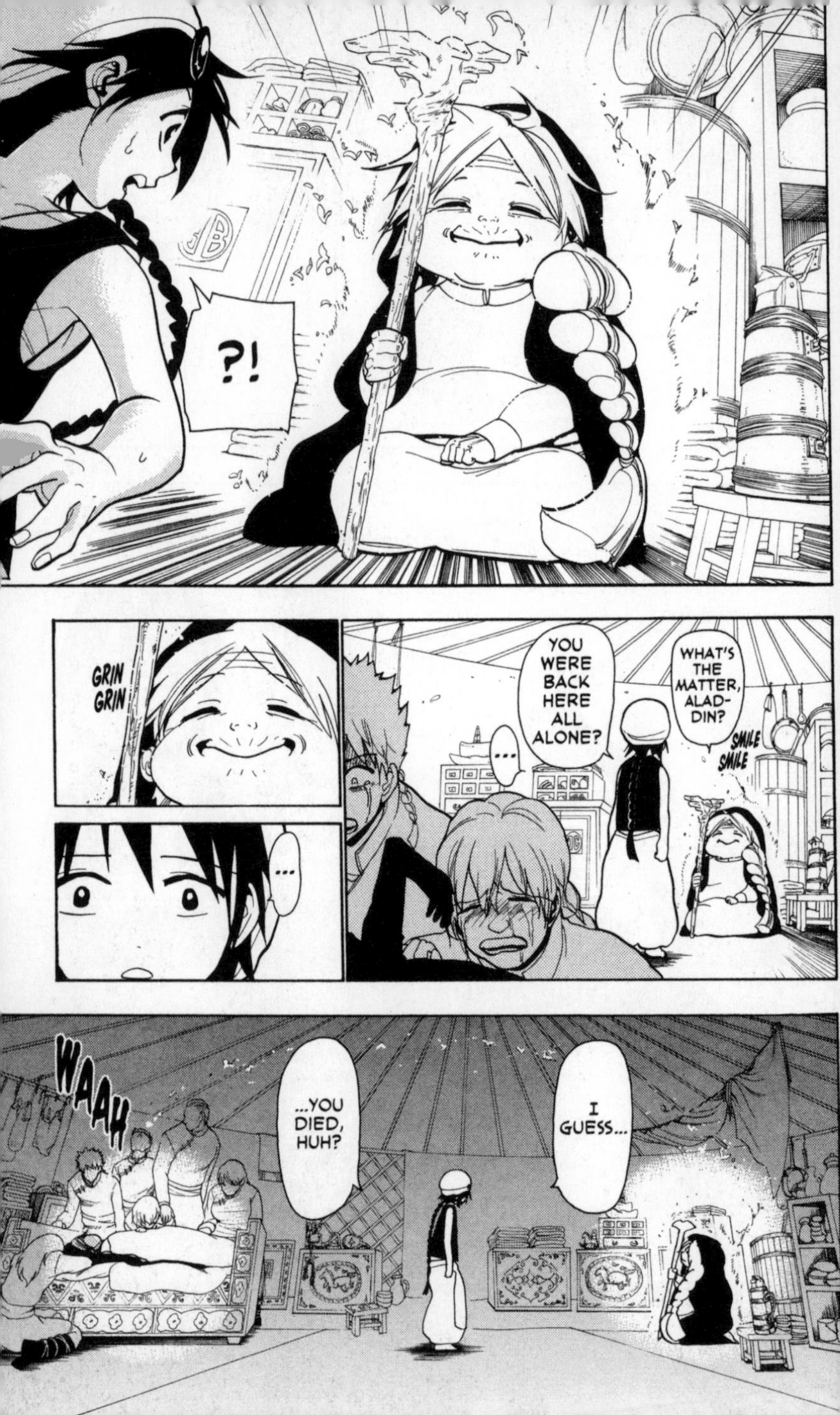
?!
WHAT'S THE MATTER, ALAD-DIN?
SMILE SMILE
YOU WERE BACK HERE ALL ALONE?
...
GRIN GRIN
...
I GUESS...
...YOU DIED, HUH?
WAAH

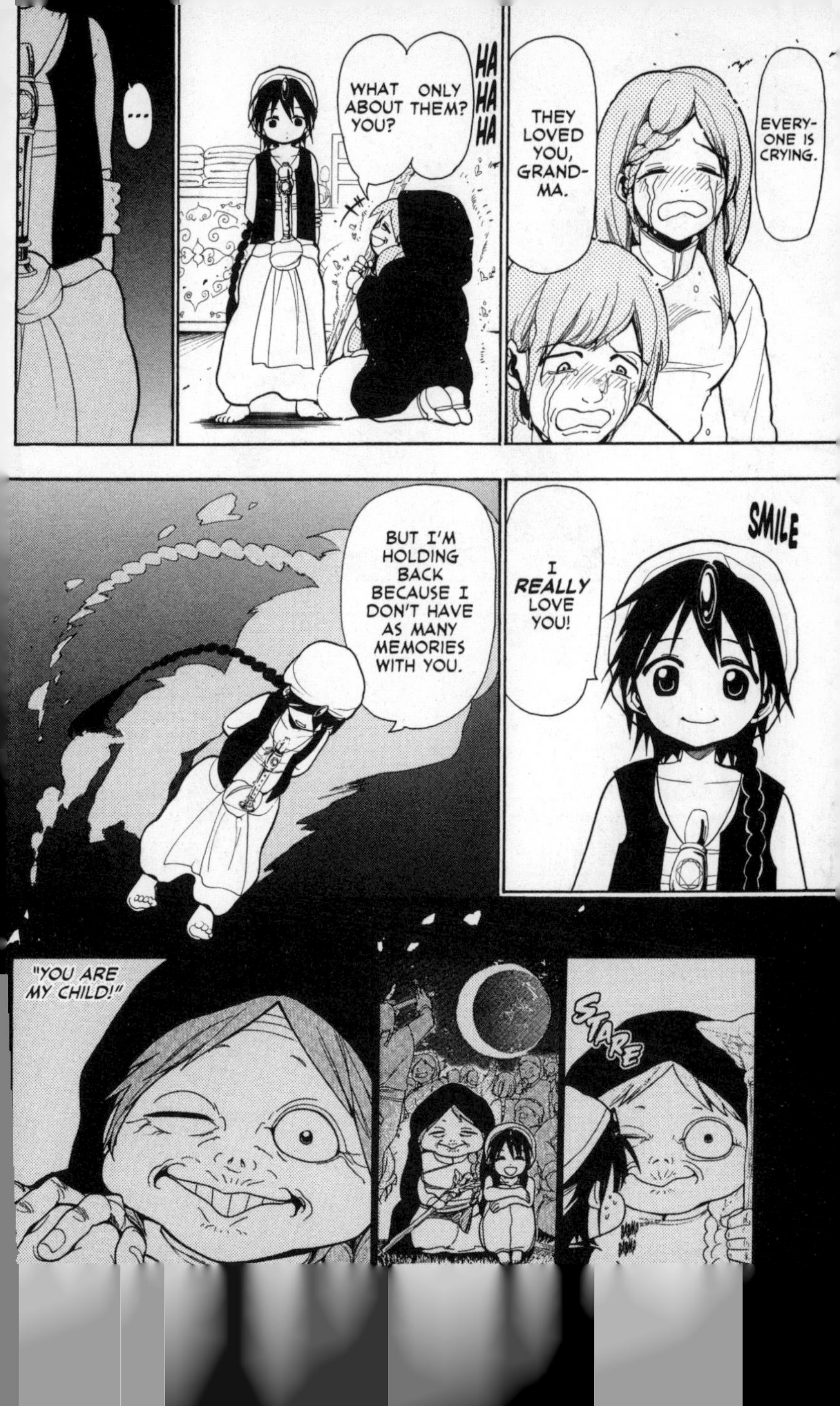
EVERY-ONE IS CRYING.
THEY LOVED YOU, GRAND-MA.
HA HA HA
ONLY THEM?
WHAT ABOUT YOU?
...
SMILE
I REALLY LOVE YOU!
BUT I'M HOLDING BACK BECAUSE I DON'T HAVE AS MANY MEMORIES WITH YOU.
STARE
"YOU ARE MY CHILD!"

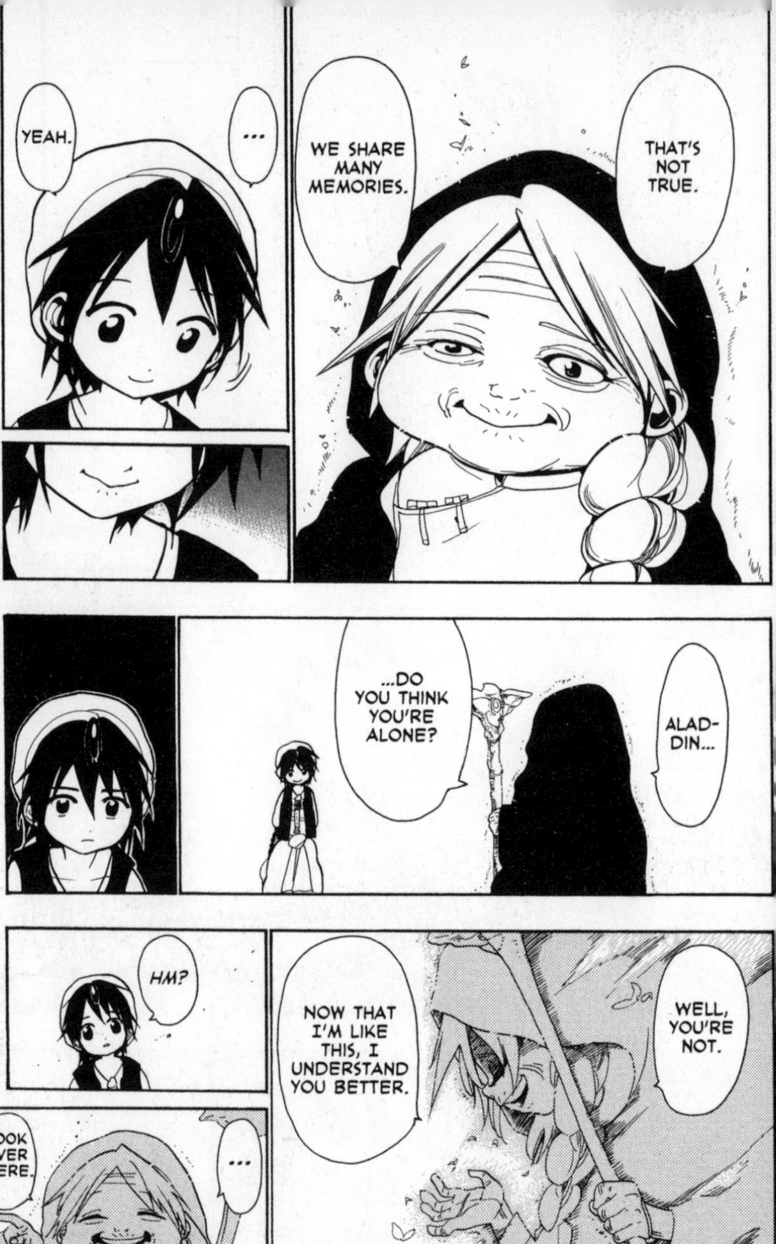
THAT'S NOT TRUE.
WE SHARE MANY MEMORIES.
...
YEAH.
ALAD-DIN...
...DO YOU THINK YOU'RE ALONE?
WELL, YOU'RE NOT.
NOW THAT I'M LIKE THIS, I UNDERSTAND YOU BETTER.
HM?
...
LOOK OVER THERE.

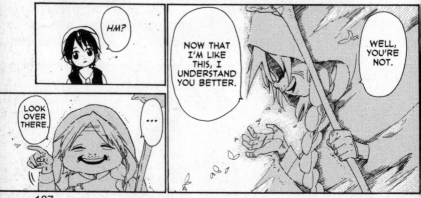

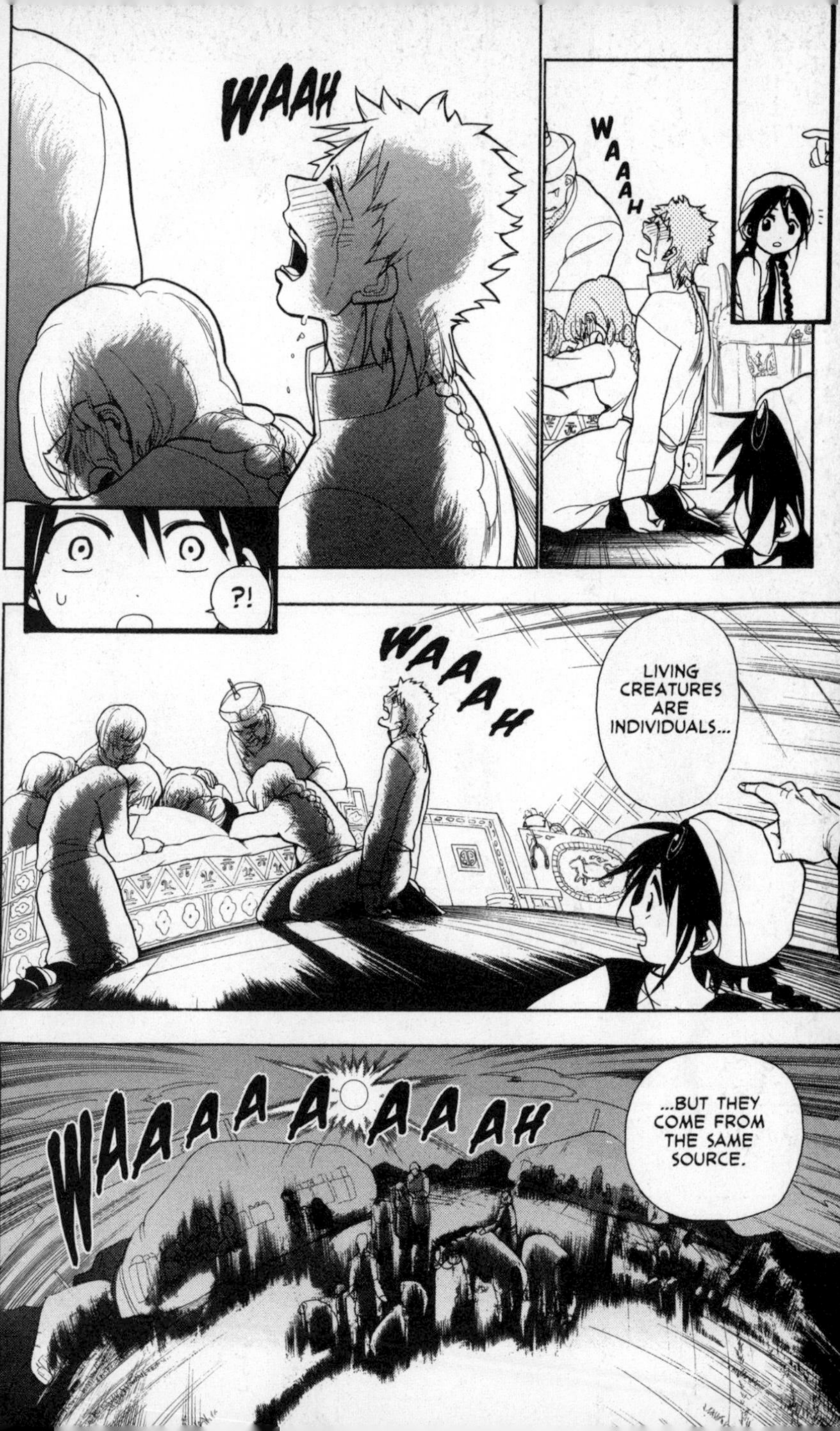
WAAAAH
WAAH
?!
WAAAAH
LIVING CREATURES ARE INDIVIDUALS...
WAAAAAAAAH
...BUT THEY COME FROM THE SAME SOURCE.

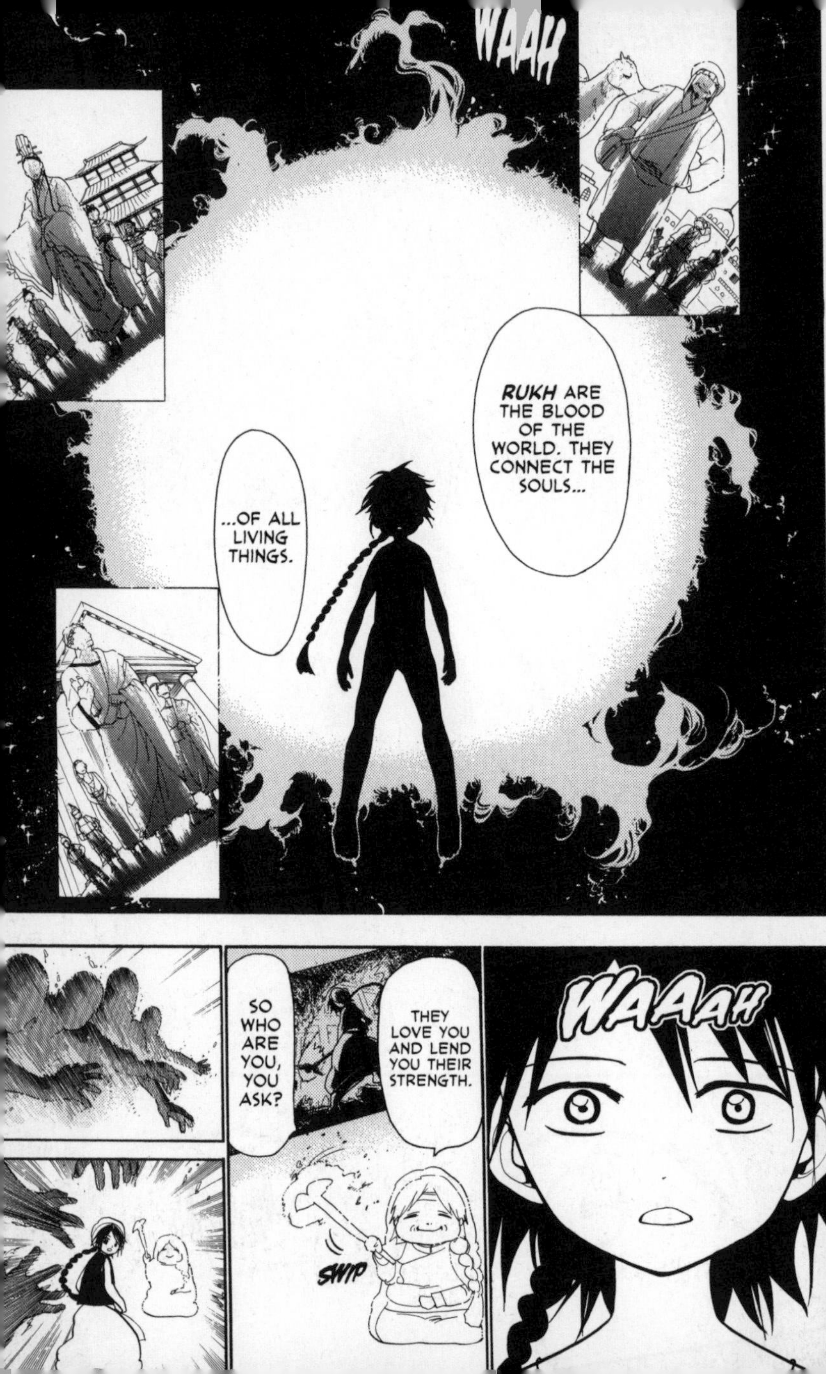
WAAH
RUKH ARE THE BLOOD OF THE WORLD. THEY CONNECT THE SOULS...
...OF ALL LIVING THINGS.
WAAAH
THEY LOVE YOU AND LEND YOU THEIR STRENGTH.
SO WHO ARE YOU, YOU ASK?
SWIP

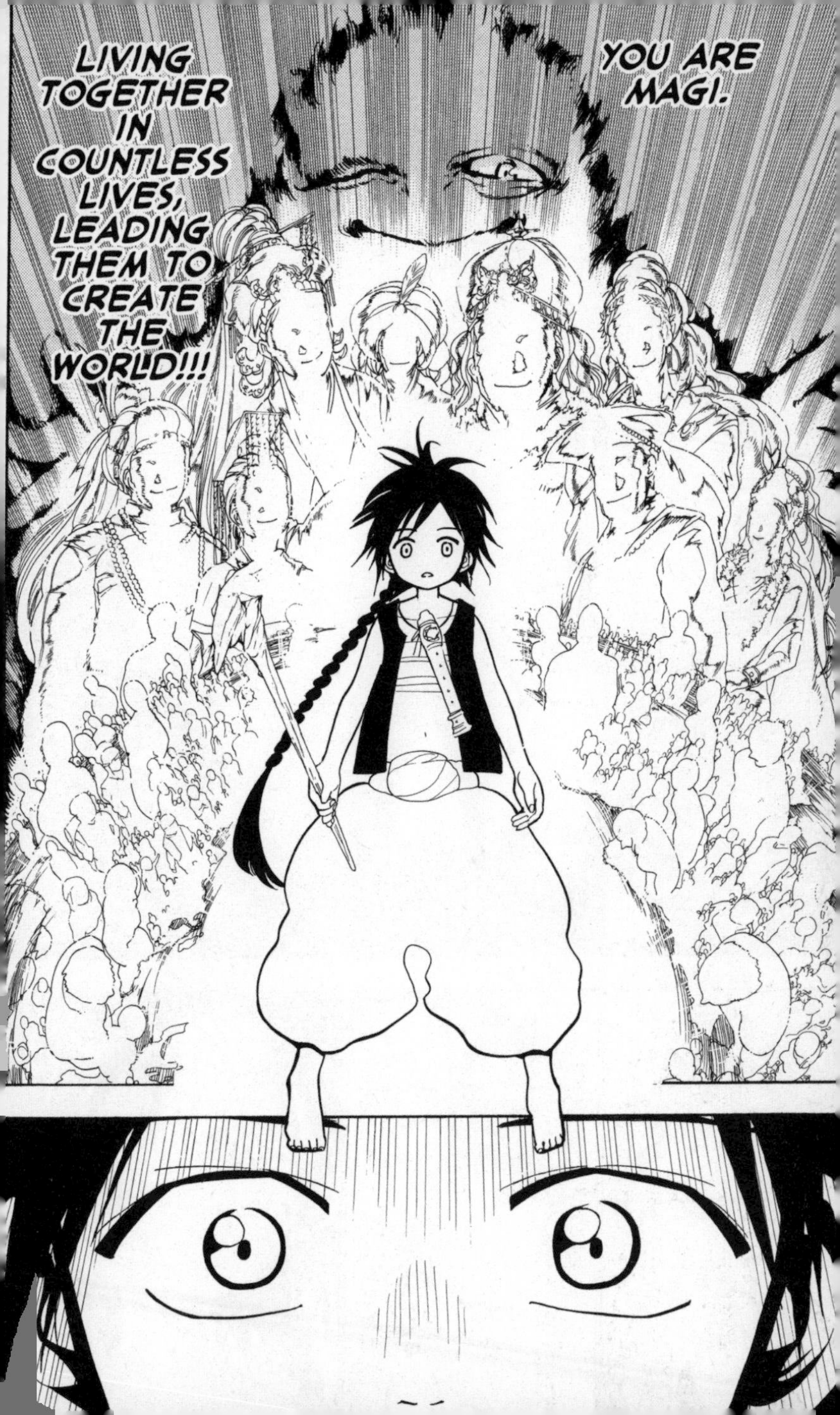
YOU ARE MAGI.
LIVING TOGETHER IN COUNTLESS LIVES, LEADING THEM TO CREATE THE WORLD!!!

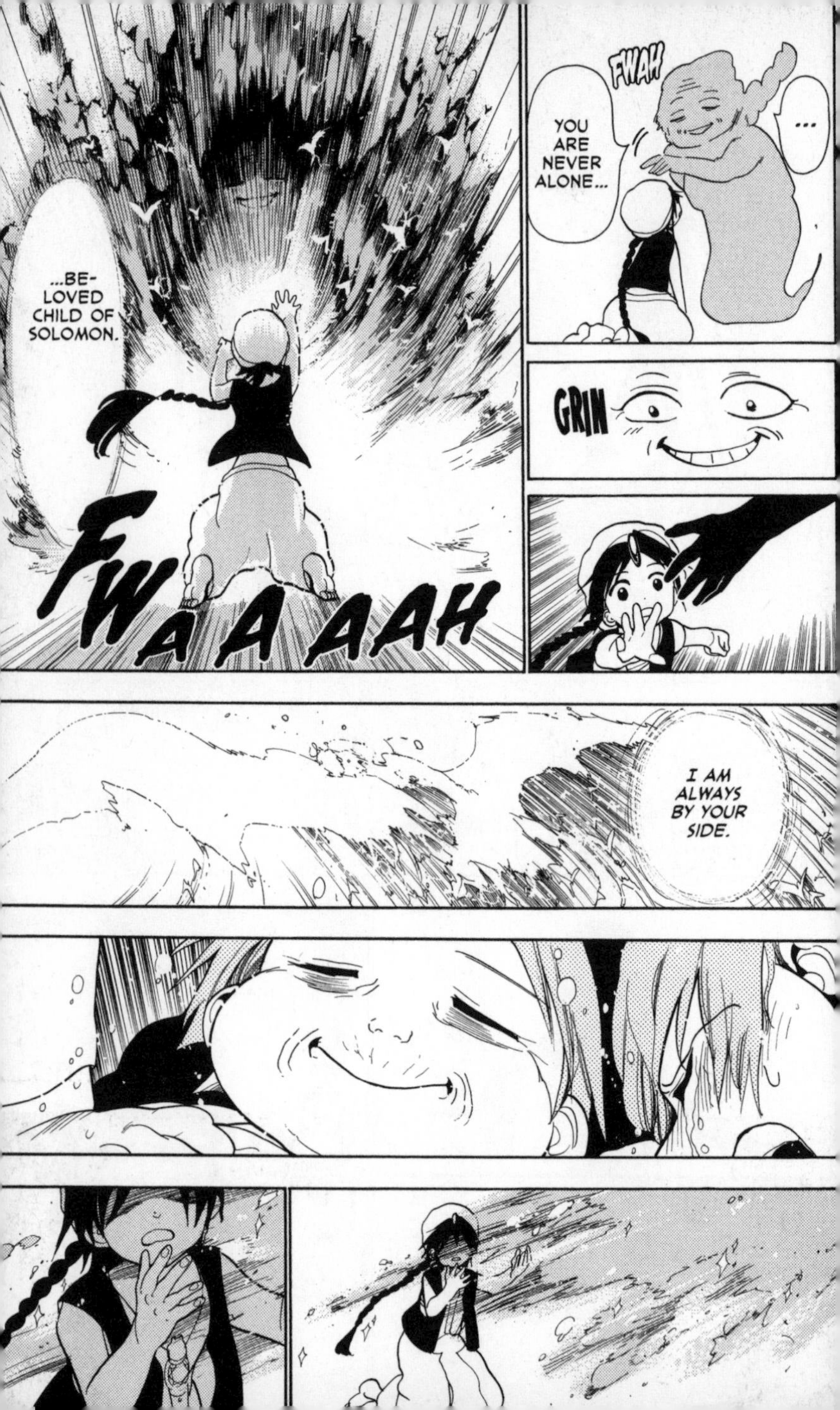
FWAH
...
YOU ARE NEVER ALONE...
GRIN
...BE-LOVED CHILD OF SOLOMON.
FWAAAAH
I AM ALWAYS BY YOUR SIDE.

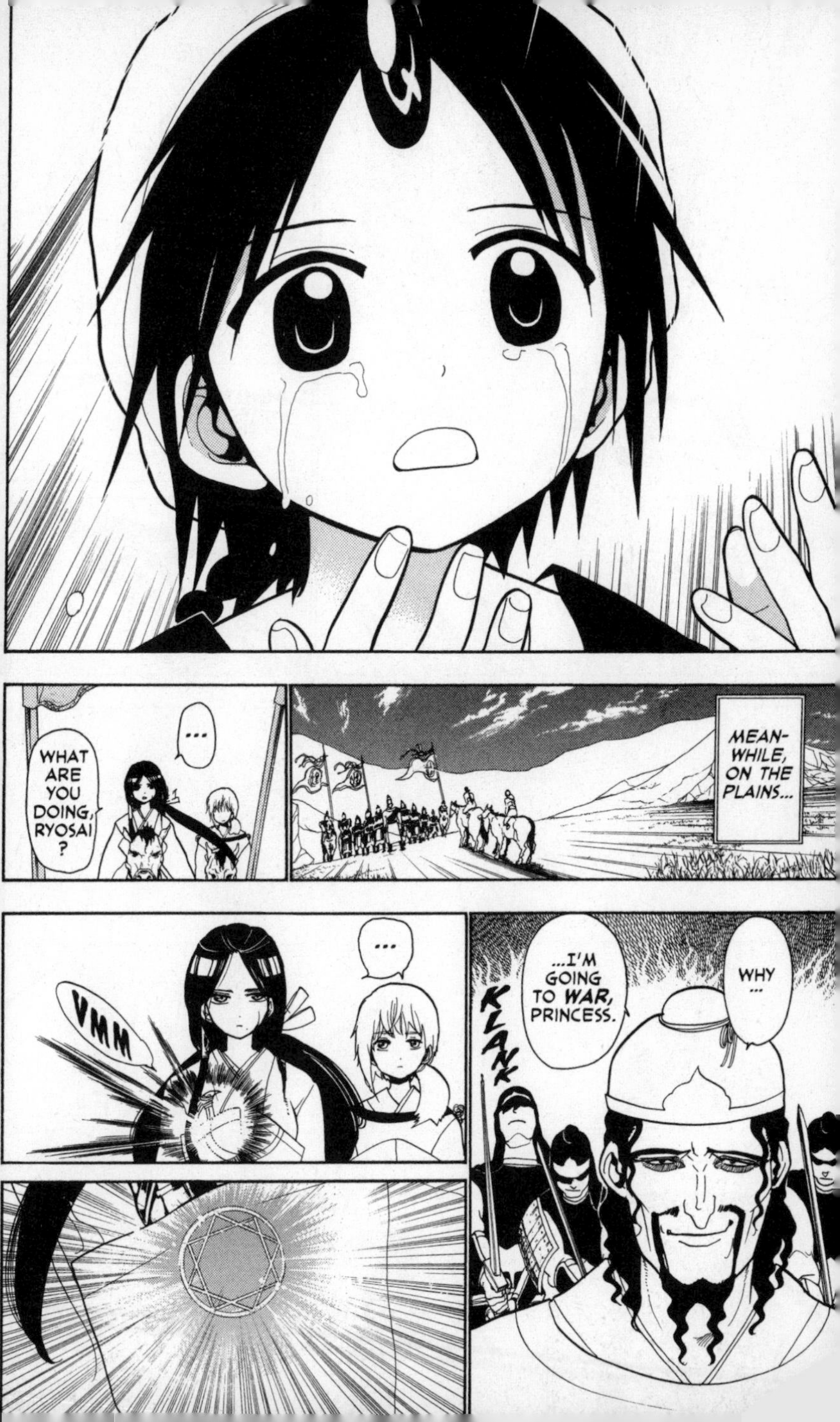
MEAN-WHILE, ON THE PLAINS...
...
WHAT ARE YOU DOING, RYOSAI?
WHY ...
...I'M GOING TO WAR, PRINCESS.
KLANK
...
VMM

Night 24: Dungeon-Capturer

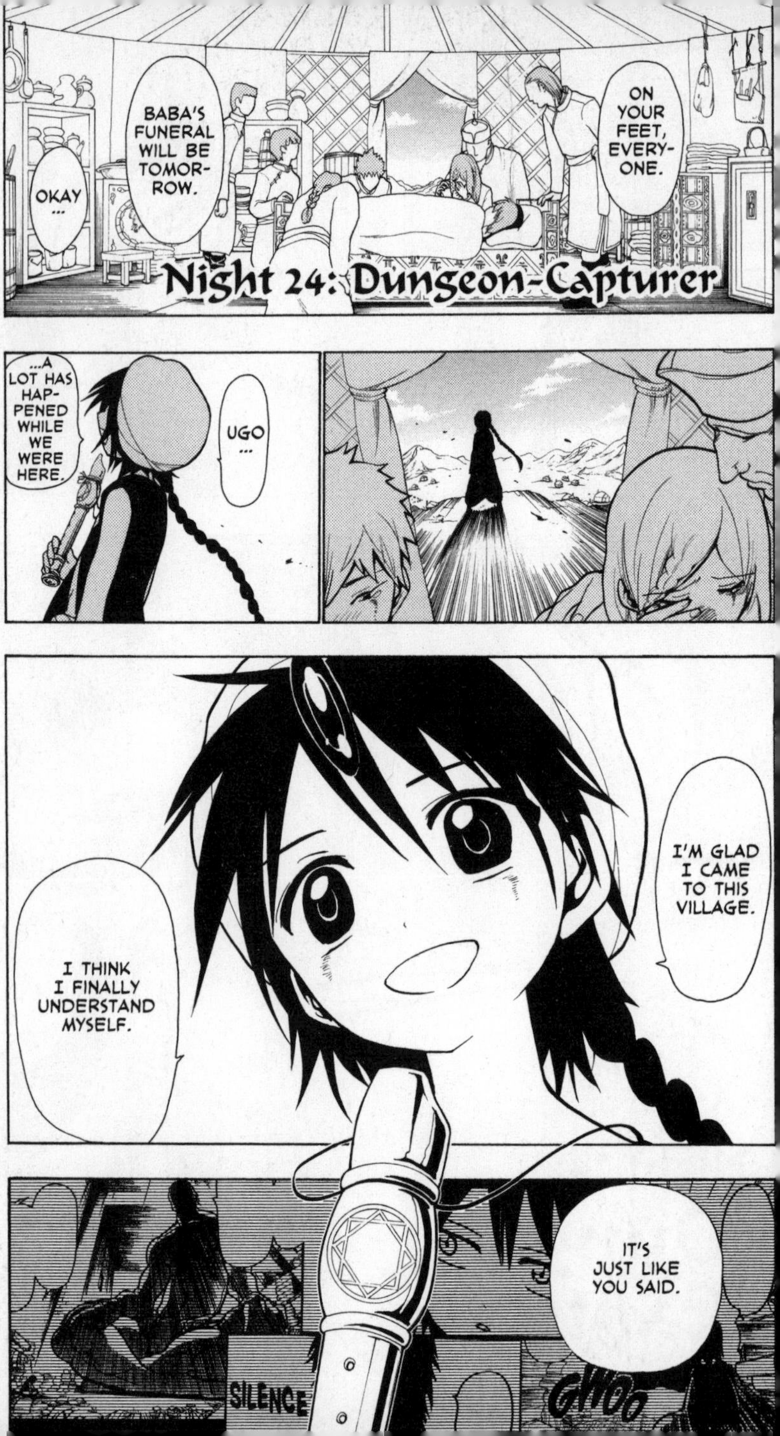

ON YOUR FEET, EVERY-ONE.
BABA'S FUNERAL WILL BE TOMOR-ROW.
OKAY ...
UGO ...
...A LOT HAS HAP-PENED WHILE WE WERE HERE.
I'M GLAD I CAME TO THIS VILLAGE.
I THINK I FINALLY UNDERSTAND MYSELF.
IT'S JUST LIKE YOU SAID.
GWOO
SILENCE

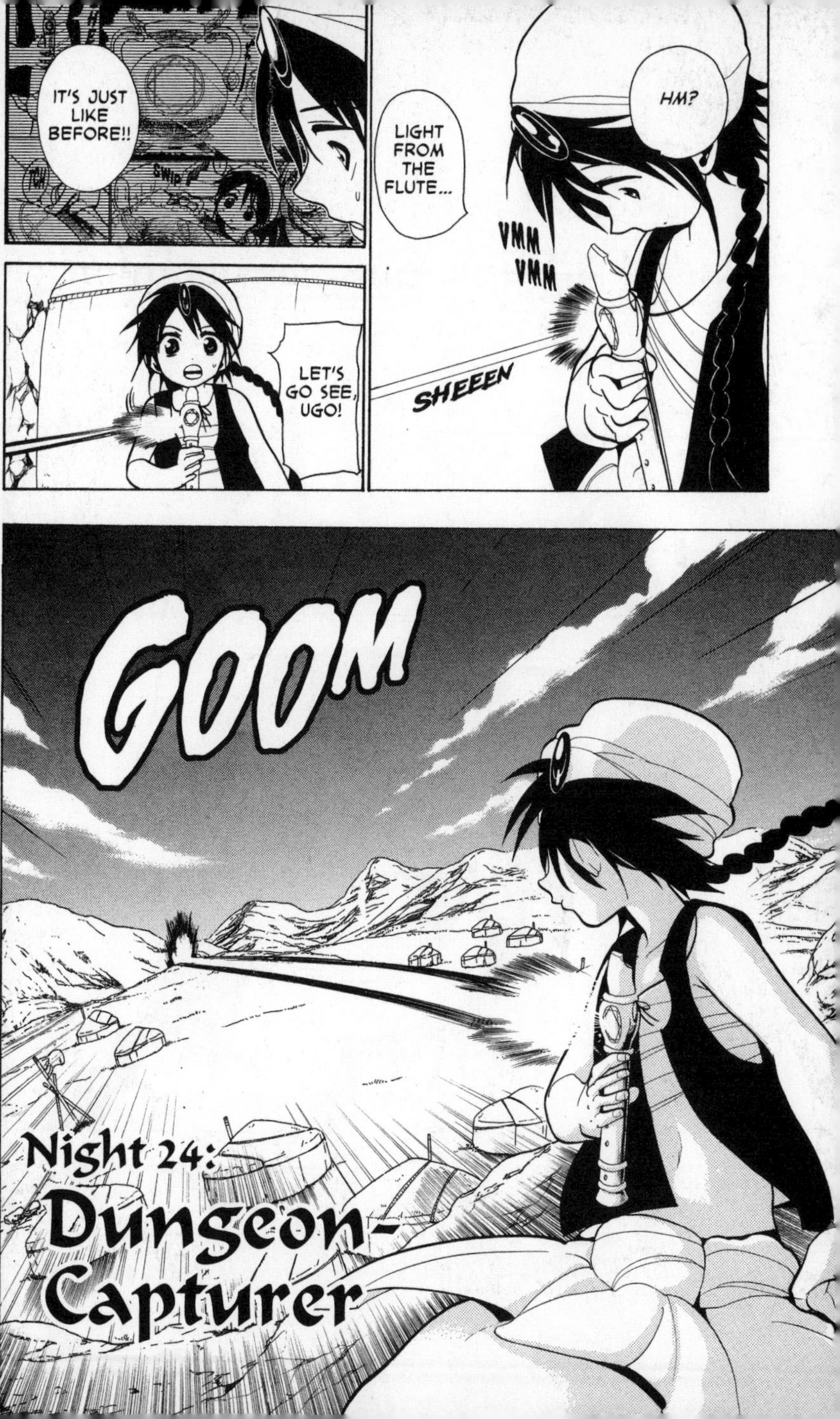
HM?
LIGHT FROM THE FLUTE...
VMM VMM
SHEEEN
IT'S JUST LIKE BEFORE!!
SWIP
LET'S GO SEE, UGO!
GOOM
Night 24:
Dungeon-Capturer

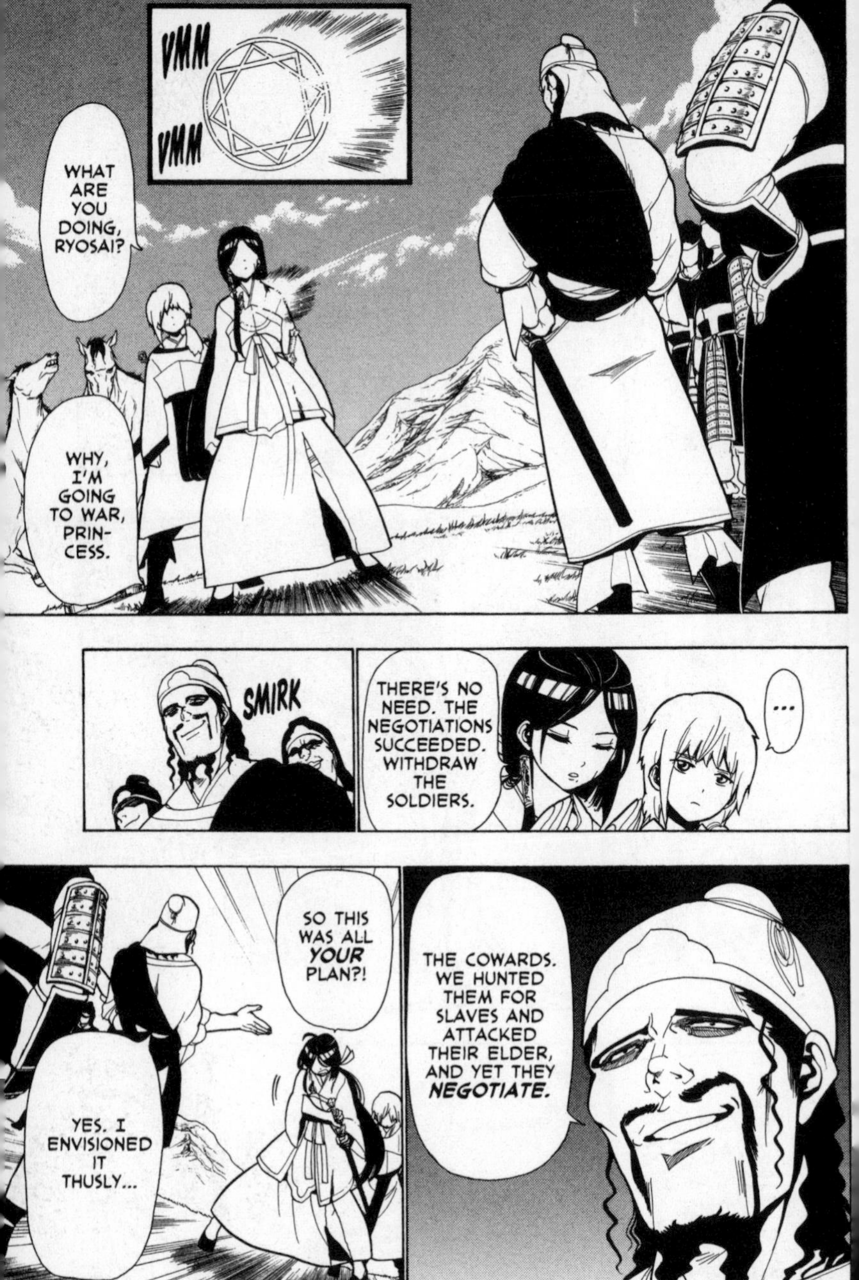
VMM
VMM
WHAT ARE YOU DOING, RYOSAI?
WHY, I'M GOING TO WAR, PRINCESS.
...
THERE'S NO NEED. THE NEGOTIATIONS SUCCEEDED. WITHDRAW THE SOLDIERS.
SMIRK
THE COWARDS. WE HUNTED THEM FOR SLAVES AND ATTACKED THEIR ELDER, AND YET THEY *NEGOTIATE.*
SO THIS WAS ALL *YOUR* PLAN?!
YES. I ENVISIONED IT THUSLY...

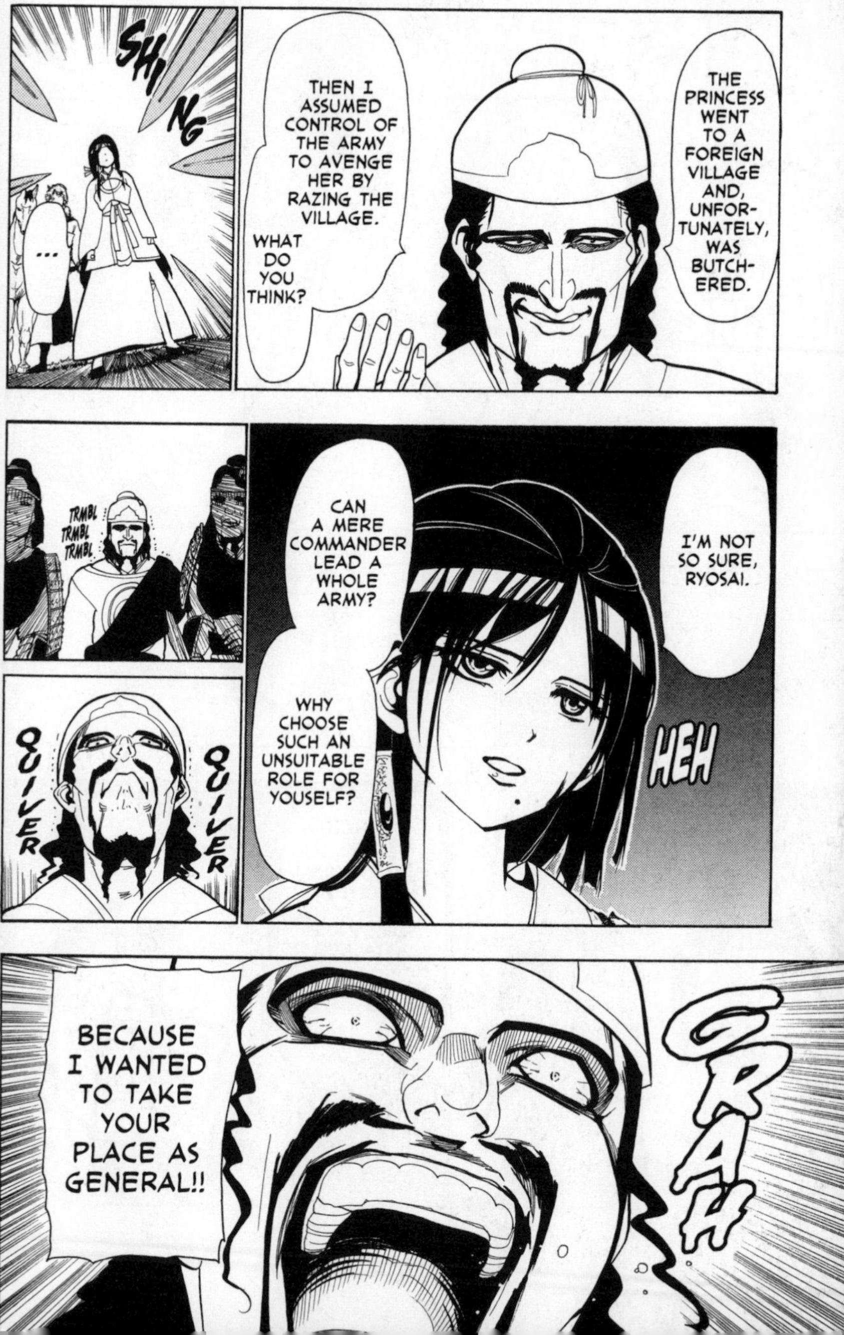
THE PRINCESS WENT TO A FOREIGN VILLAGE AND, UNFORTUNATELY, WAS BUTCHERED.
THEN I ASSUMED CONTROL OF THE ARMY TO AVENGE HER BY RAZING THE VILLAGE.
WHAT DO YOU THINK?
SHING
...
I'M NOT SO SURE, RYOSAI.
HEH
CAN A MERE COMMANDER LEAD A WHOLE ARMY?
WHY CHOOSE SUCH AN UNSUITABLE ROLE FOR YOUSELF?
TRMBL TRMBL TRMBL
QUIVER
QUIVER
GRAH
BECAUSE I WANTED TO TAKE YOUR PLACE AS GENERAL!!

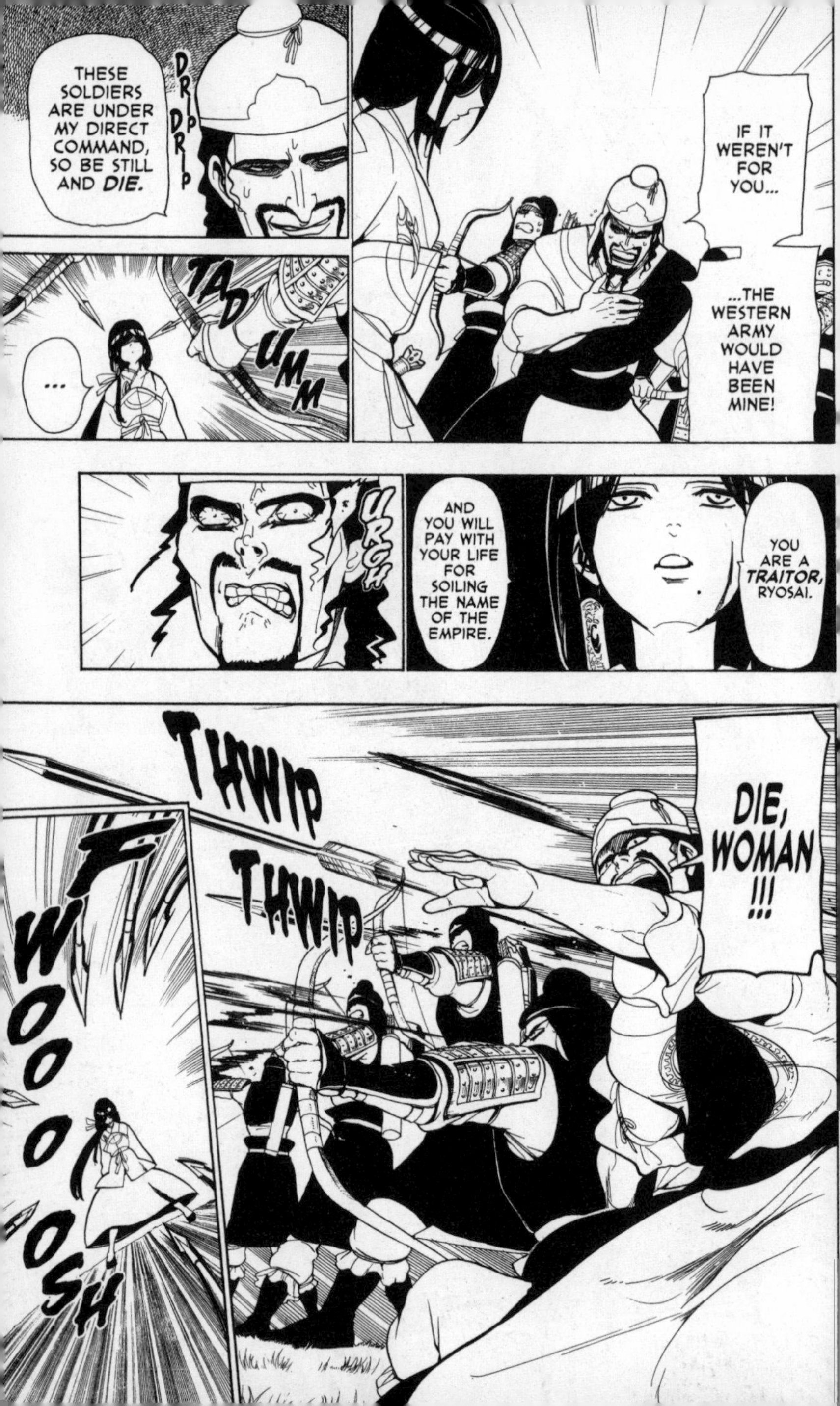
IF IT WEREN'T FOR YOU...
...THE WESTERN ARMY WOULD HAVE BEEN MINE!
THESE SOLDIERS ARE UNDER MY DIRECT COMMAND, SO BE STILL AND *DIE.*
DRIP DRIP
TADUMM
...
YOU ARE A *TRAITOR,* RYOSAI.
AND YOU WILL PAY WITH YOUR LIFE FOR SOILING THE NAME OF THE EMPIRE.
URGH
DIE, WOMAN!!!
THWIP
THWIP
FWOOOOOSH

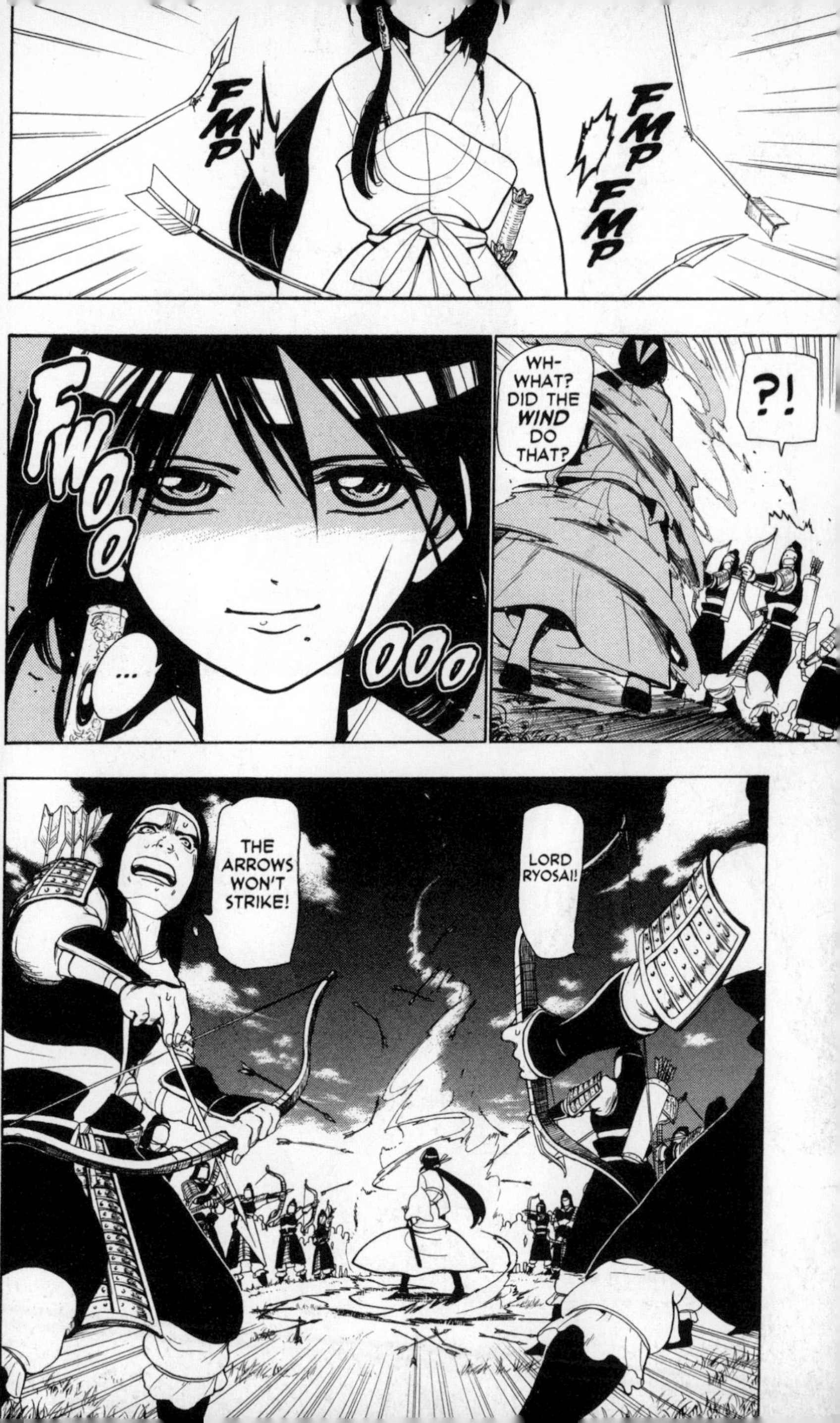
FMP FMP
FMP
?!
WH-WHAT? DID THE WIND DO THAT?
FWOOOOO
...
LORD RYOSAI!
THE ARROWS WON'T STRIKE!

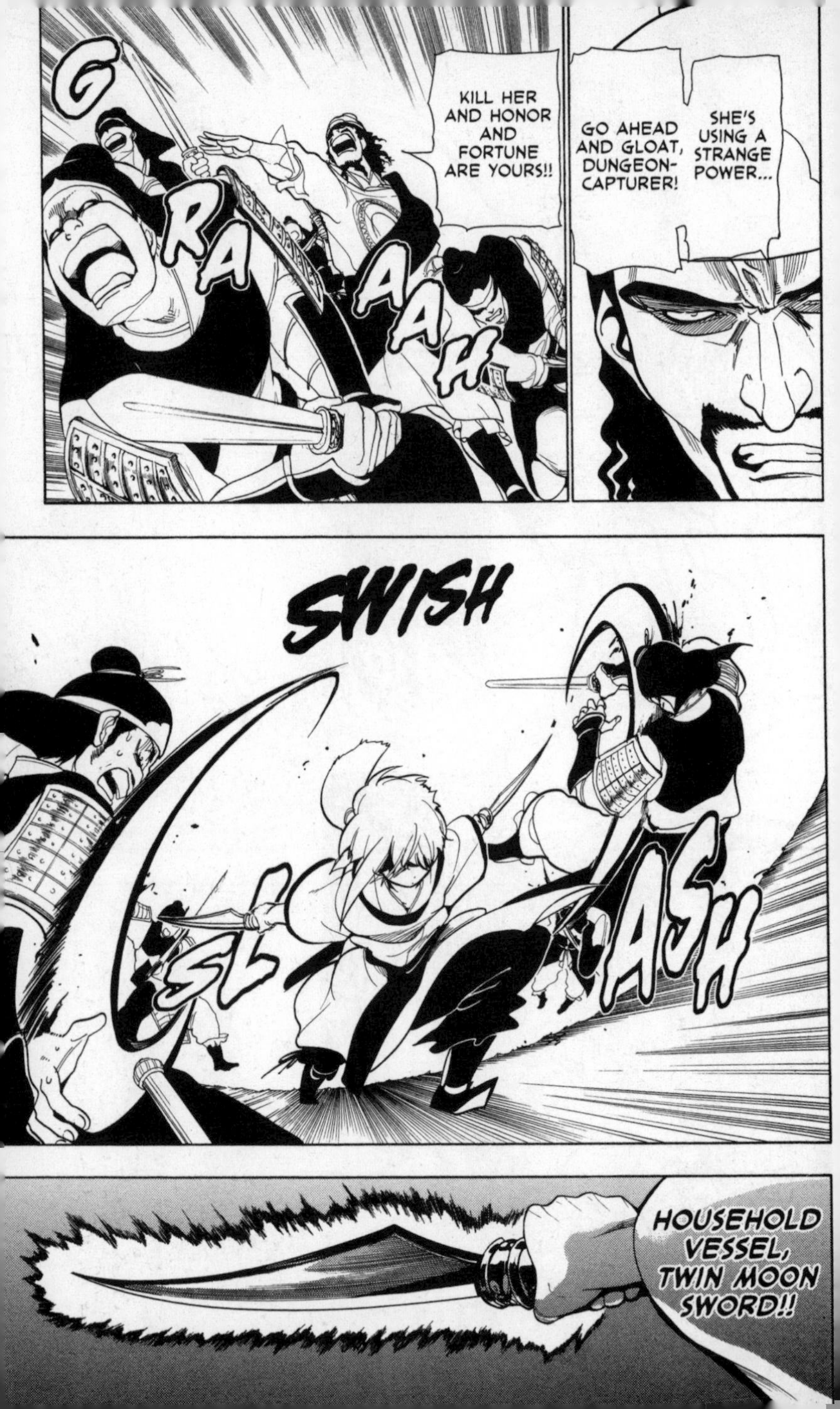
SHE'S USING A STRANGE POWER...
GO AHEAD AND GLOAT, DUNGEON-CAPTURER!
KILL HER AND HONOR AND FORTUNE ARE YOURS!!
GRAAAH
SWISH
SLASH
HOUSEHOLD VESSEL, TWIN MOON SWORD!!

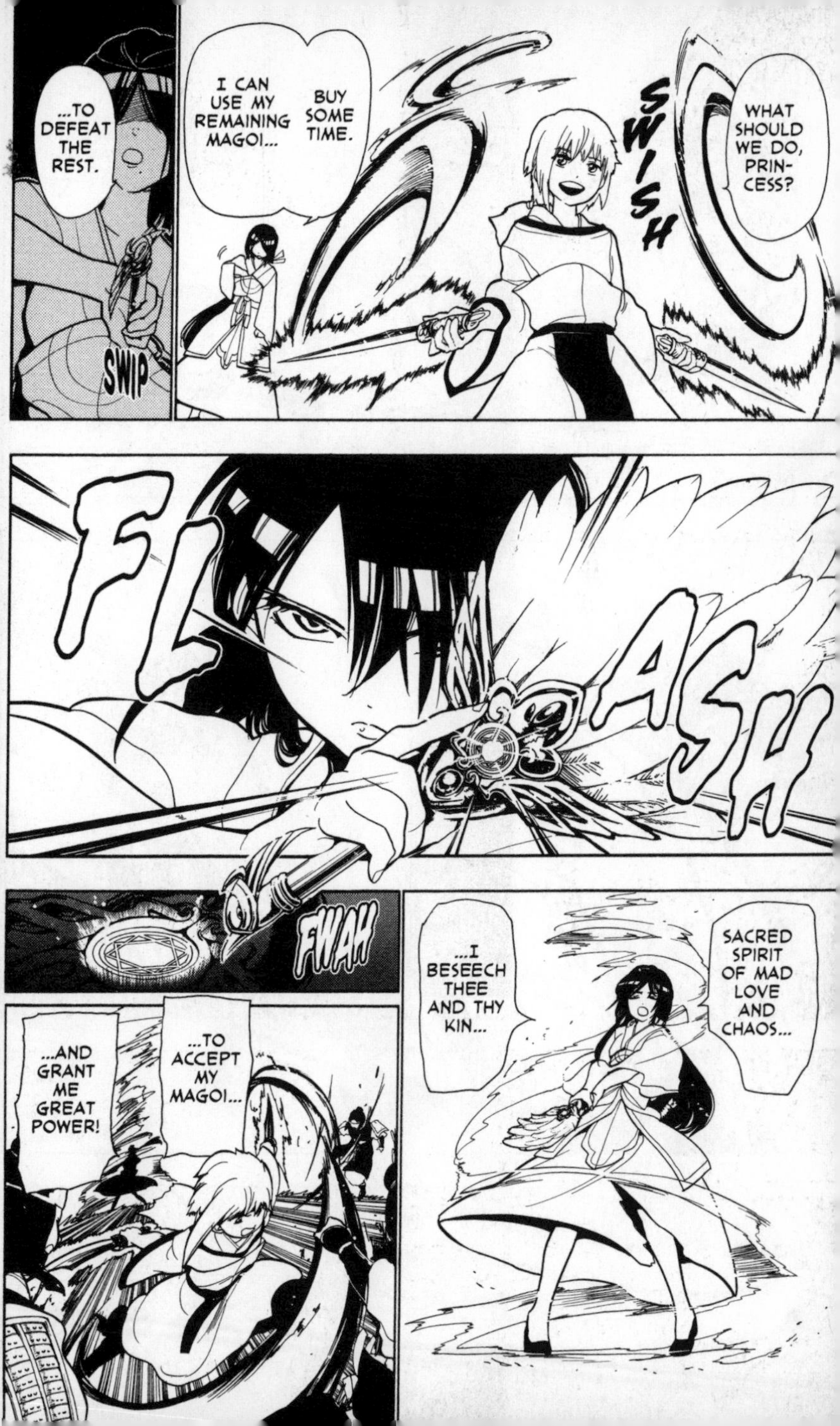
WHAT SHOULD WE DO, PRINCESS?
SWISH
I CAN USE MY REMAINING MAGOI...
BUY SOME TIME.
...TO DEFEAT THE REST.
SWIP
FLASH
SACRED SPIRIT OF MAD LOVE AND CHAOS...
...I BESEECH THEE AND THY KIN...
FWAH
...TO ACCEPT MY MAGOI...
...AND GRANT ME GREAT POWER!

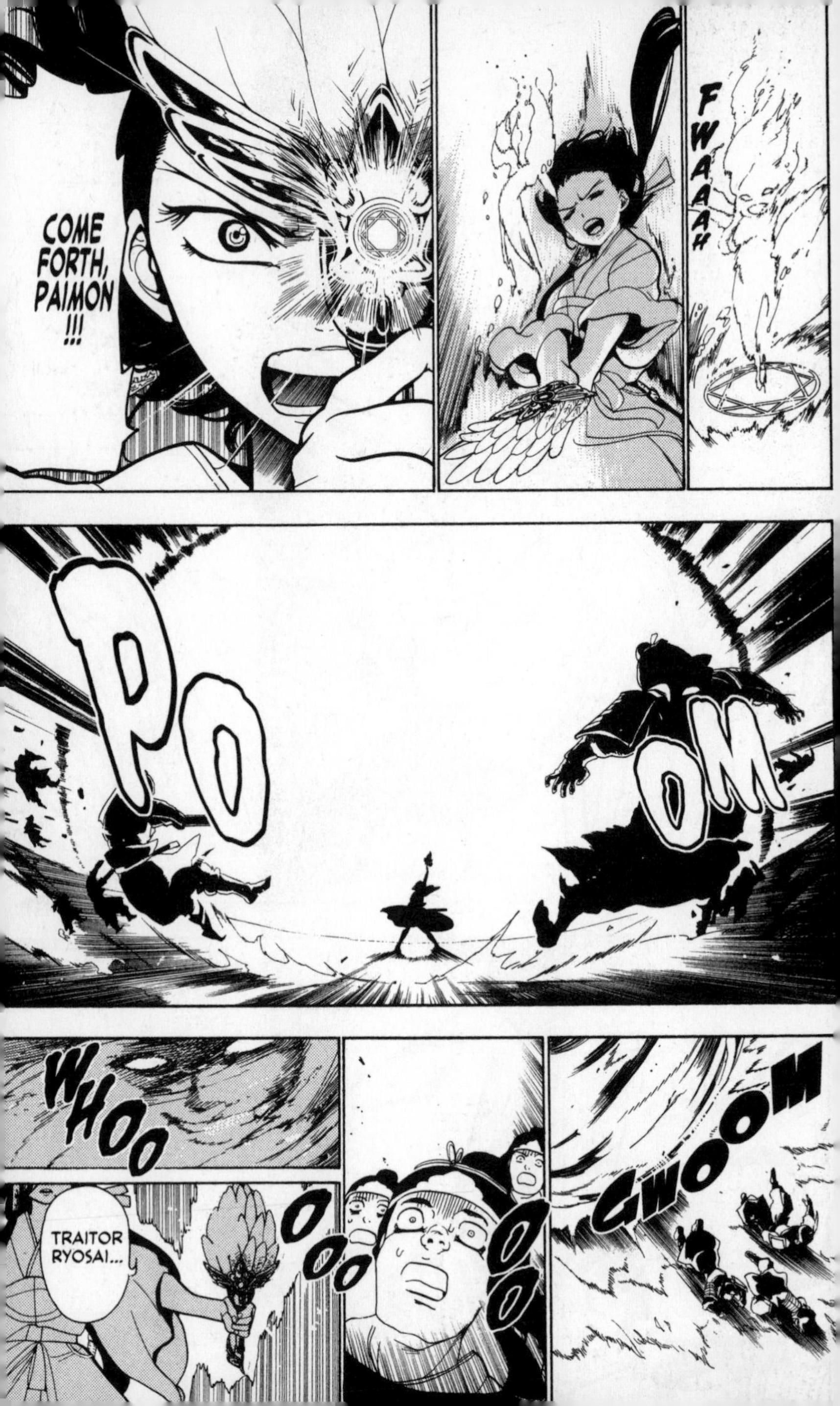
FWAAAH
COME FORTH, PAIMON!!!
POOM
GWOOOM
OOOOO
WHOOO
TRAITOR RYOSAI...

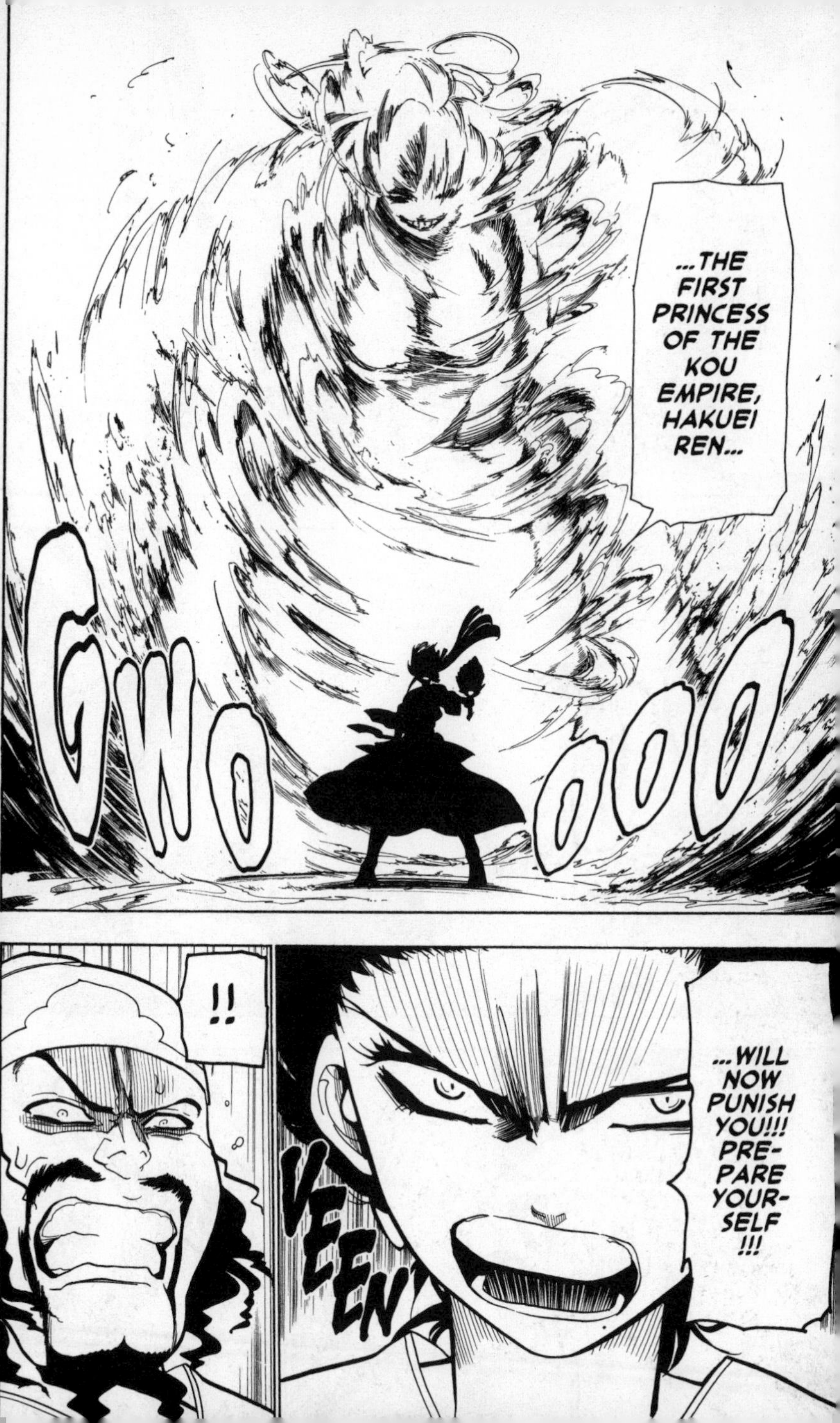
...THE FIRST PRINCESS OF THE KOU EMPIRE, HAKUEI REN...
GWOOOOO
...WILL NOW PUNISH YOU!!! PRE-PARE YOUR-SELF!!!
VEEEN
!!

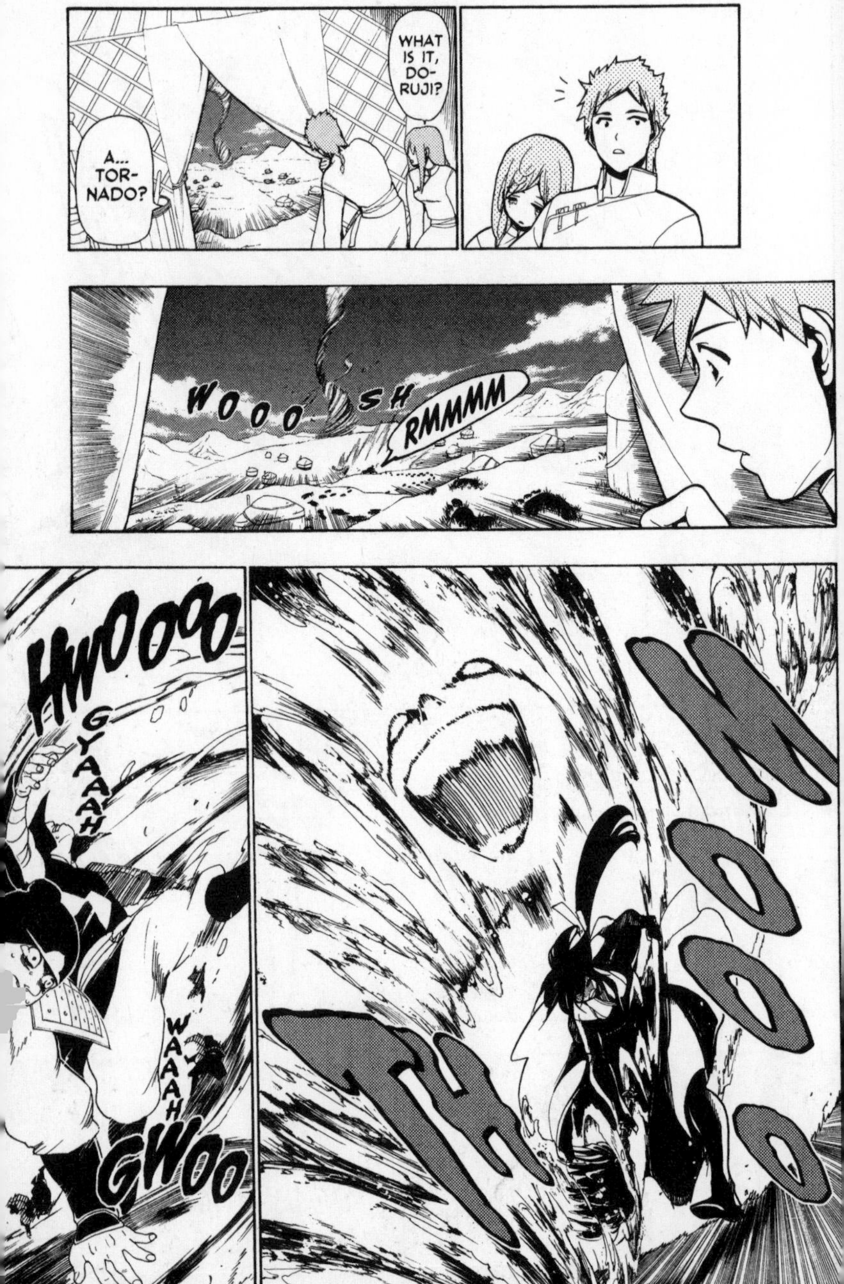
WHAT IS IT, DORUJI?
A... TOR-NADO?
WOOOSH
RMMMM
HWOOOO
GYAAAH
WAAAH
GWOO

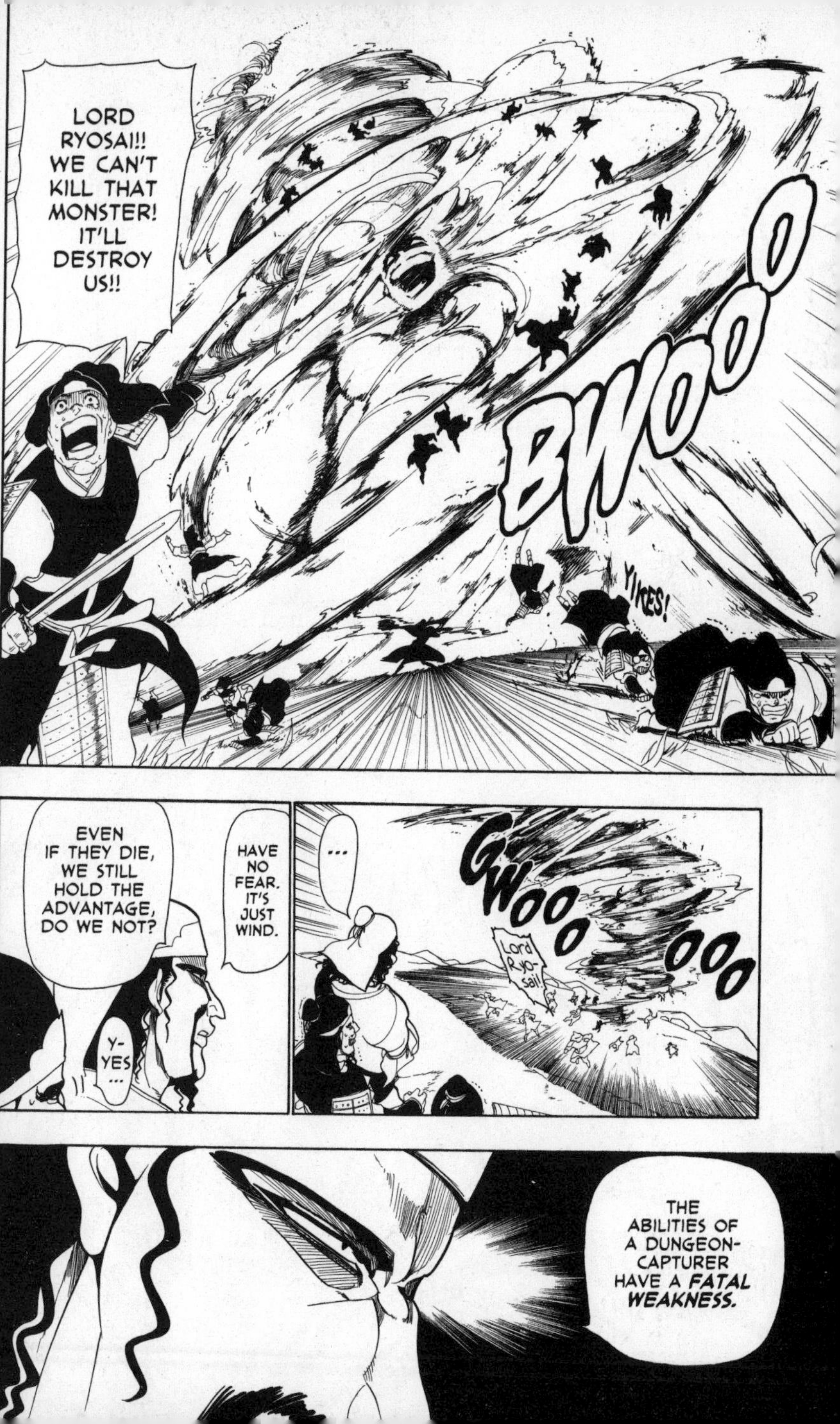
LORD RYOSAI!!! WE CAN'T KILL THAT MONSTER! IT'LL DESTROY US!!
BWOOOOO
YIKES!
...
GWOOOO
OOO
Lord Ryosai!
HAVE NO FEAR. IT'S JUST WIND.
EVEN IF THEY DIE, WE STILL HOLD THE ADVANTAGE, DO WE NOT?
Y-YES...
THE ABILITIES OF A DUNGEON-CAPTURER HAVE A *FATAL WEAKNESS.*

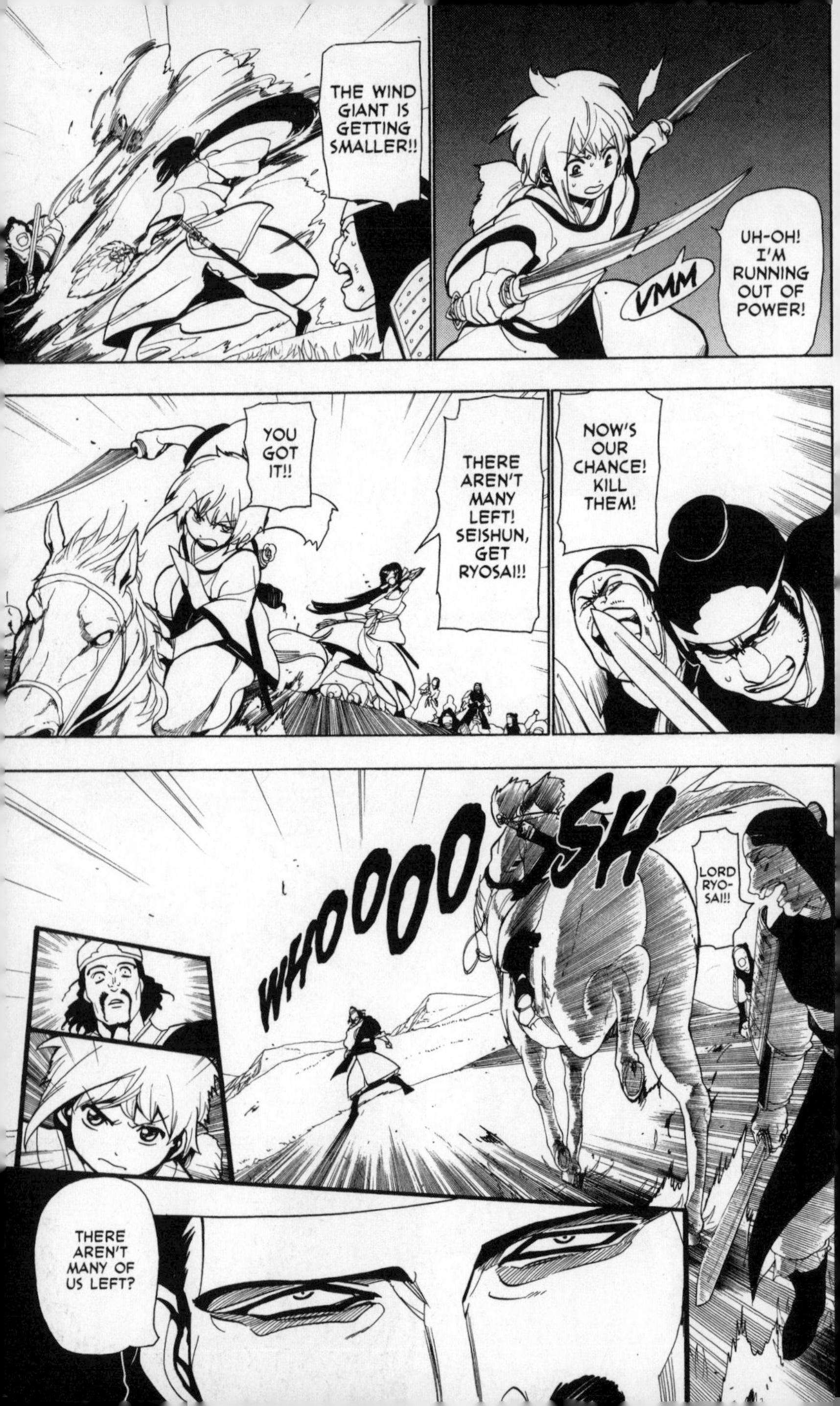
UH-OH! I'M RUNNING OUT OF POWER!
VMM
THE WIND GIANT IS GETTING SMALLER!!
NOW'S OUR CHANCE! KILL THEM!
THERE AREN'T MANY LEFT! SEISHUN, GET RYOSAI!!
YOU GOT IT!!
LORD RYO-SAI!!
WHOOOOOSH
THERE AREN'T MANY OF US LEFT?

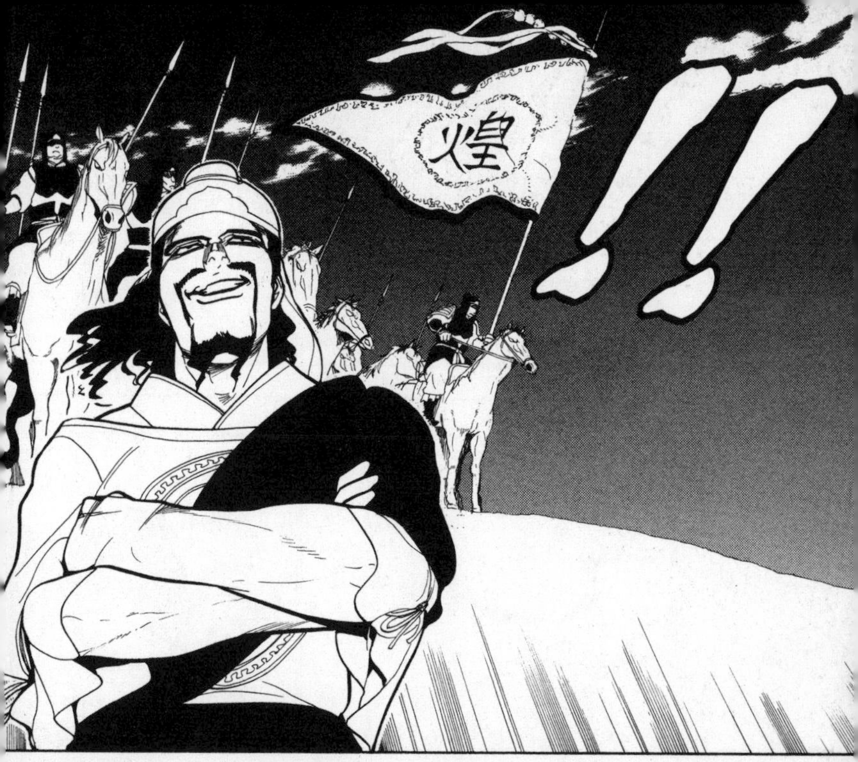
煌
!!
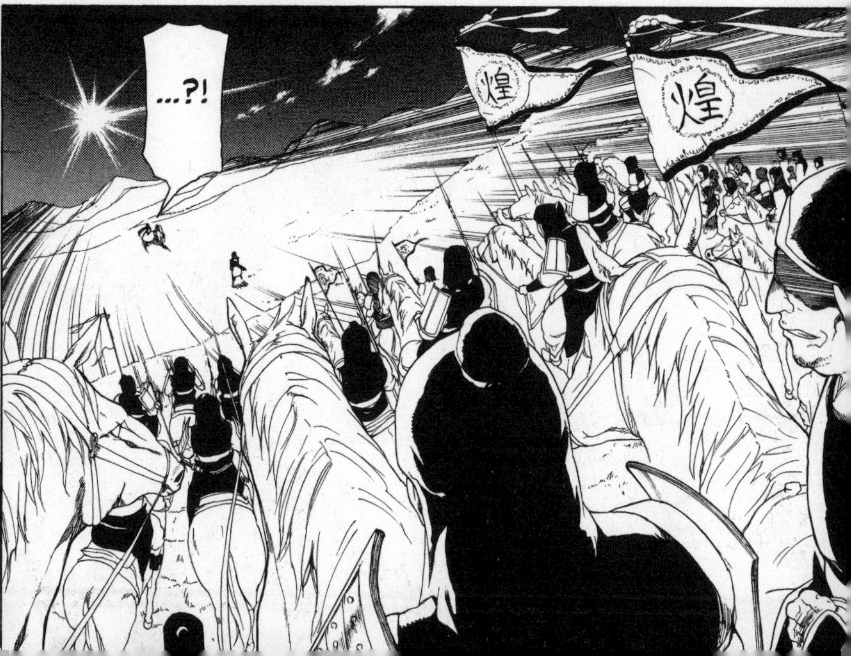
...?!
煌
煌

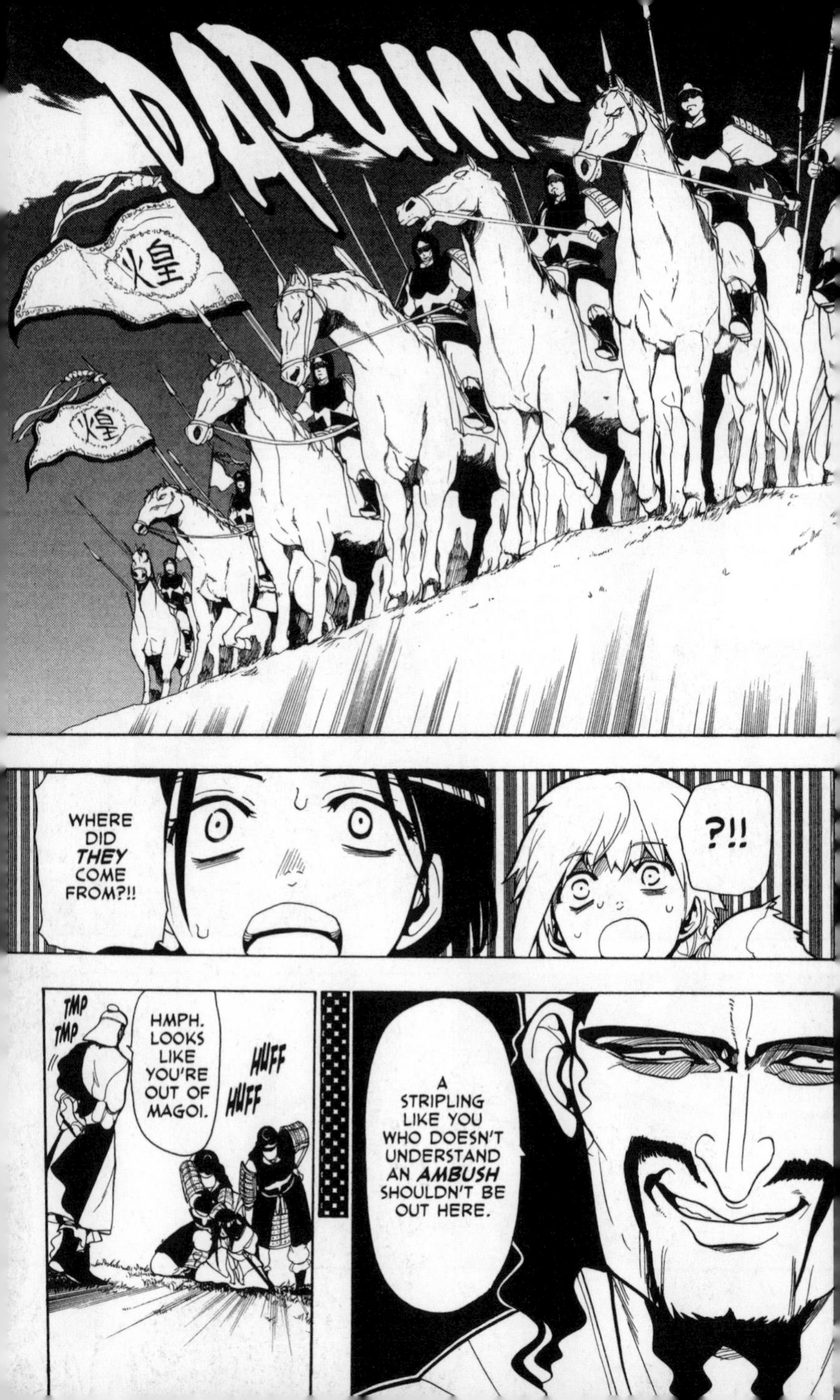
DARUMM
煌
煌
?!!
WHERE DID *THEY* COME FROM?!!
A STRIPLING LIKE YOU WHO DOESN'T UNDERSTAND AN *AMBUSH* SHOULDN'T BE OUT HERE.
TMP TMP
HMPH. LOOKS LIKE YOU'RE OUT OF MAGOI.
HUFF HUFF

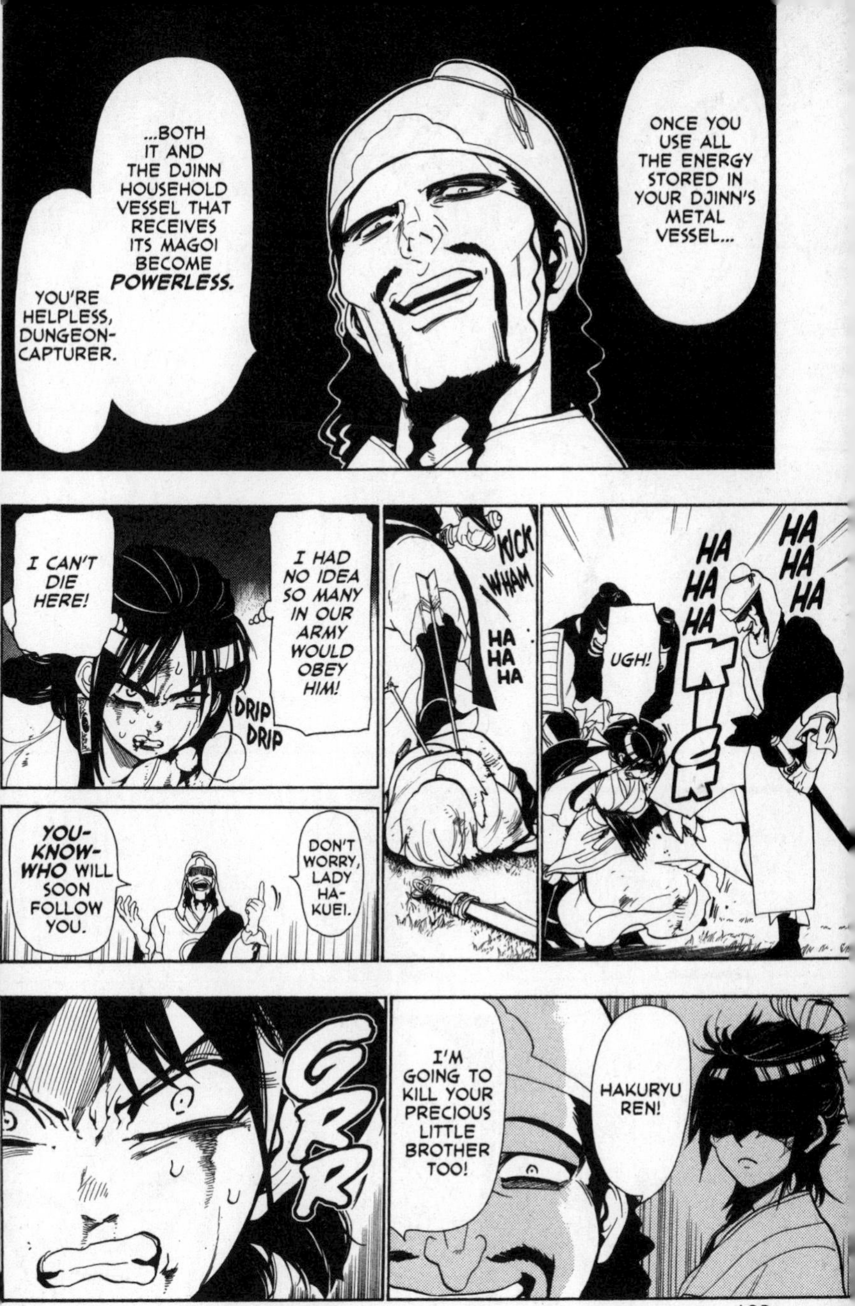
ONCE YOU USE ALL THE ENERGY STORED IN YOUR DJINN'S METAL VESSEL...
...BOTH IT AND THE DJINN HOUSEHOLD VESSEL THAT RECEIVES ITS MAGOI BECOME POWERLESS.
YOU'RE HELPLESS, DUNGEON-CAPTURER.
HA HA HA
HA HA HA HA
UGH!
KICK
KICK
WHAM
HA HA HA
I HAD NO IDEA SO MANY IN OUR ARMY WOULD OBEY HIM!
I CAN'T DIE HERE!
DRIP DRIP
DON'T WORRY, LADY HA-KUEI.
YOU-KNOW-WHO WILL SOON FOLLOW YOU.
HAKURYU REN!
I'M GOING TO KILL YOUR PRECIOUS LITTLE BROTHER TOO!
GRR

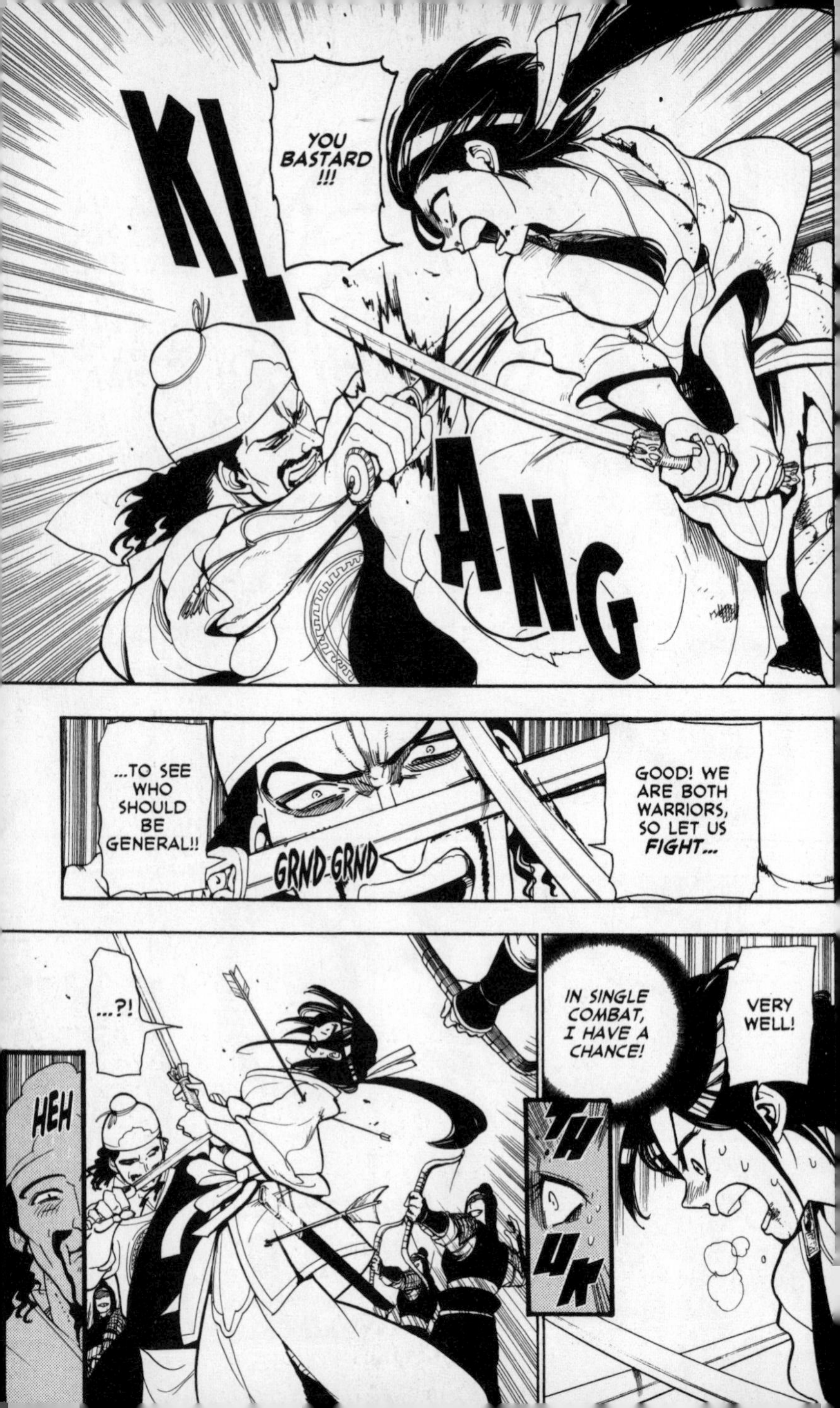

YOU BASTARD!!!
KLANG
GOOD! WE ARE BOTH WARRIORS, SO LET US FIGHT...
...TO SEE WHO SHOULD BE GENERAL!!
GRND GRND
VERY WELL!
IN SINGLE COMBAT, I HAVE A CHANCE!
THUK
...?!
HEH

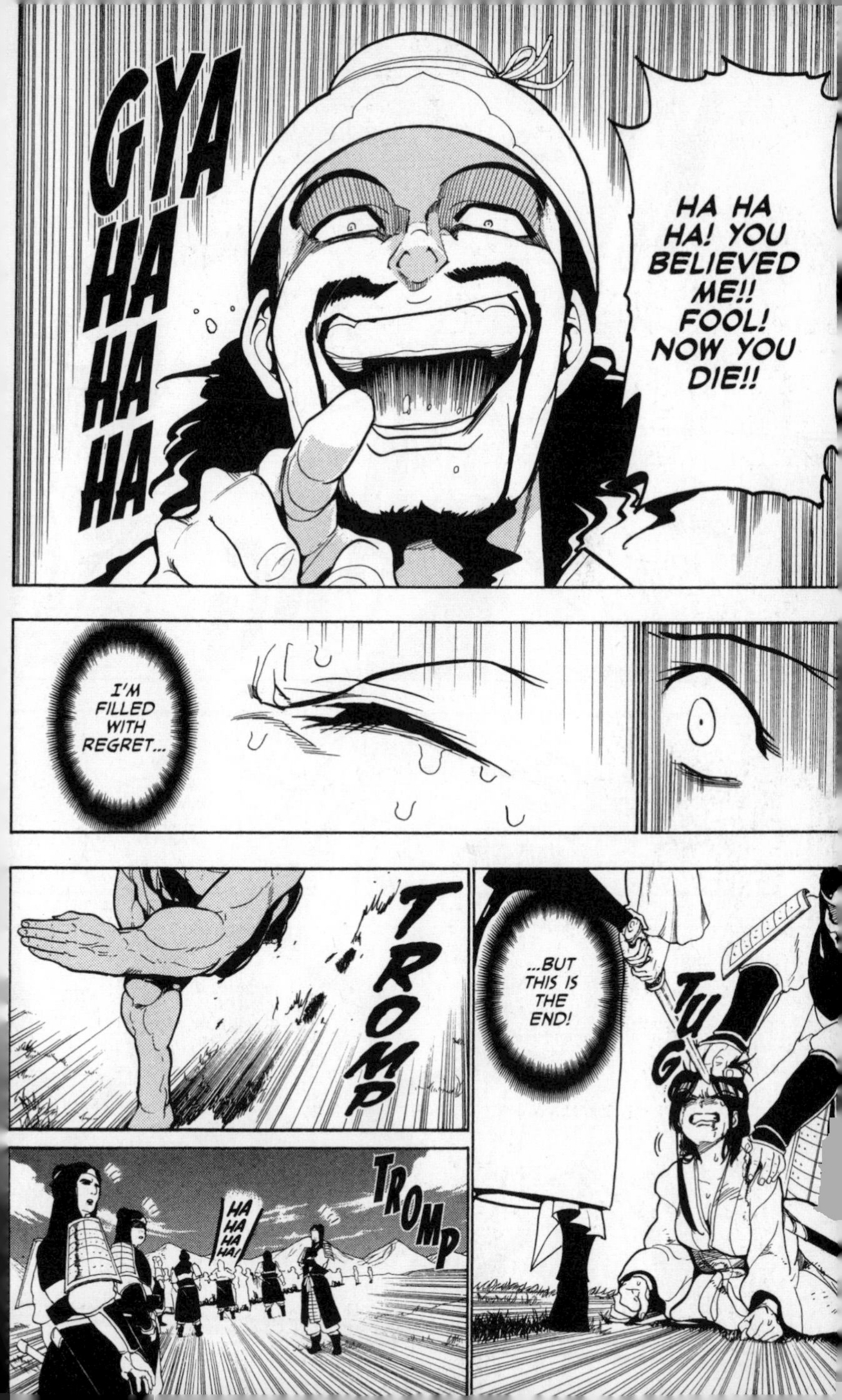
HA HA HA! YOU BELIEVED ME!! FOOL! NOW YOU DIE!!
GYA HA HA HA HA HA
I'M FILLED WITH REGRET...
...BUT THIS IS THE END!
TUG
TROMP
TROMP
HA HA HA HA!

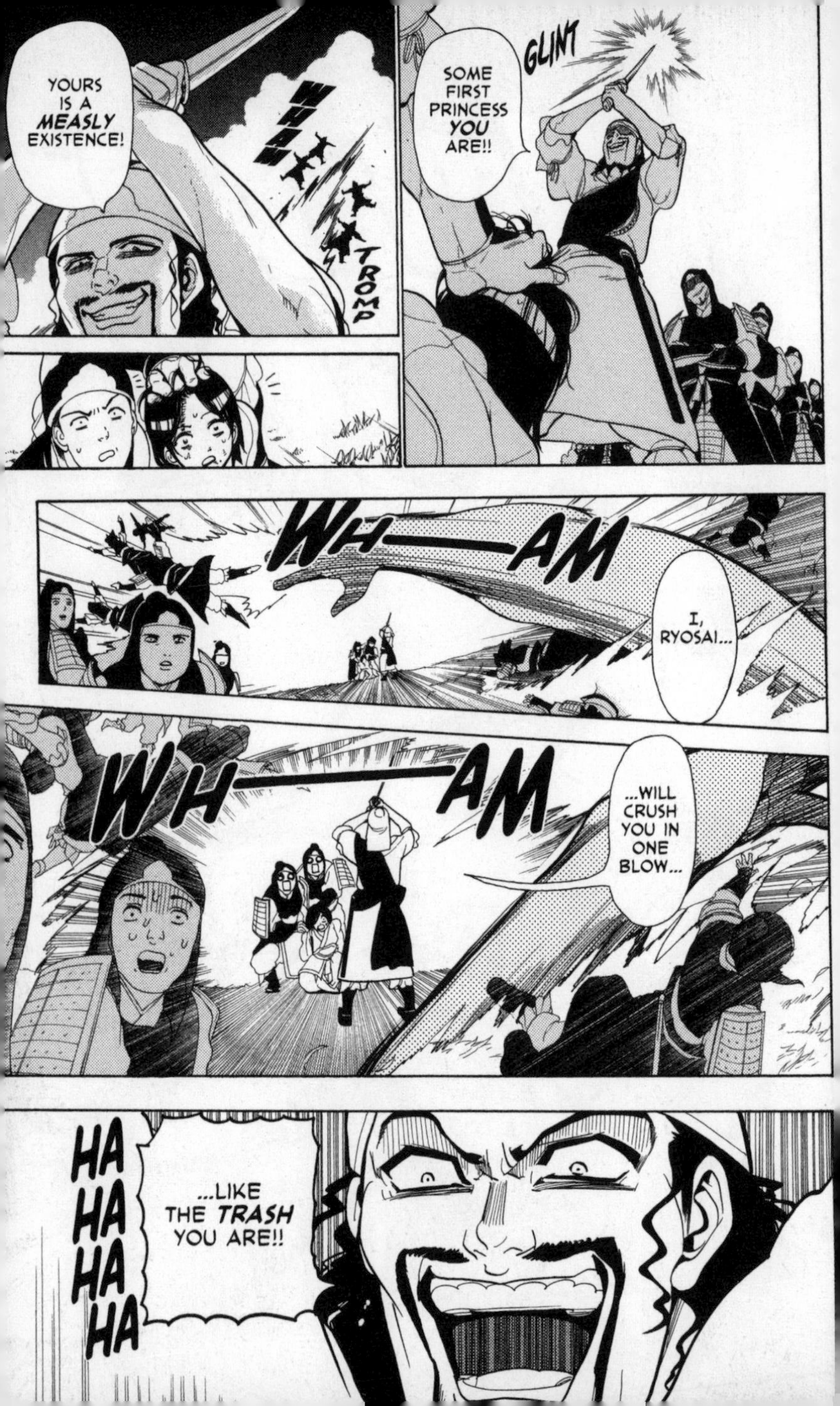
GLINT
SOME FIRST PRINCESS *YOU* ARE!!
YOURS IS A *MEASLY* EXISTENCE!
TROMP
WH—AM
I, RYOSAI...
WH—AM
...WILL CRUSH YOU IN ONE BLOW...
...LIKE THE *TRASH* YOU ARE!!
HA HA HA HA HA

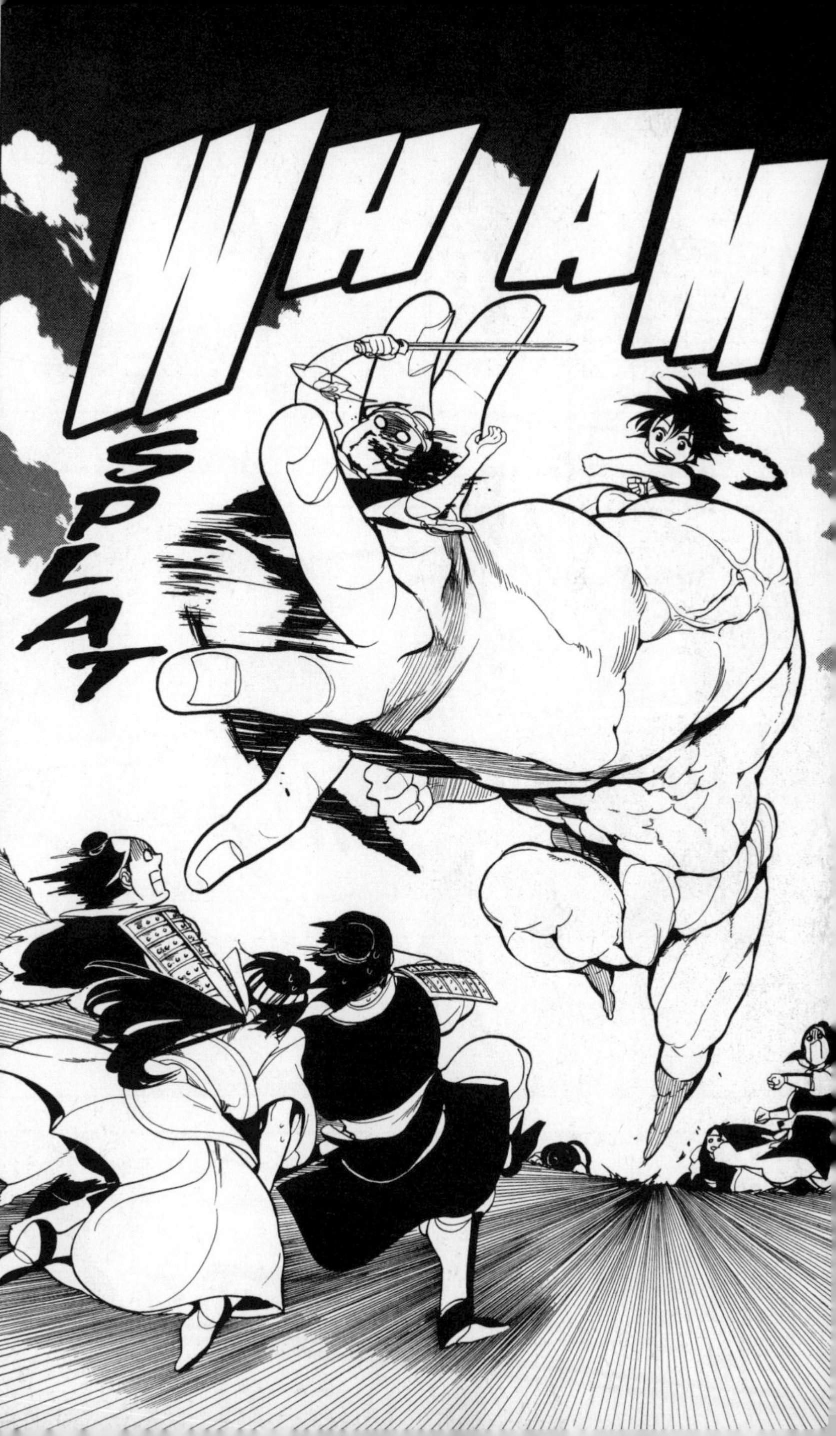
WHAM
SPLAT

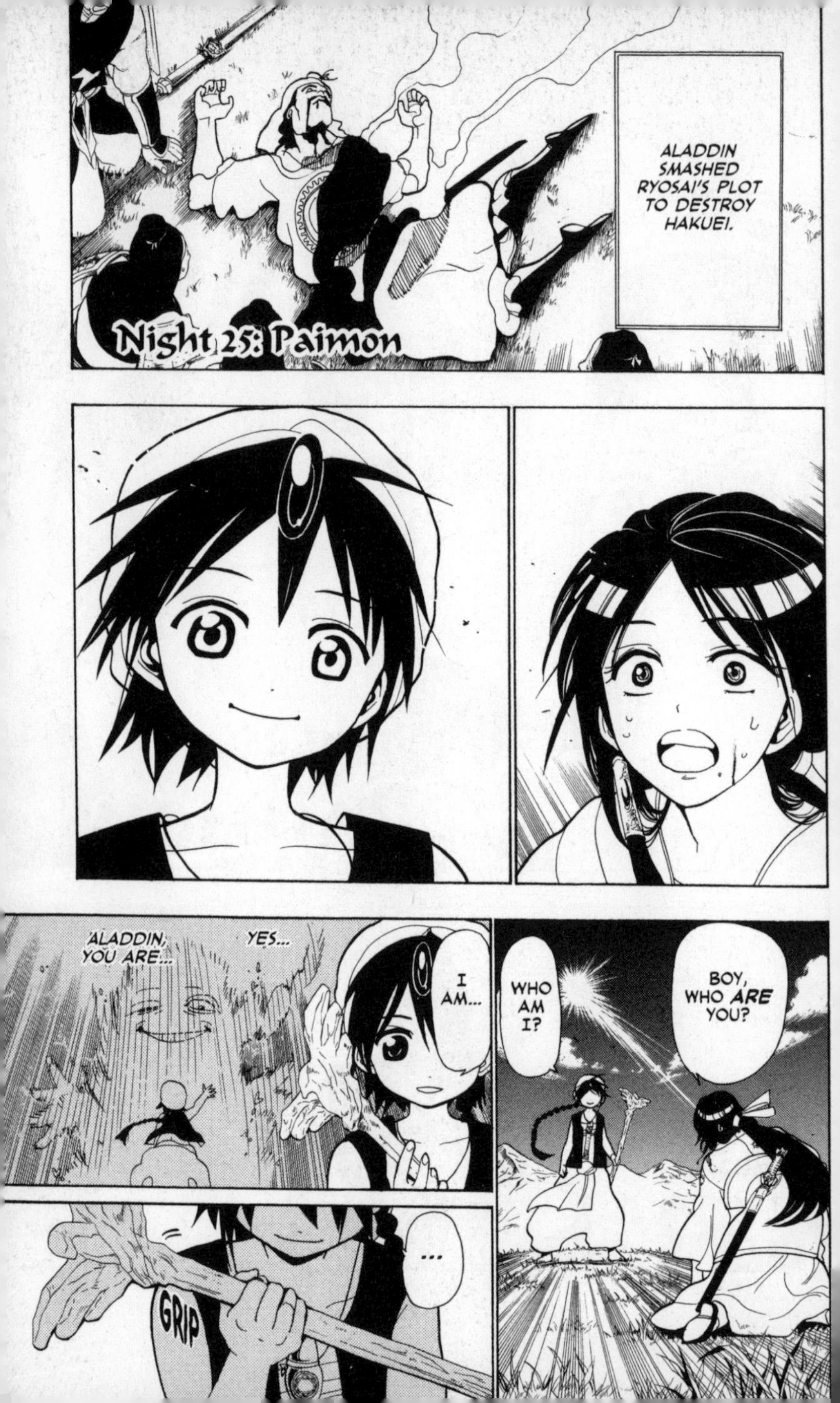
ALADDIN SMASHED RYOSAI'S PLOT TO DESTROY HAKUEI.
Night 25: Paimon
BOY, WHO ARE YOU?
WHO AM I?
I AM...
YES...
ALADDIN, YOU ARE...
...
GRIP

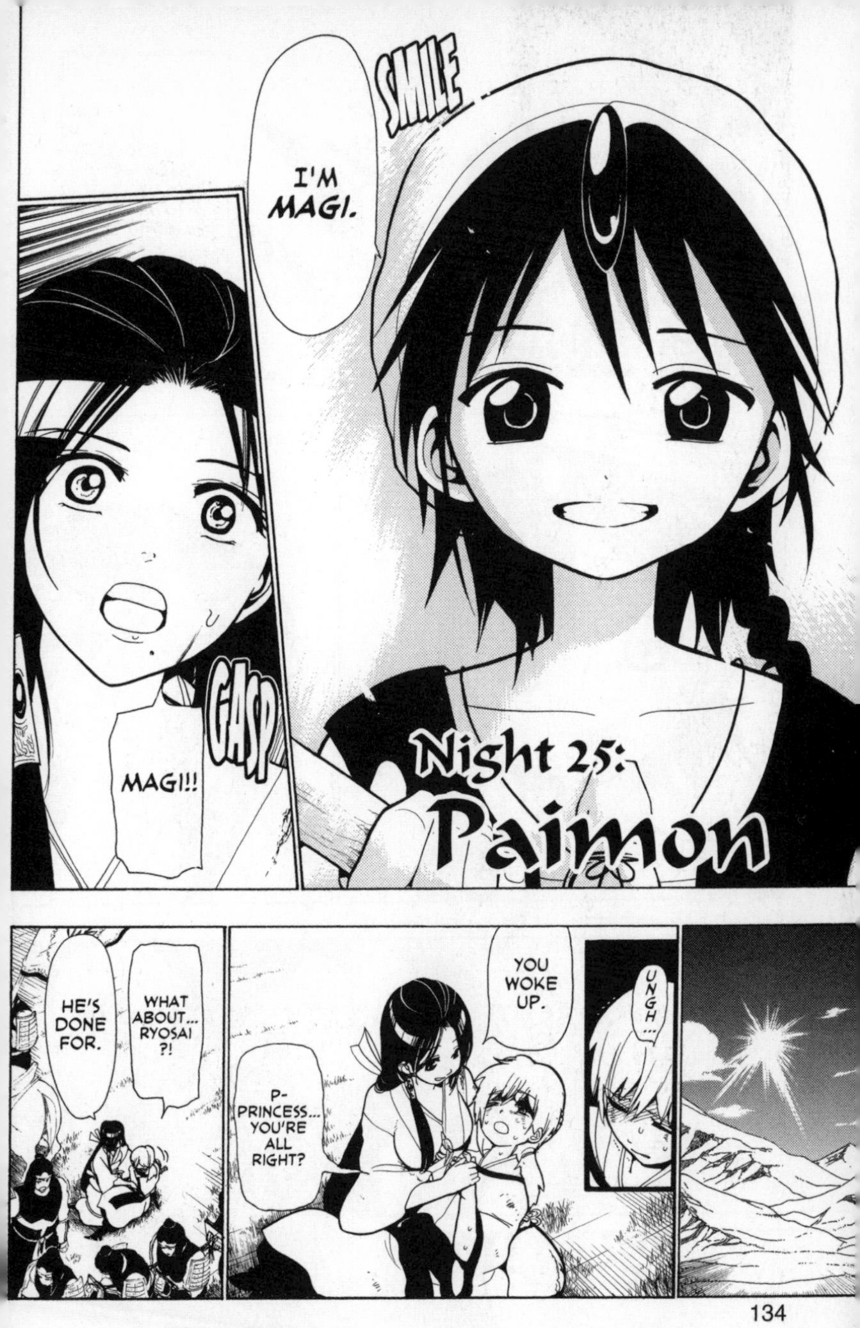
SMILE
I'M MAGI.
GASP
MAGI!!
Night 25: Paimon
UNGH...
YOU WOKE UP.
P-PRINCESS... YOU'RE ALL RIGHT?
WHAT ABOUT... RYOSAI?!
HE'S DONE FOR.

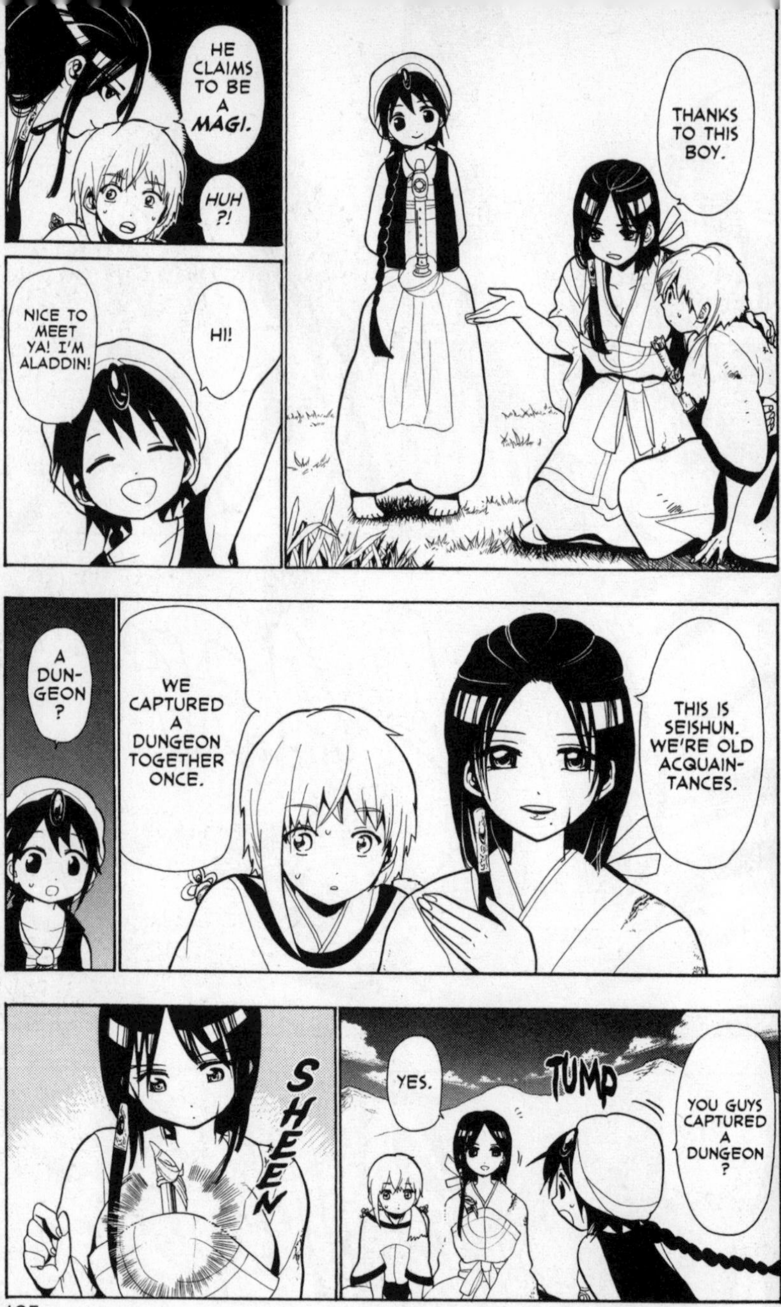
THANKS TO THIS BOY.
HE CLAIMS TO BE A MAGI.
HUH?!
HI!
NICE TO MEET YA! I'M ALADDIN!
THIS IS SEISHUN. WE'RE OLD ACQUAIN-TANCES.
WE CAPTURED A DUNGEON TOGETHER ONCE.
A DUN-GEON?
YOU GUYS CAPTURED A DUNGEON?
TUMP
YES.
SHEEN

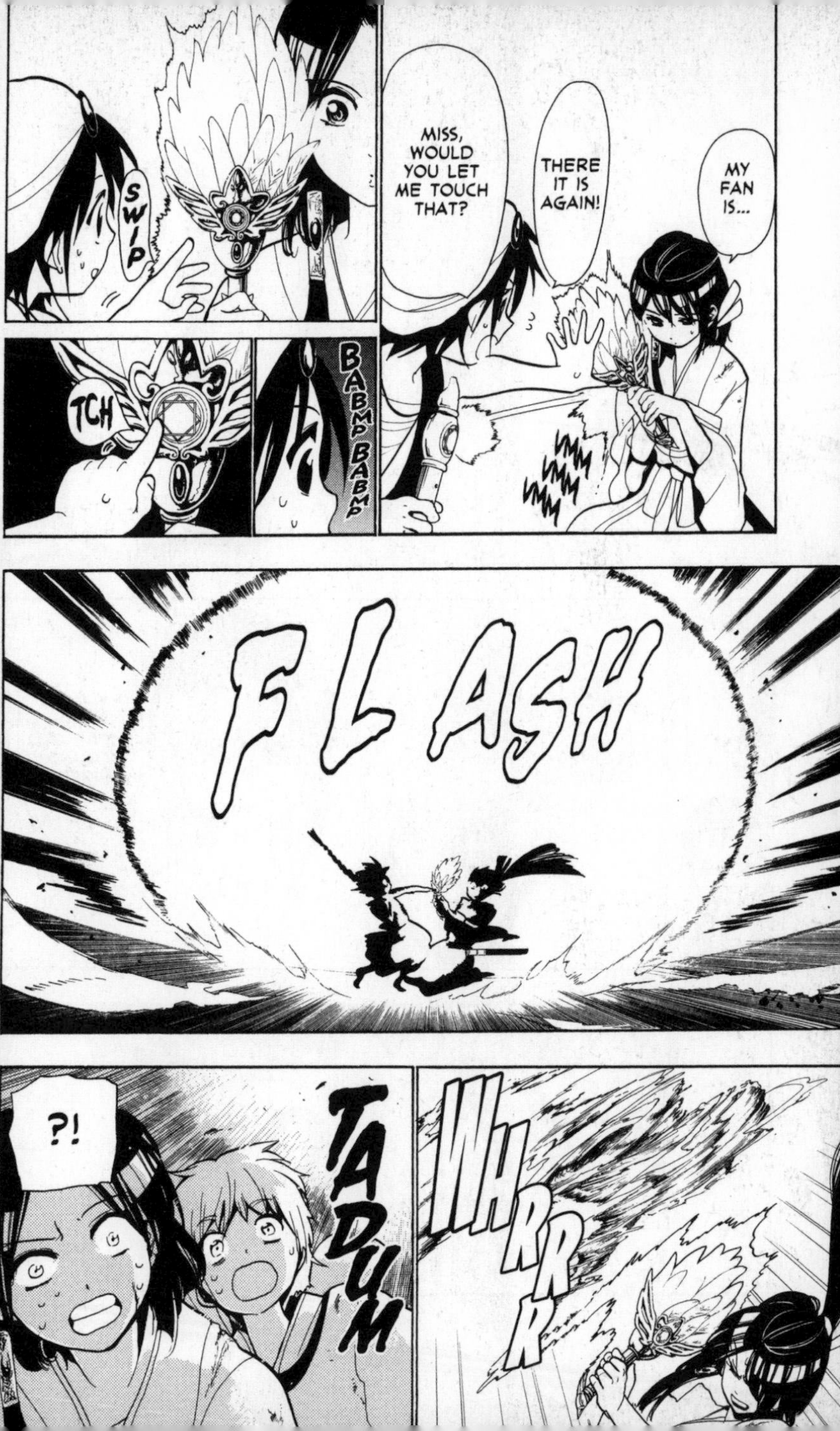
MY FAN IS...
THERE IT IS AGAIN!
MISS, WOULD YOU LET ME TOUCH THAT?
VMM VMM VMM
SWIP
BABMP BABMP
TCH
FLASH
WHRRRR
TADUM
?!

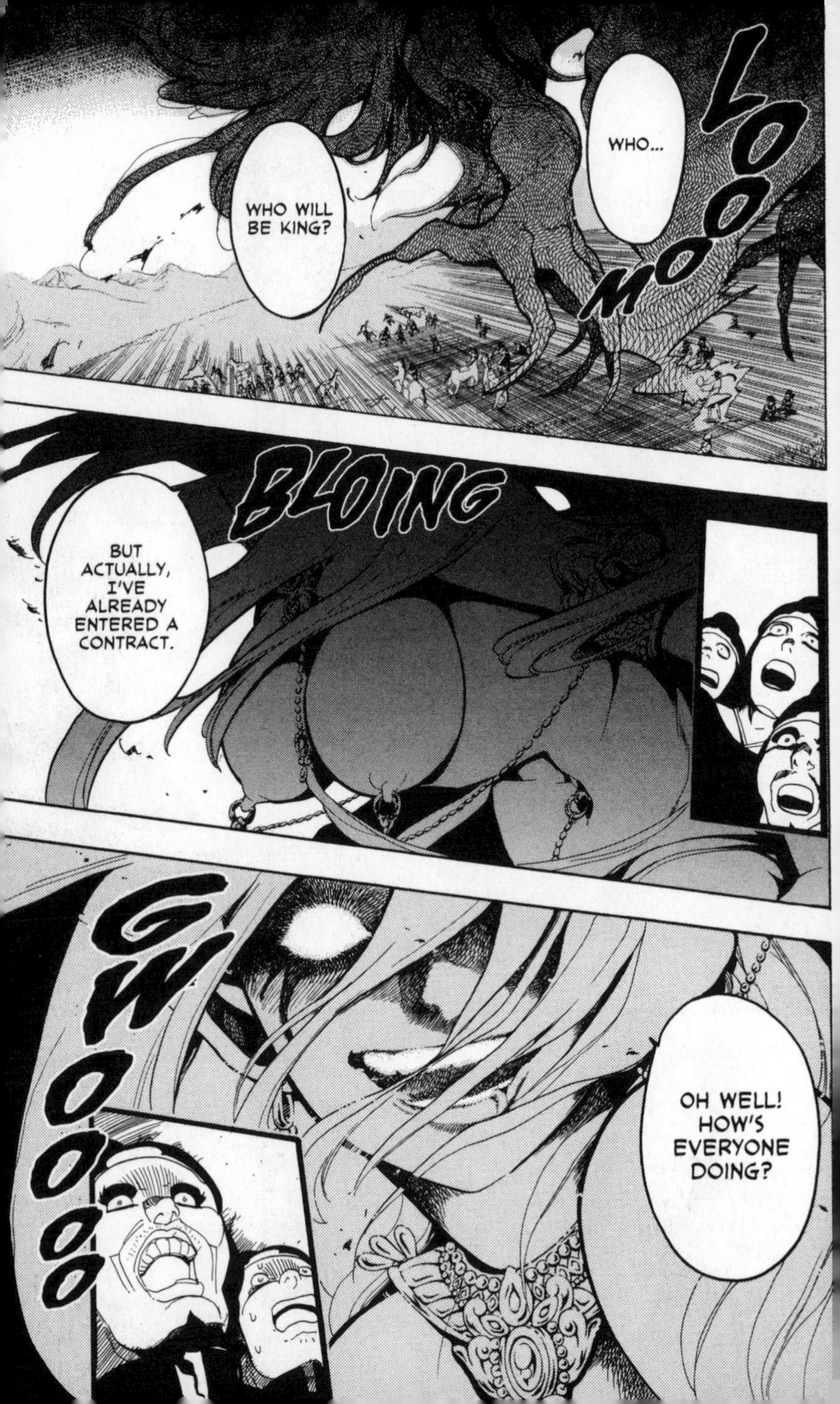
WHO...
LOOOOM
WHO WILL BE KING?
BLOING
BUT ACTUALLY, I'VE ALREADY ENTERED A CONTRACT.
OH WELL! HOW'S EVERYONE DOING?
GWOOOOOO

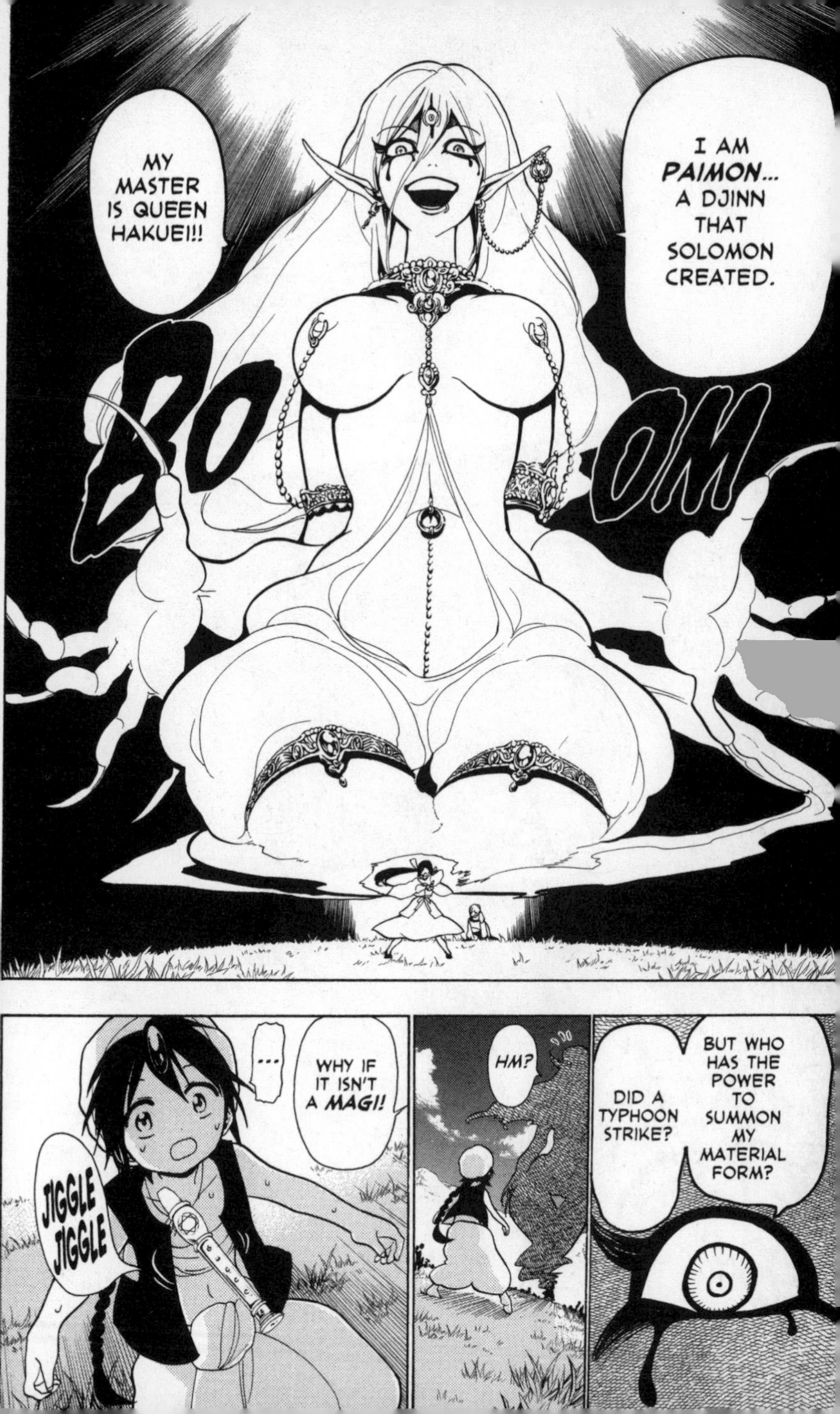
I AM PAIMON... A DJINN THAT SOLOMON CREATED.
MY MASTER IS QUEEN HAKUEI!!!
BOOM
BUT WHO HAS THE POWER TO SUMMON MY MATERIAL FORM?
DID A TYPHOON STRIKE?
HM?
WHY IF IT ISN'T A MAGI!
...
JIGGLE JIGGLE

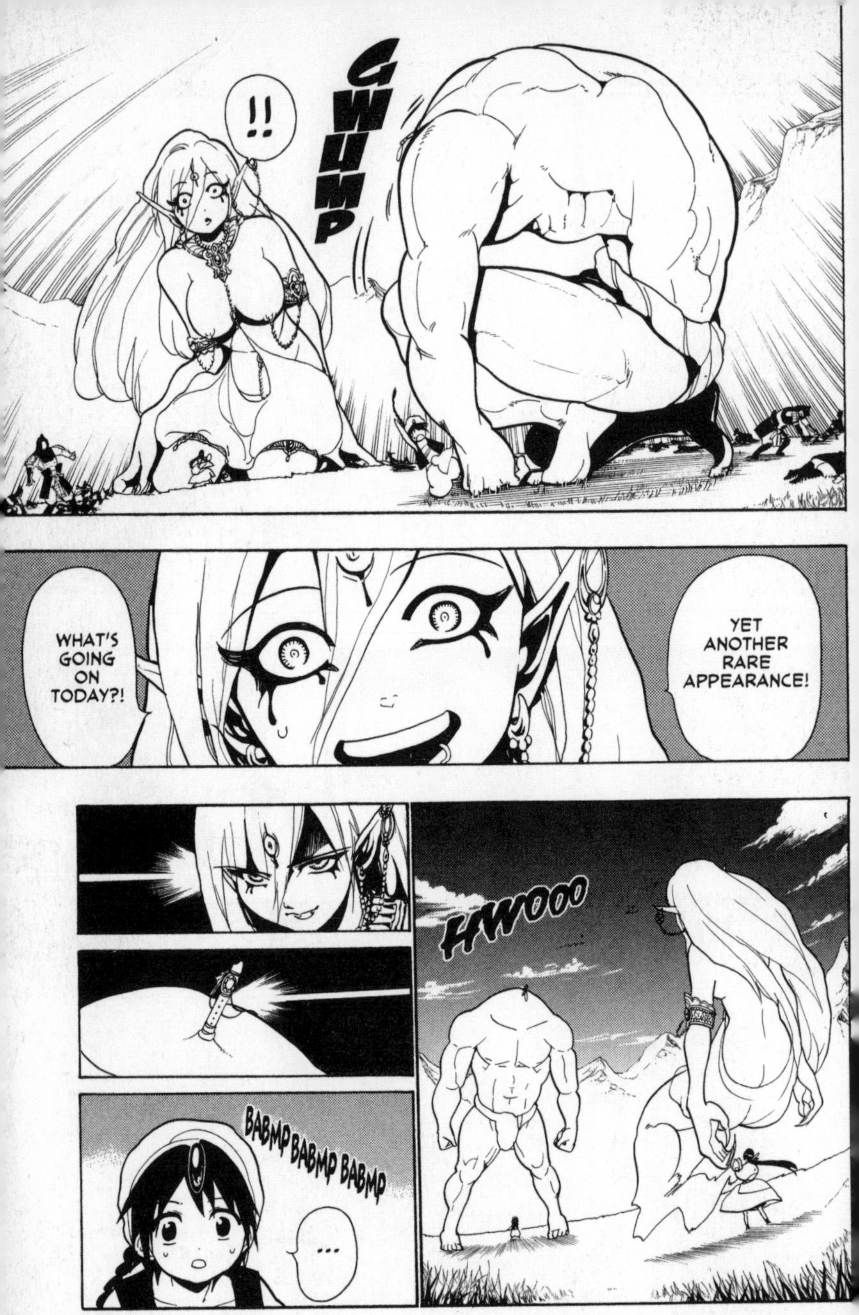
GWUMP
!!
YET ANOTHER RARE APPEARANCE!
WHAT'S GOING ON TODAY?!
HWOOO
BABMP BABMP BABMP
...

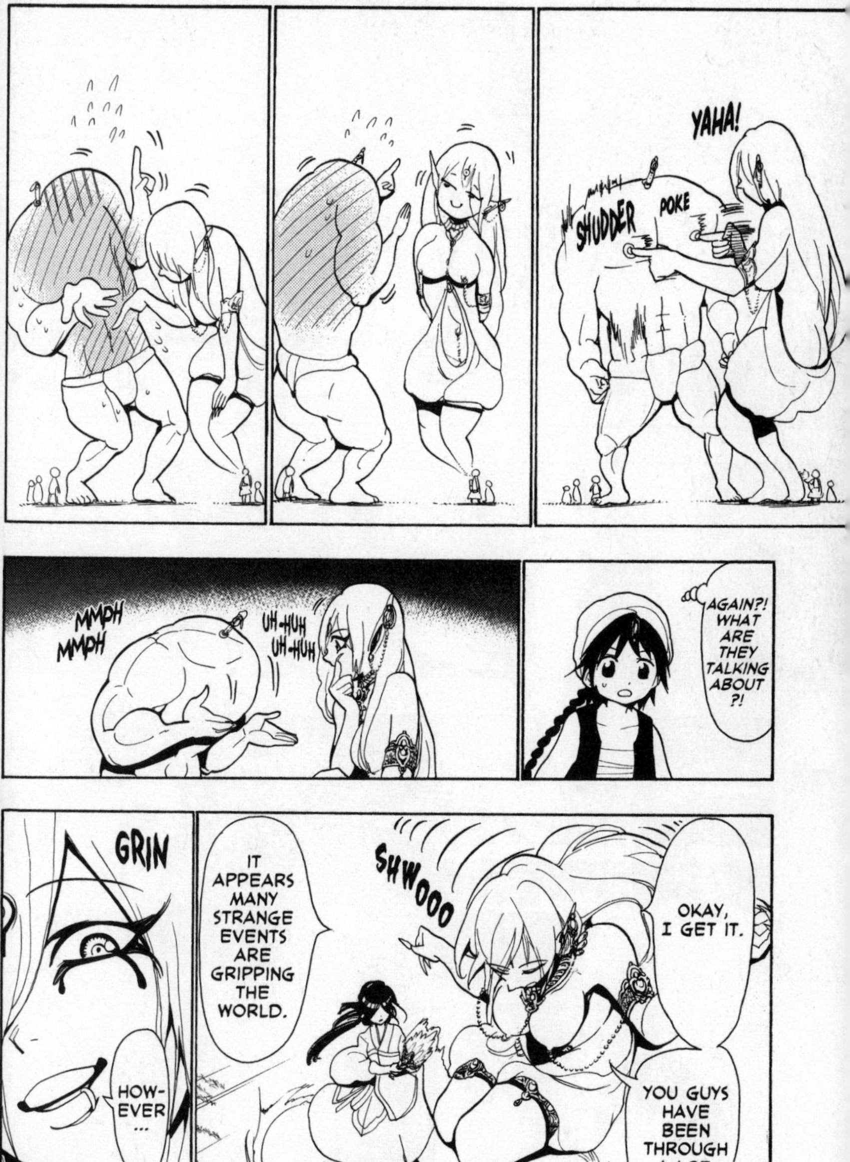
YAHA!
SHUDDER
POKE
AGAIN?! WHAT ARE THEY TALKING ABOUT ?!
UH-HUH UH-HUH
MMPH MMPH
OKAY, I GET IT.
YOU GUYS HAVE BEEN THROUGH A LOT.
SHWOOO
IT APPEARS MANY STRANGE EVENTS ARE GRIPPING THE WORLD.
GRIN
HOW-EVER ...

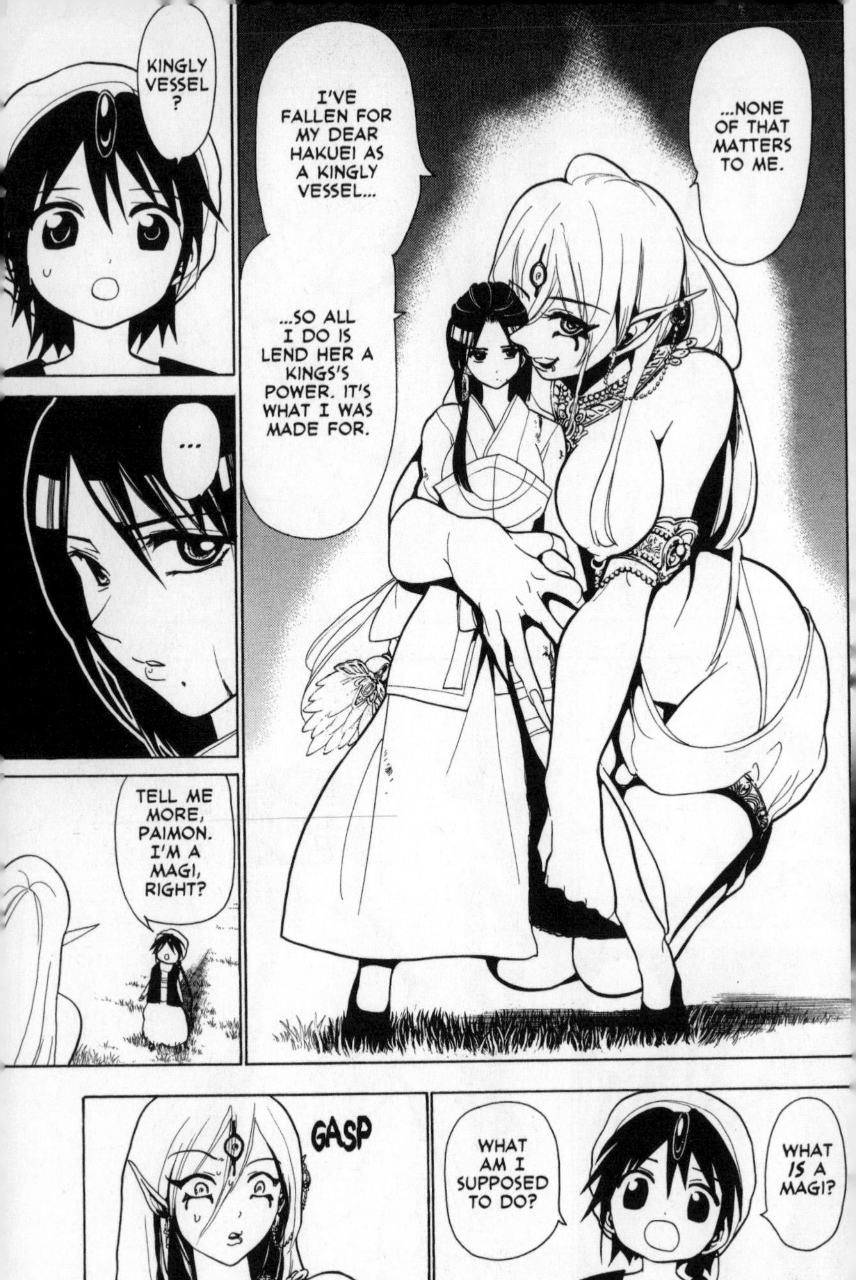
...NONE OF THAT MATTERS TO ME.
I'VE FALLEN FOR MY DEAR HAKUEI AS A KINGLY VESSEL...
...SO ALL I DO IS LEND HER A KINGS'S POWER. IT'S WHAT I WAS MADE FOR.
KINGLY VESSEL?
...
TELL ME MORE, PAIMON. I'M A MAGI, RIGHT?
WHAT *IS* A MAGI?
WHAT AM I SUPPOSED TO DO?
GASP

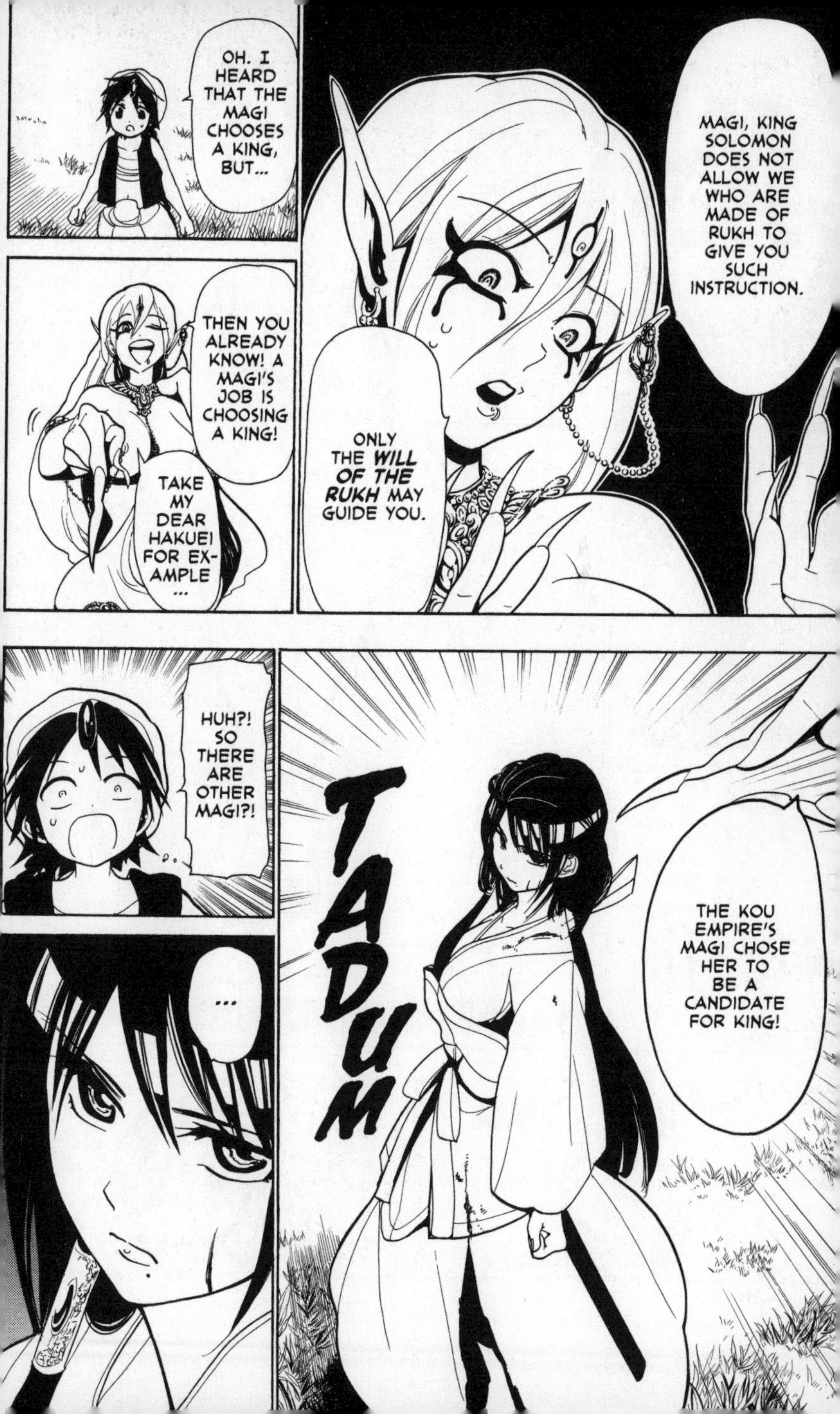

MAGI, KING SOLOMON DOES NOT ALLOW WE WHO ARE MADE OF RUKH TO GIVE YOU SUCH INSTRUCTION.
ONLY THE WILL OF THE RUKH MAY GUIDE YOU.
OH. I HEARD THAT THE MAGI CHOOSES A KING, BUT...
THEN YOU ALREADY KNOW! A MAGI'S JOB IS CHOOSING A KING!
TAKE MY DEAR HAKUEI FOR EX- AMPLE ...
THE KOU EMPIRE'S MAGI CHOSE HER TO BE A CANDIDATE FOR KING!
TADUM
HUH?! SO THERE ARE OTHER MAGI?!
...

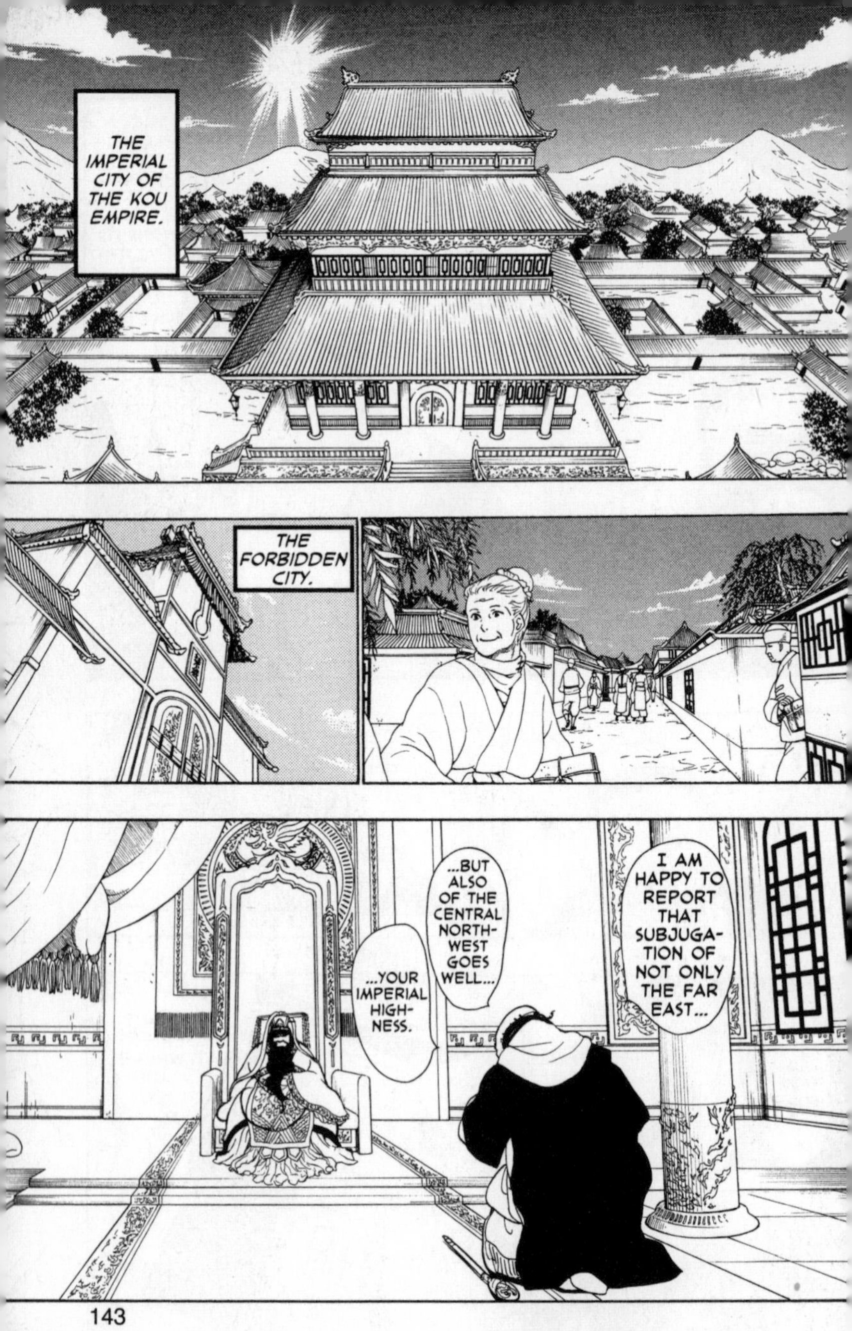
THE IMPERIAL CITY OF THE KOU EMPIRE.
THE FORBIDDEN CITY.
I AM HAPPY TO REPORT THAT SUBJUGATION OF NOT ONLY THE FAR EAST...
...BUT ALSO OF THE CENTRAL NORTH-WEST GOES WELL...
...YOUR IMPERIAL HIGHNESS.

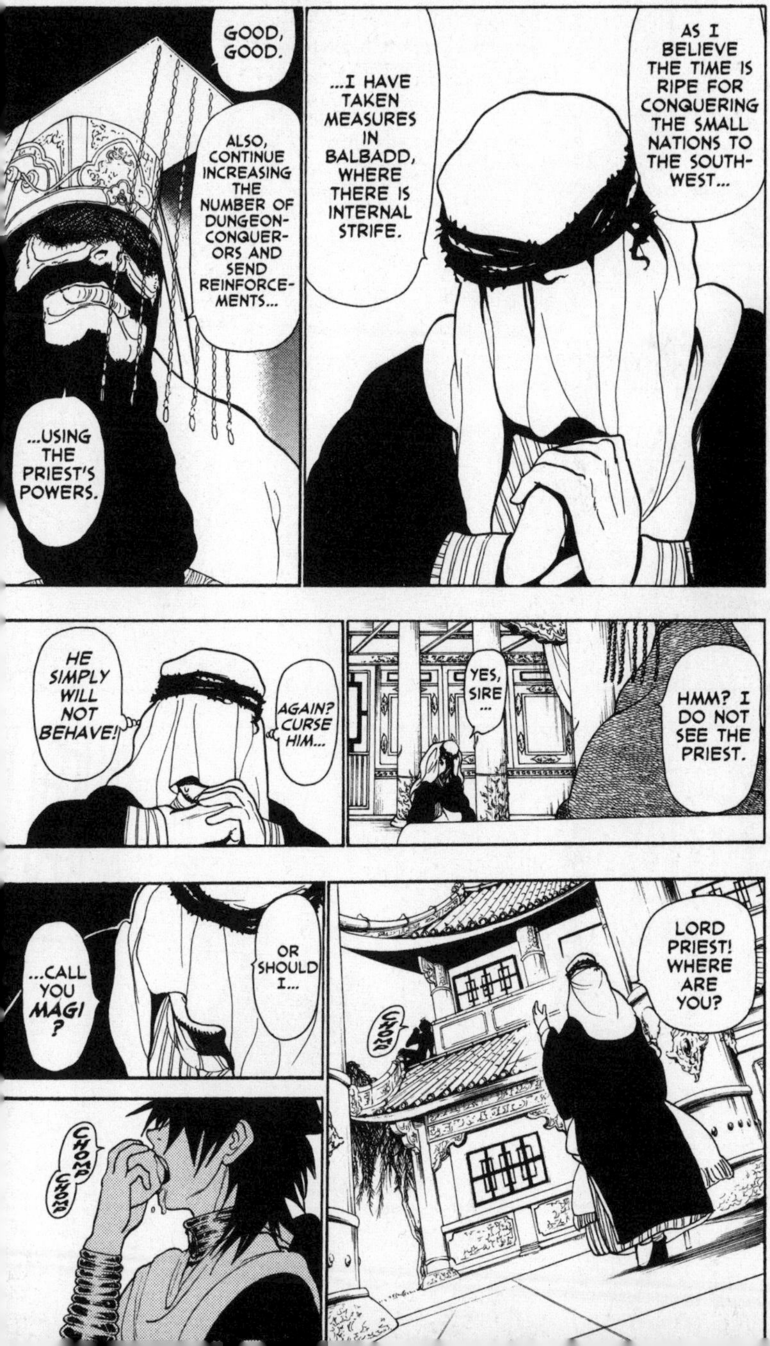
AS I BELIEVE THE TIME IS RIPE FOR CONQUERING THE SMALL NATIONS TO THE SOUTHWEST...
...I HAVE TAKEN MEASURES IN BALBADD, WHERE THERE IS INTERNAL STRIFE.
GOOD, GOOD.
ALSO, CONTINUE INCREASING THE NUMBER OF DUNGEON-CONQUERORS AND SEND REINFORCEMENTS...
...USING THE PRIEST'S POWERS.
HMM? I DO NOT SEE THE PRIEST.
YES, SIRE...
AGAIN? CURSE HIM...
HE SIMPLY WILL NOT BEHAVE!
LORD PRIEST! WHERE ARE YOU?
CHOMP
OR SHOULD I...
...CALL YOU *MAGI*?
CHOMP CHOMP

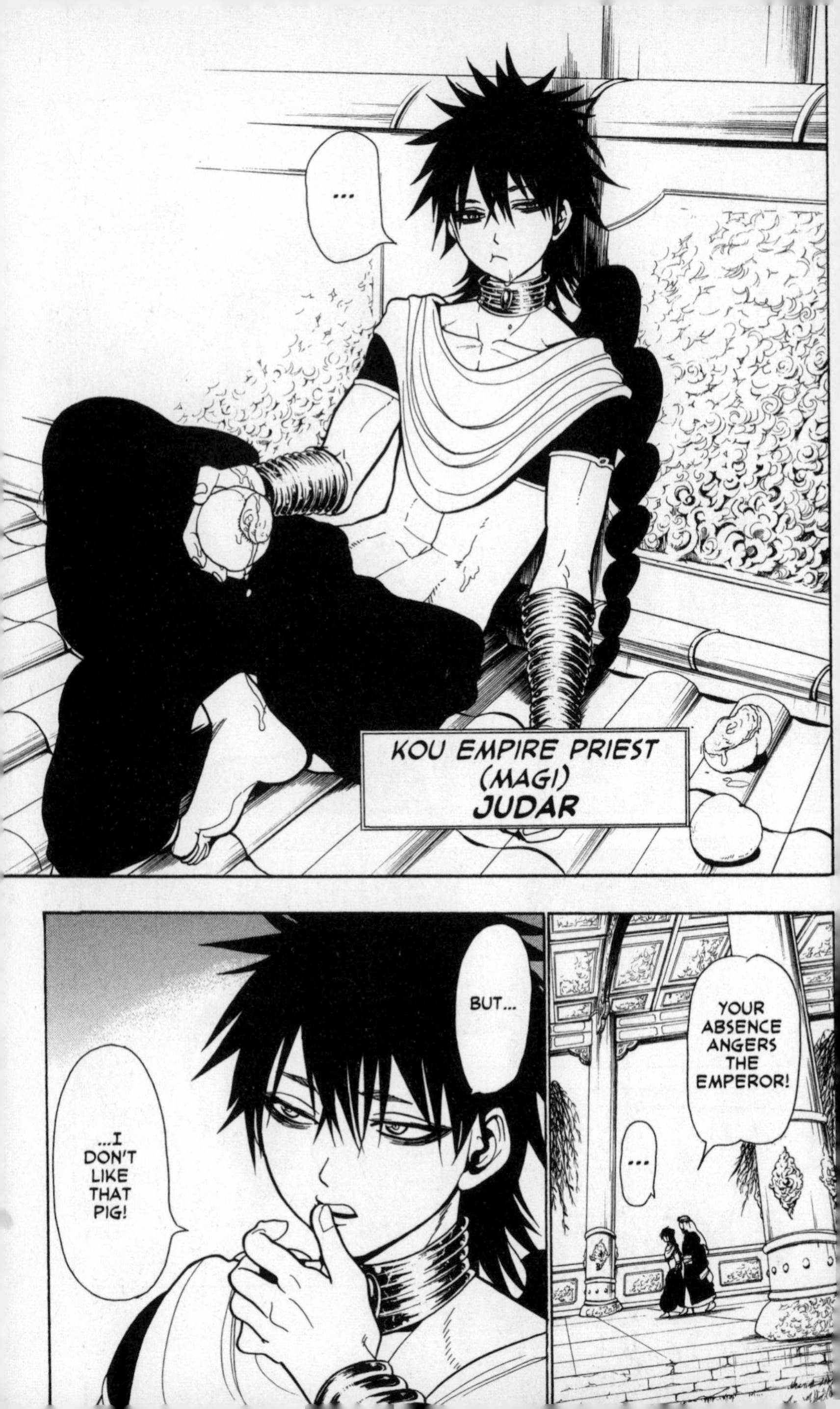
...
KOU EMPIRE PRIEST (MAGI) JUDAR
YOUR ABSENCE ANGERS THE EMPEROR!
...
BUT...
...I DON'T LIKE THAT PIG!

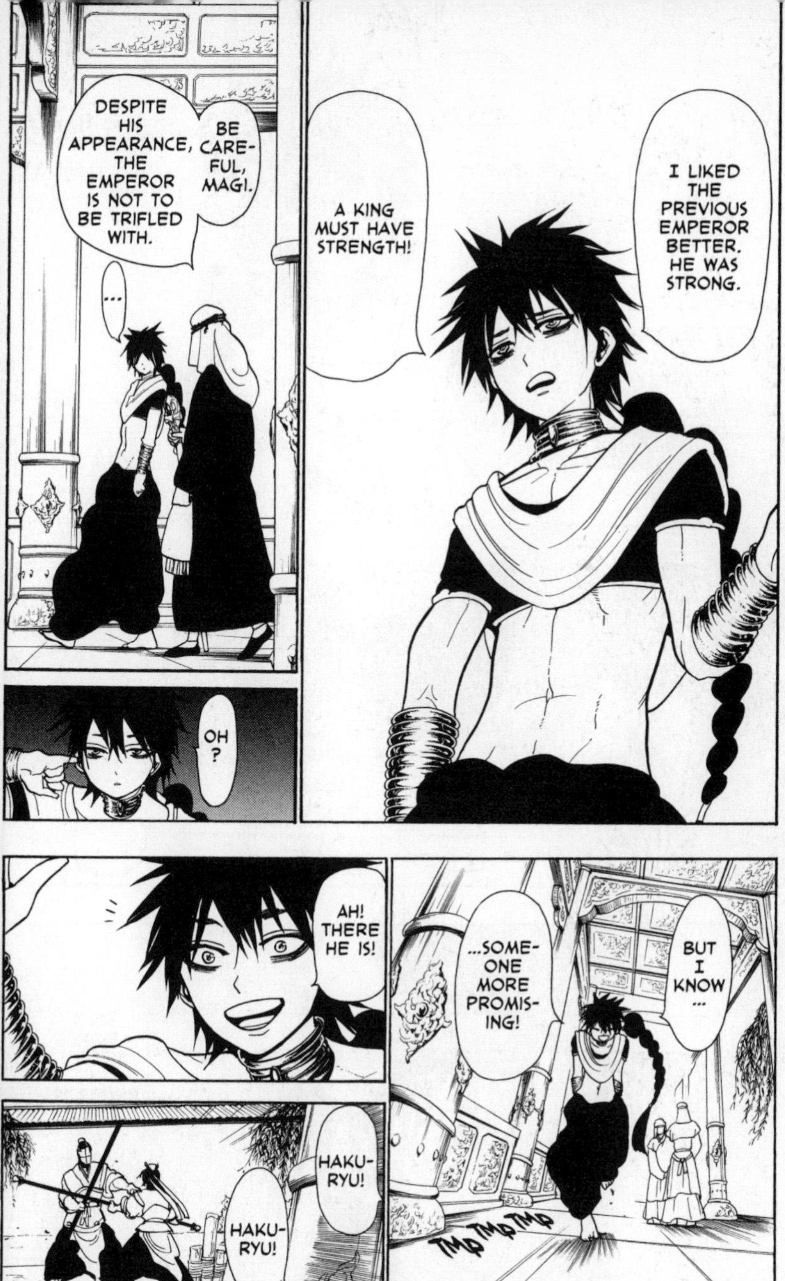
I LIKED THE PREVIOUS EMPEROR BETTER. HE WAS STRONG.
A KING MUST HAVE STRENGTH!
BE CARE-FUL, MAGI.
DESPITE HIS APPEARANCE, THE EMPEROR IS NOT TO BE TRIFLED WITH.
...
OH?
BUT I KNOW...
...SOME-ONE MORE PROMIS-ING!
TMP TMP TMP TMP
AH! THERE HE IS!
HAKU-RYU!
HAKU-RYU!

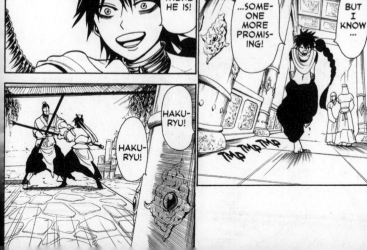

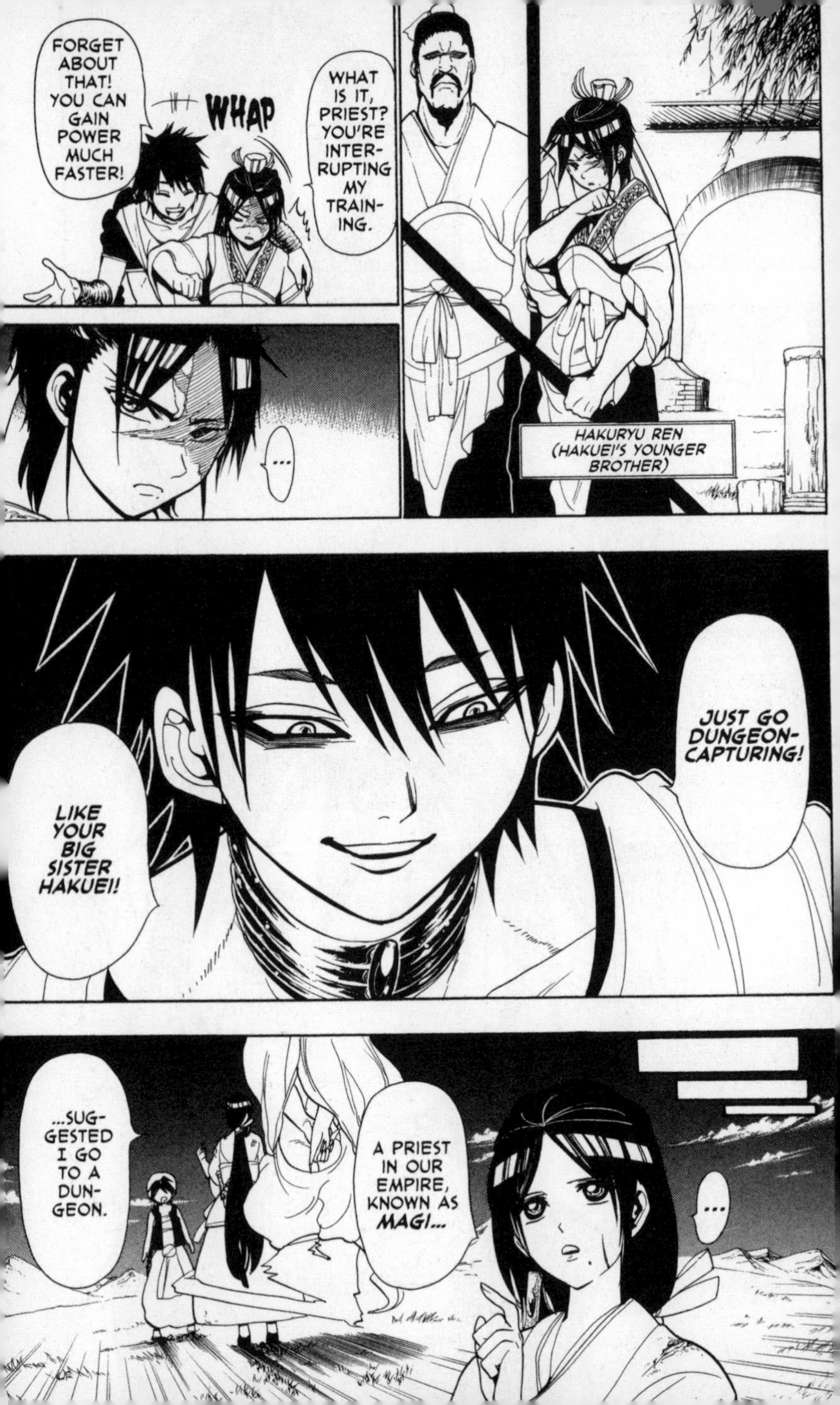
HAKURYU REN (HAKUEI'S YOUNGER BROTHER)
WHAT IS IT, PRIEST? YOU'RE INTER-RUPTING MY TRAIN-ING.
FORGET ABOUT THAT! YOU CAN GAIN POWER MUCH FASTER!
WHAP
...
JUST GO DUNGEON-CAPTURING!
LIKE YOUR BIG SISTER HAKUEI!
...
A PRIEST IN OUR EMPIRE, KNOWN AS MAGI...
...SUG-GESTED I GO TO A DUN-GEON.

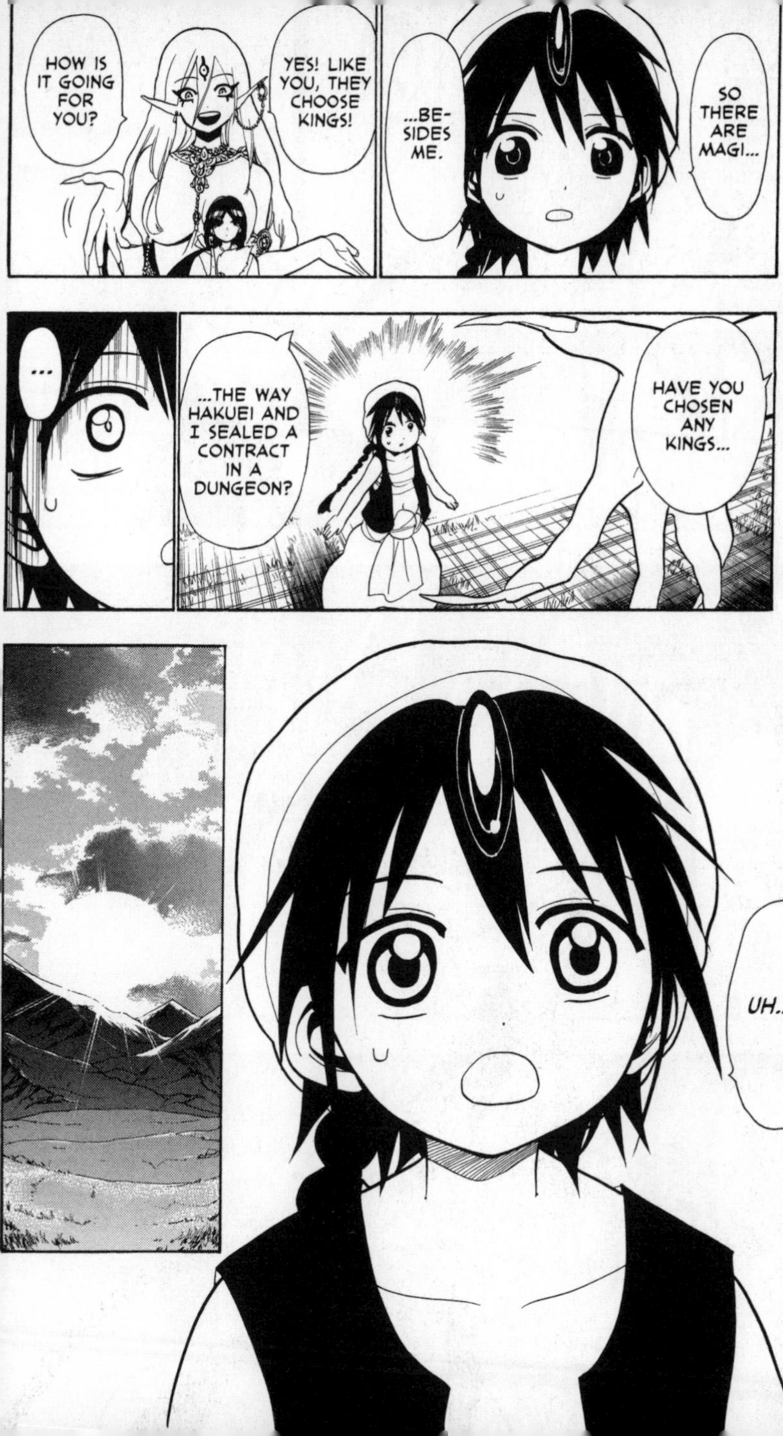
SO THERE ARE MAGI...
...BE-SIDES ME.
YES! LIKE YOU, THEY CHOOSE KINGS!
HOW IS IT GOING FOR YOU?
HAVE YOU CHOSEN ANY KINGS...
...THE WAY HAKUEI AND I SEALED A CONTRACT IN A DUNGEON?
...
UH...

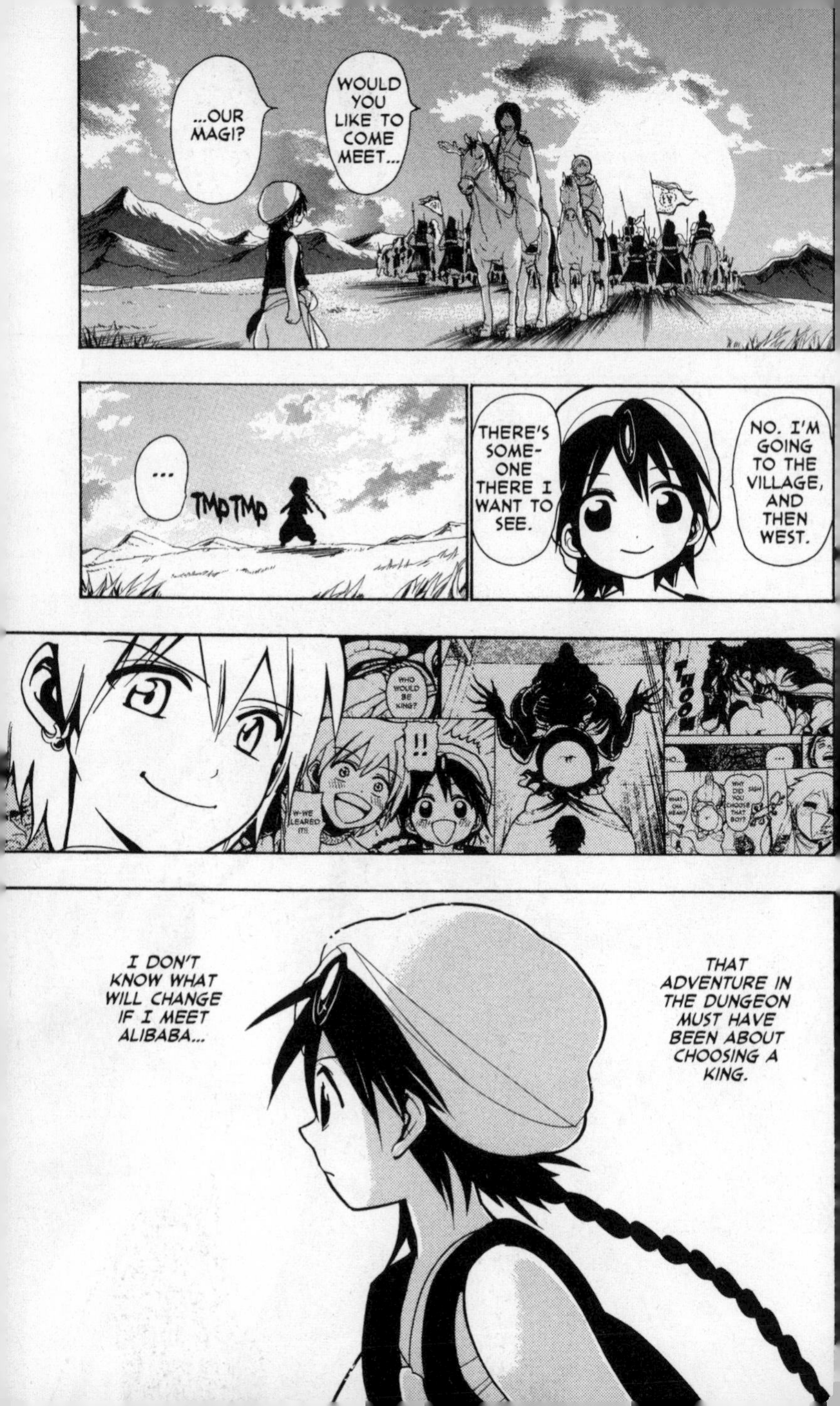
WOULD YOU LIKE TO COME MEET...
...OUR MAGI?
NO. I'M GOING TO THE VILLAGE, AND THEN WEST.
THERE'S SOME-ONE THERE I WANT TO SEE.
...
TMP TMP
THOOM
...
WHY DID YOU CHOOSE THAT BOY?
SIGH
WHAT-CHA MEAN?
WHO...
WHO WOULD BE KING?
!!
W-WE LEARED IT!
THAT ADVENTURE IN THE DUNGEON MUST HAVE BEEN ABOUT CHOOSING A KING.
I DON'T KNOW WHAT WILL CHANGE IF I MEET ALIBABA...

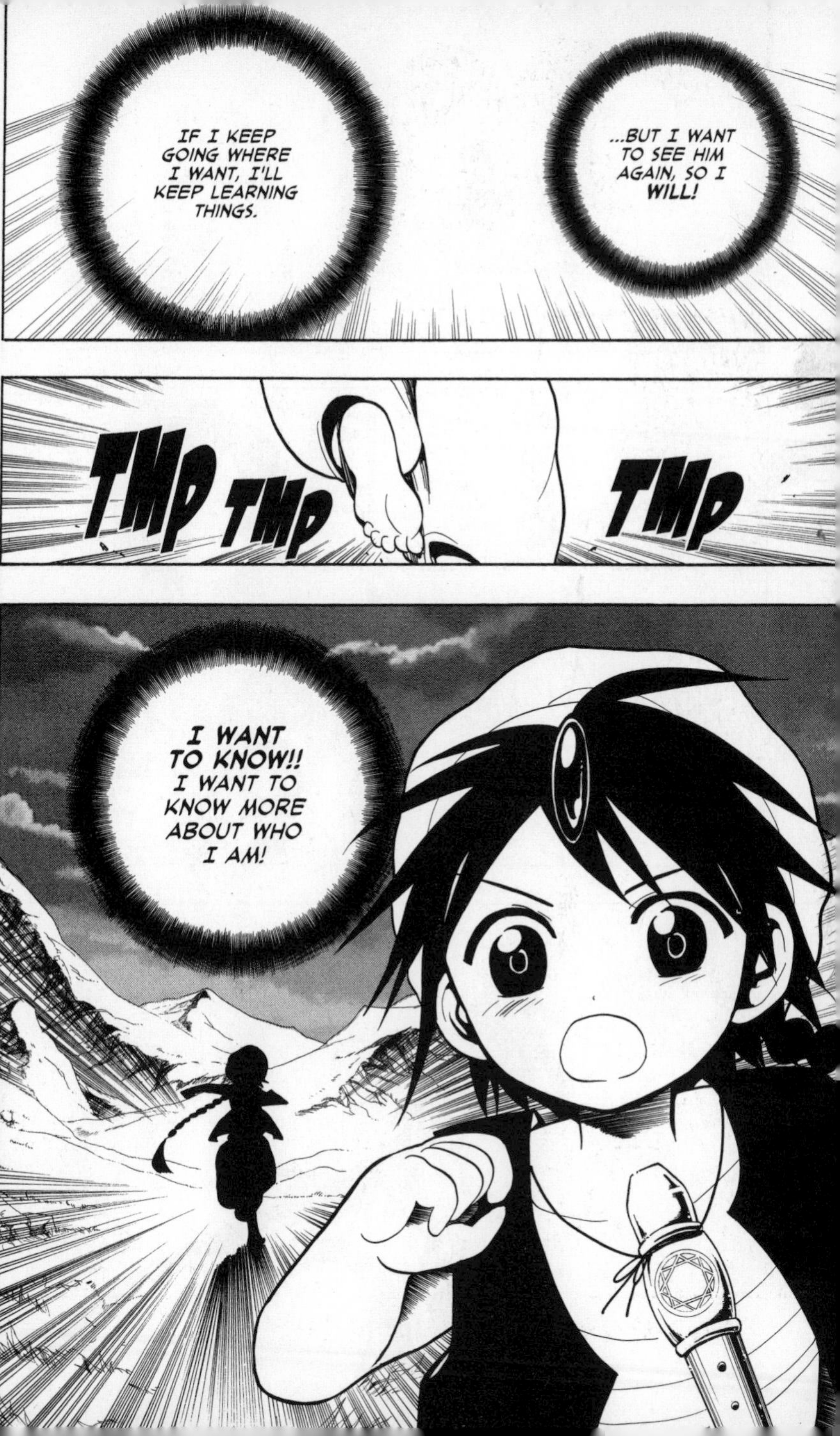
...BUT I WANT TO SEE HIM AGAIN, SO I WILL!
IF I KEEP GOING WHERE I WANT, I'LL KEEP LEARNING THINGS.
TMP
TMP TMP
I WANT TO KNOW!! I WANT TO KNOW MORE ABOUT WHO I AM!

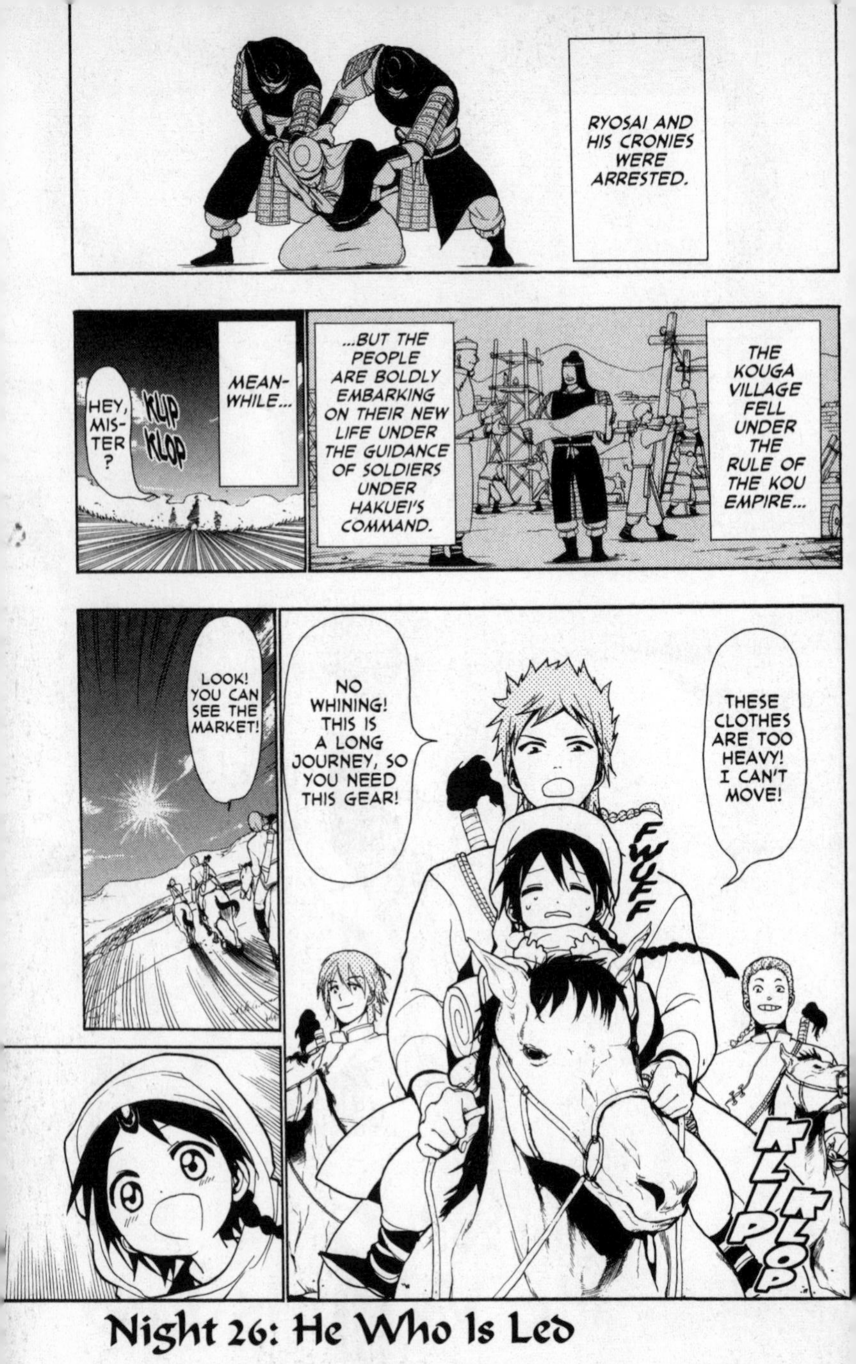
RYOSAI AND HIS CRONIES WERE ARRESTED.
THE KOUGA VILLAGE FELL UNDER THE RULE OF THE KOU EMPIRE...
...BUT THE PEOPLE ARE BOLDLY EMBARKING ON THEIR NEW LIFE UNDER THE GUIDANCE OF SOLDIERS UNDER HAKUEI'S COMMAND.
MEAN-WHILE...
KLIP KLOP
HEY, MIS-TER?
THESE CLOTHES ARE TOO HEAVY! I CAN'T MOVE!
FWUFF
NO WHINING! THIS IS A LONG JOURNEY, SO YOU NEED THIS GEAR!
KLIP KLOP
LOOK! YOU CAN SEE THE MARKET!

Night 26: He Who Is Led

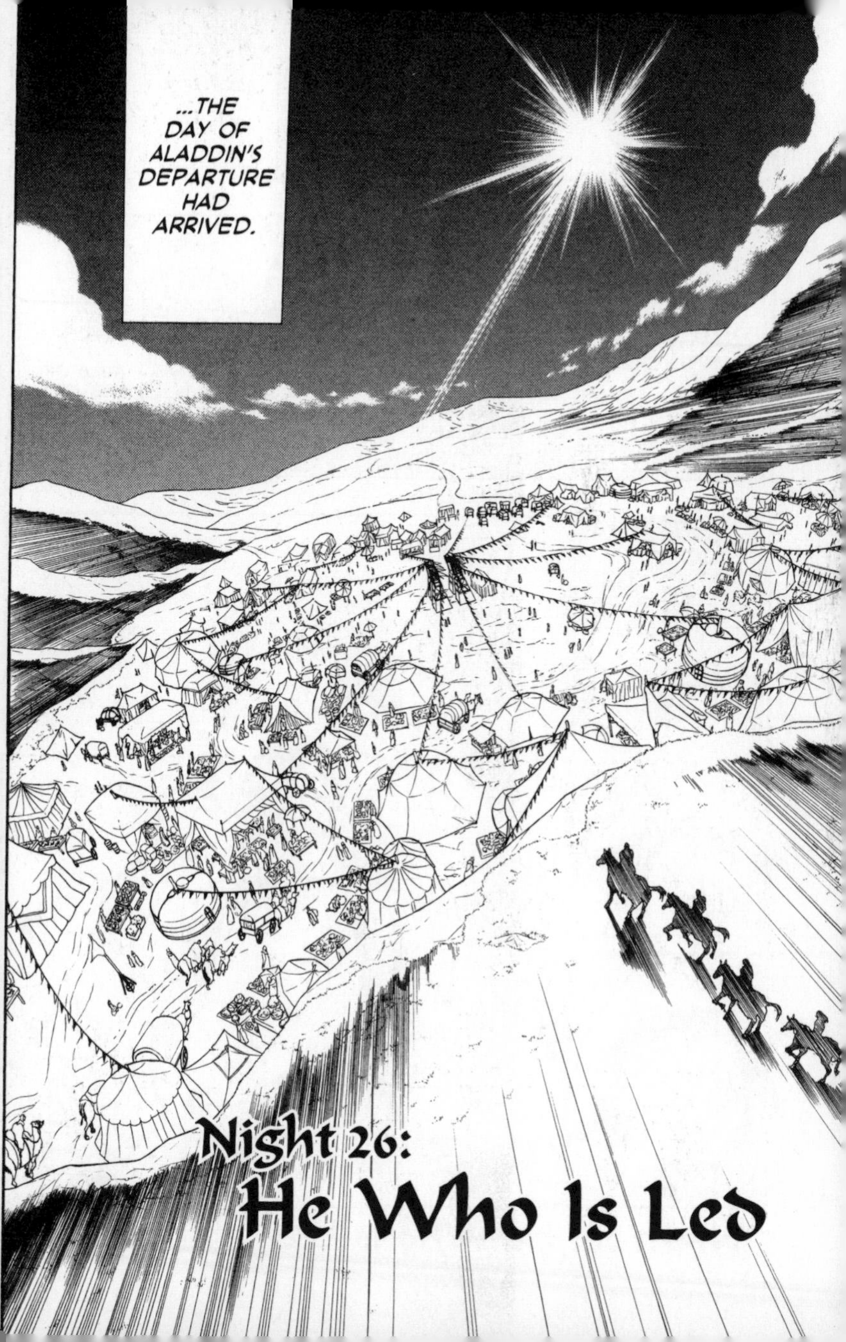
...THE DAY OF ALADDIN'S DEPARTURE HAD ARRIVED.
Night 26:
He Who Is Led

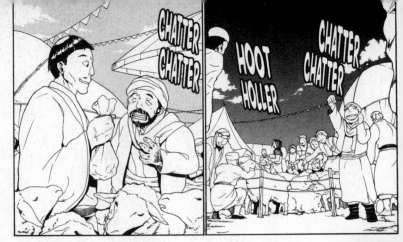

CHATTER CHATTER
HOOT HOLLER
CHATTER CHATTER
TADUM
YOU MEAN *THIS* BOY?
PLEASE TAKE HIM TO QISHAN. HE CAN WORK FOR YOU!
HMM. ONE OR TWO EXTRA RUNTS WON'T HURT.
BUT CROSSING THE DESERT IS HARD.
CAN YOU HANDLE IT, BOY?

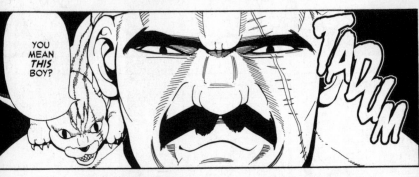

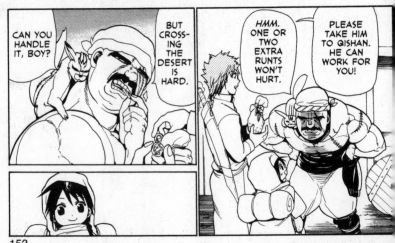

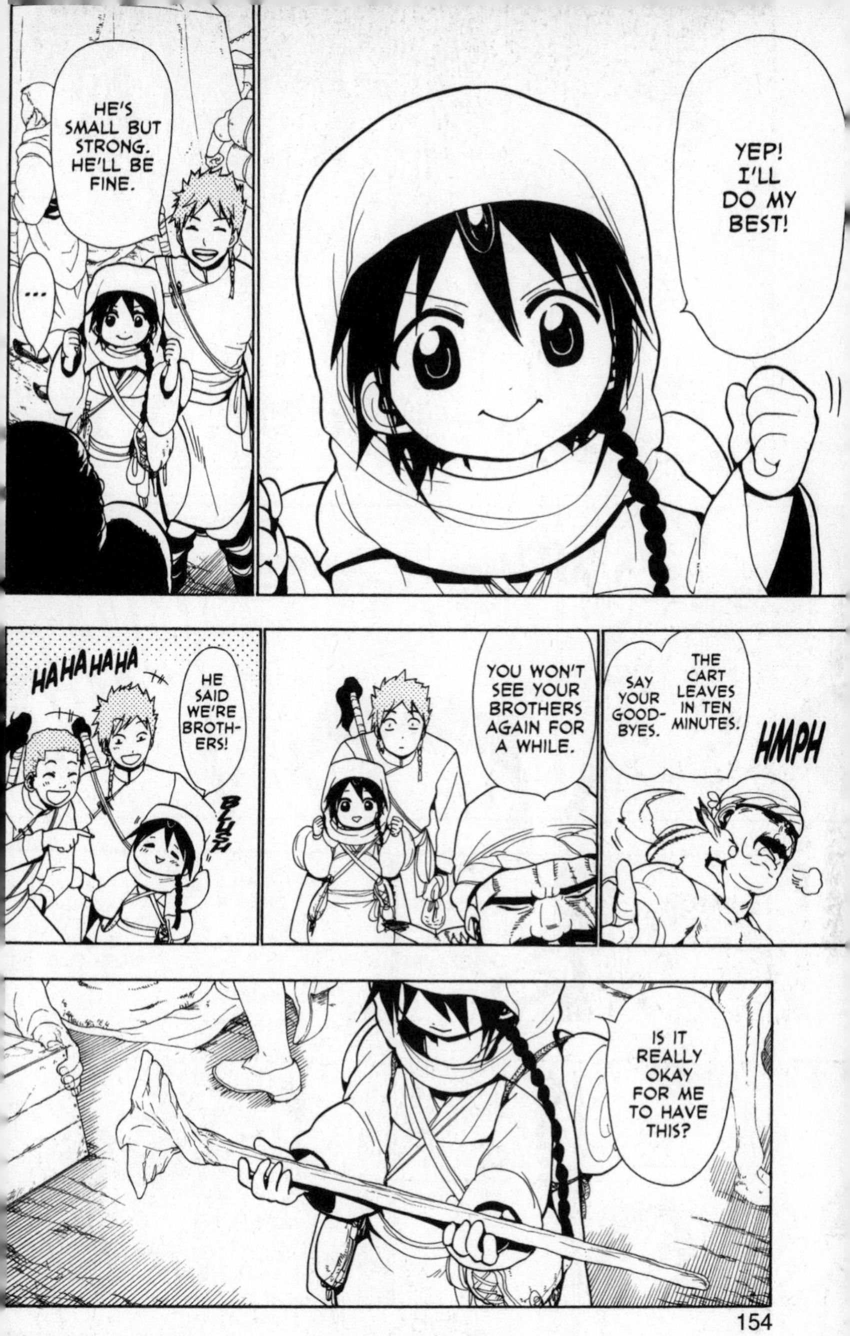
YEP! I'LL DO MY BEST!
HE'S SMALL BUT STRONG. HE'LL BE FINE.
...
THE CART LEAVES IN TEN MINUTES.
SAY YOUR GOOD-BYES.
HMPH
YOU WON'T SEE YOUR BROTHERS AGAIN FOR A WHILE.
HE SAID WE'RE BROTH-ERS!
HAHAHAHA
BLUSH
IS IT REALLY OKAY FOR ME TO HAVE THIS?

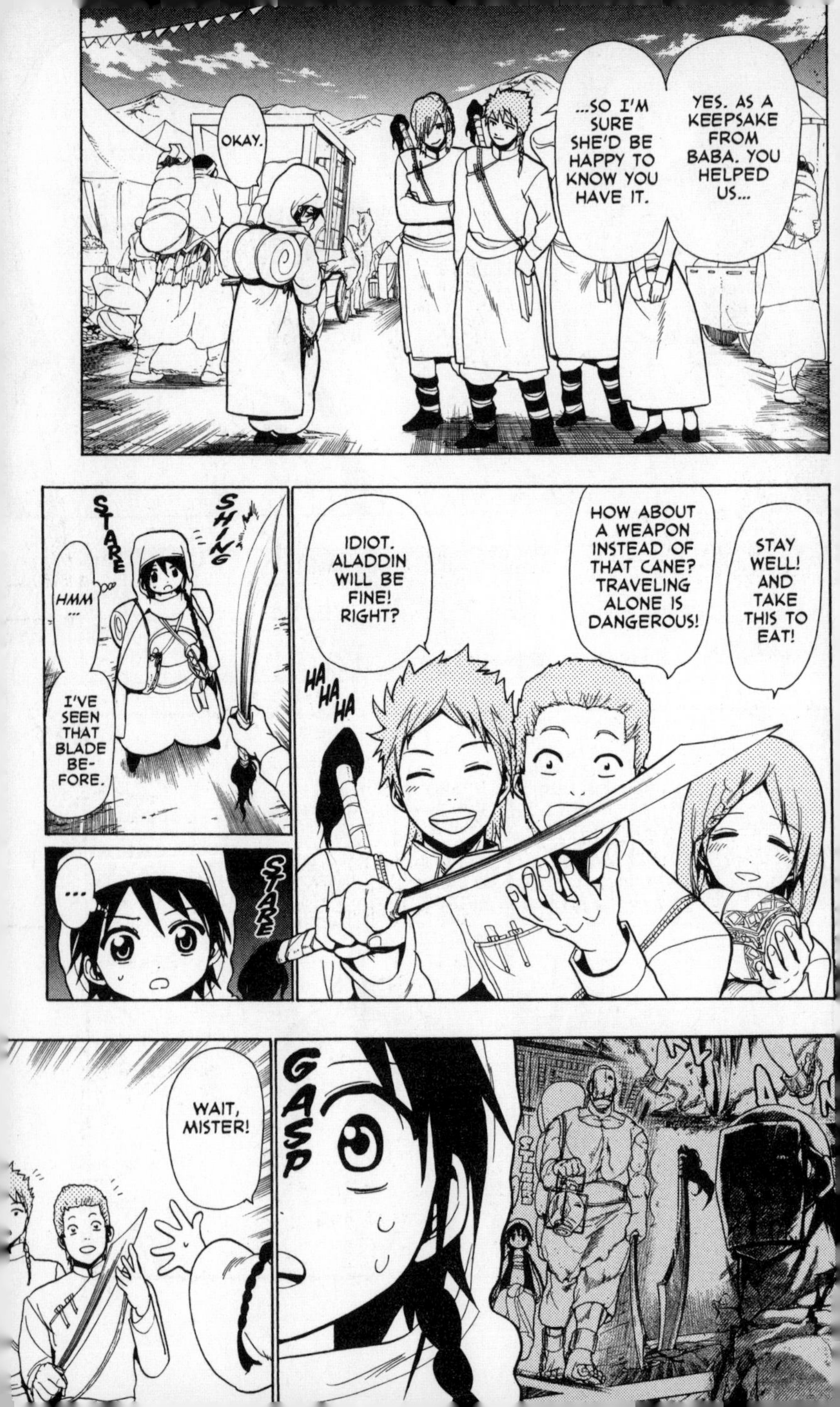

YES. AS A KEEPSAKE FROM BABA. YOU HELPED US...
...SO I'M SURE SHE'D BE HAPPY TO KNOW YOU HAVE IT.
OKAY.
STAY WELL! AND TAKE THIS TO EAT!
HOW ABOUT A WEAPON INSTEAD OF THAT CANE? TRAVELING ALONE IS DANGEROUS!
IDIOT. ALADDIN WILL BE FINE! RIGHT?
HA HA HA
SHING
STARE
HMM...
I'VE SEEN THAT BLADE BEFORE.
STARE
...
GASP
WAIT, MISTER!

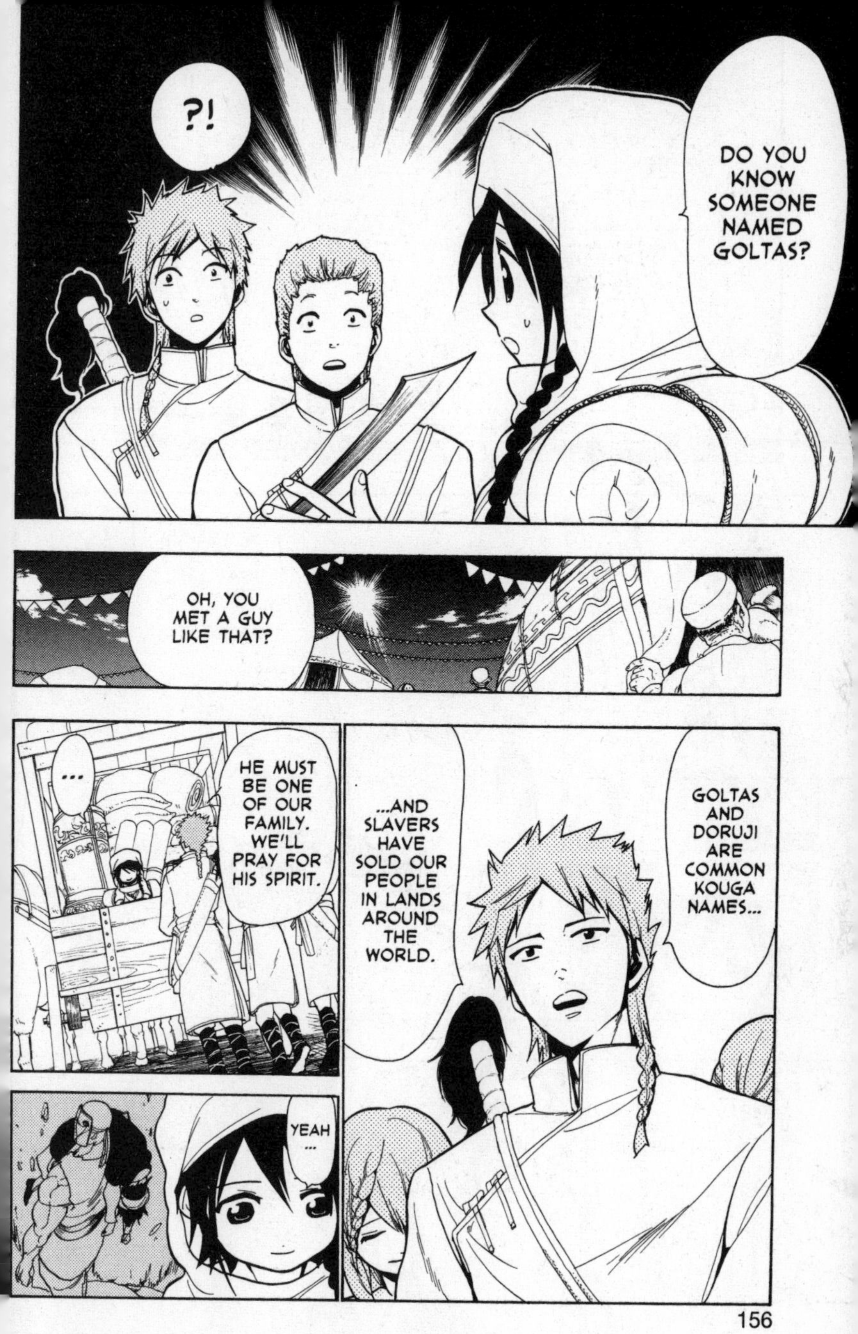
DO YOU KNOW SOMEONE NAMED GOLTAS?
?!
OH, YOU MET A GUY LIKE THAT?
GOLTAS AND DORUJI ARE COMMON KOUGA NAMES...
...AND SLAVERS HAVE SOLD OUR PEOPLE IN LANDS AROUND THE WORLD.
HE MUST BE ONE OF OUR FAMILY. WE'LL PRAY FOR HIS SPIRIT.
...
YEAH ...

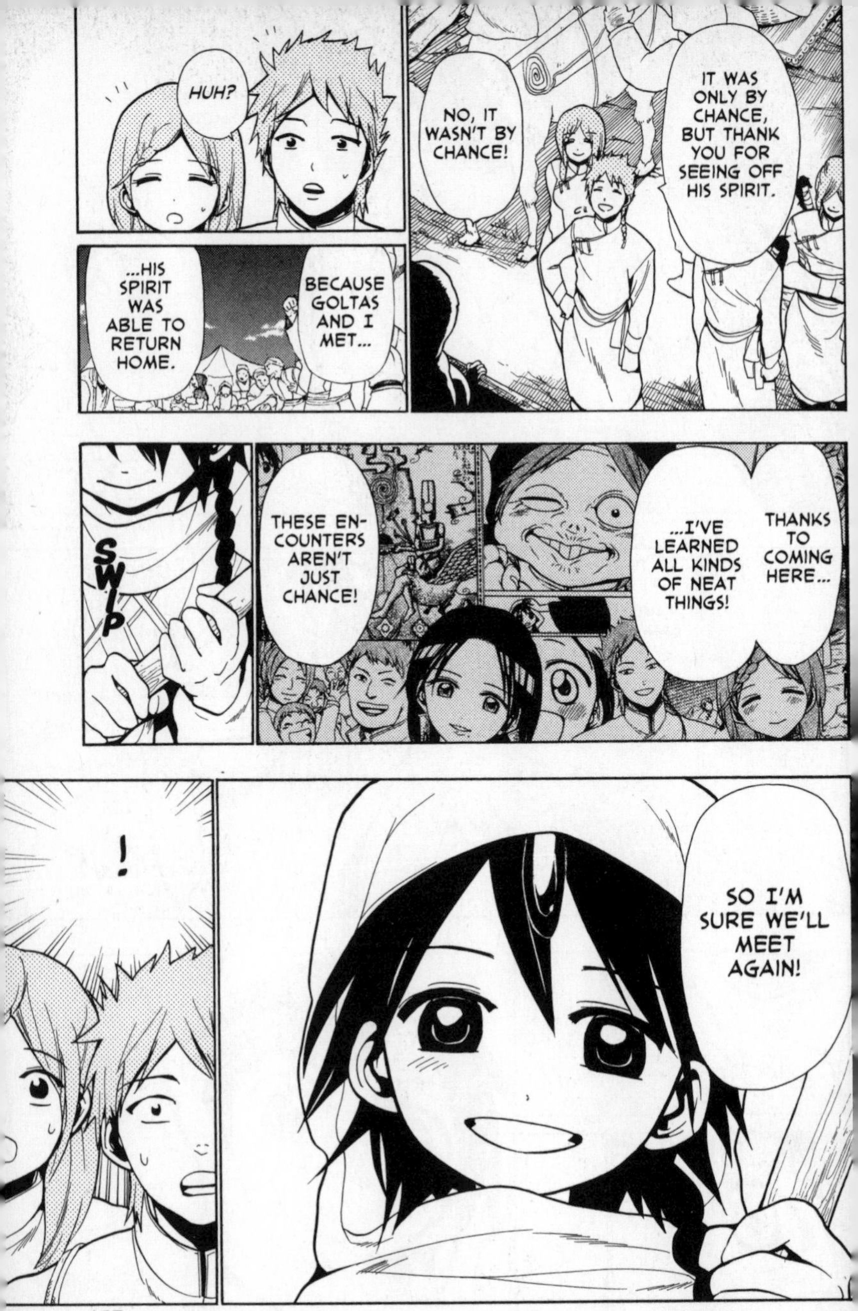

IT WAS ONLY BY CHANCE, BUT THANK YOU FOR SEEING OFF HIS SPIRIT.
NO, IT WASN'T BY CHANCE!
HUH?
BECAUSE GOLTAS AND I MET...
...HIS SPIRIT WAS ABLE TO RETURN HOME.
THANKS TO COMING HERE...
...I'VE LEARNED ALL KINDS OF NEAT THINGS!
THESE EN-COUNTERS AREN'T JUST CHANCE!
SWIP
SO I'M SURE WE'LL MEET AGAIN!
!

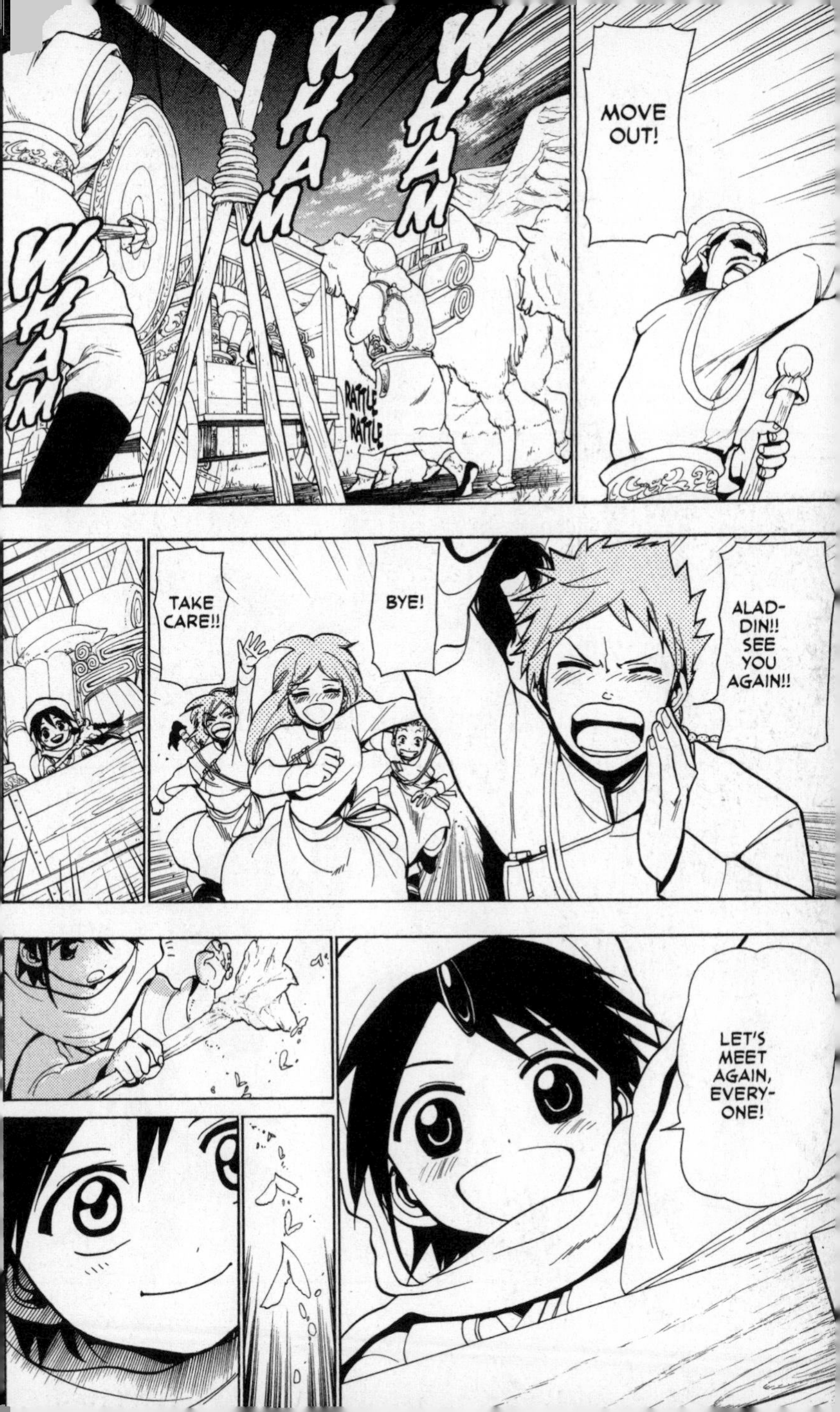
MOVE OUT!
WHAM
WHAM
WHAM
RATTLE RATTLE
ALAD-DIN!! SEE YOU AGAIN!!
BYE!
TAKE CARE!!
LET'S MEET AGAIN, EVERY-ONE!

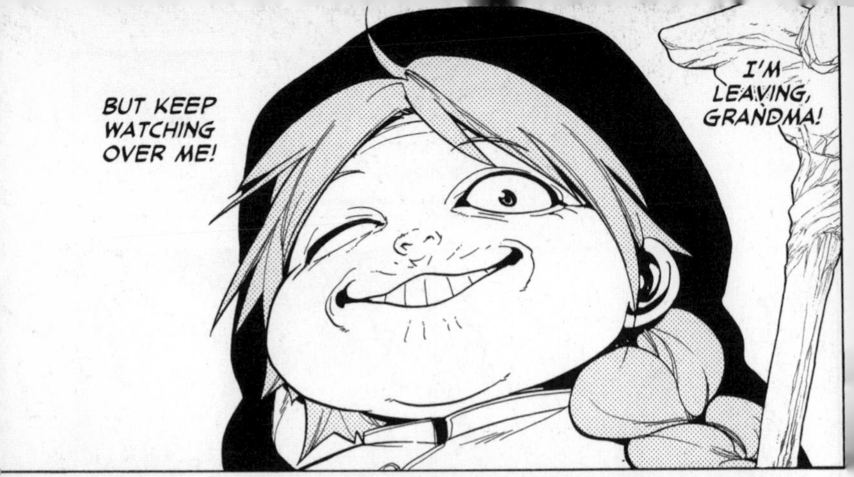
I'M LEAVING, GRANDMA!
BUT KEEP WATCHING OVER ME!
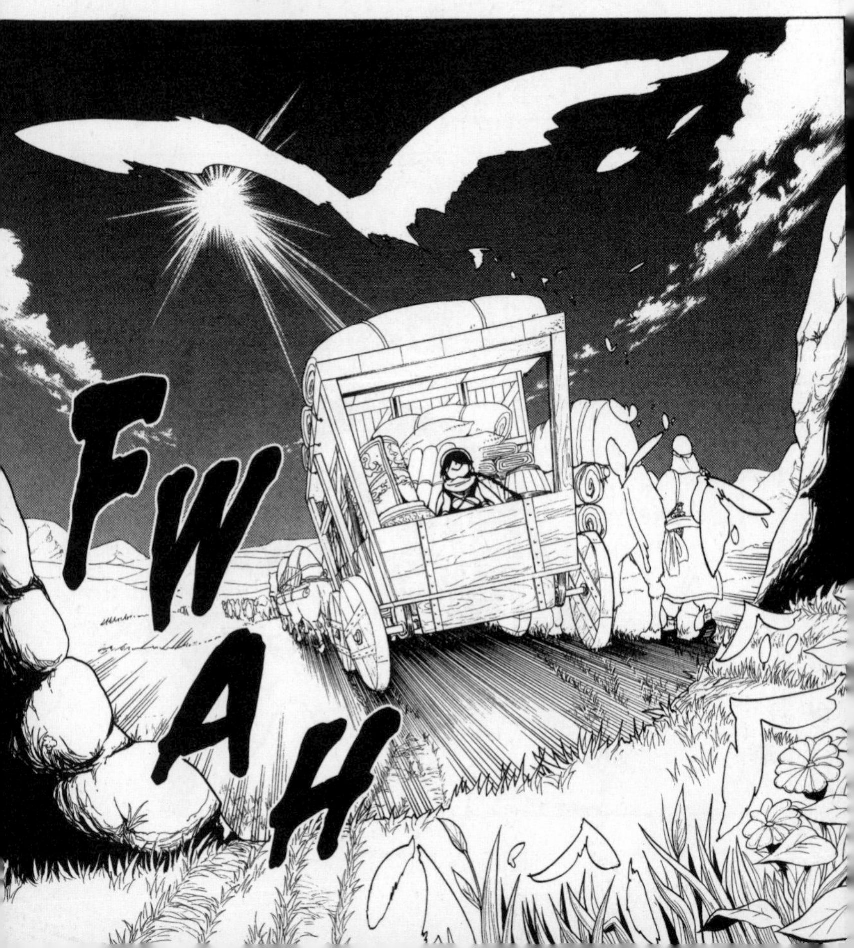
FWAH

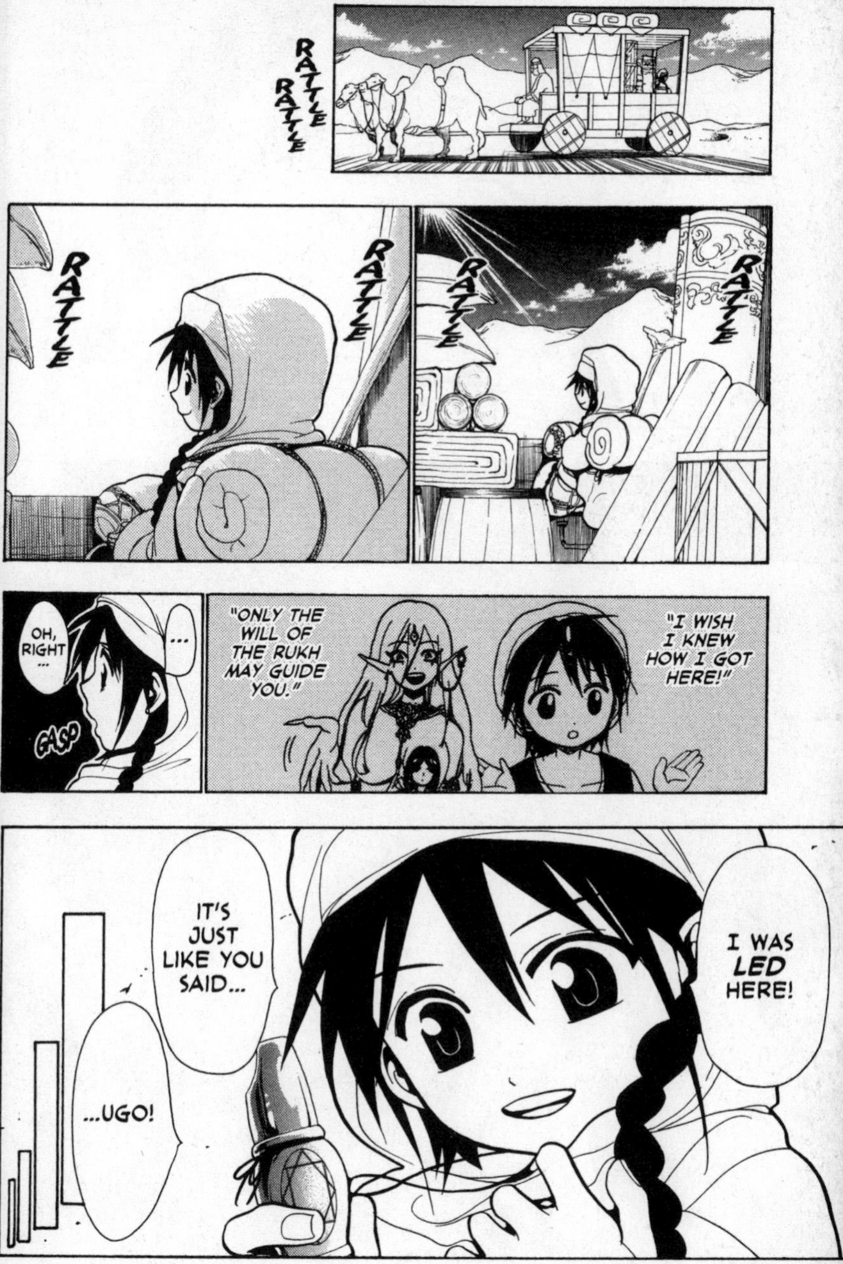
RATTLE
RATTLE
RATTLE
RATTLE
RATTLE
RATTLE
"I WISH I KNEW HOW I GOT HERE!"
"ONLY THE WILL OF THE RUKH MAY GUIDE YOU."
...
OH, RIGHT...
GASP
I WAS *LED* HERE!
IT'S JUST LIKE YOU SAID...
...UGO!

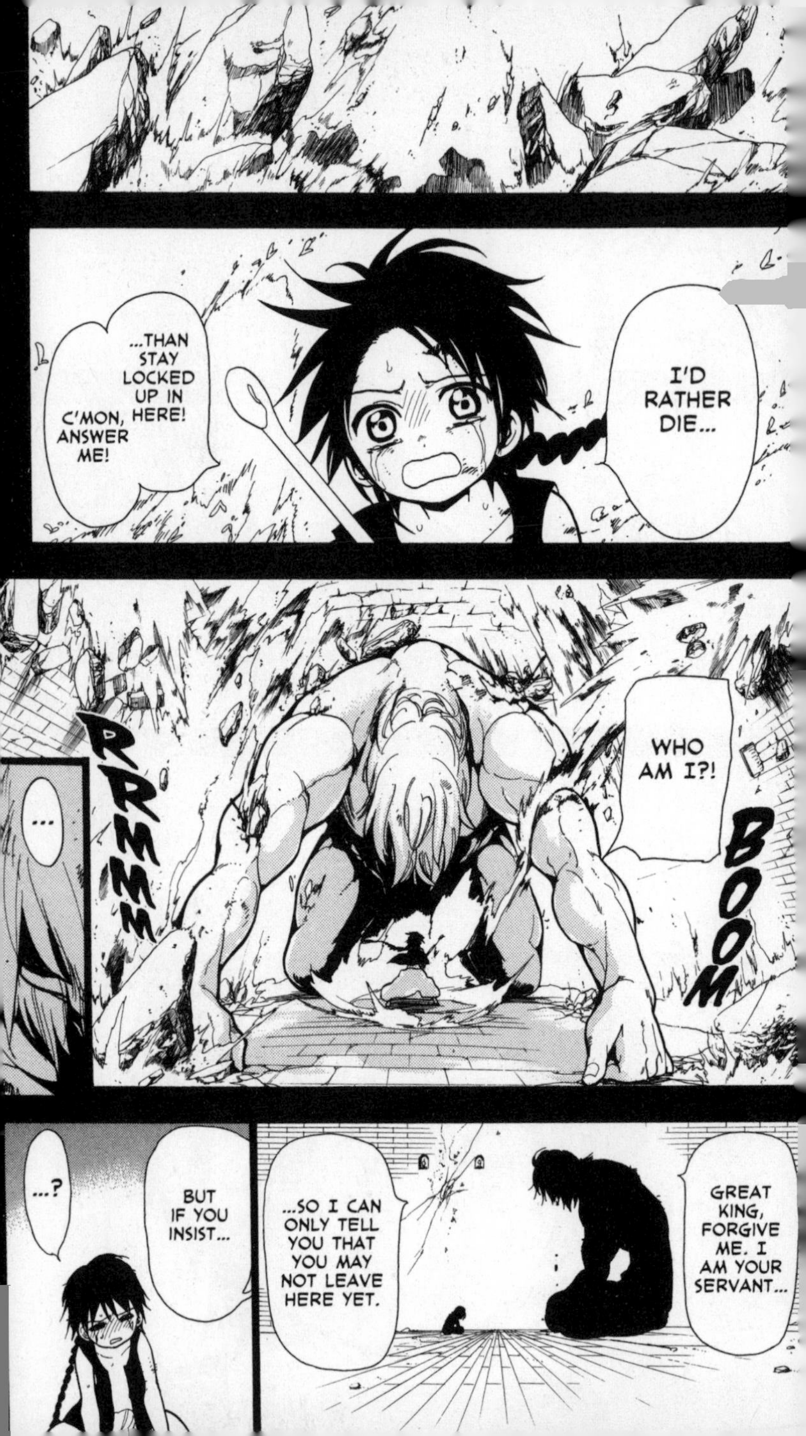
I'D RATHER DIE...
...THAN STAY LOCKED UP IN HERE!
C'MON, ANSWER ME!
WHO AM I?!
BOOM
RRMMM
...
GREAT KING, FORGIVE ME. I AM YOUR SERVANT...
...SO I CAN ONLY TELL YOU THAT YOU MAY NOT LEAVE HERE YET.
BUT IF YOU INSIST...
...?

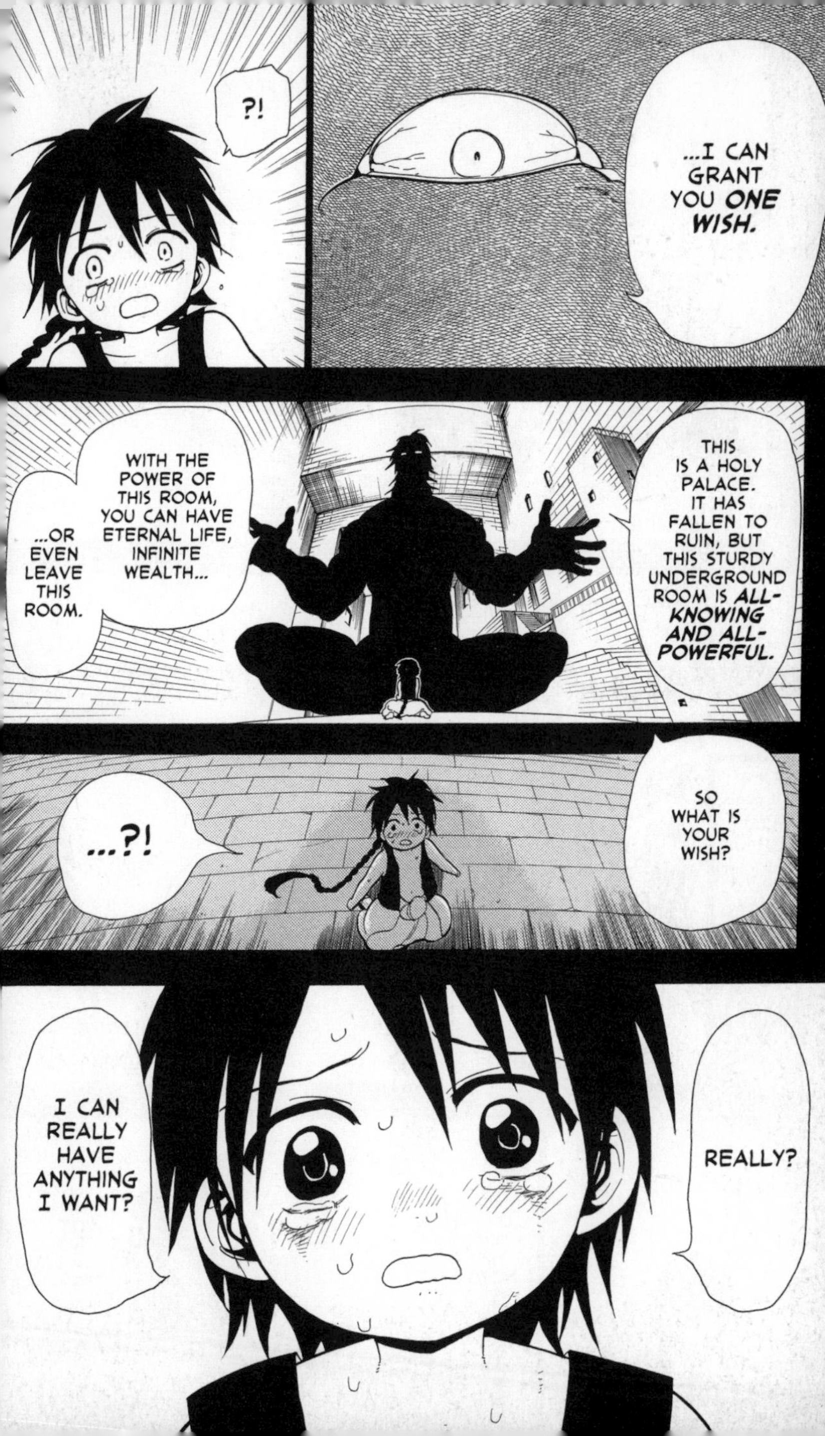
...I CAN GRANT YOU *ONE WISH.*
?!
THIS IS A HOLY PALACE. IT HAS FALLEN TO RUIN, BUT THIS STURDY UNDERGROUND ROOM IS *ALL-KNOWING AND ALL-POWERFUL.*
WITH THE POWER OF THIS ROOM, YOU CAN HAVE ETERNAL LIFE, INFINITE WEALTH...
...OR EVEN LEAVE THIS ROOM.
SO WHAT IS YOUR WISH?
...?!
REALLY?
I CAN REALLY HAVE ANYTHING I WANT?

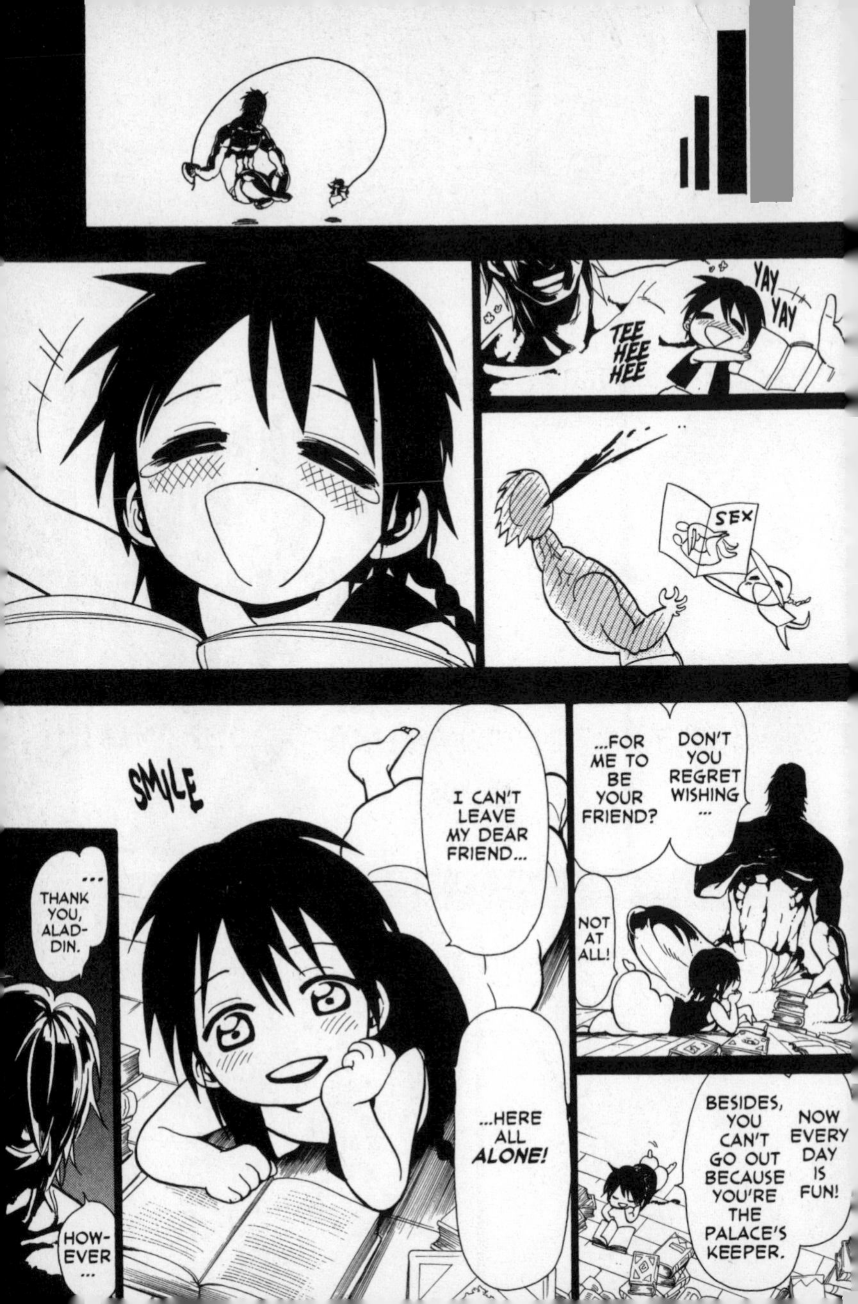
YAY YAY
TEE HEE HEE
SEX
DON'T YOU REGRET WISHING...
...FOR ME TO BE YOUR FRIEND?
NOT AT ALL!
NOW EVERY DAY IS FUN!
BESIDES, YOU CAN'T GO OUT BECAUSE YOU'RE THE PALACE'S KEEPER.
I CAN'T LEAVE MY DEAR FRIEND...
...HERE ALL ALONE!
SMILE
...THANK YOU, ALADDIN.
HOWEVER...

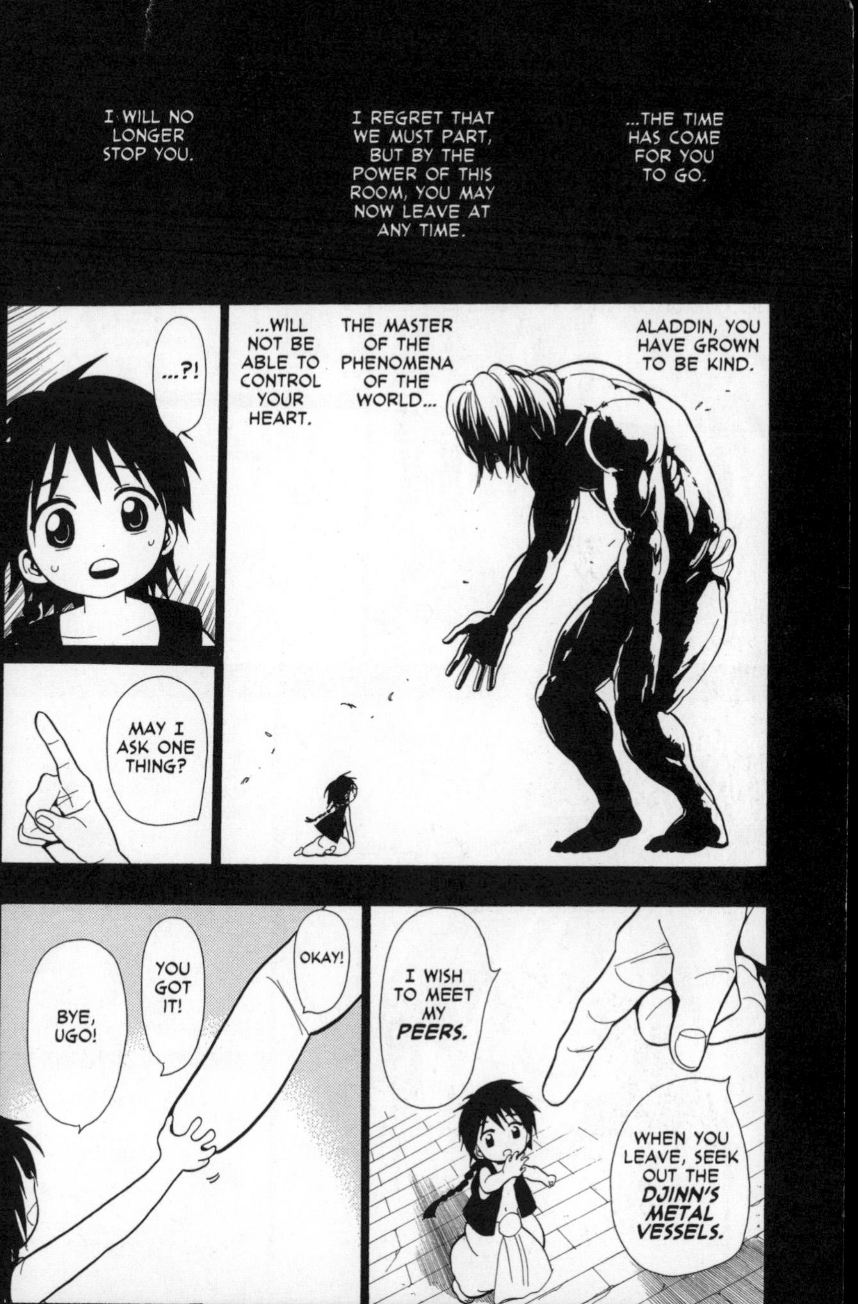
...THE TIME HAS COME FOR YOU TO GO.
I REGRET THAT WE MUST PART, BUT BY THE POWER OF THIS ROOM, YOU MAY NOW LEAVE AT ANY TIME.
I WILL NO LONGER STOP YOU.
ALADDIN, YOU HAVE GROWN TO BE KIND.
THE MASTER OF THE PHENOMENA OF THE WORLD...
...WILL NOT BE ABLE TO CONTROL YOUR HEART.
...?!
MAY I ASK ONE THING?
I WISH TO MEET MY *PEERS.*
WHEN YOU LEAVE, SEEK OUT THE *DJINN'S METAL VESSELS.*
OKAY!
YOU GOT IT!
BYE, UGO!

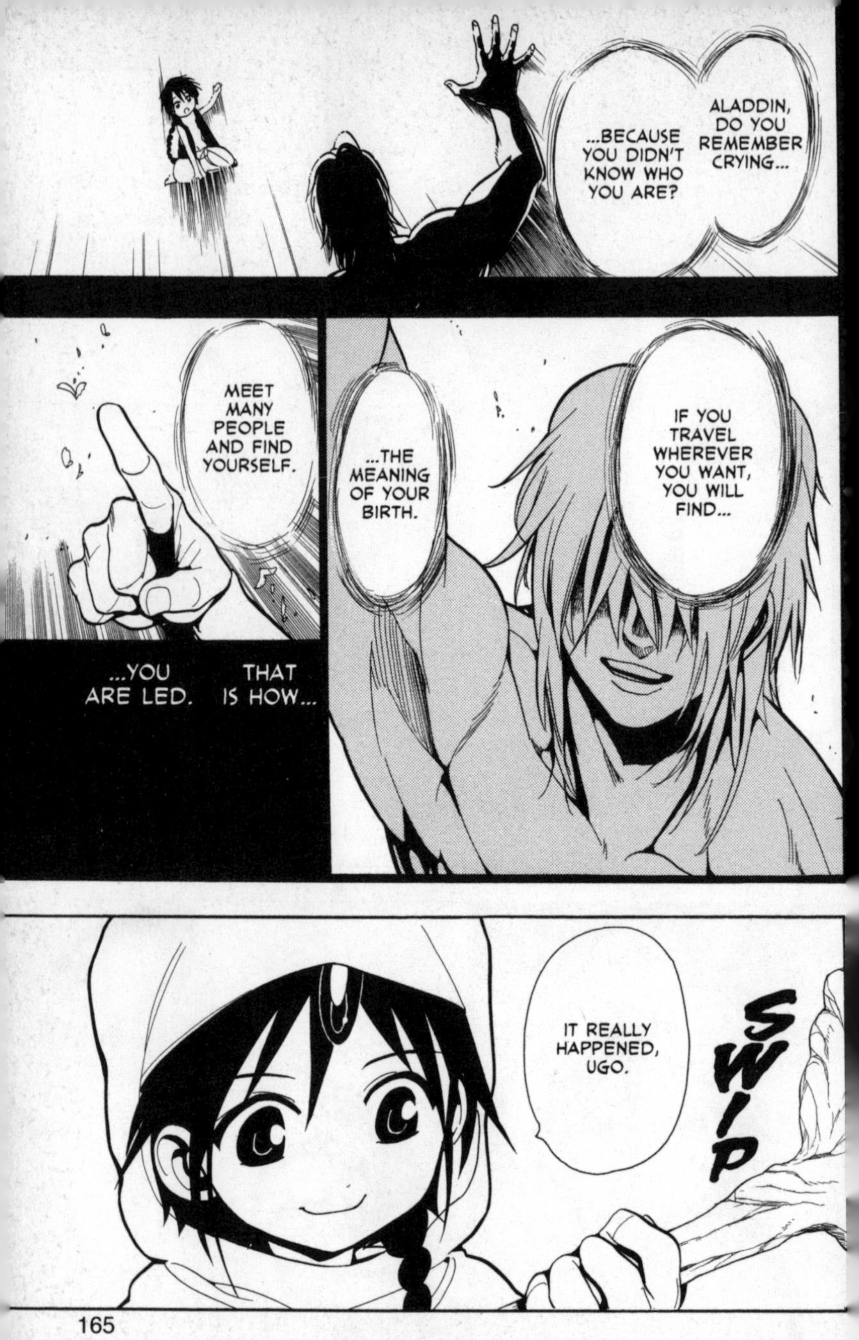
ALADDIN, DO YOU REMEMBER CRYING...
...BECAUSE YOU DIDN'T KNOW WHO YOU ARE?
IF YOU TRAVEL WHEREVER YOU WANT, YOU WILL FIND...
...THE MEANING OF YOUR BIRTH.
MEET MANY PEOPLE AND FIND YOURSELF.
THAT IS HOW...
...YOU ARE LED.
SWIP
IT REALLY HAPPENED, UGO.

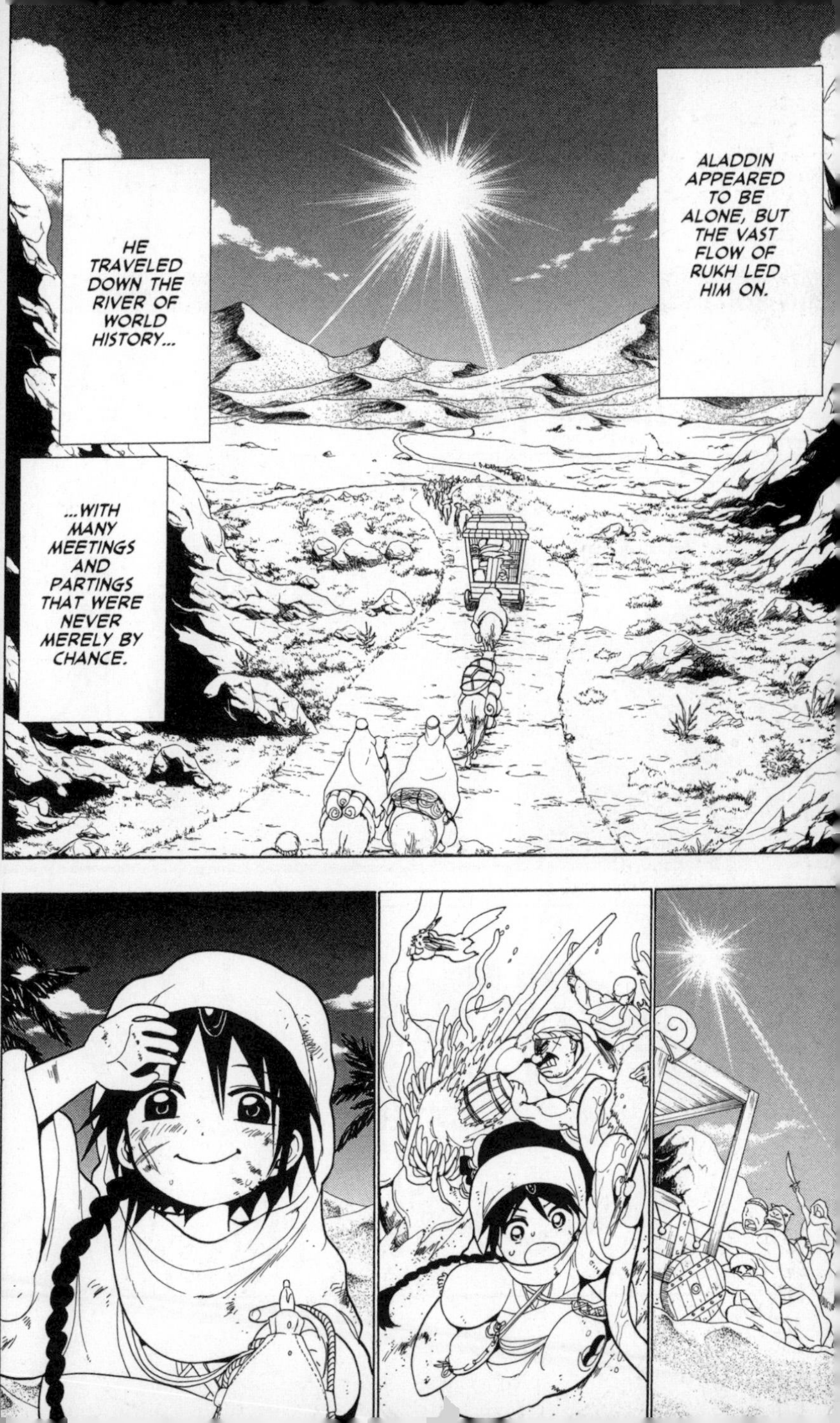
ALADDIN APPEARED TO BE ALONE, BUT THE VAST FLOW OF RUKH LED HIM ON.
HE TRAVELED DOWN THE RIVER OF WORLD HISTORY...
...WITH MANY MEETINGS AND PARTINGS THAT WERE NEVER MERELY BY CHANCE.

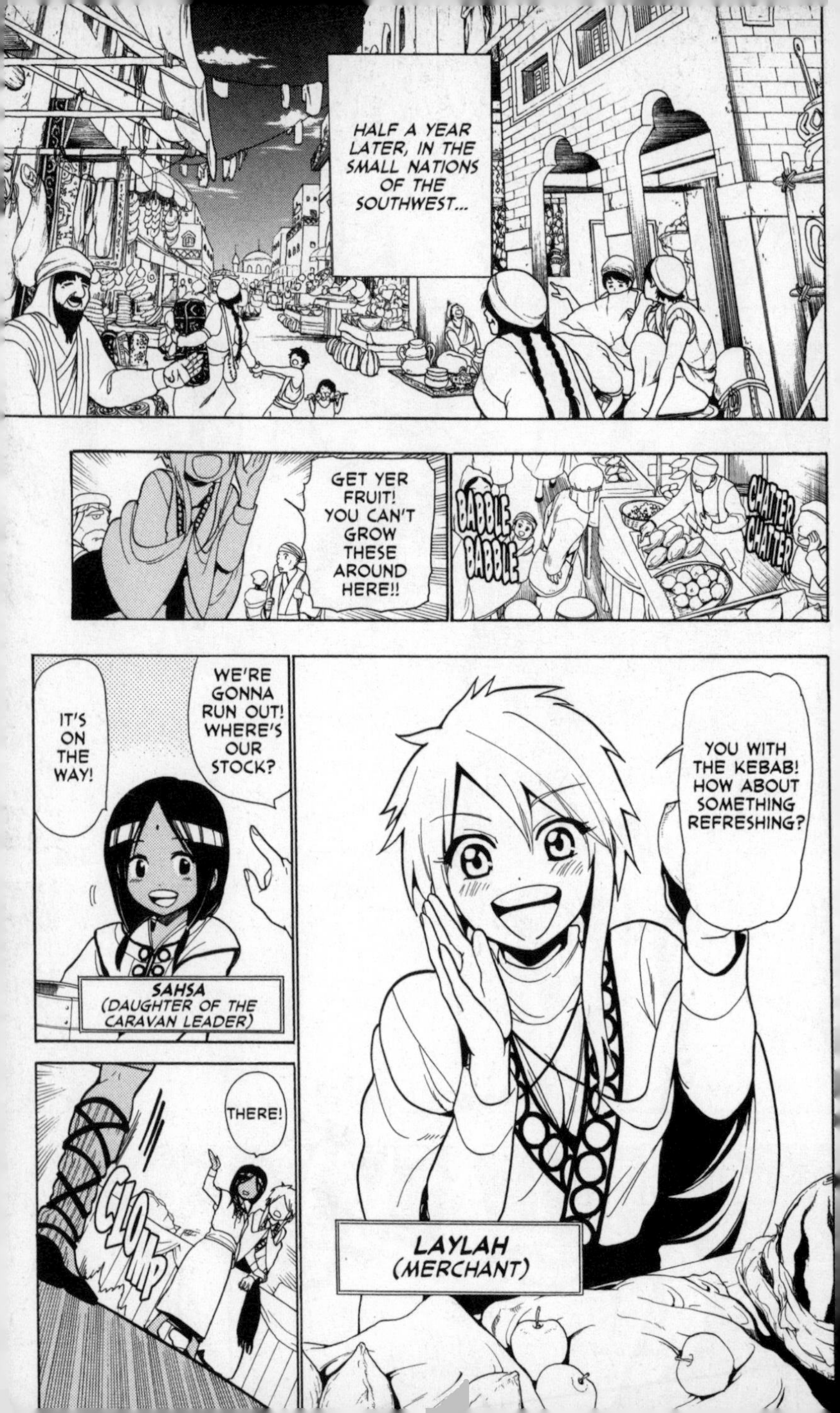
HALF A YEAR LATER, IN THE SMALL NATIONS OF THE SOUTHWEST...
CHATTER CHATTER
BABBLE BABBLE
GET YER FRUIT! YOU CAN'T GROW THESE AROUND HERE!!
YOU WITH THE KEBAB! HOW ABOUT SOMETHING REFRESHING?
LAYLAH (MERCHANT)
WE'RE GONNA RUN OUT! WHERE'S OUR STOCK?
IT'S ON THE WAY!
SAHSA (DAUGHTER OF THE CARAVAN LEADER)
THERE!
CLOMP

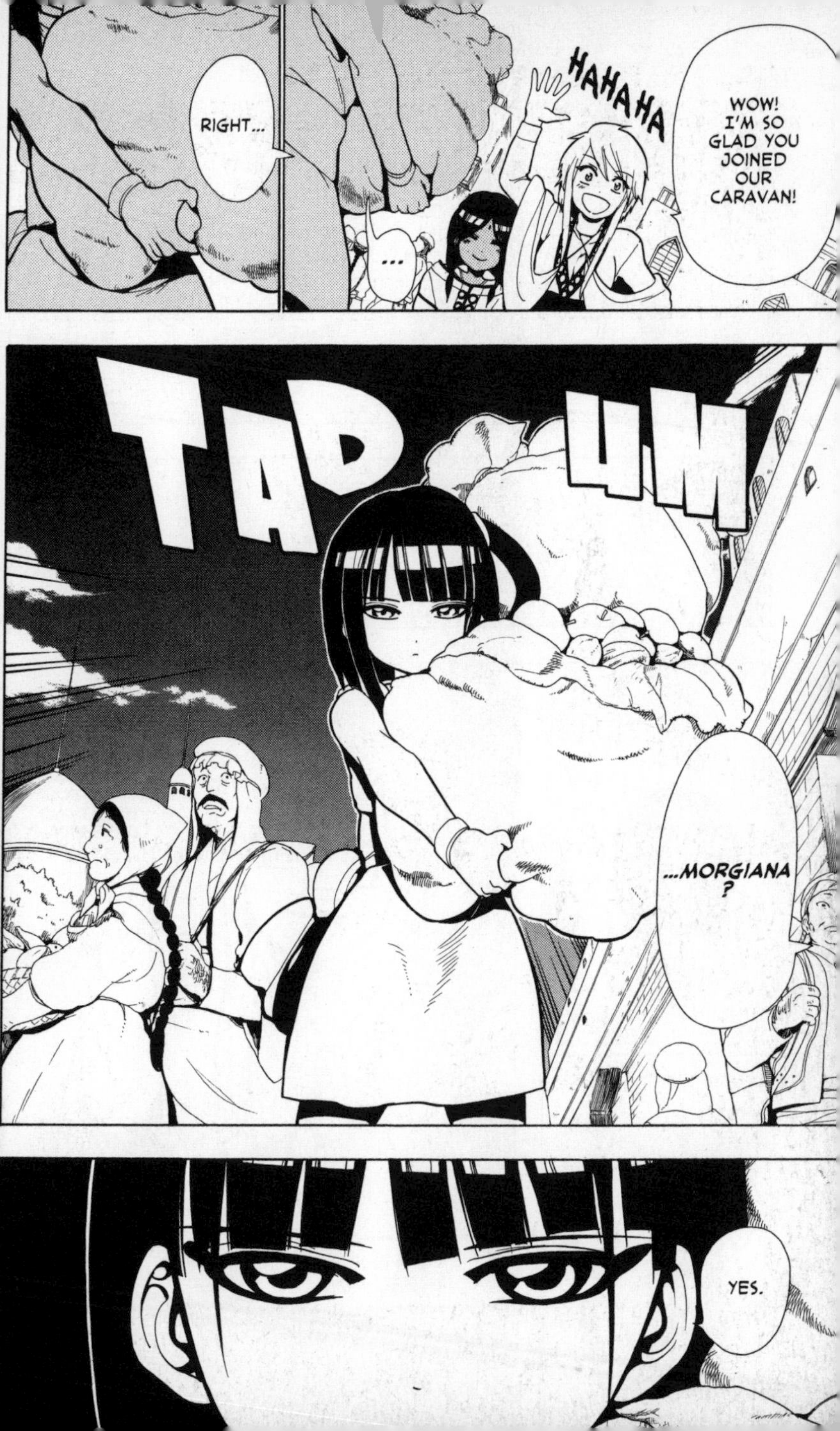
HAHAHA
WOW! I'M SO GLAD YOU JOINED OUR CARAVAN!
...
RIGHT...
TADUM
...MORGIANA?
YES.

Night 27: Bruises That Won't Fade

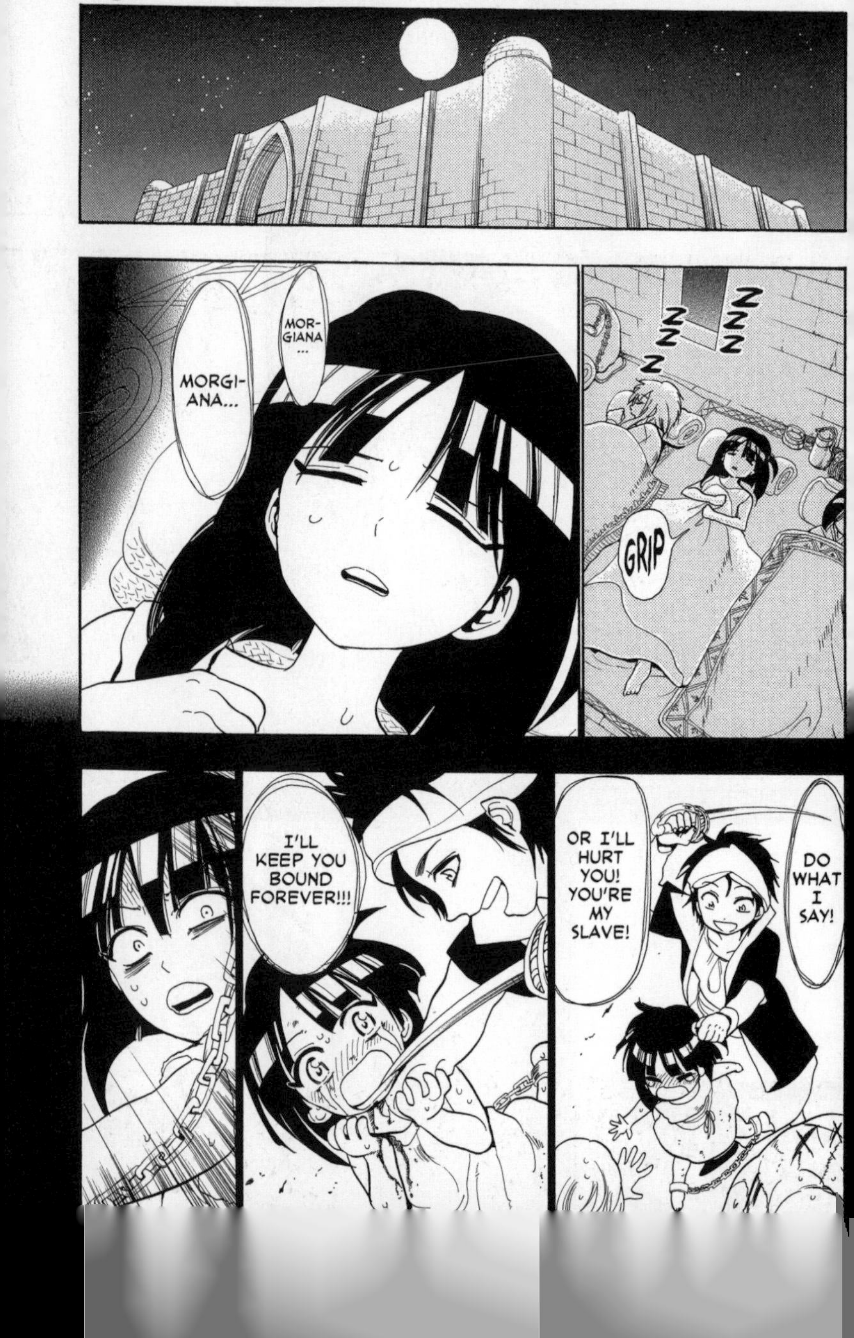

ZZZ
ZZZ
GRIP
MORGIANA...
MORGIANA...
DO WHAT I SAY!
OR I'LL HURT YOU! YOU'RE MY SLAVE!
I'LL KEEP YOU BOUND FOREVER!!!

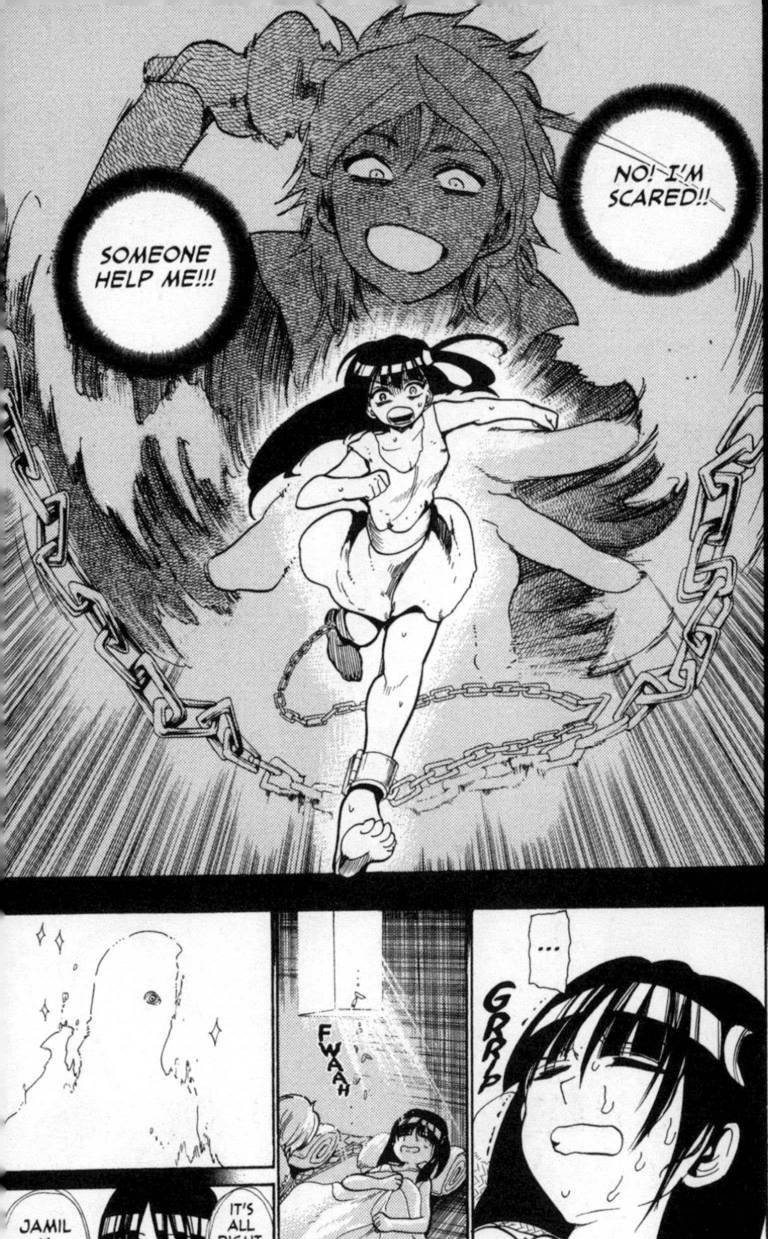
NO! I'M SCARED!!
SOMEONE HELP ME!!!
...
GRRIP
FWAAH
IT'S ALL RIGHT, MORGIANA.
JAMIL IS GONE.

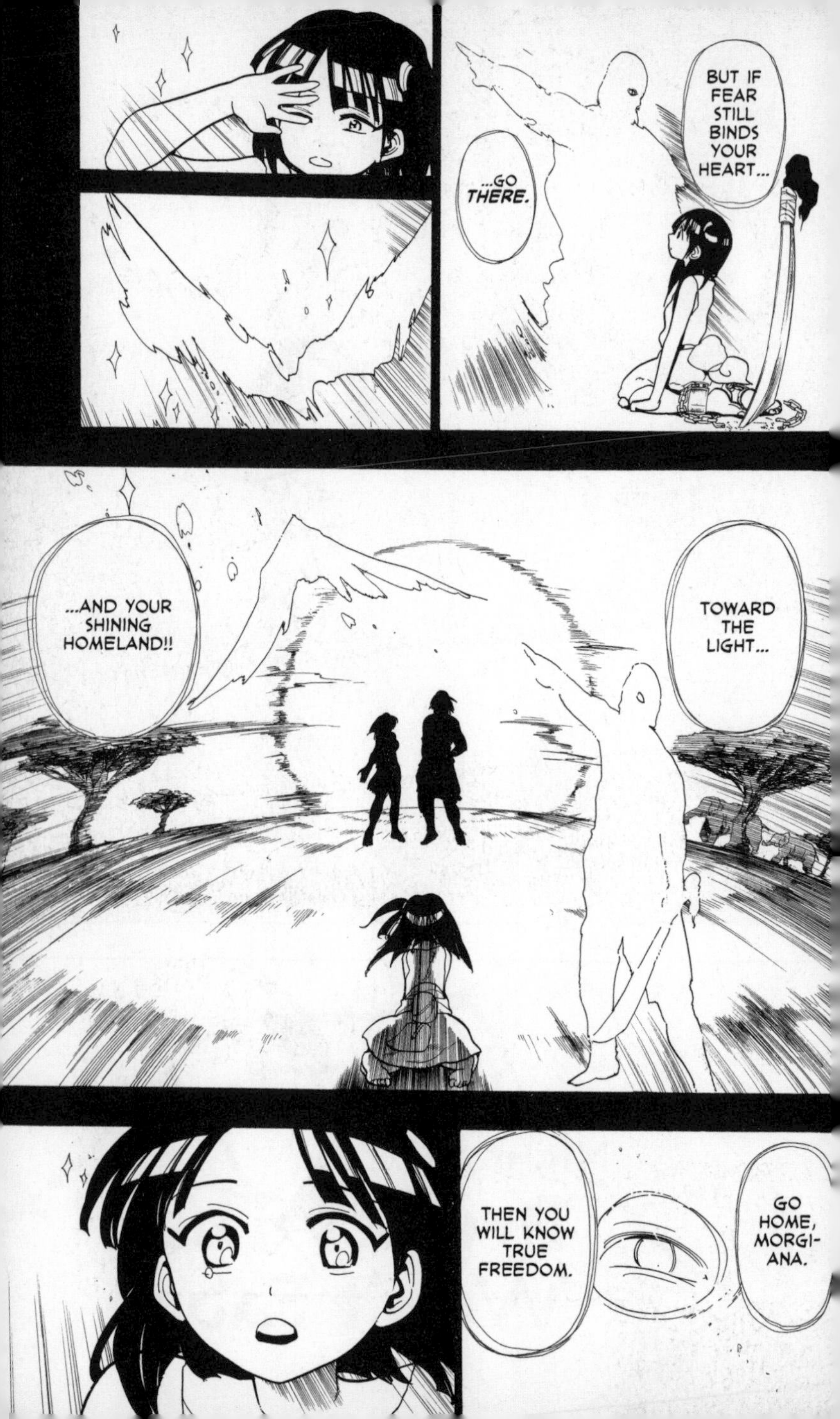
BUT IF FEAR STILL BINDS YOUR HEART...
...GO *THERE.*
TOWARD THE LIGHT...
...AND YOUR SHINING HOMELAND!!
GO HOME, MORGIANA.
THEN YOU WILL KNOW TRUE FREEDOM.

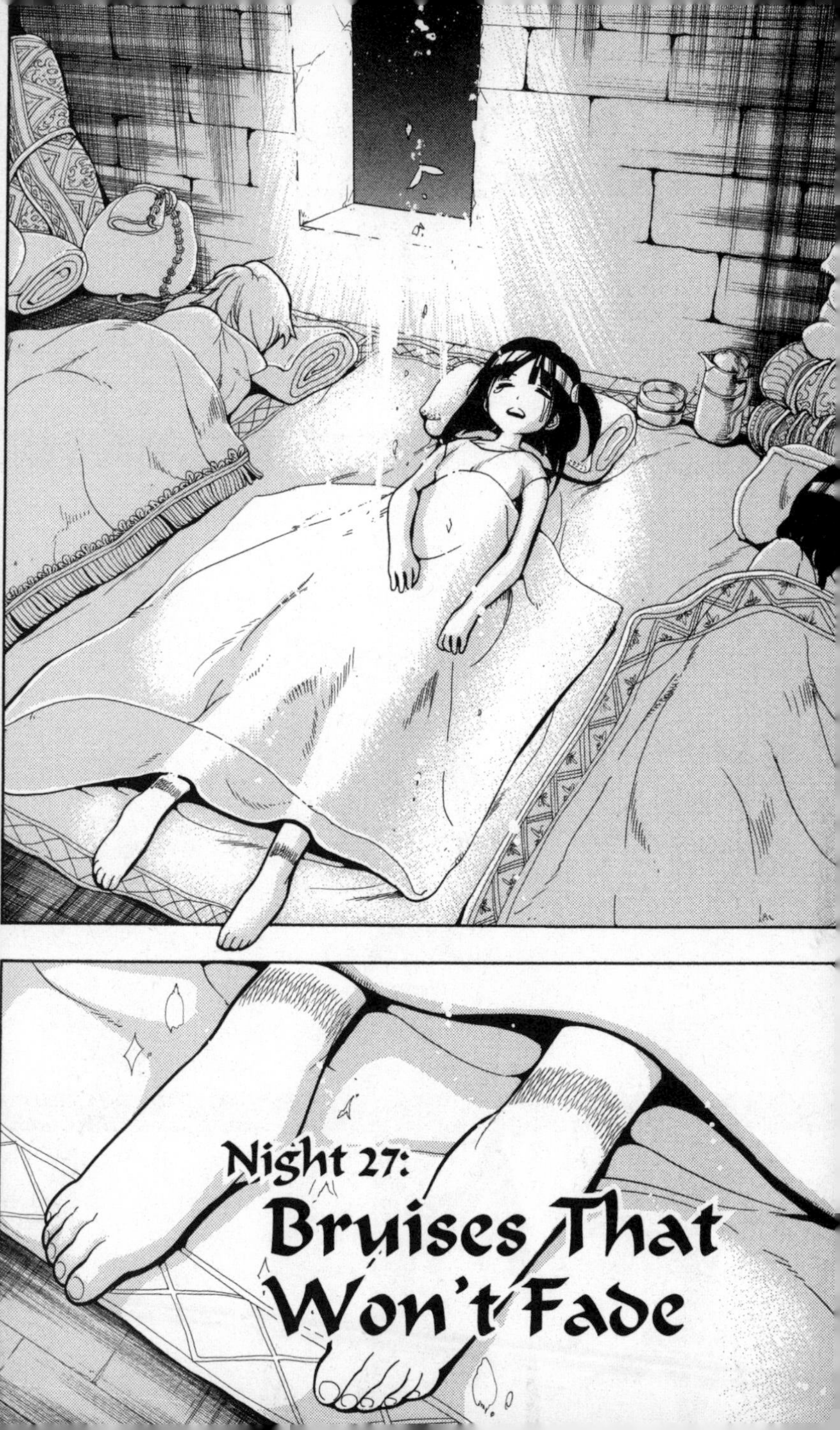
Night 27:
Bruises That Won't Fade

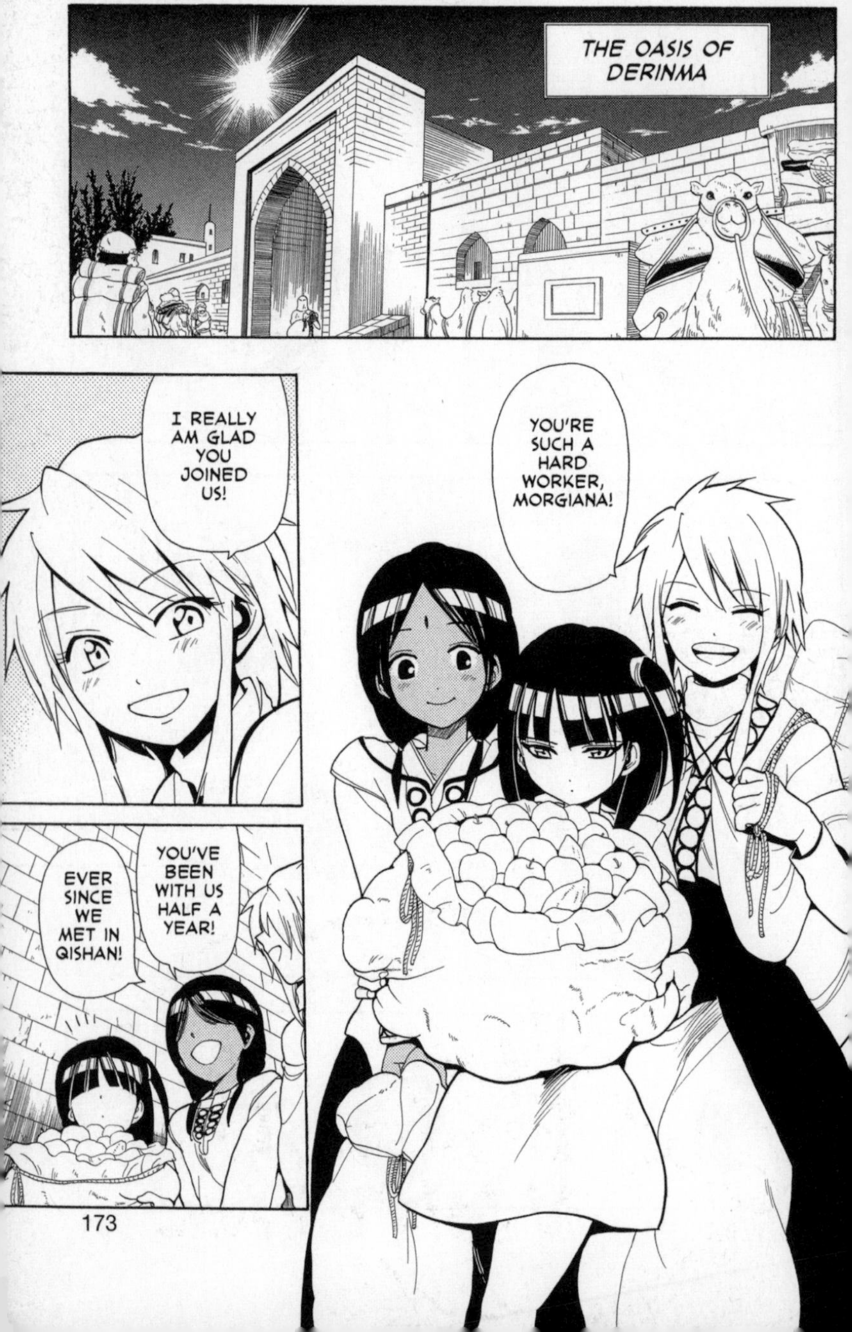
THE OASIS OF DERINMA
YOU'RE SUCH A HARD WORKER, MORGIANA!
I REALLY AM GLAD YOU JOINED US!
YOU'VE BEEN WITH US HALF A YEAR!
EVER SINCE WE MET IN QISHAN!

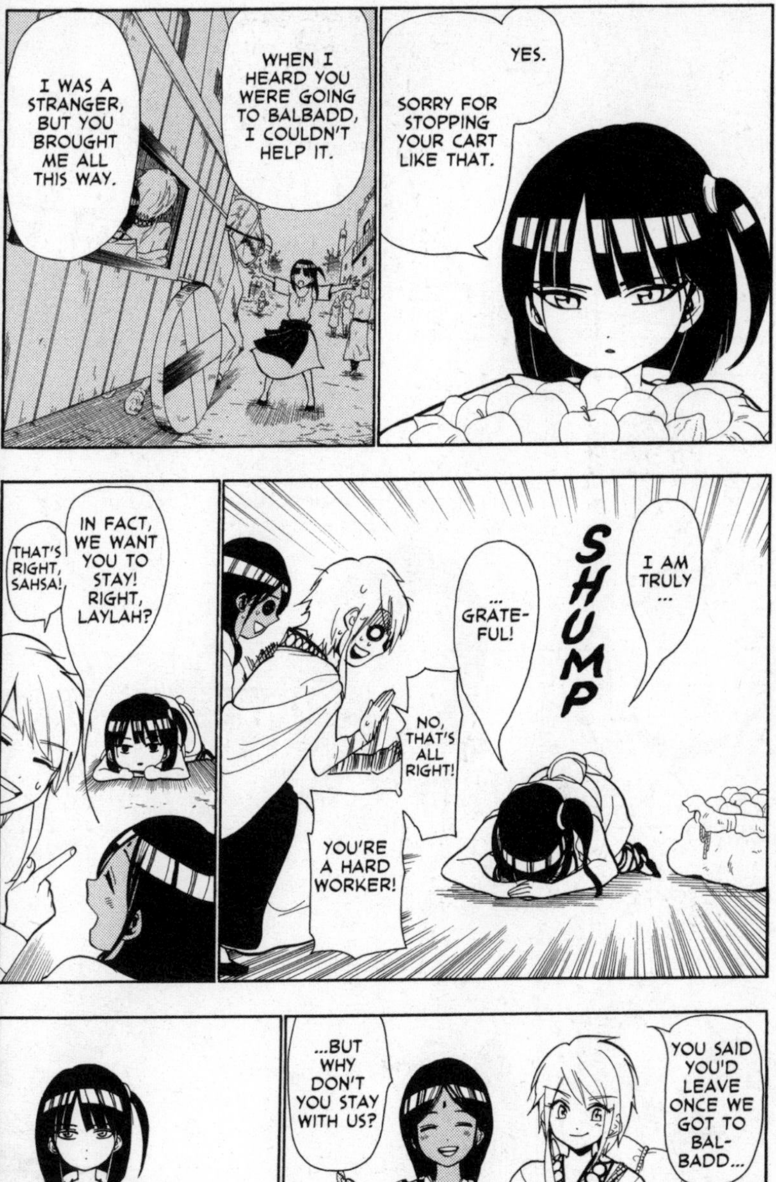
YES.
SORRY FOR STOPPING YOUR CART LIKE THAT.
WHEN I HEARD YOU WERE GOING TO BALBADD, I COULDN'T HELP IT.
I WAS A STRANGER, BUT YOU BROUGHT ME ALL THIS WAY.
I AM TRULY ...
SHUMP
... GRATE-FUL!
NO, THAT'S ALL RIGHT!
YOU'RE A HARD WORKER!
IN FACT, WE WANT YOU TO STAY! RIGHT, LAYLAH?
THAT'S RIGHT, SAHSA!
YOU SAID YOU'D LEAVE ONCE WE GOT TO BAL-BADD...
...BUT WHY DON'T YOU STAY WITH US?

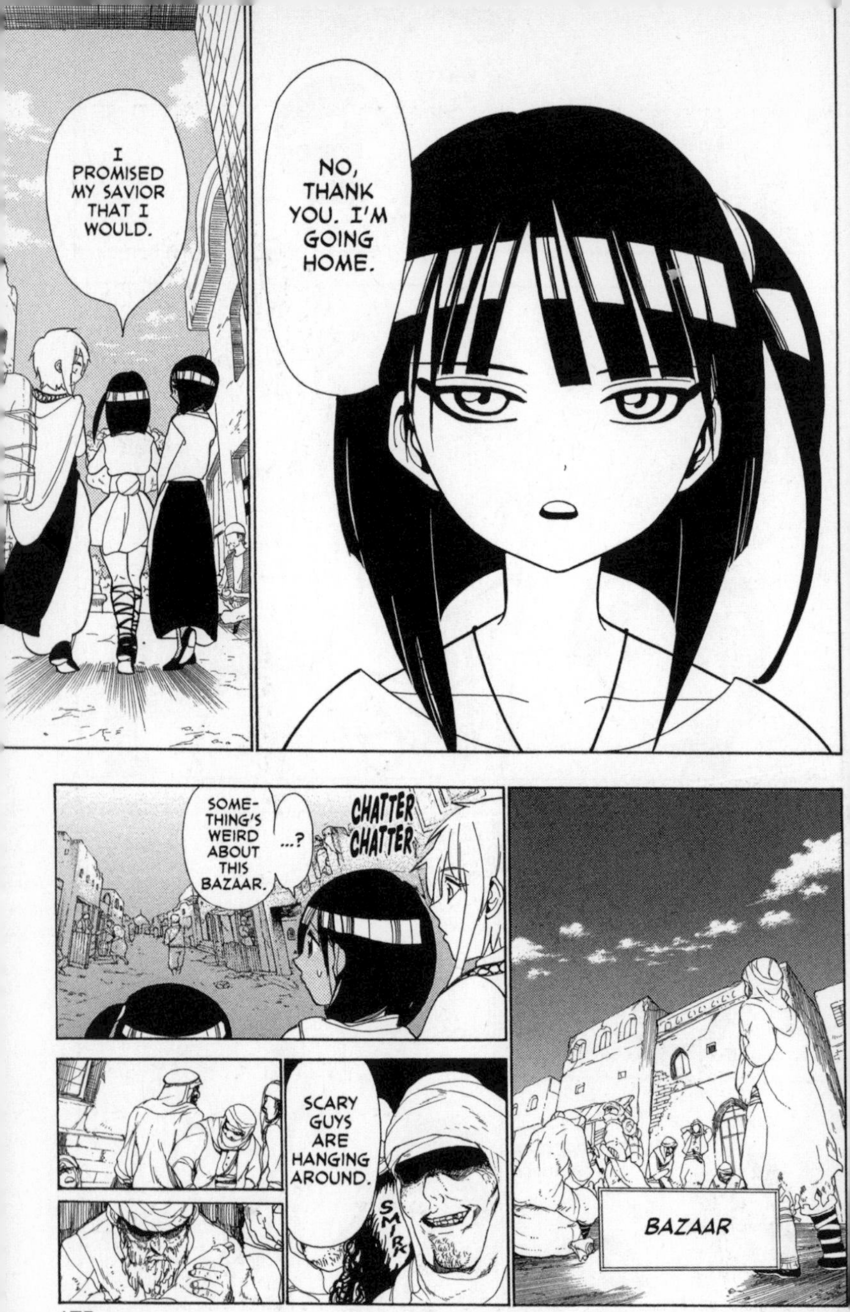
NO, THANK YOU. I'M GOING HOME.
I PROMISED MY SAVIOR THAT I WOULD.
BAZAAR
CHATTER CHATTER
...?
SOME-THING'S WEIRD ABOUT THIS BAZAAR.
SCARY GUYS ARE HANGING AROUND.
SMIRK

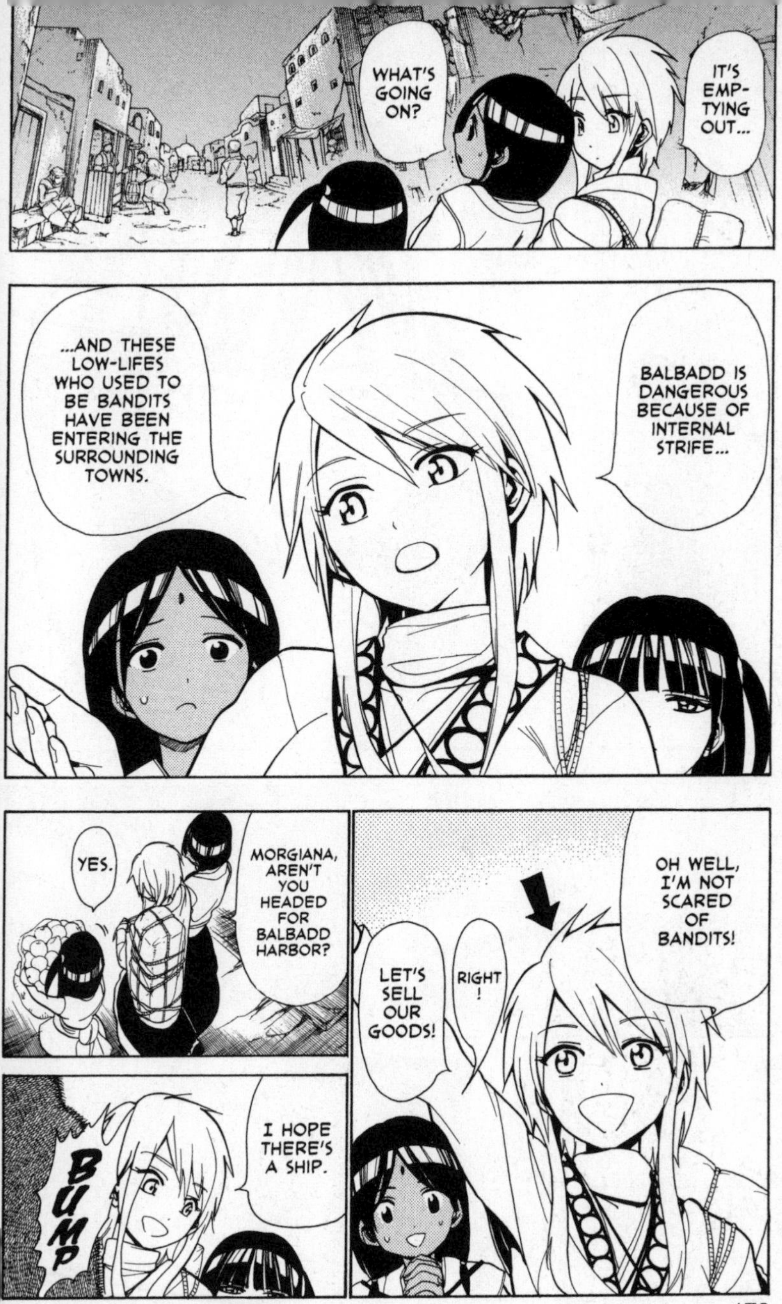
IT'S EMPTYING OUT...
WHAT'S GOING ON?
BALBADD IS DANGEROUS BECAUSE OF INTERNAL STRIFE...
...AND THESE LOW-LIFES WHO USED TO BE BANDITS HAVE BEEN ENTERING THE SURROUNDING TOWNS.
OH WELL, I'M NOT SCARED OF BANDITS!
RIGHT!
LET'S SELL OUR GOODS!
MORGIANA, AREN'T YOU HEADED FOR BALBADD HARBOR?
YES.
I HOPE THERE'S A SHIP.
BUMP

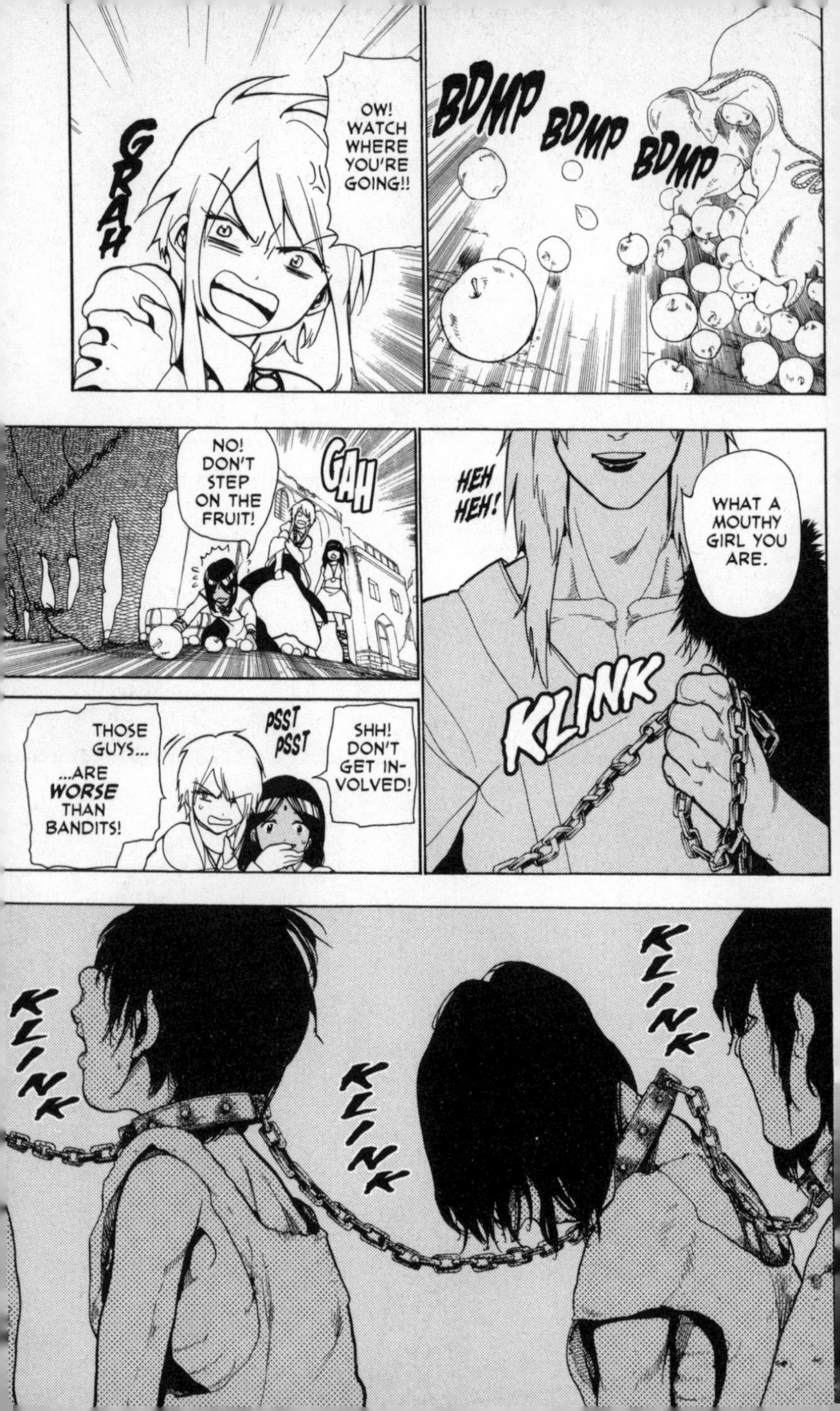
BDMP BDMP BDMP
OW! WATCH WHERE YOU'RE GOING!!
GRAH
WHAT A MOUTHY GIRL YOU ARE.
HEH HEH!
KLINK
GAH
NO! DON'T STEP ON THE FRUIT!
SHH! DON'T GET IN-VOLVED!
PSST PSST
THOSE GUYS...
...ARE **WORSE** THAN BANDITS!
KLINK
KLINK
KLINK

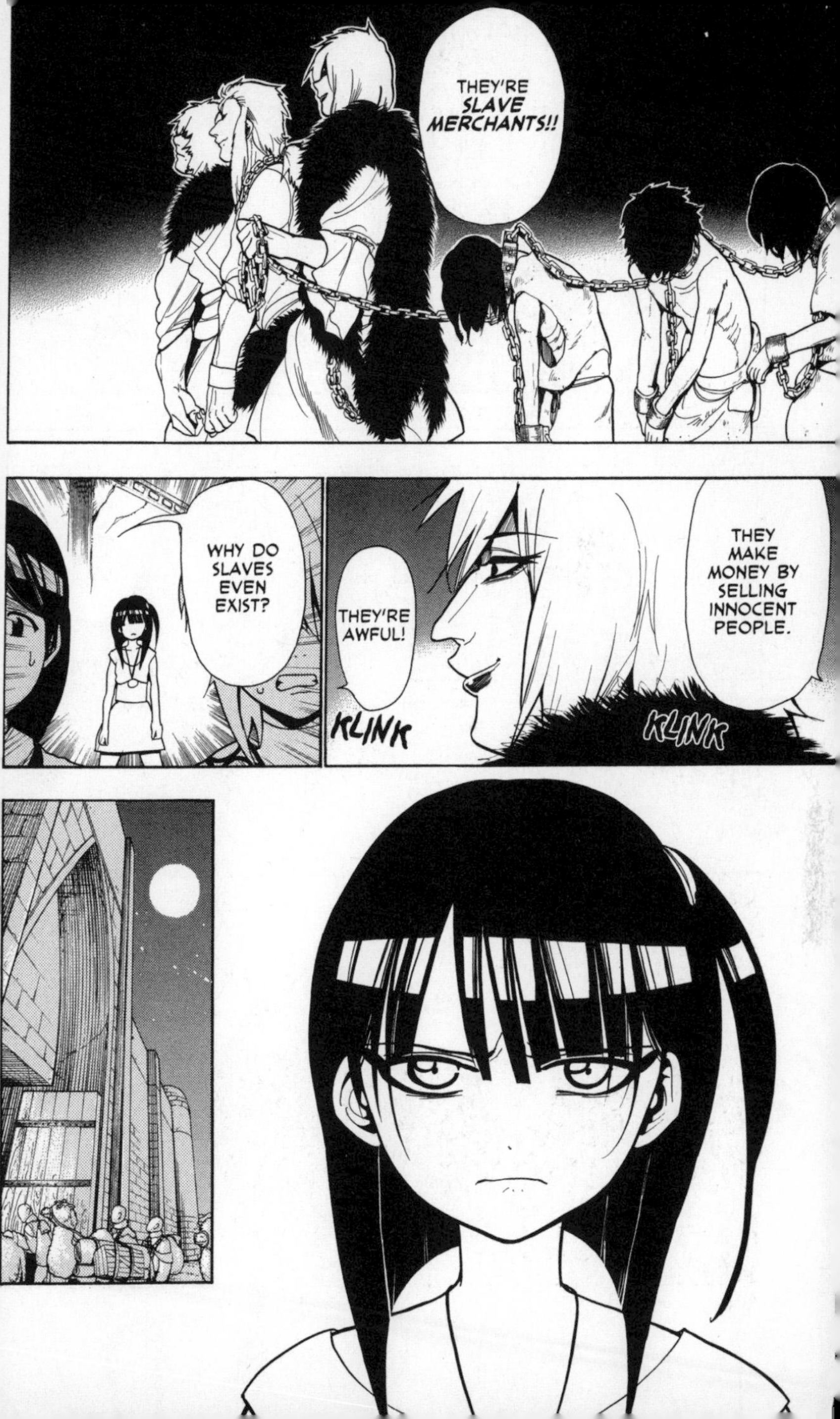
THEY'RE SLAVE MERCHANTS!!
THEY MAKE MONEY BY SELLING INNOCENT PEOPLE.
KLINK
THEY'RE AWFUL!
KLINK
WHY DO SLAVES EVEN EXIST?

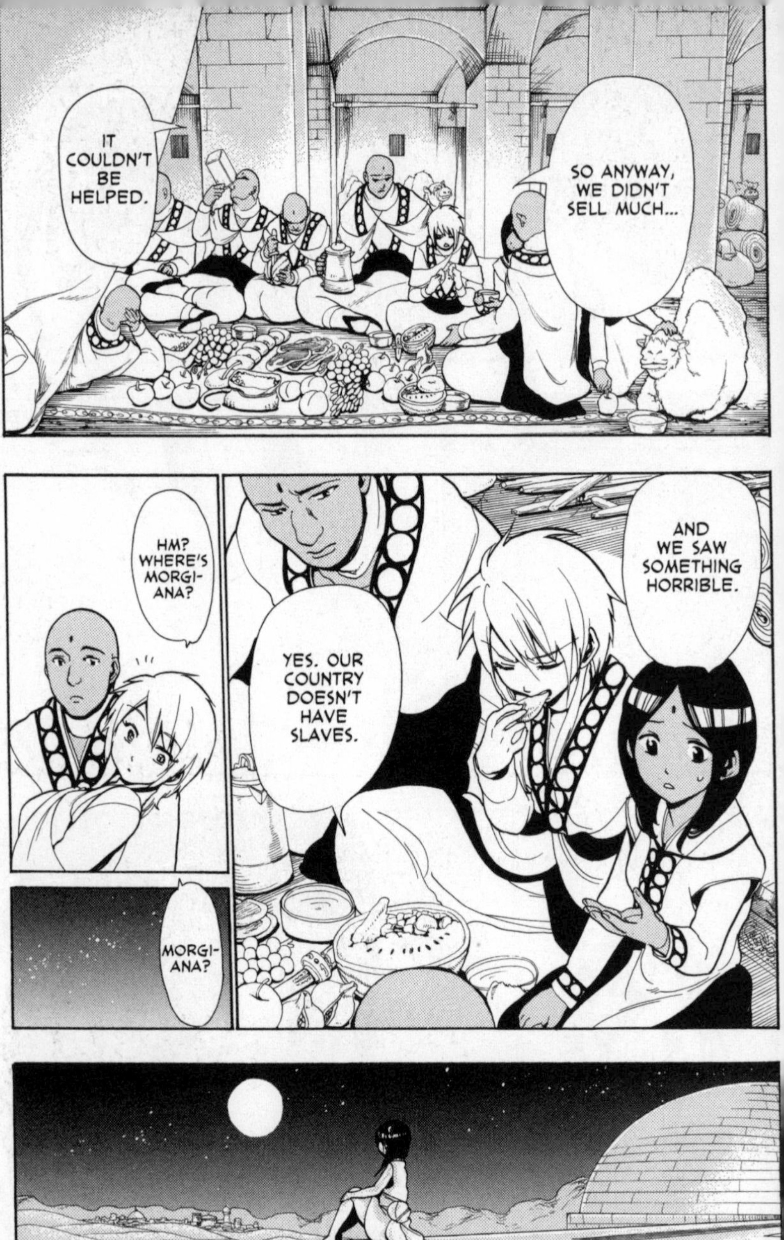
SO ANYWAY, WE DIDN'T SELL MUCH...
IT COULDN'T BE HELPED.
AND WE SAW SOMETHING HORRIBLE.
YES. OUR COUNTRY DOESN'T HAVE SLAVES.
HM? WHERE'S MORGI-ANA?
MORGI-ANA?

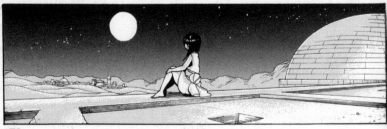

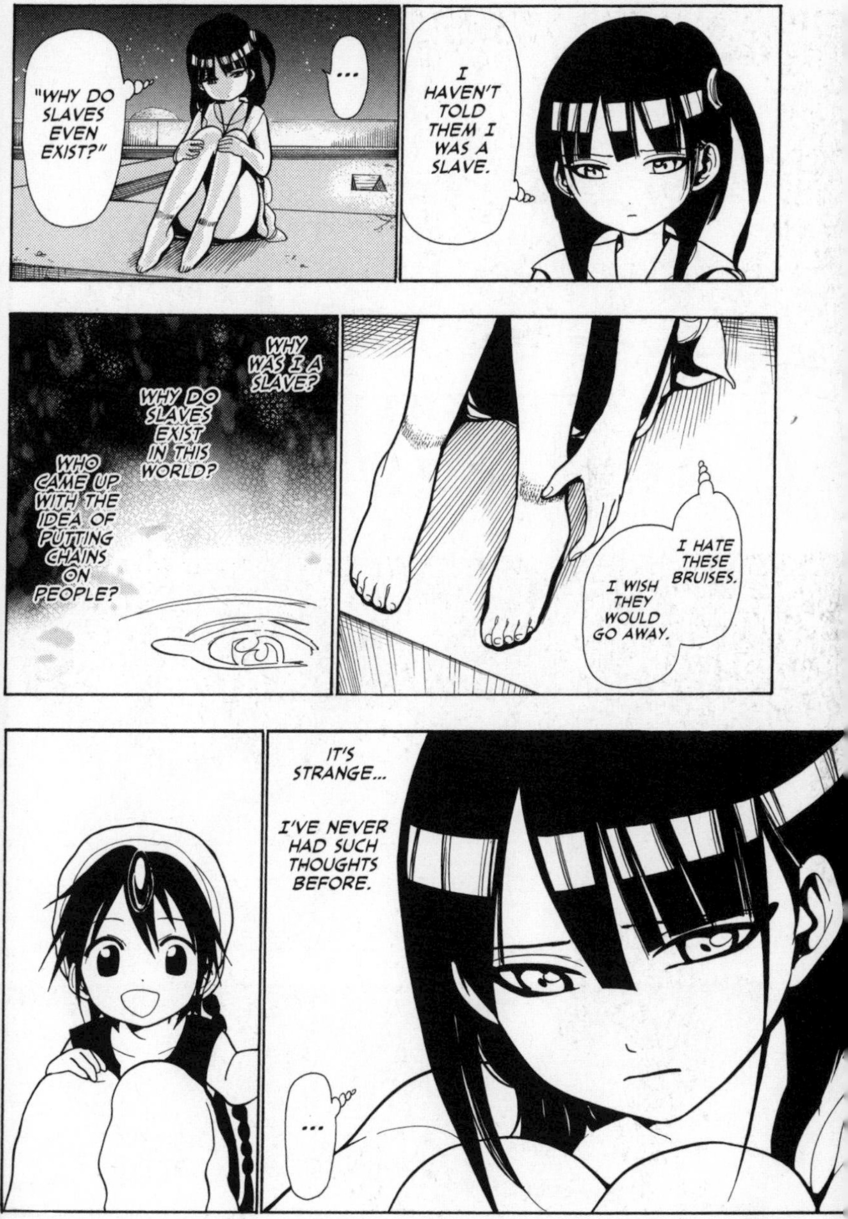
I HAVEN'T TOLD THEM I WAS A SLAVE.
...
"WHY DO SLAVES EVEN EXIST?"
I HATE THESE BRUISES.
I WISH THEY WOULD GO AWAY.
WHY WAS I A SLAVE?
WHY DO SLAVES EXIST IN THIS WORLD?
WHO CAME UP WITH THE IDEA OF PUTTING CHAINS ON PEOPLE?
IT'S STRANGE...
I'VE NEVER HAD SUCH THOUGHTS BEFORE.
...

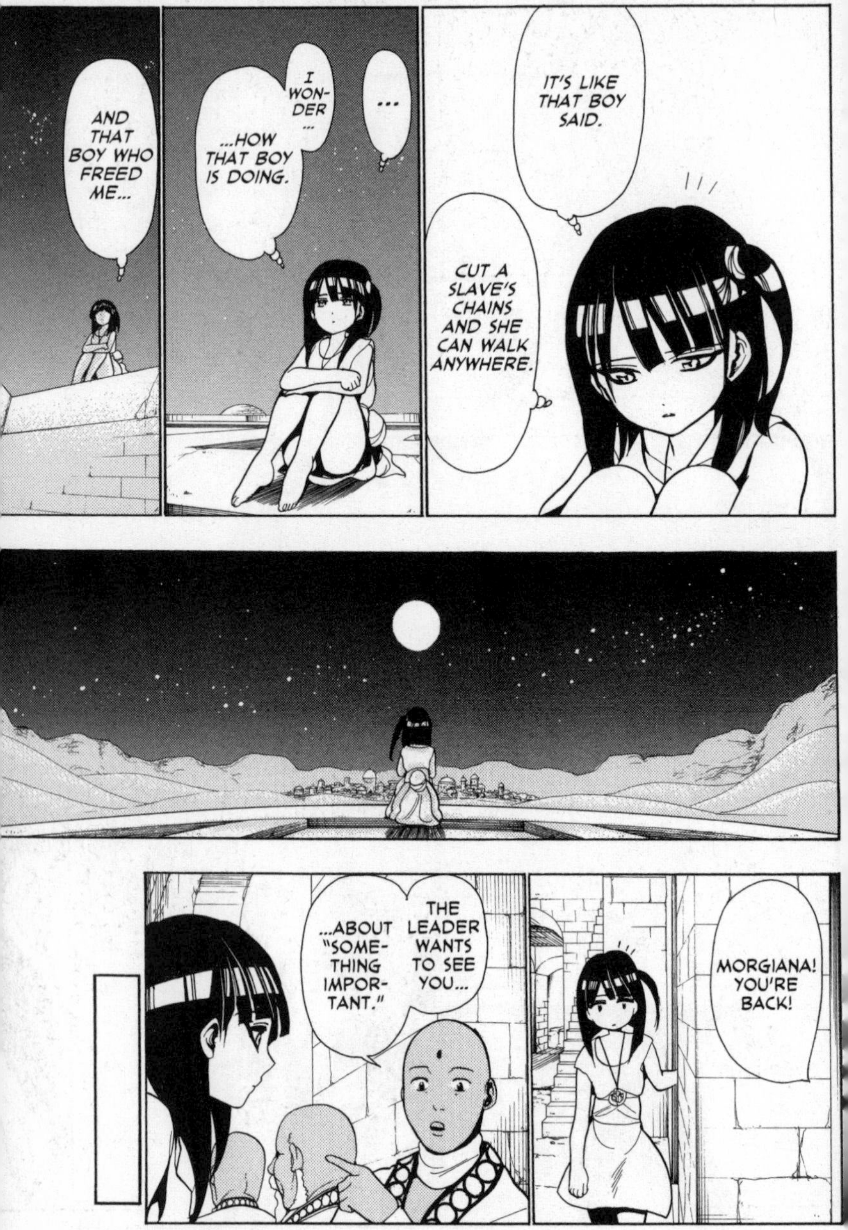
IT'S LIKE THAT BOY SAID.
CUT A SLAVE'S CHAINS AND SHE CAN WALK ANYWHERE.
...
I WONDER...
...HOW THAT BOY IS DOING.
AND THAT BOY WHO FREED ME...
MORGIANA! YOU'RE BACK!
THE LEADER WANTS TO SEE YOU...
...ABOUT "SOMETHING IMPORTANT."

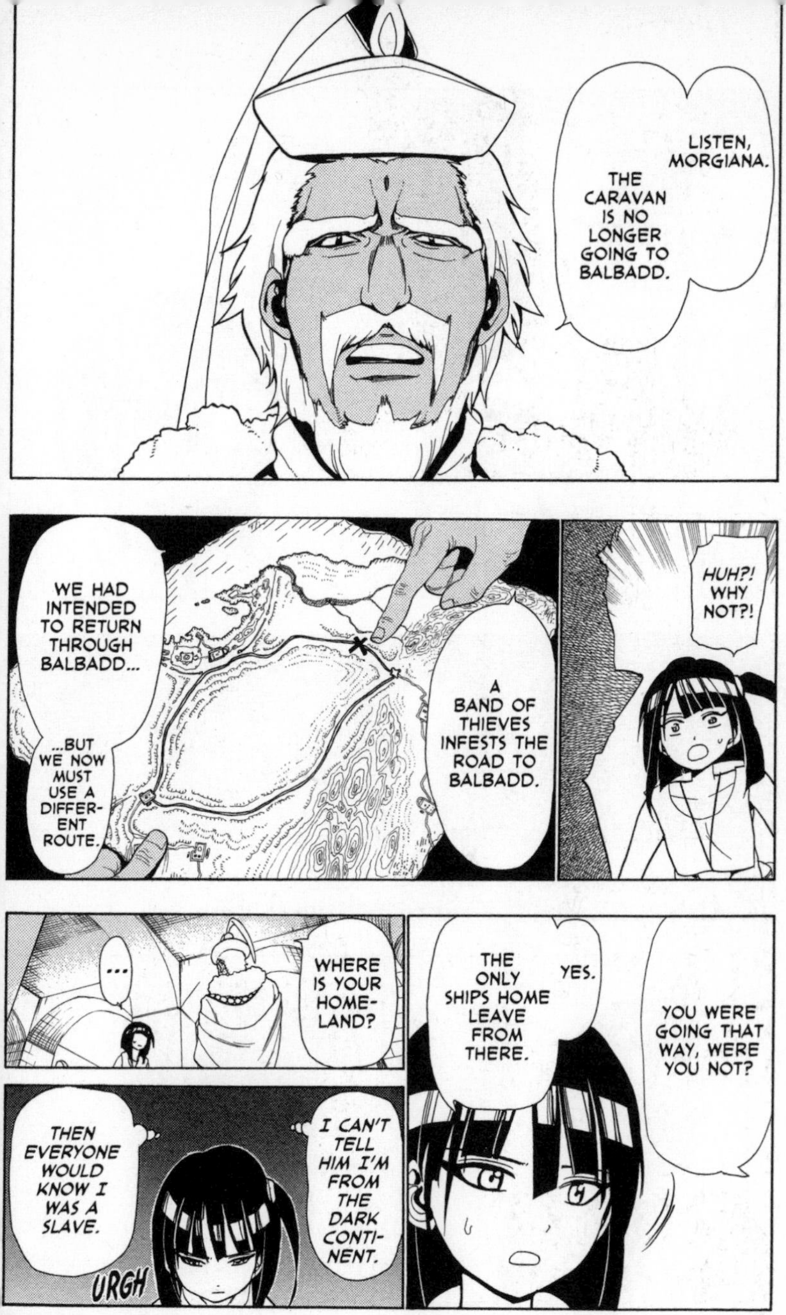
LISTEN, MORGIANA.
THE CARAVAN IS NO LONGER GOING TO BALBADD.
HUH?! WHY NOT?!
A BAND OF THIEVES INFESTS THE ROAD TO BALBADD.
WE HAD INTENDED TO RETURN THROUGH BALBADD...
...BUT WE NOW MUST USE A DIFFERENT ROUTE.
YOU WERE GOING THAT WAY, WERE YOU NOT?
YES.
THE ONLY SHIPS HOME LEAVE FROM THERE.
WHERE IS YOUR HOMELAND?
...
I CAN'T TELL HIM I'M FROM THE DARK CONTINENT.
THEN EVERYONE WOULD KNOW I WAS A SLAVE.
URGH

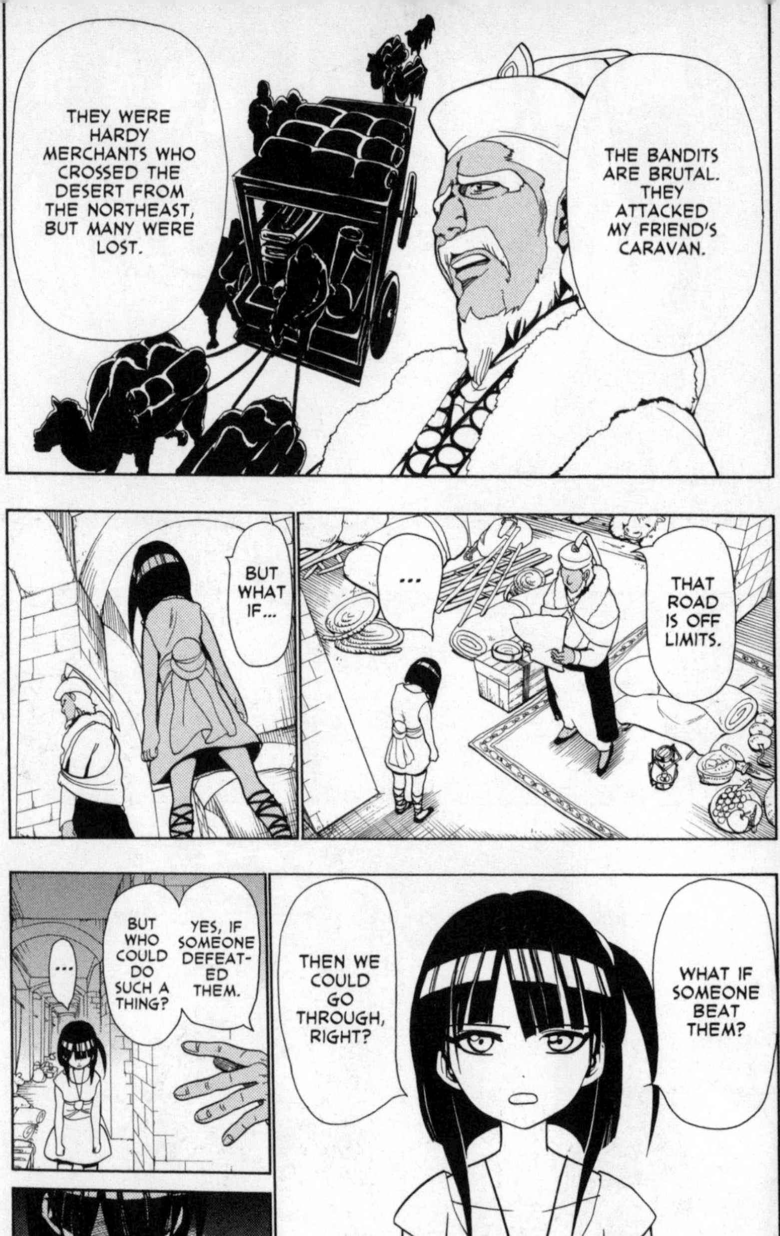
THE BANDITS ARE BRUTAL. THEY ATTACKED MY FRIEND'S CARAVAN.
THEY WERE HARDY MERCHANTS WHO CROSSED THE DESERT FROM THE NORTHEAST, BUT MANY WERE LOST.
THAT ROAD IS OFF LIMITS.
...
BUT WHAT IF...
WHAT IF SOMEONE BEAT THEM?
THEN WE COULD GO THROUGH, RIGHT?
YES, IF SOMEONE DEFEAT-ED THEM.
BUT WHO COULD DO SUCH A THING?
...

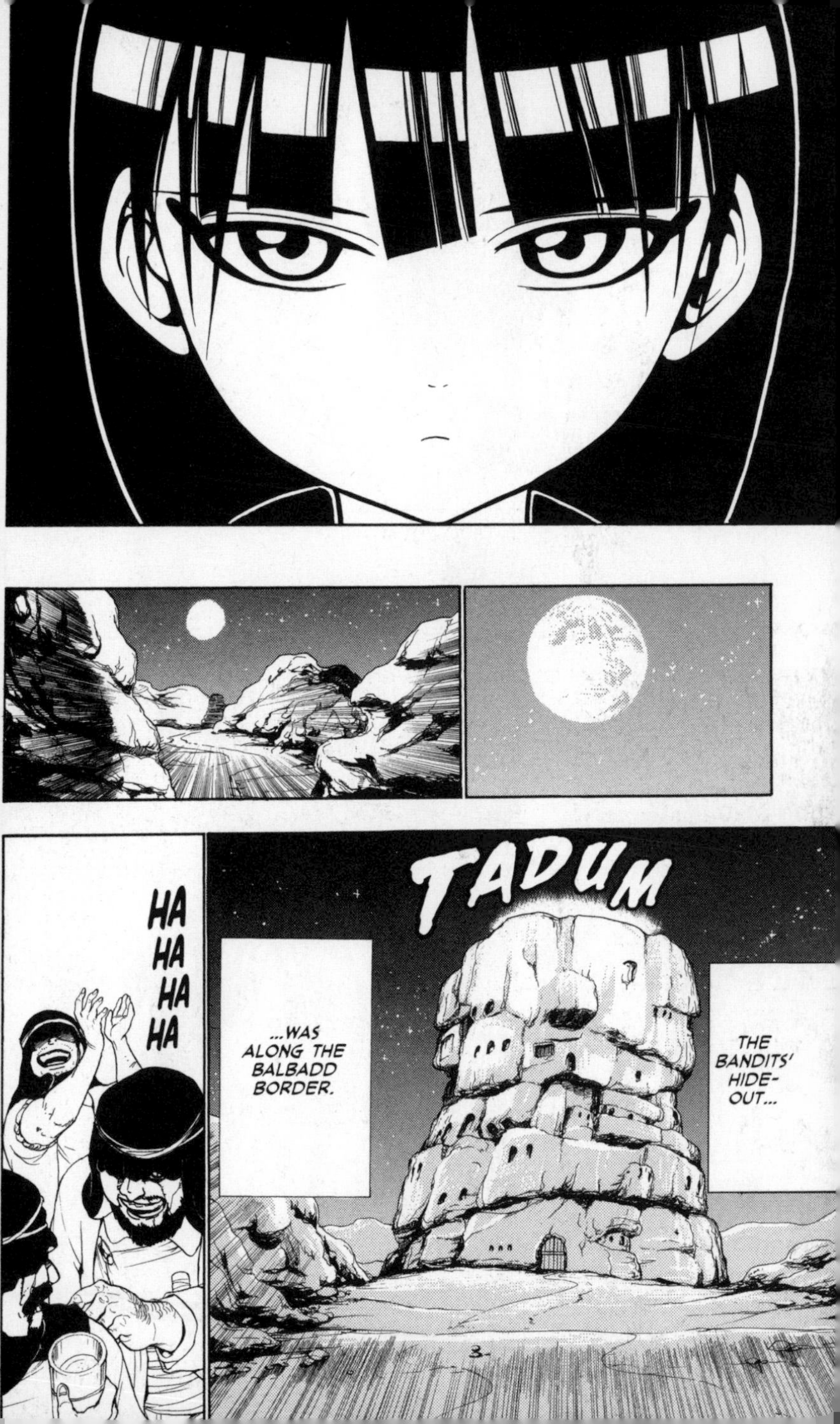
TADUM
THE BANDITS' HIDE-OUT...
...WAS ALONG THE BALBADD BORDER.
HA HA HA HA

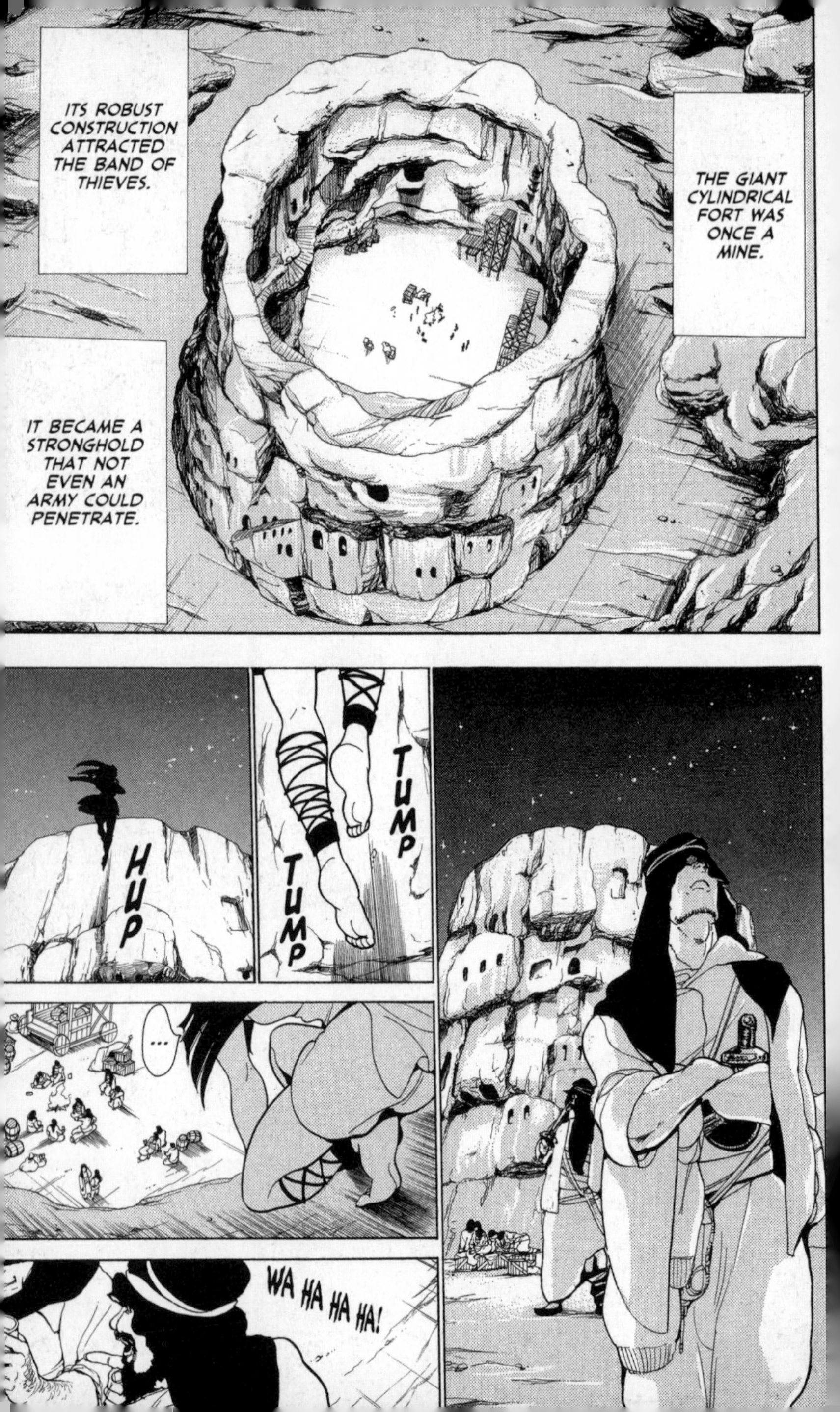
THE GIANT CYLINDRICAL FORT WAS ONCE A MINE.
ITS ROBUST CONSTRUCTION ATTRACTED THE BAND OF THIEVES.
IT BECAME A STRONGHOLD THAT NOT EVEN AN ARMY COULD PENETRATE.
TUMP
TUMP
HUP
...
WA HA HA HA!

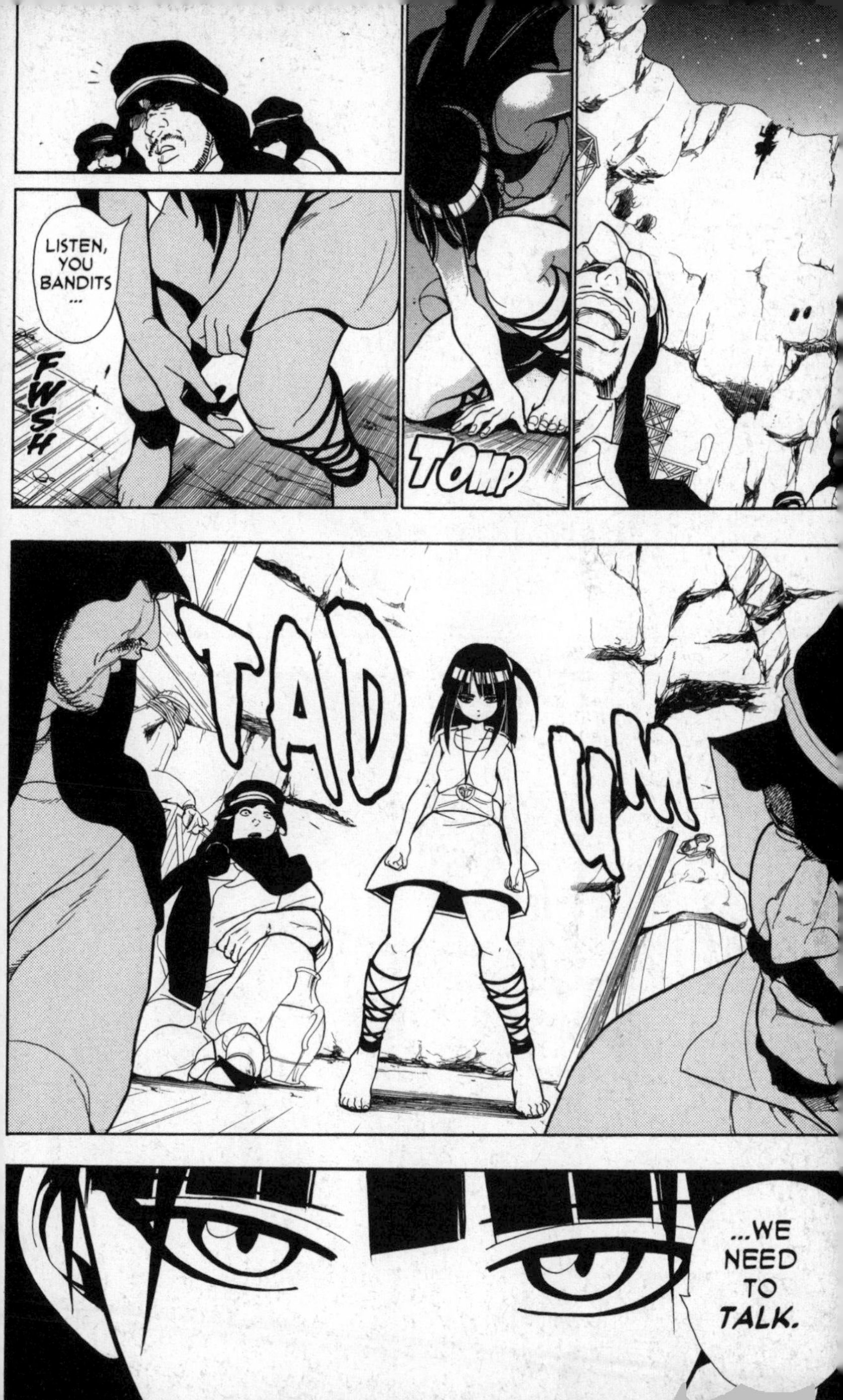
TOMP
LISTEN, YOU BANDITS...
FWSH
TAD UM
...WE NEED TO TALK.

MAGI
The labyrinth of magic
3

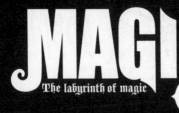

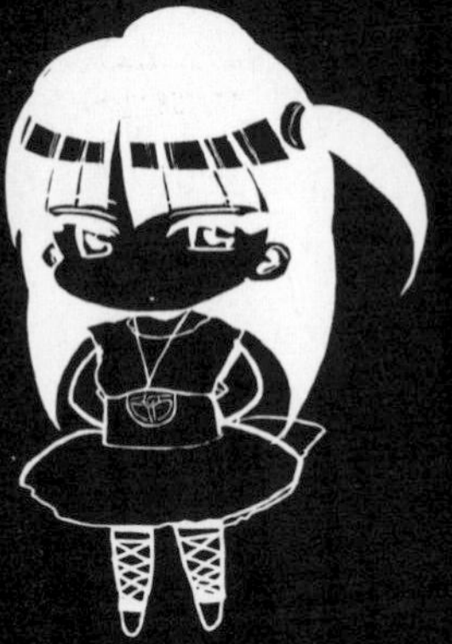

Staff

■ Story & Art

Shinobu Ohtaka
Shinobu Ohtaka

■ Regular Assistants

Matsubara

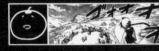

Miho Isshiki

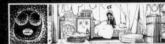

Akira Sugito

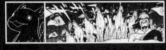

Tanimoto

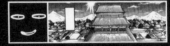

Maru

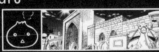

■ Editor

Kazuaki Ishibashi

■ Sales & Promotion

Akira Ozeki
Shinichirou Todaka

■ Designers

Yasuo Shimura + Bay Bridge Studio

■ Special Thanks

Mutsumi Ogasawara

BONUS MANGA HELP ME, ALADDIN!

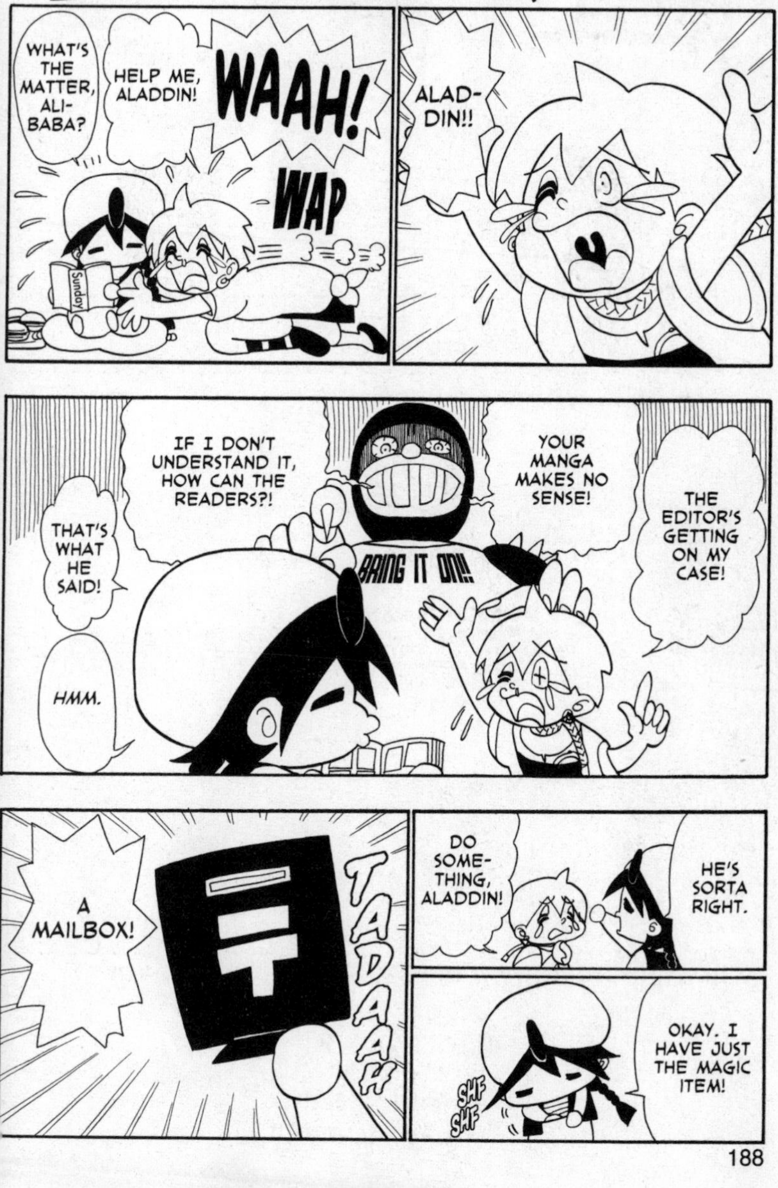

ALAD-DIN!!
WAAH!
HELP ME, ALADDIN!
WHAT'S THE MATTER, ALI-BABA?
WAP
THE EDITOR'S GETTING ON MY CASE!
YOUR MANGA MAKES NO SENSE!
IF I DON'T UNDERSTAND IT, HOW CAN THE READERS?!
BRING IT ON!!
THAT'S WHAT HE SAID!
HMM.
HE'S SORTA RIGHT.
DO SOME-THING, ALADDIN!
OKAY. I HAVE JUST THE MAGIC ITEM!
SHF SHF
TADAAH
A MAILBOX!

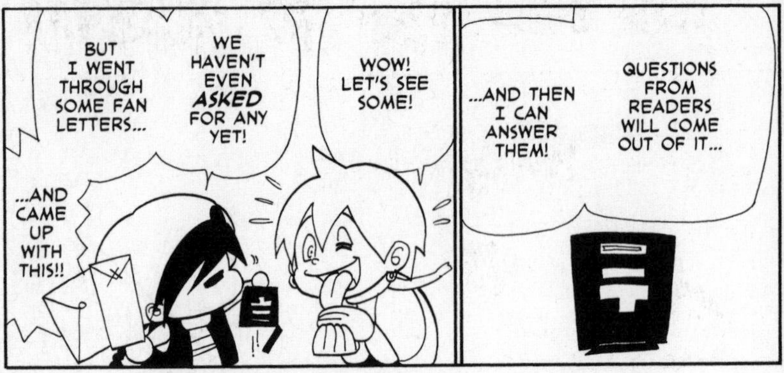
QUESTIONS FROM READERS WILL COME OUT OF IT...
...AND THEN I CAN ANSWER THEM!
WOW! LET'S SEE SOME!
WE HAVEN'T EVEN ***ASKED*** FOR ANY YET!
BUT I WENT THROUGH SOME FAN LETTERS...
...AND CAME UP WITH THIS!!

Q. HOW IS ALIBABA'S OUTFIT ASSEMBLED?
I CAN'T MAKE ANY SENSE OF IT AT ALL!

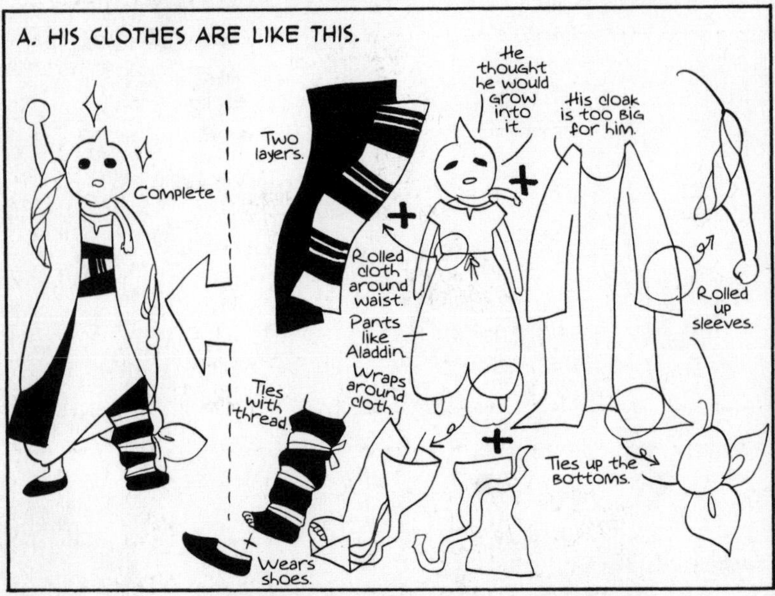
A. HIS CLOTHES ARE LIKE THIS.
Complete
Two layers.
Rolled cloth around waist.
Pants like Aladdin.
He thought he would grow into it.
His cloak is too big for him.
Rolled up sleeves.
Ties with thread.
Wraps around cloth.
Wears shoes.
Ties up the bottoms.

SO CAN YOU MAKE ANY SENSE OF IT NOW? SEND QUESTIONS TO...

MAGI EDITOR
C/O VIZ MEDIA
P.O. BOX 77010
SAN FRANCISCO, CA 94107

SHINOBU OHTAKA

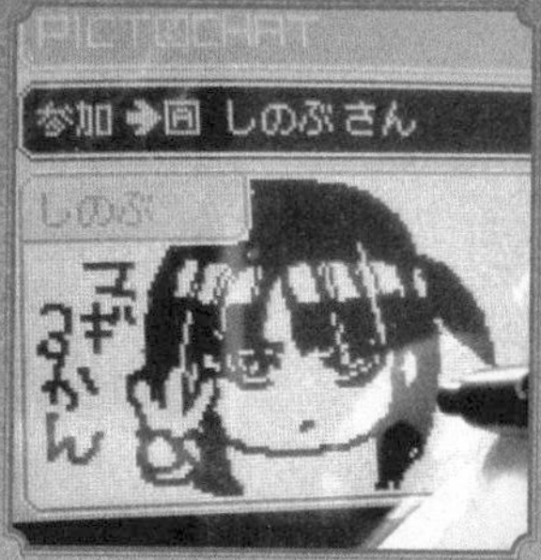
PICTOCHAT
しのぶさん
しのぶ
マギ3かん

* Pictochat Shinobu-san
Magi volume 3

Thanks for reading!

MAGI

Volume 3

Shonen Sunday Edition

Story and Art by
SHINOBU OHTAKA

MAGI Vol.3
by Shinobu OHTAKA
© 2009 Shinobu OHTAKA
All rights reserved.
Original Japanese edition published by SHOGAKUKAN.
English translation rights in the United States of America, Canada,
the United Kingdom and Ireland arranged with SHOGAKUKAN.

Translation & English Adaptation ◆ John Werry

Touch-up Art & Lettering ◆ Stephen Dutro

Editor ◆ Mike Montesa

Printed in the U.S.A.

Published by VIZ Media, LLC
P.O. Box 77010
San Francisco, CA 94107

10 9 8 7 6 5 4 3 2 1
First printing, December 2013

WWW.SHONENSUNDAY.COM

www.viz.com

You're reading the WRONG WAY

MAGI reads from right to left, starting in the upper-right corner. Japanese is read from **right** to **left**, meaning that action, sound effects, and word-balloon order are completely reversed from English order.

1
2
1
3
4
2
5
6
3
7
8
4
9
5
142

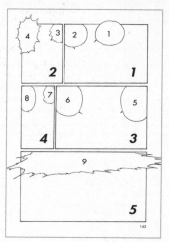

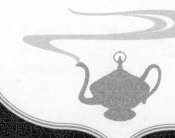